BIBLICAL ESSAYS

BIBLICAL ESSAYS

BY THE LATE

J. B. LIGHTFOOT, D.D., D.C.L., LL.D.,

LORD BISHOP OF DURHAM.

PUBLISHED BY
THE TRUSTEES OF THE LIGHTFOOT FUND.

London:

MACMILLAN AND CO.

AND NEW YORK.

1893

Cambridge:

PRINTED BY C. J. CLAY, M.A. AND SONS,

AT THE UNIVERSITY PRESS.

INTRODUCTORY NOTE.

ABOUT one-third of the present volume has already seen the light. The opening essay 'On the Internal Evidence for the Authenticity and Genuineness of St John's Gospel' was published in the 'Expositor' in the early months of 1890, and has been reprinted since; the essay 'On the Mission of Titus to the Corinthians' appeared in the 'Journal of Sacred and Classical Philology' nearly thirty years ago, while the ninth essay 'On the Structure and Destination of the Epistle to the Romans' consists of three famous articles contributed within the years 1869 and 1871 to the 'Journal of Philology,' two by Dr Lightfoot and one by Dr Hort. Beginning with a criticism of M. Renan's theory that our present Epistle to the Romans represents no less than four letters addressed to different Churches, Dr Lightfoot proceeded to formulate a counter-theory of an original letter (our complete Epistle) addressed to the Church of Rome, and a shorter recension of a more general character reissued by the Apostle at a later period and intended for a wider circle of readers. This theory did not commend itself to Dr Hort, and his criticism of Dr Lightfoot's arguments and Dr Lightfoot's reply, which form the second and third of the articles in question, are published herewith, while for a restatement of Dr Hort's view the reader is referred to the 'Notes on Selected Readings' which form an appendix to the Introduction to the edition of the New Testament edited by

Drs Westcott and Hort[1]. A singular pathos attaches to the republication of these articles in the thought that he who so recently gave his consent to their insertion in this volume, and whose counsel was so reverently listened to by his co-trustees, has been called to his rest, before the volume has passed into circulation.

And the pathos of the situation is only increased as we turn to the main part of the volume, to that which appears in print for the first time. When in 1879 Dr Lightfoot was called away from Cambridge to undertake the Bishopric of Durham, apprehension was felt and expressed in many quarters that the continual claims of diocesan engagements would seriously impair his literary productiveness. How heroically he struggled to belie this anticipation is well known. But the marvellous steadfastness of purpose with which he devoted to literary work every available moment which could be snatched from official duties can be fully appreciated by those only who had the privilege of watching the great bishop's life from day to day. By sheer strength of will he completed the five massive volumes on the Apostolic Fathers. But the issue of commentaries on St Paul's Epistles was checked absolutely. From time to time rumours were circulated that some particular commentary was in progress, nay more, in type and within a measurable distance of publication; but alas! these surmises were entirely devoid of foundation. The Bishop was heard more than once to declare that, his edition of the Apostolic Fathers finished, he hoped with what leisure he could secure in two years to be able to bring out a commentary upon any one of the Pauline Epistles on which he had lectured when at Cambridge. But the necessary relief from pressure never came, and after his death it was found, as had been anticipated

---

[1] *The New Testament in the original Greek* (1881), vol. 2, Appendix, pp. 100 sq.

by those who knew his methods, that the notes on the New Testament had remained untouched since the day when he left Cambridge for Auckland Castle. There were moreover sad gaps in the commentaries and in the introductory matter, sketches of work which had never been filled in, and jottings which needed the master-mind of the writer to interpret them adequately. In accordance therefore with a report furnished to the Trustees by Dr Hort, it was decided to abandon all attempts to bring out a complete edition of any epistle on the lines of the published commentaries, and instead to gather into one volume such of the prolegomena as it was possible to publish, reserving for another volume selections from commentaries on the text which appeared to be fullest and most valuable. The present volume of 'Biblical Essays' represents the first of these undertakings. The contents can easily be assigned to the places which they would have occupied had the Bishop been able to complete his projected series of commentaries on all the Pauline Epistles. The second and third essays on St John's Gospel form part of a subject which, as he tells us himself, he considered to have 'passed into other and better hands,' and they would probably never have been published by Dr Lightfoot himself. The next four essays were intended to appear as excursuses in the Commentary on the Thessalonians; the three which follow would have supplied material for introductions to the Epistles to the Corinthians, Romans and Ephesians respectively, while the last two would have found a place in an edition of the Pastoral Epistles.

To edit the writings of one who is no longer at hand to explain and to correct must always present grave difficulties; but when the material to be edited is to appear as the work of a scholar of the widest reputation for learning and accuracy, to venture upon the task is little short of presumption. In the present instance the difficulty is enhanced by Dr Lightfoot's method of work, to which the present Bishop of Durham draws attention in his prefatory note to the posthumous edition of St Clement of Rome. Possessed of a remarkably retentive memory, he preferred to trust to outlines, rather than write out in full what he intended to deliver in the lecture-room. Accordingly, in those essays which are described as printed from lecture-notes, it has been found necessary to frame into sentences page after page which, in the original notes, exists only in the briefest summary. It is inevitable therefore, that in places the Bishop's meaning will have been obscurely expressed, if not entirely missed. That this inadequacy of treatment is not more glaring is due to the kindness of those who, in response to the appeal of the Trustees, have placed their notes of Dr Lightfoot's professorial lectures at the disposal of the editor. The cordial thanks of the Trustees are tendered to the Rev. G. F. Browne, Canon of St Paul's, to W. P. Turnbull, Esq., formerly Fellow of Trinity College and now one of Her Majesty's Inspectors of Schools, to the Rev. H. F. Gore-Booth, Rector of Sacred Trinity, Salford, for the loan of their valuable notes; and to the Rev. W. E. Barnes, Fellow and Lecturer of St Peter's College, for kind assistance in looking over the proof-sheets of the third essay.

As some of the lectures were delivered at Cambridge on more than one occasion, it may be well to state that the date placed at the end of each essay represents the year of delivery, after which apparently no fresh material was added in the notes in writing.

In conclusion, the Trustees desire to thank the officers and workmen of the University Press for intelligent criticism and for unfailing courtesy during the time that these sheets have been passing through the press.

J. R. H.

Corpus Christi College, Cambridge.
July 15, 1893.

EXTRACT FROM THE LAST WILL AND TESTAMENT OF THE LATE
JOSEPH BARBER LIGHTFOOT, LORD BISHOP OF DURHAM.

"I bequeath all my personal Estate not hereinbefore other-
"wise disposed of unto [my Executors] upon trust to pay and
"transfer the same unto the Trustees appointed by me under
"and by virtue of a certain Indenture of Settlement creating a
"Trust to be known by the name of 'The Lightfoot Fund for
'the Diocese of Durham' and bearing even date herewith but
"executed by me immediately before this my Will to be ad-
"ministered and dealt with by them upon the trusts for the
"purposes and in the manner prescribed by such Indenture of
"Settlement."

EXTRACT FROM THE INDENTURE OF SETTLEMENT OF 'THE
LIGHTFOOT FUND FOR THE DIOCESE OF DURHAM.'

"WHEREAS the Bishop is the Author of and is absolutely
"entitled to the Copyright in the several Works mentioned in
"the Schedule hereto, and for the purposes of these presents he
"has assigned or intends forthwith to assign the Copyright in
"all the said Works to the Trustees. Now the Bishop doth
"hereby declare and it is hereby agreed as follows:—

"The Trustees (which term shall hereinafter be taken to
"include the Trustees for the time being of these presents)

" shall stand possessed of the said Works and of the Copyright
" therein respectively upon the trusts following (that is to say)
" upon trust to receive all moneys to arise from sales or other-
" wise from the said Works, and at their discretion from time
" to time to bring out new editions of the same Works or any
" of them, or to sell the copyright in the same or any of them,
" or otherwise to deal with the same respectively, it being the
" intention of these presents that the Trustees shall have and
" may exercise all such rights and powers in respect of the said
" Works and the copyright therein respectively, as they could
" or might have or exercise in relation thereto if they were the
" absolute beneficial owners thereof....

    " The Trustees shall from time to time, at such discretion as
" aforesaid, pay and apply the income of the Trust funds for or
" towards the erecting, rebuilding, repairing, purchasing, en-
" dowing, supporting, or providing for any Churches, Chapels,
" Schools, Parsonages, and Stipends for Clergy, and other Spiri-
" tual Agents in connection with the Church of England and
" within the Diocese of Durham, and also for or towards such
" other purposes in connection with the said Church of England,
" and within the said Diocese, as the Trustees may in their ab-
" solute discretion think fit, provided always that any payment
" for erecting any building, or in relation to any other works in
" connection with real estate, shall be exercised with due regard
" to the Law of Mortmain ; it being declared that nothing here-
" in shall be construed as intended to authorise any act contrary
" to any Statute or other Law....

    " In case the Bishop shall at any time assign to the Trustees
" any Works hereafter to be written or published by him, or
" any Copyrights, or any other property, such transfer shall be
" held to be made for the purposes of this Trust, and all the

"provisions of this Deed shall apply to such property, subject
"nevertheless to any direction concerning the same which the
"Bishop may make in writing at the time of such transfer, and
"in case the Bishop shall at any time pay any money, or trans-
"fer any security, stock, or other like property to the Trustees,
"the same shall in like manner be held for the purposes of this
"Trust, subject to any such contemporaneous direction as afore-
"said, and any security, stock or property so transferred, being
"of a nature which can lawfully be held by the Trustees for the
"purposes of these presents, may be retained by the Trustees,
"although the same may not be one of the securities herein-
"after authorised.

"The Bishop of Durham and the Archdeacons of Durham
"and Auckland for the time being shall be *ex-officio* Trustees,
"and accordingly the Bishop and Archdeacons, parties hereto,
"and the succeeding Bishops and Archdeacons, shall cease to be
"Trustees on ceasing to hold their respective offices, and the
"number of the other Trustees may be increased, and the power
"of appointing Trustees in the place of Trustees other than
"Official Trustees, and of appointing extra Trustees, shall be
"exercised by Deed by the Trustees for the time being, pro-
"vided always that the number shall not at any time be less
"than five.

"The Trust premises shall be known by the name of 'The
"Lightfoot Fund for the Diocese of Durham.'"

TABLE OF CONTENTS.

I.

INTERNAL EVIDENCE FOR THE AUTHENTICITY AND GENUINENESS OF ST JOHN'S GOSPEL.

Reprinted from the 'Expositor' of January, February, March, 1890.

I.

INTERNAL EVIDENCE FOR THE AUTHENTICITY AND GENUINENESS OF ST JOHN'S GOSPEL.

THIS lecture originally formed one of a series connected with Christian evidences, and delivered in St George's Hall in 1871. The other lectures were published shortly afterwards; but, not having been informed beforehand that publication was expected, I withheld my own from the volume. It seemed to me that in the course of a single lecture I could only touch the fringes of a great subject, and that injustice would be done by such imperfect treatment as alone time and opportunity allowed. Moreover I was then, and for some terms afterwards, engaged in lecturing on this Gospel at Cambridge, and I entertained the hope that I might be able to deal with the subject less inadequately if I gave myself more time. Happily it passed into other and better hands, and I was relieved from this care.

A rumour got abroad at the time, and has (I am informed) been since repeated, that I did not allow the lecture to be published, because I was dissatisfied with it. I was only dissatisfied in the sense which I have already explained. It could not be otherwise than unsatisfactory to bring forward mere fragmentary evidence of an important conclusion, when there was abundant proof in the background. The present publication of the lecture is my answer to this rumour. I give it after eighteen years exactly in the same form in which it was originally written, with the exception of a few verbal alterations. Looking over it again after this long lapse of time, I have nothing to withdraw. Additional study has only strengthened my conviction that this narrative of St John could not have been written by any one but an eye-witness.

As I have not dealt with the external evidence except for the sake of supplying a statement of the position of antagonists, the treatment suffers less than it would otherwise have done from not being brought down to date. I have mentioned by way of illustration two respects in which later discoveries had falsified Baur's contentions. The last eighteen years would supply several others. I will single out three: (1) The antagonists of the Ignatian Epistles are again put on their defence. The arguments which were adduced against the genuineness of these epistles will hold no longer. Ignatius has the testimony of his friend and contemporary Polycarp, and Polycarp has the testimony of his own personal disciple Irenæus. The testimony of Irenæus is denied by no one; the testimony of Polycarp is only denied because it certifies to the Ignatian letters. Before we are prepared to snap this chain of evidence rudely, and to break with an uninterrupted tradition, we require far stronger reasons than have been hitherto adduced. (2) Justin Martyr wrote before or about the middle of the second century. His use of the Fourth Gospel was at one time systematically denied by the impugners of its apostolic authorship. Now it is acknowledged almost universally, even by those who do not allow that this evangelical narrative was written by St John himself. (3) The *Diatessaron* of Tatian was written about A.D. 170, and consisted of a 'Harmony of Four Gospels.' Baur and others contended that at all events St John was not one of the four. Indeed how could it be? For it had not been written, or only recently written, at this time. The *Diatessaron* itself has been discovered, and a commentary of Ephraem Syrus upon it in Armenian has likewise been unearthed within the last few years, both showing that it began with the opening words of St John.

[1889.]

The fourth of our canonical gospels has been ascribed by the tradition of the Church to St John the son of Zebedee, the personal disciple of our Lord, and one of the twelve apostles. Till within a century (I might almost say, till within a generation) of the present time, this has been the universal belief—with one single and unimportant exception—of all ages, of all churches, of all sects, of all individuals alike.

This unanimity is the more remarkable in the earlier ages of the Church, because the language of this gospel has a very intimate bearing on numberless theological controversies which started up in the second, third, and fourth centuries of the Christian era; and it was therefore the direct interest of one party or other to deny the apostolic authority, if they had any ground for doing so. This happened not once or twice only, but many times. It would be difficult to point to a single heresy promulgated before the close of the fourth century, which might not find some imaginary points of coincidence or some real points of conflict—some relations whether of antagonism or of sympathy—with this gospel. This was equally true of Montanism in the second century, and of Arianism in the fourth. The Fourth Gospel would necessarily be among the most important authorities—we might fairly say *the* most important authority—in the settlement of the controversy, both from the claims which it made as a product of the beloved apostle himself, and from the striking representations which it gives of our Lord's teaching. The defender or the impugner of this or that theological opinion would have had a direct interest in disproving its genuineness and denying its authority. Can we question that this would have been done again and again, if there had been any haze of doubt hanging over its origin, if the antagonist could have found even a *primâ facie* ground for an attack?

And this brings me to speak of that one exception to the universal tradition to which I have already alluded. Once, and once only, did the disputants in a theological controversy yield to the temptation, strong though it must have been. A small, unimportant, nameless sect—if indeed they were compact enough to form a sect—in the latter half of the second century, denied that the Gospel and the Apocalypse were written by St John. These are the two canonical writings which especially attribute the title of the Word of God, the Logos, to our Lord: the one, in the opening verses, 'In the beginning was the Word, and the Word was with God, and the Word was God'; the other, in the vision of Him who rides on the white horse, whose garments are stained with blood, and whose name is given as the 'Word of God.' To dispose of the doctrine they discredited the writings. Epiphanius calls them *Alogi*, 'the opponents of the Word,' or (as it might be translated, for it is capable of a double meaning) 'the irrational ones.' The name is avowedly his own invention. Indeed they would scarcely have acknowledged a title which had this double sense, and could have been so easily turned against themselves. They appear only to disappear. Beyond one or two casual allusions, they are not mentioned; they have no place in history.

This is just one of those exceptions which strengthen the rule. What these *Alogi* did, numberless other sectaries and heretics would doubtless have done, if there had been any sufficient ground for the course. But even these *Alogi* lend no countenance to the views of modern objectors. Modern critics play off the Apocalypse against the Gospel, allowing the genuineness of the former, and using it to impugn the genuineness of the latter. Moreover there is the greatest difference between the two. The modern antagonist places the composition of the Fourth Gospel in the middle or the latter half of the second century; these ancient heretics ascribed it to the early heresiarch Cerinthus, who lived at the close of the first century, and was a contemporary of St John. Living themselves in the latter half of the second century, they knew (as their opponents would have reminded them, if they had found it convenient to forget the fact) that the Gospel was not a work of yesterday, that it had already a long history, and that it went back at all events to the latest years of the apostolic age; and in their

theory they were obliged to recognise this fact. I need hardly
say that the doctrine of the Person of Christ put forward in the
Gospel and the Apocalypse is diametrically opposed to the
teaching of Cerinthus, as every modern critic would allow. I
only allude to this fact, to show that these very persons, who
form the single exception to the unanimous tradition of all the
churches and all the sects alike, are our witnesses for the
antiquity of the Gospel (though not for its authenticity), and
therefore are witnesses *against* the modern impugners of its
genuineness.

With this exception, the early testimony to the authenticity and genuineness of the Gospel is singularly varied.
It is a remarkable and an important fact, that the most
decisive and earliest testimony comes, not from Fathers of
the orthodox Church, but from heretical writers. I cannot
enter upon this question at length, for I did not undertake
this afternoon to speak of the external evidence; and I ask
you to bear in mind, that any inadequate and cursory
treatment necessarily does a great injustice to a subject
like this; for the ultimate effect of testimony must depend
on its fulness and variety. I only call attention to the fact
that within the last few years most valuable additions have
been made to this external testimony, and these from the
opposite extremes of the heretical scale. At the one extreme
we have *Ebionism,* which was the offspring of Judaizing tendencies; at the other, *Gnosticism,* which took its rise in Gentile
license of speculation and practice. Ebionism is represented by
a remarkable extant work belonging to the second century,
possibly to the first half of the second century, the *Clementine
Homilies.* The greater part of this work has long been known,
but until within the last few years the printed text was taken
from a MS. mutilated at the end; so that of the twenty Homilies
the last half of the nineteenth and the whole of the twentieth
are wanting. These earlier Homilies contained more than one
reference to gospel history which could not well be referred to
any of the three first evangelists, and seemed certainly to have

been taken from the fourth. Still the reference was not absolutely certain, and the impugners of St John's Gospel availed
themselves of this doubt to deny the reference to this gospel.
At length, in the year 1853, Dressel published for the first
time, from a Vatican MS., the missing conclusion of these
Homilies; and this was found to contain a reference to the
incidents attending the healing of the man born blind, related
only by St John, and related in a way distinctly characteristic
of St John—a reference so distinct, that no one from that time
has attempted to deny or to dispute it.

So much for the testimony of Ebionism—of the *Judaic*
sects of early Christianity. But equally definite, and even
more full, is the testimony which recent discovery has brought
to light on the side of *Gnosticism*. Many of my hearers will
remember the interest which was excited a few years ago by
the publication of a lost treatise on heresies, which Bunsen and
others ascribed (and, as is now generally allowed, correctly
ascribed) to Hippolytus, in the earlier part of the third century.
This treatise contains large and frequent extracts from previous
Gnostic writers of diverse schools—Ophites, Basilideans, Valentinians; among them, from a work which Hippolytus quotes as
the production of Basilides himself, who flourished about A.D.
130–140. And in these extracts are abundant quotations from
the Gospel of St John.

I have put these two recent accessions to the external
testimony in favour of the Fourth Gospel side by side, because,
emanating from the most diverse quarters, they have a peculiar
value, as showing the extensive circulation and wide reception
of this gospel at a very early date; and because also, having
been brought to light soon after its genuineness was for the
first time seriously impugned, they seem providentially destined
to furnish an answer to the objections of recent criticism.

If we ask ourselves why we attribute this or that ancient
writing to the author whose name it bears—why, for instance,
we accept this tragedy as a play of Sophocles, or that speech as
an oration of Demosthenes,—our answer will be, that it bears

the name of the author, and (so far as we know) has always been ascribed to him. In very many cases we know nothing, or next to nothing, about the history of the writing in question. In a few instances we are fortunate enough to find a reference to it, or a quotation from it, in some author who lived a century or two later. The cases are exceptionally rare when there is an indisputable allusion in a contemporary, or nearly contemporary, writer. For the most part, we accept the fact of the authorship, because it comes to us on the authority of a MS. or MSS. written several centuries after the presumed author lived, supported in some cases by quotations in a late lexicographer, or grammarian, or collection of extracts.

The external testimony in favour of St John's Gospel reaches back much nearer to the writer's own time and is far more extensive than can be produced in the case of most classical writings of the same antiquity. From the character of the work also, this testimony gains additional value; for where the contents of a book intimately affect the cherished beliefs and the practical conduct of all who receive it, the universality of its reception, amidst jarring creeds and conflicting tendencies, is far more significant than if its contents are indifferent, making no appeal to the religious convictions, and claiming no influence over the life. We may be disposed to complain that the external testimony is not so absolutely and finally conclusive in itself that no door is open for hesitation, that all must, despite themselves, accept it, and that any investigation into the internal evidence is superfluous and vain. But this we have no right to demand. If it is as great, and more than as great, as would satisfy us in any other case, this should suffice us. In all the most important matters which affect our interests in this world and our hopes hereafter, God has left some place for diversity of opinion, because He would not remove all opportunity of self-discipline.

If then the genuineness of this gospel is supported by greater evidence than in ordinary cases we consider conclusive, we approach the investigation of its internal character with a very strong presumption in its favour. The *onus probandi* rests with those who would impugn its genuineness, and nothing short of the fullest and most decisive marks of spuriousness can fairly be considered sufficient to counterbalance this evidence.

As I proceed, I hope to make it clear that, allowing their full weight to all the difficulties (and it would be foolish to deny the existence of difficulties) in this gospel, still the internal marks of authenticity and genuineness are so minute, so varied, so circumstantial, and so unsuspicious, as to create an over-whelming body of evidence in its favour.

But before entering upon this investigation, it may be worth while to inquire whether the hypotheses suggested by those who deny the genuineness of this gospel are themselves free from all difficulties. For if it be a fact (as I believe it is) that any alternative which has been proposed introduces greater perplexities than those which it is intended to remove, we are bound (irrespective of any positive arguments in its favour) to fall back upon the account which is exposed to fewest objections, and which at the same time is supported by a continuous and universal tradition.

We may take our start from Baur's theory, for he was the first to develop and systematize the attack on the genuineness of the Fourth Gospel. According to Baur it was written about the year 170. The external testimony however is alone fatal to this very late epoch; for, after all wresting of evidence and post-dating of documents, it is impossible to deny that at this time the gospel was, not only in existence, but also received far and wide as a genuine document; that it was not only quoted occasionally, but had even been commented upon as the actual work of St John. Consequently the tendency of later impugners has been to push the date farther back, and to recede from the extreme position of this, its most determined and ablest anta-gonist. Hilgenfeld, who may be regarded as the successor of Baur, and the present representative of the Tübingen school (though it has no longer its headquarters at Tübingen), would place its composition about the year 150; and Tayler, who a few years ago (1867) reproduced the argument of Baur and others in England, is disposed to assign it to about the same date. With a strange inconsistency he suggests, towards the close of his book, that its true author may have been John the presbyter, though John the presbyter is stated by Papias (who had conversed with this John, and from whom all the information we possess respecting him is derived) to have been a personal disciple of our Lord, and therefore could hardly have been older than John the apostle, and certainly could not have been living towards the middle of the second century.

This tendency to recede nearer and nearer to the evangelist's own age shows that the pressure of facts has begun to tell on the theories of antagonistic criticism, and we may look forward to the time when it will be held discreditable to the reputation of any critic for sobriety and judgment to assign to this gospel any later date than the end of the first century, or the very beginning of the second.

But meanwhile, let us take the earliest of these dates (A.D. 150) as less encumbered with difficulties, and therefore more favourable to the opponents of its genuineness, and ask whether a gospel written at such a time would probably have presented the phenomena which we actually find in the fourth canonical gospel. We may interrogate alike its omissions and its contents. On this hypothesis, how are we to account for what it has left unsaid, and for what it has said?

Certainly it must be regarded as a remarkable phenomenon, that on many ecclesiastical questions which then agitated the minds of Christians it is wholly silent, while to others it gives no distinct and authoritative answer. Our Lord's teaching has indeed its bearing on the controversies of the second century, as on those of the fourth, or of the twelfth, or of the sixteenth, or of the nineteenth: but, as in these latter instances, its lessons are inferential rather than direct, they are elicited by painful investigation, they are contained implicitly in our Lord's life and person, they do not lie on the surface, nor do they offer definite solutions of definite difficulties.

Take, for instance, the dispute concerning the episcopate. Contrast the absolute silence of this gospel respecting this institution with the declarations in the Epistles of Ignatius. A modern defender of the episcopate will appeal to the commission given to the apostles (John xx. 22, 23). I need not stop here to inquire to what extent it favours his views. But obviously it is quite insufficient by itself. It would serve almost equally well for an apostolically ordained ministry of any kind, for a presbyteral as for an episcopal succession. Is it possible that a writer, composing a gospel at the very time when the authority of this office had been called in question, if a supporter of the power of the episcopate, would have resisted the temptation of inserting something which would convey a sanction, if an opponent, something which would convey a disparagement, of this office, in our Lord's own name ?

Or, again : take the Gnostic theories of emanations. Any one who has studied the history of the second century will know how large a place they occupy in the theological disputes of the day; what grotesque and varied forms they assume in the speculations of different heretical teachers; what diverse arguments, some valid, some fanciful, are urged against them by orthodox writers. Would a forger have hesitated for a moment to slay this many-headed hydra by one well-aimed blow ? What can we suppose to have been the object of such a forger, except to advance certain theological views ? And why should he have let slip the very opportunity, which (we must suppose) he was making for himself, of condemning the worst forms of heresy from our Lord's own lips ? It is true that you and I think we see (and doubtless think rightly), that the doctrine of God the Word taught in St John's Gospel is the real answer to the theological questionings which gave rise to all these theories about æons or emanations, and involves implicitly and indirectly the refutation of all such theories. But it is only by more or less abstruse reasoning that we arrive at this conclusion. The early Gnostics did not see it so ; they used St John's Gospel, and retained their theories notwithstanding. A forger would have taken care to provide a direct refutation which it was impossible to misunderstand.

Or, again: about the middle of the second century the great controversy respecting the time of celebrating Easter was beginning to lift up its head. For the latter half of this century the feud raged, bursting out ever afresh and disturbing the peace of the Church again and again, until it was finally set at rest in the fourth century at the Council of Nicæa. Was the festival of the Lord's resurrection to be celebrated always on the same day of the week, the Sunday? Or was it to be guided by the time of the Jewish Passover, and thus to take place on the same day of the month, irrespective of the day of the week? Each community, each individual, took a side in this controversy. Unimportant in itself, it seriously endangered the existence of the Church. The daring adventurer who did not hesitate to forge a whole gospel would certainly not be deterred by any scruple from setting the matter at rest by a few strokes of the pen. His narrative furnished more than one favourable opportunity for interposing half a dozen decisive words in our Lord's name: and yet he abstained.

Thus we might take in succession the distinctive ecclesiastical controversies of the second century, and show how the writer of the Fourth Gospel holds aloof from them all: certainly a strange and almost incredible fact, if this writer lived about the middle, or even in the latter half, of the century, and, as a romancer, was not restrained by those obligations of fact which fetter the truthful historian who is himself a contemporary of the events recorded!

But if the omissions of the writer are strange and unaccountable on the assumption of the later date of the Gospel, the actual contents present still greater difficulties on the same hypothesis. In the interval between the age when the events are recorded to have taken place and the age in which the writer is supposed to have lived, a vast change had come over the civilized world. In no period had the dislocation of Jewish history been so complete. Two successive hurricanes had swept over the land and nation. The devastation of Titus had been succeeded by the devastation of Hadrian. What the locust of the first siege had left the cankerworm of the second had devoured. National polity, religious worship, social institutions, all were gone. The city had been razed, the land laid desolate, the law and the ordinances proscribed, the people swept into captivity or scattered over the face of the earth. 'Old things had passed away; all things had become new.'

Now let us place ourselves in the position of one who wrote about the middle of the second century, after the later Roman invasion had swept off the scanty gleanings of the past which had been spared from the earlier. Let us ask how a romancer so situated is to make himself acquainted with the incidents, the localities, the buildings, the institutions, the modes of thought and feeling, which belonged to this past age and (as we may almost say) this bygone people. Let it be granted that here and there he might stumble upon a historical fact, that in one or two particulars he might reproduce a national characteristic. More than this would be beyond his reach. For, it will be borne in mind, he would be placed at a great disadvantage, compared with a modern writer; he would have to reconstruct history without those various appliances, maps and plates, chronological tables, books of travel, by which the author of a historical novel is so largely assisted in the present day.

And even if he had been furnished with all these aids, would he have known how to use them? The uncritical character of the apostolic age is a favourite commonplace with those who impugn the genuineness of the canonical Scriptures, or the trustworthiness of the evangelical narratives. I do not deny that the age (compared with our own) was uncritical, though very exaggerated language is often used on the subject. But obviously this argument has a double edge. And the keener of these two edges lies across the very throat of recent negative criticism. For it requires a much higher flight of critical genius to invent an extremely delicate fiction than to detect it when invented. The age which could not expose a coarse forgery was incapable of constructing a subtle historical romance. This one thing I hope to make clear in the short time that is allowed me this afternoon. The Fourth Gospel, if a forgery, shows the most consummate skill on the part of the forger; it is (as we should say in modern phrase) thoroughly in keeping. It is replete with historical and geographical details; it is interpenetrated with the Judaic spirit of the times; its delineations of character are remarkably subtle; it is perfectly natural in the progress of the events; the allusions to incidents or localities or modes of thought are introduced in an artless and unconscious way, being closely interwoven with the texture of the narrative; while throughout, the author has exercised a silence and a self-restraint about his assumed personality which is without a parallel in ancient forgeries, and which deprives his work of the only motive that, on the supposition of its spuriousness, would account for his undertaking it at all.

In all these respects it forms a direct contrast to the known forgeries of the apostolic or succeeding ages. I will only ask my hearers who are acquainted with early apocryphal literature to compare St John's Gospel with two very different and yet equally characteristic products of the first and second centuries of the Christian era—with the *Protevangelium*, or Gospel of the Infancy of Jesus, on the one hand, and with the *Clementine Homilies*, on the other: the former, a vulgar daub dashed in by a coarse hand in bright and startling colours; the other, a subtle philosophical romance, elaborately drawn by an able and skilful artist. But both the one and the other are obviously artificial in all their traits, and utterly alien to the tone of genuine history.

Such productions as these show what we might expect to find in a gospel written at the middle or after the middle of the second century.

If then my description of the Fourth Gospel is not over-charged (and I will endeavour to substantiate it immediately), the supposition that this gospel was written at this late epoch by a resident at Alexandria or at Ephesus will appear in the highest degree incredible; and, whatever difficulties the traditional belief may involve, they are small indeed compared with the improbabilities created by the only alternative hypothesis.

I have already proved that the absence of certain topics in this gospel seems fatal to its late authorship. I shall now proceed to investigate those phenomena of its actual contents which force us to the conclusion that it was written by a Jew contemporary with and cognisant of the facts which he relates, and more especially those indications which fix the authorship on the Apostle St John. It is necessary however to premise by way of caution, that exhaustive treatment is impossible in a single lecture, and that I can only hope to indicate a line of investigation which any one may follow out for himself.

First of all then, the writer was a Jew. This might be inferred with a very high degree of probability from his Greek style alone. It is not ungrammatical Greek, but it is distinctly Greek of one long accustomed to think and speak through the medium of another language. The Greek language is singularly rich in its capabilities of syntactic construction, and it is also well furnished with various connecting particles. The two languages with which a Jew of Palestine would be most familiar—the Hebrew, which was the language of the sacred Scriptures, and the Aramaic, which was the medium of communication in daily life—being closely allied to each other, stand in direct contrast to the Greek in this respect. There is comparative poverty of inflexions, and there is an extreme paucity of connecting and relative particles. Hence in Hebrew and Aramaic there is little or no syntax, properly so called.

Tested by his style then, the writer was a Jew. Of all the New Testament writings the Fourth Gospel is the most distinctly Hebraic in this respect. The Hebrew simplicity of diction will at once strike the reader. There is an entire absence of periods, for which the Greek language affords such facility. The sentences are co-ordinated, not subordinated.

The clauses are strung together, like beads on a string. The very monotony of arrangement, though singularly impressive, is wholly unlike the Greek style of the age.

More especially does the influence of the Hebrew appear in the connecting particles. In this language the single connecting particle ׀ is used equally, whether co-ordination or opposition is implied; in other words, it represents 'but' as well as 'and.' The Authorized Version does not adequately represent this fact, for our translators have exercised considerable license in varying the renderings: 'then,' 'moreover,' 'and,' 'but,' etc. Now it is a noticeable fact, that in St John's Gospel the capabilities of the Greek language in this respect are most commonly neglected; the writer falls back on the simple 'and' of Hebrew diction, using it even where we should expect to find an adversative particle. Thus v. 39, 40, 'Ye search the Scriptures, for in them ye think that ye have eternal life: *and* they are they which testify of Me: *and* ye will not come to Me '; vii. 19, ' Did not Moses give you the law, *and* none of you keepeth the law ? ' where our English version has inserted an adversative particle to assist the sense, 'and *yet* '; vii. 30, ' Then they sought to take Him: *and* no man laid hands on Him,' where the English version substitutes '*but* no man '; vii. 33, ' Then said Jesus unto them, Yet a little while am I with you, *and* I go to Him that sent Me,' where again our translators attempt to improve the sense by reading 'and *then*.' And instances might be multiplied.

The Hebrew character of the diction moreover shows itself in other ways: by the parallelism of the sentences, by the repetition of the same words in different clauses, by the order of the words, by the syntactical constructions, and by individual expressions. Indeed so completely is this character maintained throughout, that there is hardly a sentence which might not be translated literally into Hebrew or Aramaic, without any violence to the language or to the sense.

I might point also to the interpretation of Aramaic words, as Cephas, Gabbatha, Golgotha, Messias, Rabboni, Siloam,

Thomas, as indicating knowledge of this language. On such isolated phenomena however no great stress can fairly be laid, because such interpretations do not necessarily require an extensive acquaintance with the language; and when the whole cast and colouring of the diction can be put in evidence, an individual word here and there is valueless in comparison.

There are however two examples of proper names in this Gospel on which it may be worth while to remark; because the original is obscured in our English Bibles by a false reading in the Greek text used by our translators, and because they afford incidentally somewhat strong testimony to the writer's knowledge both of the language and of contemporary facts.

The first of these is *Iscariot*. In the other three gospels this name is attributed to the traitor apostle Judas alone. In St John's Gospel also, as represented in the received text and in our English version, this is the case. But if the more correct readings be substituted, on the authority of the ancient copies, we find it sometimes applied to Judas himself (xii. 4, xiii. 2, xiv. 22), and sometimes to Judas' father Simon (*e.g.* vi. 71, 'He spake of Judas the son of Simon Iscariot'; xiii. 26, 'He giveth it to Judas the son of Simon Iscariot'). Now this shows that the evangelist knew this not to be a proper name strictly so called, but to describe the native place of the person, 'the man of Kerioth,' and hence to be applicable to the father and the son alike.

The other instance which I shall give, at first sight presents a difficulty; but when further investigated it only adds fresh testimony to the exact knowledge of the Fourth Evangelist. In St Matthew, Simon Peter is called Bar-Jona (Matt. xvi. 17); *i.e.* son of Jona (or Jonan or Jonas). Accordingly in the received text of St John also he appears in not less than four passages (i. 42, xxi. 15–17) as Simon son of Jona (or Jonan or Jonas). But there can be no reasonable doubt that the correct reading in all these four passages is 'Simon son of Joannes'— the Hebrew and Aramaic Johanan, the English John—and

that later transcribers have altered it to make it accord with
the form adopted by St Matthew. Here there is an apparent
discrepancy, which however disappears on examination; for we
find that Jona or Jonan or Jonas is more than once used in the
LXX version of the Old Testament as a contracted form of the
name Johanan, Johannes, or John. Thus the statements of
the two evangelists are reconciled; and we owe it to the special
knowledge derived from the Fourth Gospel that the full and
correct form is preserved. For, when we have once got this
key to the fact, we can no longer question that John was the
real name of Peter's father, since it throws great light on our
Lord's words in St Matthew. The ordinary name Jonah, which
was borne by the prophet, and which is generally supposed to
be the name of Simon's father, signifies 'a dove'; but the
name Johanan or John is 'the grace of God.' Hence the
Baptist is called not Zechariah, as his relatives thought natural,
but John, in accordance with the heavenly message (Luke i. 13),
because he was specially given to his parents by God's grace.
So too the call of St Peter (John i. 42) becomes full of meaning:
'Thou art Simon the son of the grace of God; thou shalt be
called Cephas'; and the final commission given to the same
apostle is doubly significant, when we interpret the thrice
repeated appeal as 'Simon son of God's grace, lovest thou Me?'
for without this interpretation the studied repetition of his
patronymic seems somewhat meaningless. Bearing this fact in
mind, we turn to the passage of St Matthew (xvi. 17, 18): 'Jesus
answered and said unto him, Blessed art thou, Simon Bar-Jona
(son of the grace of God): for flesh and blood hath not revealed
it unto thee, but My Father which is in heaven. And I say
unto thee, That thou art Peter, and upon this rock I will build
My Church.' His name and his surname alike are symbols and
foreshadowings of God's special favour to him in his call and
commission. This is only one of many instances in which the
authenticity of the statements of the Fourth Gospel is confirmed
by the fact that they incidentally explain what is otherwise unexplained in the narrative of the synoptic evangelists.

Another evidence that the writer was acquainted with the Hebrew language is furnished by the quotations from the Old Testament. This evangelist, like St Paul, sometimes cites from the current Greek version of the Seventy, and sometimes translates directly from the Hebrew. When a writer, as is the case in the Epistle to the Hebrews, quotes largely and quotes uniformly from the LXX version, this is at least an indication that he was not acquainted with the original; and hence we infer that the epistle just mentioned was not written by St Paul, a Hebrew of the Hebrews, but by some disciple, a Hellenistic Jew, thoroughly interpenetrated with the apostle's mind and teaching, but ignorant of the language of his fore-fathers. If on any occasion the quotations of a writer accord with the original Hebrew against the LXX version, we have a right to infer that he was acquainted with the sacred language, was, in fact, a Hebrew or Aramaic-speaking Jew. Several decisive examples might be produced, but one must suffice. In xix. 37 is a quotation from Zechariah xii. 10, which in the original is, 'They shall look upon Me whom they pierced.' Accordingly it is given in St John, 'They shall look on Him whom they pierced' (ὄψονται εἰς ὃν ἐξεκέντησαν). But the LXX rendering is, 'They shall gaze upon Me, because they insulted' (ἐπιβλέψονται πρός με, ἀνθ᾽ ὧν κατωρχήσαντο), where the LXX translators had a different reading, רָקְדוּ for דָּקְרוּ, and where their Greek rendering has not a single word in common with St John's text.

In xii. 40 again, the evangelist quotes Isaiah vi. 10, 'Because that Esaias said again, He hath blinded their eyes, and hardened their heart; that they should not see with their eyes,' etc. Now this quotation is far from being verbally exact; for in the Hebrew the sentence is imperative, 'Make fat the heart of this people, and make heavy their ears, and close their eyes, that they should not see with their eyes,' etc. Yet, on the other hand, it does not contain any of the characteristic renderings of the LXX; and this is one distinct proof that, however loosely quoted, it was derived, not from the

LXX, but from the original. For the LXX translators, taking
offence, as it would seem, at ascribing the hardening of the
heart to God's own agency, have thrown the sentence into a
passive form : ' The heart of this people was made fat, and with
their ears they heard heavily, and their eyes they closed,' etc.,
so as to remove the difficulty. If therefore the evangelist had
derived the passage from the LXX, it is inconceivable that he
would have reintroduced the active form, thus wantonly reviving
a difficulty, unless he had the original before him.

I will only add one other example. In xiii. 18 occurs a
quotation from Psalm xli. 9 (xl. 10). Here the expression
which in the original signifies literally ' made great ' or ' made
high' his heel is correctly translated 'lifted up his heel' (ἐπῆρεν
τὴν πτέρναν αὐτοῦ), as in the A.V. of the Psalms. The LXX
version however gives ἐμεγάλυνεν πτερνισμόν, ' he multiplied
(or increased) tripping up with the heel,' or ' treachery,' which
has given rise to the paraphrastic rendering in our Prayer-
Book version, ' laid great wait for me.' Here again it is
obvious that the evangelist's quotation could not have been
derived from the LXX, but must have been rendered either
directly from the Hebrew, or (what for my purpose is equally
decisive) indirectly through some Chaldee Targum.

If therefore we had no other evidence than the language,
we might with confidence affirm that this gospel was not
written either by a Gentile or by a Hellenistic Christian, but
by a Hebrew accustomed to speak the language of his fathers.
This fact alone negatives more than one hypothesis which has
been broached of late years respecting its authorship, for it is
wholly inconsistent with the strictly Gentile origin which most
recent theories assign to it. But, though irreconcilable with
Gentile authorship, it is not wholly inconsistent with the later
date; for we cannot pronounce it quite impossible that there
should be living in Asia Minor or in Egypt, in the middle
or after the middle of the second century, a Judaic Christian
familiar with the Hebrew or Aramaic language, however rare
such instances may have been.

Having thus established the fact that the writer was neither a Gentile nor a Hellenist, but a Hebrew of the Hebrews, we will proceed to inquire further whether he evinces an acquaintance with the manners and feelings, and also with the geography and history (more especially the contemporary history) of Palestine, which so far as our knowledge goes (and in dealing with such questions we must not advance one step beyond our knowledge) would be morally impossible with even a Hebrew Christian at the supposed date, long after the political existence of the nation had been obliterated, and when the disorganization of Jewish society was complete.

As I am obliged to compress my remarks within the space of a single lecture, I cannot place the evidence fully before you; but my hope is, that I may indicate the lines of investigation which will enable you to answer it more completely for yourselves. I will only say, that we obtain from the Fourth Gospel details at once fuller and more minute on all these points than from the other three. Whether we turn to the Messianic hopes of the chosen people, with all the attendant circumstances with which imagination had invested this expected event, or to the mutual relations of Samaritans, Jews, Galilæans, Romans, and the respective feelings, prejudices, beliefs, customs of each, or to the topography as well of the city and the temple as of the rural districts—the Lake of Gennesaret, and the cornfields and mountain ridges of Shechem —or to the contemporary history of the Jewish hierarchy and the Herodian sovereignty, we are alike struck at every turn with subtle and unsuspicious traces, betokening the familiarity with which the writer moves amidst the ever-shifting scenes of his wonderful narrative.

This minuteness of detail in the Fourth Evangelist is very commonly overlooked, because our gaze is arrested by still more important and unique features in this Gospel. The striking character of our Lord's discourses as recorded in St John—their length and sequence, their simplicity of language,

their fulness and depth of meaning—dazzles the eye of the
critic and blinds him to the historical aspects of the narrative.
Only by concentrating our view on these latter shall we realize
the truth that the evangelist is not floating in the clouds of
airy theological speculations, that though with his eye he peers
into the mysteries of the unseen, his foot is planted on the solid
ground of external fact; that, in short, the incidents are not
invented as a framework for the doctrine, but that the doctrine
arises naturally out of, and derives its meaning from, the incidents.

One example will serve at once to illustrate the double
characteristic of this Gospel, the accurate historical narrative of
facts which forms the basis of the Gospel, and the theological
teaching which is built as a superstructure upon this foundation, and which the evangelist keeps distinctly and persistently
in view in his selection and arrangement of the facts, and also
to introduce the investigation which I purpose instituting.

The narrative and the discourses alike are thoroughly
saturated with the Messianic ideas of the time. The Christ,
as expected by the Jews, is the one central figure round which
all the facts are grouped, the one main topic on which all the
conversations hinge. This is the more remarkable, because the
leading conception in the writer's own mind is not the Messiah,
but the Word, the Logos,—not the deliverance of Israel, but
the manifestation of God in the flesh. This main purpose is
flung out at the opening of the Gospel, and it is kept steadily
in view in the selection of materials throughout the work.
But it does not once enter into the mind of the Jews, who are
wholly absorbed in the Messianic idea. Nay, the word Logos
does not once occur even on our Lord's own lips, though the
obvious motive of His teaching is to enforce this higher aspect
of His person, to which they were strangers. And I cannot
but think that this distinct separation is a remarkable testimony to the credibility of the writer, who, however strongly
impressed with his mission as the teacher of a great theological
conception, nevertheless keeps it free from his narrative of

facts; though obviously there would be a very strong temptation to introduce it, a temptation which to a mere forger would
be irresistible.

The Messianic idea, for instance, is turned about on all
sides, and presented in every aspect. On this point we learn
very much more of contemporary Jewish opinion from the
Fourth Gospel than from the other three. At the commencement and at the close of the narrative—in the preaching of the
Baptist and in the incidents of the Passion—it is equally
prominent. In Galilee (i. 41, 46, 49; vi. 15, 28, 30 *sq.*), in
Samaria (iv. 25, 29, 42), in Judæa (v. 39, 45 *sq.*; vii. 26 *sq.*,
40–43; viii. 30 *sq.*; x. 24), it is the one standard theme of
conversation. Among friends, among foes, among neutrals
alike it is mooted and discussed. The person and character of
Jesus are tried by this standard. He is accepted or He is
rejected, as He fulfils or contradicts the received ideal of the
Messiah.

The accessories also of the Messiah's coming, as conceived
by the Jews, are brought out with a completeness beyond the
other gospels. I will only ask you, as an illustration of this,
to consider the discourse on the manna in the sixth chapter.
The key to the meaning of the conversation is the fact that the
Jews expected a miracle similar to the gift of manna in the
wilderness, as an accompaniment of the appearance of the
great deliverer. This expectation throws a flood of light on
the whole discourse. But the fact is not communicated in the
passage itself. There is only a bald, isolated statement, which
apparently is suggested by nothing, and itself fails to suggest
anything: 'Our fathers did eat manna in the wilderness.'
Then comes an aposiopesis. The inference is unexpressed.
The expectation, which explains all, is left to be inferred,
because it would be mentally supplied by men brought up
among the ideas of the time. We ourselves have to get it by
the aid of criticism and research from rabbinical authorities.
But, when we have grasped it, we can unlock the meaning of
the whole chapter.

Connected with Messiah's coming are other conceptions on which it may be worth while to dwell for a moment. One of these is the appearance of a mysterious person called 'the prophet.' This expectation arose out of the announcement in Deuteronomy xviii. 15, 'The Lord thy God will raise up unto thee a prophet from the midst of thee, like unto me.' To this anticipation we have allusions in not less than four places in St John (i. 21, 25; vi. 14; vii. 40), in all of which 'the prophet' is mentioned, though in the three first the distinctness of the expectation is blurred in the English version by the rendering 'that prophet.' In all these passages the mention of 'the prophet' without any explanation is most natural on the lips of contemporary Jews, whose minds were filled with the Messianic conceptions of the times; while such language is extremely unlikely to have been invented for them more than a century after the date of the supposed occurrences. But the point especially to be observed is, that the form which the conception takes is strictly Jewish, and not Christian. Christian teachers identified the prophet foretold by Moses with our Lord Himself, and therefore with the Christ. This application of the prophecy is made directly in St Peter's speech (Acts iii. 22), and inferentially in St Stephen's (Acts vii. 37); and later Christian teachers followed in their steps. But these Jews in St John's Gospel conceive 'the Christ' and 'the prophet' as two different persons. If He is not 'the Christ,' they adopt the alternative that He may be 'the prophet' (i. 21, 25); if not 'the prophet,' then 'the Christ' (vii. 40). It is hardly conceivable to my mind that a Christian writer, living in or after the middle of the second century, calling on his imagination for facts, should have divested himself so absolutely of the Christian idea and fallen back on the Jewish.

But before I have done with 'the prophet,' there is yet one more point worthy of notice. After the miracle of feeding the five thousand, we are told that 'those men who had seen the miracle that Jesus did said, This is of a truth the prophet that should come into the world' (vi. 14). The connexion is not

obvious, and the writer has not explained himself.   Here again
the missing link is supplied by the Messianic conception of
the age.   The prophet foretold was to be like Moses himself.
Hence it was inferred that there must be a parallel in the works
of the two.   Hence a repetition of the gift of the manna—the
bread from heaven—might be expected.   Was not this miracle
then the very fulfilment of their expectation ?   Hence we read
that on the day following (after several incidents have intervened, but with the miracle still fresh on their minds), they
seek Him out, and still try to elicit a definite answer from Him:
' What sign showest thou then ?   Our fathers did eat manna in
the desert.'   Thus a casual and indistinct reference in one part
of the chapter is explained by an equally casual and indistinct
reference in another, and light emerges from darkness.

From the Messianic ideas I turn to the Jewish sects and the
Levitical hierarchy.

The Sadducees, with whom we are familiar in other gospels,
are not once mentioned by the Fourth Evangelist.   How are we
to account for this fact ?   Have we here a discrepancy, or (if
not a discrepancy) at least an incongruity ?   Is there in St
John's picture an entire omission of that group which occupies
a prominent place on the canvas of the other evangelists,
especially of St Matthew ?

The common connexion, when describing the adversaries of
our Lord, is ' the Pharisees and Sadducees ' in the synoptic
evangelists, ' the chief priests and the Pharisees ' in St John.
In the comparison of these phrases lies the solution.   The high
priests at this time belonged to the sect of the Sadducees.   How
this happened we do not know.   It may be that their Roman
rulers favoured this party, as being more lukewarm than the
Pharisees in religious matters, and therefore less likely to give
trouble to the civil powers.   At all events, the fact appears distinctly from more than one notice in the narrative of the Acts
(iv. 1, v. 17); and the same is stated in a passage of Josephus
(*Ant.* xx. 9. 1).   Thus a real coincidence arises from an apparent
incongruity.

But Josephus elsewhere (*Ant.* xviii. 1. 4) makes another
statement respecting the Pharisees, which throws great light on
the narrative of the Fourth Evangelist.   He tells us that the
Sadducees were few in number, though of the highest rank;
and that when they were in office, they were forced, even
against their will, to listen to the Pharisees, because otherwise
they would not be tolerated by the people.   Now this is
precisely the order of events in St John.   The Pharisees (with
one single exception) always take the initiative; they are the
active opponents of our Lord, and the chief priests step in to
execute their will.

The single exception is remarkable.   Once only we find
chief priests acting alone and acting promptly (xii. 10).   They
form a plot for putting Lazarus to death.   This was essentially
a Sadducees' question.   It was necessary that a living witness
to the great truth, which the high-priestly party denied, should
be got rid of at all hazards.   Hence they bestir themselves and
throw off their usual apathy; just as, turning from the Gospels
to the Acts of the Apostles, they have taken the place of the
Pharisees as the foremost persecutors of the new faith, because
the resurrection from the dead was the cardinal topic of the
preaching of the apostles.

But there is one other notice of the Jewish historian with
which the narrative of the Fourth Evangelist presents a striking
but unsuspicious coincidence.   We are somewhat startled with
the outburst of rudeness which marks the chief of the party on
one occasion (xi. 49, 50).   'One of them, Caiaphas, being high
priest that year, said unto them, Ye know nothing at all, and
ye do not reflect that it is expedient for you that one man
should die for the people, and that the whole nation should not
perish.'   As a comment on this, take the words of Josephus:
'The behaviour of the Sadducees to one another is not a little
rude, and their intercourse with their peers is brusque, as
if addressing strangers' (*B. J.* ii. 8. 14).

These coincidences need little comment.   I will only add
that the Fourth Evangelist does not himself give us the key to

the incidents, that the references have been gathered from three different parts of Josephus, that the statements in the evangelist are not embroideries on his narrative, but are woven into its very texture; and that nevertheless all these several notices dovetail together and create one harmonious whole, which bears the very impress of strict historical truth.

After reviewing these coincidences, it will appear strange that from the passage last quoted Baur derived what he obviously considered to be one of his strongest arguments against the authenticity of the Gospel. Because the evangelist three times speaks of Caiaphas as 'high priest that year' (xi. 49, 51; xviii. 13), he argues that the writer supposed the high priesthood to be an annual office, and therefore could not have been the Apostle John.

Now unless I have entirely misled you and myself, this is incredible. You cannot imagine that one who shows an acquaintance, not only with the language, but also with the customs, feelings, history, topography of the race, even in their minute details, should yet be ignorant of this most elementary fact of Jewish institutions. Whether the Gospel is authentic or whether it is not, such a supposition is equally incredible. If the writing is a forgery, the forger was certainly highly informed and extremely subtle; he must have ransacked divers histories for his facts; and yet here he is credited with a degree of ignorance which a casual glance at a few pages of his Old Testament or his Josephus would at once have served to dissipate. Suppose a parallel case. Imagine one, who writing (we will say) a historical work, shows a subtle appreciation of political feeling in England, and a minute acquaintance with English social institutions, and yet falls into the error of supposing that the premier is elected annually by vote of the people, or that the lord-mayoralty is a hereditary office tenable for life.

If therefore this supposition is simply impossible, we must explain the expression, 'high priest that year,' in some other way. And the explanation seems to be this. The most important duty of the high priest was an annual function, the sacrifice and intercession for the people on the great day of atonement. 'Once every year,' says the writer of the Epistle to the Hebrews (ix. 7), 'the high priest alone entereth into the second tabernacle (the inner sanctuary), not without blood, which he offereth for himself and for the errors of the people.' The year of which the evangelist speaks was the year of all years; 'the acceptable year of the Lord,' as it is elsewhere called; the year in which the great sacrifice, the one atonement, was made, the atonement which annulled once and for ever the annual repetitions. It so happened that it was the duty of Caiaphas, as high priest, to enter the holy of holies, and offer the atonement for *that* year. The evangelist sees, if we may use the phrase without irreverence, a dramatic propriety in the fact that he of all men should make this declaration. By a Divine irony he is made unconsciously to declare the truth, proclaiming Jesus to be the great atoning sacrifice, and himself to be instrumental in offering the victim. This irony of circumstances is illustrated in the case of Pilate, as in the case of Caiaphas. The latter, the representative of the Jewish hierarchy, pronounces Jesus the great atoning sacrifice; the former, the representative of the civil power, pronounces Him as the sovereign of the race, 'Behold your King!' The malignity of Caiaphas and the sneer of Pilate alike bear witness to a higher truth than they themselves consciously apprehend.

From the sects and the hierarchy we may turn to the city and the temple. Here too we should do well to bear in mind how largely we owe the distinctive features of the topography and architecture with which we are familiar to the Fourth Gospel. Within the sacred precincts themselves the Porch of Solomon, within the Holy City the pools of Bethsaida[1] and Siloam, are brought before our eyes by this evangelist alone. And when we pass outside of the walls, he is still our guide. From him we trace the steps of the Lord and His disciples on

[1] 'Bethsaida' or 'Bethzatha' should probably be read in S. John v. 2 rather than 'Bethesda.'

that fatal night crossing the brook Kedron into the garden; it is he who, relating the last triumphal entry into Jerusalem, specifies 'the branches of the palm trees' (the other evangelists use general expressions, 'boughs of the trees,' or the like)— 'the palm trees' on which he had so often gazed, of which the sight was still so fresh in his memory, which clothed the eastern slopes of Olivet, and gave its name to the village of Bethany, 'the house of dates.' How simple and natural the definite articles are on the lips of an eye-witness I need not say. How awkward they sound to later ears, and how little likely to have been used by a later writer, unfamiliar with the scene itself, we may infer from the fact that in our own version they are suppressed, and the evangelist is made to say, 'they took branches of palm trees.'

Moreover the familiarity of the Fourth Evangelist, not only with the site and the buildings of the temple, but also with the history, appears in a striking way from a casual allusion. After the description of the cleansing of the temple by our Lord, —a description which though brief is given with singular vividness of detail—the Jews ask for some sign, as the credential which might justify this assumption of authority and right of chastisement. His answer is, 'Pull down this temple, and in three days I will build it up.' Their astonishment is expressed in their reply, 'This temple has been forty-six years in building, and wilt Thou raise it again in three days?' (ii. 19, 20).

Now I think it will be allowed that this mention of time is quite undesigned. It has no appearance of artifice, it occurs naturally in the course of conversation, and it is altogether free from suspicion, as having been introduced to give a historical colouring to a work of fiction. If so, let us examine its historical bearing.

For this purpose it is necessary to follow two distinct lines of chronological research. We have to investigate the history of the building of the Herodian temple, and we have to ascertain the dates of our Lord's life.

Now by comparison of several passages in Josephus, and

by the exercise of historical criticism upon them, we arrive at
the conclusion that Herod commenced his temple about A.U.C.
735, *i.e.* B.C. 18. It took many years in building, and was not
finally completed until A.U.C. 817, *i.e.* A.D. 64. Thus the works
were going on during the whole of the period comprised in the
New Testament history. If we add forty-six years to the date
of its commencement (A.U.C. 735) we are brought down to A.U.C.
781 or 782, *i.e.* A.D. 28 or 29.

The chronology of Herod's temple involves one considerable
effort of historical criticism. The chronology of our Lord's life
requires another. Into this question however I need not enter
in detail. It is sufficient to remind you that the common date
of the Christian era is now generally allowed to be a little wide
of the mark, and that our Lord's birth actually took place three
or four years before this era. The point to be observed here is,
that St Luke places the baptism of our Lord in or about the
fifteenth year of Tiberius, which comprised the interval between
the autumn of 781 and the autumn of 782. Now the occurrence
related by St John took place, as we may infer from his narrative, in the first passover after the baptism; that is, according
to St Luke's chronology probably at the passover of 782.

Thus we are brought to the same date by following two
lines of chronology; and we arrive at the fact that forty-six
years there or thereabouts had actually elapsed since the commencement of Herod's building to this point in our Lord's
ministry. I am anxious not to speak with too great precision,
because the facts do not allow it. The exact number might
have been forty-five or forty-seven years, for fragments of years
may be reckoned in or not in our calculation, and the data are
not sufficiently exact to determine the date to a nicety. But,
after all allowance made for this margin of uncertainty, the
coincidence is sufficiently striking.

And now let us suppose the Gospel to have been written in
the middle of the second century, and ask ourselves what strong
improbabilities this hypothesis involves.

The writer must first have made himself acquainted with

a number of facts connected with the temple of Herod. He must not only have known that the temple was commenced in a particular year, but also that it was still incomplete at the time of our Lord's ministry. So far as we know, he could only have got these facts from Josephus. Even Josephus however does not state the actual date of the commencement of the temple. It requires some patient research to arrive at this date by a comparison of several passages. We have therefore to suppose, first, that the forger of the Fourth Gospel went through an elaborate critical investigation for the sake of ascertaining the date. But, secondly, he must have made himself acquainted with the chronology of the gospel history. At all events, he must have ascertained the date of the commencement of our Lord's ministry. The most favourable supposition is, that he had before him the Gospel of St Luke, though he nowhere else betrays the slightest acquaintance with this gospel. Here he would find the date which he wanted, reckoned by the years of the Roman emperors. Thirdly, after arriving at these two results by separate processes, he must combine them; thus connecting the chronology of the Jewish kings with the chronology of the Roman emperors, the chronology of the temple erection with the chronology of our Lord's life.

When he has taken all these pains, and worked up the subject so elaborately, he drops in the notice which has given him so much trouble in an incidental and unobtrusive way. It has no direct bearing on his history; it does not subserve the purpose of his theology. It leads to nothing, proves nothing. Certainly the art of concealing art was never exercised in a more masterly way than here. And yet this was an age which perpetrated the most crude and bungling forgeries, and is denounced by modern criticism for its utter incapacity of criticism.

Nor, when we travel beyond the city and its suburbs, does the writer's knowledge desert him. One instance must suffice; but it is, if I mistake not, so convincing, that it may well serve in place of many.

The country of the Samaritans lay between Judæa and Galilee, so that a person journeying from the one region to the other, unless he were prepared to make a detour, must necessarily pass through it. This was the case with our Lord and His Apostles, as related in the fourth chapter. The high-road from Jerusalem passes through some very remarkable scenery. The mountain ridges of Ebal and Gerizim run parallel to each other from east to west, not many hundred feet apart, thus inclosing a narrow valley between them. Eastward this valley opens out into a plain, a rare phenomenon in this country—'one mass of corn unbroken by a boundary or hedge,' as it is described by one who has seen it. Up the valley westward, shut in between these mountain barriers, lies the modern town of Nablûs, the ancient Shechem. The road does not enter the valley, but traverses the plain, running at right angles to the gorge, and thus touching the eastern bases of the mountain ridges as they fall down into the level ground. Here at the mouth of the valley is a deep well, even now descending 'to a depth of seventy feet or more,' and formerly, before it had been partially filled with accumulated rubbish, we may well believe deeper still. In the words of Dean Stanley:

"Of all the *special* localities of our Lord's life in Palestine, this is almost the only one absolutely undisputed. By the edge of this well, in the touching language of the ancient hymn, 'quaerens me sedisti lassus.' Here on the great road through which 'He must needs go' when 'He left Judæa, and departed into Galilee,' He halted, as travellers still halt, in the noon or evening of the spring day by the side of the well. Up that passage through the valley His disciples 'went away into the city,' which He did not enter. Down the same gorge came the woman to draw water, according to the unchanged custom of the East. . . . Above them, as they talked, rose 'this mountain' of Gerizim, crowned by the temple, of which vestiges still remain, where the fathers of the Samaritan sect 'said men ought to worship.' . . . And round about them, as He and she thus sate or stood by the well, spread far and wide the noble plain of waving corn. It was still winter, or early spring, 'four months yet to the harvest,' and the bright golden ears of those fields had not yet 'whitened' their unbroken expanse of verdure. But as He gazed upon them, they served to suggest the glorious vision of the distant harvest of the Gentile world, which with each successive turn of the conversation unfolded itself more and more distinctly before Him, as He sate (so we gather from the narrative) absorbed in the opening prospect, silent amidst His silent and astonished disciples."

The scrupulous accuracy of the geographical and archæological details in St John's account of the conversation with the Samaritan woman will have appeared already from this quotation. I will only ask you to consider for a moment how naturally they occur in the course of the narrative, so naturally and so incidentally that without the researches of modern travellers the allusions would be entirely lost to us. I think that this consideration will leave but one alternative. Either you have here written, as we are constantly reminded, in an uncritical age and among an uncritical people, the most masterly piece of romance-writing which the genius and learning of man ever penned in any age; or you have (what universal tradition represents it to be) a genuine work of an eye-witness and companion of our Lord. Which of these two suppositions does less violence to historical probability I will leave to yourselves to determine.

Follow then the narrative in detail. An unknown Traveller is sitting at the well. His garb, or His features, or His destination, show Him to be a Jew. A woman of the country comes to draw water from the well, and He asks her to give Him to drink. She is surprised that He, a Jew, is willing to talk so freely to her, a Samaritan. And here I would remark that the explanation which follows, ' For the Jews have no dealings with ' (or rather, ' do not associate with') 'the Samaritans,' is the evangelist's own, a fact obscured by the ordinary mode of printing in our English Bibles. Hitherto, though the scene is very natural and very real, there is nothing which a fairly clever artist might not have invented. But from this point onwards follow in rapid succession various historical and geographical allusions, various hints of individual character in the woman, various aspects of Divine teaching on our Lord's part, all closely interwoven together, each suggesting and suggested by another, in such a manner as to preclude any hypothesis of romance or forgery. 'Thou wouldest have asked, and I would have given thee living water.' 'Sir, Thou hast nothing to draw with, and the well is *deep*. . . . Art Thou greater than our father Jacob?' And so the conversation proceeds, one point suggesting the next in the most natural way. Take, for instance, the reference to Gerizim. 'Sir, I perceive that Thou art a prophet. Our fathers worshipped in this mountain.' Observe that there is no mention in the context of any mountain in the neighbourhood; that even here, where it is mentioned, its name is not given: but suddenly the woman, partly to divert the inconvenient tenour of the conversation, partly to satisfy herself on one important point of difference between the Samaritans and the Jews, avails herself of the newly found prophet's presence, and, pointing to the over-hanging heights of Gerizim, puts the question to Him. The mention of the sacred mountain, like the mention of the depths of the well, draws forth a new spiritual lesson. 'Not in this mountain, nor yet at Jerusalem. . . . God is a spirit.' The woman saith, 'When Messias cometh, He will tell us all things.' Jesus saith, 'I that speak unto thee am He.'

At this point the disciples approach from the valley, with the provisions which they had purchased in the city, and rejoin their Master. They are surprised to find Him so engaged. Here again an error in the English version obscures the sense. Their marvel was, not that He talked with *the* woman, but that He talked with *a* woman. It was a rabbinical maxim, 'Let no man talk with a woman in the street (in public), no, not with his own wife.' The narrowness of His disciples was shocked that He, their own rabbi, should be so wanting to Himself as to disregard this recognised precept of morality. The narrator assumes the knowledge with which he himself was so familiar.

So the conversation with the woman closes. With natural eagerness she leaves her pitcher, and hurries back to the city with her news. With natural exaggeration she reports there that the stranger has told her all things that ever she did.

A conversation with the disciples follows, which is hardly

less remarkable, but from which I must be content to select one illustration only. I think that it must be allowed, that the reference to the harvest is wholly free from suspicion, as regards the manner of its introduction. It is unpremeditated, for it cannot be severed from the previous part of the conversation, out of which it arises. It is unobtrusive, for the passage itself makes no attempt to explain the local allusion (which, without the experience of modern travellers would escape notice): 'There are yet four months, and then cometh the harvest. Behold, I say unto you, Lift up your eyes, and look on the fields ; for they are white already to harvest.' And yet, when we once realize the scene, when in imagination our eye ranges over that vast expanse of growing corn—so unusual in Palestine, however familiar in corn-growing England—we are at once struck with the truthfulness and the significance of this allusive parable.

I have thus endeavoured to show, by taking a few instances, the accuracy of the writer's knowledge in all that relates to the history, the geography, the institutions, the thoughts and feelings of the Jews. If however we had found accuracy, and nothing more, we might indeed have reasonably inferred that the narrative was written by a Jew of the mother-country, who lived in a very early age, before time and circumstance had obliterated the traces of Palestine, as it existed in the first century ; but we could not safely have gone beyond this. But unless I have entirely deceived myself, the manner in which this accurate knowledge betrays itself justifies the further conclusion that we have before us the genuine narrative of an eye-witness, who records the events just as they occurred in natural sequence.

I have discussed the accuracy of the external allusions. Let me now apply another test. The representation of character is perhaps the most satisfactory criterion of a true narrative, as applied to an age before romance-writing had been studied as an art.

We are all familiar with the principal characters in the

Gospel history: Peter, John, Philip, Thomas, Pilate, the sisters Mary and Martha, and several others which I might mention; each standing before us with an individuality, which seems to place him or her within the range of our own personal knowledge. Have we ever asked ourselves to which evangelist above the rest we owe this personal acquaintance with the actors in this great drama?

When the question is once asked, the answer cannot be doubtful. It is true indeed that we should have known St Peter without the narrative of the Fourth Evangelist, though he adds several minute points, which give additional life to the portrait. It is true that Pilate is introduced to us in the other Gospels, though without St John we should not have been able to read his heart and character, his proud Roman indifference and his cynical scorn. But, on the other hand, take the case of Thomas. Of this Apostle nothing is recorded in the other Evangelists, and yet he stands out before us, not as a mere lay figure, on whose stiff, mechanical form the artist may hang a moral precept or a doctrinal lesson by way of drapery, but as a real, living, speaking man, at once doubtful and eager, at once hesitating and devoted—sceptical, not because his nature is cold and unsympathetic, but because his intellect moves more cautiously than his heart, because the momentous issues which belief involves bid him pause before he closes with it; at one moment endeavouring to divert his Master's purpose of going up to Jerusalem, where certain destruction awaits him: at the next, ready to share the perils with Him, 'Let us also go with Him'; at one moment resisting the testimony of direct eye-witnesses and faithful friends to his Master's resurrection: at the next, overwhelmed by the evidence of his senses, and expressing the depth of his conviction in the earnest confession 'My Lord and my God.'

I must satisfy myself with one other example. The character of the sisters Martha and Mary presents a striking contrast. They are mentioned once only in the other Gospels, in the familiar passage of St Luke, where they appear respectively as

the practical, bustling housewife, who is busied about many
things, and the devout, contemplative, absorbed disciple, who
chooses the one thing needful. In St John also this contrast
reappears; but the characteristics of the two sisters are brought
out in a very subtle way. In St Luke the contrast is summed
up, as it were, in one definite incident; in St John it is developed gradually in the course of a continuous narrative. And
there is also another difference. In St Luke the contrast is
direct and trenchant, a contrast (one might almost say) of light
and darkness. But in St John the characters are shaded off, as
it were, into each other. Both alike are beloved by our Lord,
both alike send to Him for help, both alike express their faith
in His power, both alike show deep sorrow for their lost brother.
And yet, notwithstanding this, the difference of character is
perceptible throughout the narrative. It is Martha who, with
her restless activity, goes out to meet Jesus, while Mary remains
in the house weeping. It is Martha who holds a conversation
with Jesus, argues with Him, remonstrates with Him, and in
the very crisis of their grief shows her practical common sense
in deprecating the removal of the stone. It is Mary who goes
forth silently to meet Him, silently and tearfully, so that the
bystanders suppose her to be going to weep at her brother's
tomb; who, when she sees Jesus, falls down at His feet; who,
uttering the same words of faith in His power as Martha, does
not qualify them with the same reservation; who infects all
the bystanders with the intensity of her sorrow, and crushes
the human spirit of our Lord Himself with sympathetic grief.

And when we turn to the second occasion in which the two
sisters are introduced by St John, the contrast is still the same.
Martha is busied in the homely duties of hospitality towards
Jesus and her other guests; but Mary brings her choicest and
most precious gift to bestow upon Him, at the same time
showing the depth of her humility and the abandonment of her
devotion by wiping His feet with her hair.

In all this narrative the Evangelist does not once direct
attention to the contrast between the two sisters. He simply

relates the events of which he was an eye-witness without a comment. But the two were real, living persons, and therefore the difference of character between them develops itself in action.

I have shown hitherto that, whatever touchstone we apply, the Fourth Gospel vindicates itself as a trustworthy narrative, which could only have proceeded from a contemporary and an eye-witness. But nothing has hitherto been adduced which leads to the identification of the author as the Apostle St John. Though sufficient has been said to vindicate the *authenticity*, the *genuineness* is yet untouched.

It is said by those who deny its apostolic origin, that the unknown author, living in the middle of the second century, and wishing to gain a hearing for a modified gospel suited to the wants of his age, dropped his own personality and shielded himself under the name of St John the son of Zebedee.

Is this a true representation of the fact? Is it not an entire though unconscious misrepresentation? John is not once mentioned by name throughout the twenty-one chapters of this Gospel. James and John, the sons of Zebedee, occupy a prominent place in all the other Evangelists. In this Fourth Gospel alone neither brother's name occurs. The writer does once, it is true, speak of the 'sons of Zebedee'; but in this passage, which occurs in the last chapter (xxi. 2), there is not even the faintest hint of any connexion between the writer himself and this pair of brothers. He mentions them in the third person, as he might mention any character whom he had occasion to introduce.

Now is not this wholly unlike the proceeding of a forger who was simulating a false personality? Would it not be utterly irrational under these circumstances to make no provision for the identification of the author, but to leave everything to the chapter of accidents? No discredit, indeed, is thrown on the genuineness of a document by the fact that the author's name appears on the forefront. This is the case with the histories of Herodotus and Thucydides; it is the case also with the Epistles of Paul and Peter and James, and with the Apocalypse of John. But, on the supposition of forgery, it was a matter of vital moment that the work should be accepted as the genuine production of its pretended author. The two instances of early Christian forgeries which I brought forward in an earlier part of this lecture will suffice as illustrations. The *Gospel of the Infancy* closes with a distinct declaration that it was written by James. The *Clementine Homilies* affirm the pretended authorship in the opening words, 'I Clement, being a Roman citizen.' Even if our supposed forger could have exercised this unusual self-restraint in suppressing the simulated author's name, would he not have made it clear by some allusion to his brother James, or to his father Zebedee, or to his mother Salome? The policy which he has adopted is as suicidal as it is unexpected.

How then do we ascertain that it was written by John the son of Zebedee? I answer, first of all, that it is traditionally ascribed to him, as the *Phædo* is ascribed to Plato, or the *Antigone* to Sophocles; and, secondly, that from a careful examination of indirect allusions and casual notices, from a comparison of things said and things unsaid, we arrive at the same result by a process independent of external tradition. But a forger could not have been satisfied with trusting to either of these methods. External tradition was quite beyond the reach of his control. In this particular case, as we shall see, the critical investigation requisite is so subtle, and its subject-matter lies so far below the surface, that a forger, even supposing him capable of constructing the narrative, would have defeated his own purpose by making such demands on his readers.

For let us follow out this investigation. In the opening chapter of the Gospel there is mention of a certain disciple whose name is not given (i. 35, 37, 40). This anonymous person (for it is a natural, though not a certain inference, that

the same is meant throughout) reappears again in the closing
scene before and after the passion, where he is distinguished as
'the disciple whom Jesus loved.' At length, but not till the
concluding verses of the Gospel, we are told that this anonymous disciple is himself the writer: ' This is the disciple which
testifieth of these things, and wrote these things.'

In accordance with this statement we find that those
particular scenes in which this anonymous disciple is recorded
as taking a part are related with peculiar minuteness and
vividness of detail. Such is the case, for instance, with the
notices of the Baptist and of the call of the earliest disciples.
Such again is the case with the conversation at the last supper,
with the scene over the fire in the hall of Caiaphas's house,
with certain other incidents connected with the crucifixion, and
with the scene on the Lake of Galilee after the resurrection.

Who then is this anonymous disciple? On this point the
Gospel furnishes no information. We arrive at the identification, partly by a process of exhaustion, partly by attention to
some casual incidents and expressions.

Comparing the accounts in the other Gospels, it seems safe
to assume that he was one of the inner circle of disciples. This
inner circle comprised the two pairs of brothers, Peter and
Andrew, James and John—if indeed Andrew deserves a place
here. Now he cannot have been Andrew, because Andrew
appears in company with him in the opening chapter; nor can
he have been Peter, because we find him repeatedly associated
with Peter in the closing scenes. Again, James seems to be
excluded; for James fell an early martyr, and external and
internal evidence alike point to a later date for this Gospel.
Thus by a process of exhaustion we are brought to identify him
with John the son of Zebedee.

With this identification all the particulars agree.

First. He is called among the earliest disciples; and from
his connexion with Andrew (i. 40, 44) it may be inferred that
he was a native of Bethsaida in the neighbourhood.

Secondly. At the close of his Master's life, and after his

Master's resurrection, we find him especially associated with Simon Peter. This position exactly suits John, who in the earliest days of the Church takes his place by the side of Peter in the championship of faith.

Thirdly. Unless the beloved disciple be John the son of Zebedee, this person who occupies so prominent a place in the account of the other Evangelists, and who stood in the foremost rank in the estimation of the early Church as a pillar Apostle, does not once appear in the Fourth Gospel, except in the one passage where 'the sons of Zebedee' are mentioned and summarily dismissed in a mere enumeration of names. Such a result is hardly credible.

Lastly. Whereas in the other Evangelists John the Baptist is very frequently distinguished by the addition of this surname, and always so distinguished where there is any possibility of confusing him with the son of Zebedee, in this Gospel alone the forerunner is never once called John the Baptist. To others some distinguishing epithet seemed needed. To the son of Zebedee there was only one famous John; and therefore when he had occasion to mention him, he naturally spoke of him as John simply, without any addition. Is it conceivable, I would ask, that any forger would have lost sight of himself so completely, and used natural language of John the son of Zebedee with such success, as to observe this very minute and unobtrusive indication of personality?

I have addressed myself more directly to the theory of the Tübingen school, either as propounded by Baur, or as modified by later critics, which denies at once the historical character of this Gospel and its apostolic authorship, and places it in the middle or latter half of the second century. But there is an intermediate position between rejecting its worth as a historic record and accepting St John as its author, and this position has been taken up by some. They suppose it to have been composed by some disciple or disciples of St John from reminiscences of their master's teaching, and thus they are prepared to allow that it contains some historical matter which is valuable. You will have seen however that most of the arguments adduced, though not all, are equally fatal to this hypothesis as the other. The process by which, after establishing its authenticity, we succeeded in identifying its author is, if I mistake not, alone sufficient to overthrow this solution. Indeed this theory is exposed to a double set of objections, and it has nothing to recommend it.

I have already taken up more time than I had intended, and yet I feel that very much has been left unsaid. But I venture to hope that certain lines of investigation have been indicated, which, if carefully and soberly followed out, can only lead to one result. Whatever consequences may follow from it, we are compelled on critical grounds to accept this Fourth Gospel as the genuine work of John the son of Zebedee.

Some among my hearers perhaps may be disappointed that I have not touched on some well-known difficulties, though these have been grossly exaggerated. Some have to be satisfactorily explained; of others probable, or at least possible, solutions have been given; while others still remain on which we are obliged to suspend judgment until some new light of history is vouchsafed. It is not from too much light, but from too little light, that the historical credibility of this Gospel has suffered. Each new discovery made, each old fact elucidated, sets at rest some disputed question. If the main fact of the genuineness be established, the special difficulties can well afford to wait.

One word more, and I conclude. I have treated this as a purely critical question, carefully eschewing any appeal to Christian instincts. As a critical question I wish to take a verdict upon it. But as I could not have you think that I am blind to the theological issues directly or indirectly connected with it, I will close with this brief confession of faith. I believe from my heart that the truth which this Gospel more especially enshrines—the truth that Jesus Christ is the very Word Incarnate, the manifestation of the Father to mankind—is the one lesson which, duly apprehended, will do more than all our feeble efforts to purify and elevate human life here by imparting to it hope and light and strength, the one study which alone can fitly prepare us for a joyful immortality hereafter.

[1871.]

II.

EXTERNAL EVIDENCE FOR THE AUTHENTICITY
AND GENUINENESS OF ST JOHN'S GOSPEL.

Printed from Lecture-notes.

II.

EXTERNAL EVIDENCE FOR THE AUTHENTICITY
AND GENUINENESS OF ST JOHN'S GOSPEL.

THE genuineness of St John's Gospel is the centre of the
position of those who uphold the historical truth of the
record of our Lord Jesus Christ given us in the New Testament.
Hence the attacks of the opponents of revealed religion are concentrated upon it. So long however as it holds its ground, these
assaults must inevitably prove ineffective. The assailants are
of two kinds: (1) those who deny the miraculous element in
Christianity—Rationalists, (2) those who deny the distinctive
character of Christian doctrine—Unitarians. The Gospel con-
fronts both. It relates the most stupendous miracle in the
history of our Lord (short of the Incarnation and the Resurrection), the raising of Lazarus. Again, it enunciates in the most
express terms the Divinity, the Deity, of our Lord. And yet at
the same time it professes to have been written by the one man,
of all others, who had the greatest opportunities of knowing the
truth. The testimony of St Paul might conceivably be set
aside, as of one who was not an eye-witness. But here we
have, not an ἔκτρωμα[1], not a personal disciple merely, not one
of the twelve only, but *the one* of the twelve—the Apostle who
leaned on his Master's bosom, who stood by his Master's cross,
who entered his Master's empty grave. If therefore the claim
of this Gospel to be the work of John the son of Zebedee be
true, if in other words the Fourth Gospel be genuine, the most

---

[1] 1 Cor. xv. 8.

formidable, not to say an insuperable, obstacle stands in the way of both classes of antagonists.   Hence the persistence and the ingenuity of the attacks; and hence also the necessity of a thoroughness in the defence.   No apology therefore is needed, if the subject should seem dry and uninviting.

And details too are necessary.   For the nature of the proof is cumulative.   Some points which I shall have to urge may seem weak.   The allusions to the Gospel in many cases are uncertain or anonymous.   But they must be taken *pro tanto*. To borrow a mechanical simile, evidence for the authenticity of a document is not like a chain, where the strength of the whole is the strength of its weakest link.   It is like the supports of a building, where the strength is in the aggregate.   One pillar may be weak, or may fall; but the superstructure will still remain, for each instance is independent of the others.

Consequently, considerable mental effort is necessary in order to keep in view all the elements of a cumulative proof. We are apt to concentrate our attention on that which is last, or that which is exceptional.   If then the last argument stated is weak, or if anywhere there is one argument exceptionally weak, we may leap to the conclusion that the whole is weak. This is manifestly a false mode of arguing, and we must constantly be on our guard against its subtle influence.

Hence the necessity of keeping the whole in view.   We shall be occupied during the present term with the *external evidence*.   But the external evidence is not all.   And in summing up in our own minds the results which we shall obtain, we must not forget what lies beyond—what will occupy us probably next term—the reinforcement of the *internal evidence*. For the present however we shall confine ourselves to the former.   And we cannot help being struck at the outset by the inadequacy of treatment which the question has met with in the *prolegomena* of the majority of commentators.   An allusion to Theophilus, to Irenæus, to Eusebius, an apology, somewhat lame, for the silence of Papias, and the whole subject is briefly and summarily dismissed.   Now the injury

done to the cause of revealed truth by this method of treatment is very serious, and has resulted in an undue disparagement of the external evidence for the Fourth Gospel. On this
point I cannot do better than quote so temperate and judicious
a writer as Mr Sanday, who, in his introduction to his work on
the *Authorship and Historical Character of the Fourth Gospel*,
when stating his reasons for confining himself to the internal
evidence, writes as follows:

> 'Several reasons seem to make this limitation of treatment desir-
> able. The subject of the external evidence has been pretty well fought
> out. The opposing parties are probably as near to an agreement as
> they ever will be. It will hardly be an unfair statement of the case
> for those who reject the Johannean authorship of the Gospel to say
> that the external evidence is compatible with that supposition. And
> on the other hand, we may equally say for those who accept the Johan-
> nean authorship, that the external evidence would not be sufficient
> alone to prove it. As it at present stands, the controversy may
> be regarded as drawn; and it is not likely that the position of
> parties will be materially altered' (p. 3).

Now I hope to show that there is no deficiency of testimony
(considering the nature of the subject), that on the contrary
there is a vast body of evidence of various kinds, which cannot
be set aside; that the result is a very powerful argument in
favour of the genuineness; and that therefore, when we enter
upon the question of internal evidence, we shall enter upon it
with a very strong weight of evidence in support of St John's
authorship, which can only be counterbalanced by powerful considerations on the other side.

But, before commencing the investigation, let us first see
what is the nature of the antagonism with which we have to
deal. The history of the controversy may be seen in Bleek[1].
Briefly stated, the position of affairs is this. The universal
reception of the Gospel as the work of St John (with the
exception of an obscure sect[2]) up to the close of the last
century has been assailed in the early years of the present

---

[1] Bleek *Beiträge zur Evangelien-
Kritik* (1846).

[2] The Alogi, on whom see below,
pp. 115 sq.

century by a series of writers, who unite in denying the Johannine authorship, and place the date somewhere in the middle or latter half of the second century.

I give the names of the principal exponents of the new view, with the dates which they respectively assign for the authorship :—

BRETSCHNEIDER *Probabilia de Evangelii et Epistolarum Joannis Apostoli indole et origine* Leipzig 1820. He expressed himself vaguely as to the date, but apparently placed it at the beginning or middle of the second century. After two years, in the preface to his *Handbuch der Dogmatik* 1822, he withdrew his conclusions, and declared his conviction that the Johannine authorship was finally established.

LÜTZELBERGER *Die kirchliche Tradition über den Apostel Johannes und seine Schriften in ihrer Grundlosigkeit nachgewiesen* Leipzig 1840. He considers that the Gospel was written near Edessa, about 135–140.

BAUR first expressed his views on the Johannine question in the *Theologische Jahrbücher* Tübingen 1844. He fixes the date somewhere about 160–170, and this is the view of the older Tübingen School.

HILGENFELD *Das Evangelium und die Briefe Johannis nach ihrem Lehrbegriff* (1849). He considers that the Fourth Gospel took its rise in the middle of the second century owing to the prevalence of the Valentinian Gnosis.

SCHOLTEN, professor at Leyden, and head of the modern Dutch negative school, in his work entitled *Het Evangelie naar Johannes* (1864–6) places the writing of the Fourth Gospel in 150, but considers that it was interpolated subsequently. In a later work *De oudste getuigenissen* (1867) he throws the date back later still to 170.

TAYLER, J. J. *An attempt to ascertain the character of the Fourth Gospel, especially in its relation to the Three First* London 1867. In reading this work we cannot fail to be struck with its evident sincerity ; at the same time it exhibits singular deficiency in the enumeration of facts, and looseness in the treatment of them. Tayler's conclusion is that the Fourth Gospel was written after 135 and before 163 (p. 151). And yet (p. 155) he suggests that 'John the Presbyter' is the author of the book—John the Presbyter, of whom we only know that he was a personal disciple of our Lord.

KEIM *Geschichte Jesu von Nazara* (1867) ascribes the Fourth Gospel to the reign of Trajan, A.D. 98–117.

RENAN in the first edition of his *Vie de Jésus* (1863) considers that our Fourth Gospel is based upon the genuine work of St John, but edited by his disciples at the end of the first century. M. Renan's view has fluctuated in subsequent editions of his book.

In reviewing this list of writers, we cannot fail to be struck with two facts: (1) the variety of their opinions; (2) their gradual retrogression from the extreme position taken up at first. The pressure of facts has compelled them to abandon one position after another, and to approximate more and more closely to the traditional view.

I. THE CHURCHES OF ASIA MINOR.

Unless we are prepared to reject without a hearing all the traditions of Christianity, we cannot refuse to believe that the latest years of the Apostle St John were spent in the Roman province of Asia and chiefly in Ephesus its capital. This tradition is singularly full, consistent and well-authenticated[1]. Here he gathered disciples about him, organized churches, appointed bishops and presbyters. A whole chorus of voices unite in bearing testimony to its truth. One who passed his earlier life in these parts and had heard his aged master, a disciple of St John himself, recount his personal reminiscences of the great Apostle[2]; another, who held this very see of Ephesus and writing less than a century after the Apostle's death was linked with the past by a chain of relatives all bishops in the Christian Church[3]; a third who also flourished about the close of the century and numbered among his teachers an old man from this very district[4]—are the principal, because the most distinct, witnesses to a fact which is implied in several other notices of earlier or contemporary writers.

As to the time at which St John left his original home and settled in this new abode no direct account is preserved; but a very probable conjecture may be hazarded. The impending

---

[1] Papias in Eus. *H. E.* iii. 39; Iren. ii. 22. 5, Fragm. 2 (p. 822 Stieren) etc.; Polycrates in Eus. *H. E.* v. 24; Apollonius in Eus. *H. E.* v. 18; Clem. Alex. *Quis div. salv.* 42 (p. 958); cf. *Can. Mur.* (p. 17 ed. Tregelles), Tertull. *adv. Marc.* iv. 5, *Praescr. Haer.* 32, *Ancient Syriac Documents* pp. 32, 34 (*ed.* Cureton). The variety of the sources of these quotations—Gaul, Asia Minor, Alexandria, Rome, Carthage, Syria—is worth noticing.

[2] Irenæus.

[3] Polycrates.

[4] Clement of Alexandria. One of his teachers was an Ionian Greek (*Strom.* I. 1. § 11 p. 322); see below, p. 92.

fall of the Holy City was the signal for the dispersion of the followers of Christ. About this same time the three other great Apostles, St Peter, St Paul and St James, died a martyr's death ; and on St John, the last surviving of the four great pillars of the Church, devolved the work of developing the theology of the Gospel and completing the organization of the Church. It was not unnatural that at such a crisis he should fix his residence in the centre of a large and growing Christian community, which had been planted by the Apostle of the Gentiles, and watered by the Apostle of the Circumcision[1]. The missionary labours of St Paul and St Peter in Asia Minor were confirmed and extended by the prolonged residence of their younger contemporary. At all events such evidence as we possess is favourable to this view of the date of St John's settlement at Ephesus. Assuming that the Apocalypse is the work of the beloved Apostle[2], and accepting the view which assigns it to the close of Nero's reign or thereabouts, we find him now for the first time in the immediate neighbourhood of Asia Minor and in direct communication with Ephesus and the neighbouring Churches.

St John however was not alone. Whether drawn thither by the attraction of his presence or acting in pursuance of some common agreement, the few surviving personal disciples of the Lord would seem to have chosen Asia Minor as their permanent abode, or at all events as their recognised headquarters. Here at least we meet with the friend of St John's youth and perhaps his fellow-townsman, Andrew of Bethsaida[3], who with him had first listened to John the Baptist and with him also had been the earliest to recognise Jesus as the Christ[4]. Here too we

---

[1] On the relation of the Apostles to the Ephesian Church see Theod. Mops. *praef. in epist. ad Ephesos.*

[2] If the Apocalypse be conceded, the testimony is decisive. And as opponents with very few exceptions (Scholten is one) allow the genuineness, and indeed use it against the Gospel, it may be urged.

[3] See the account in *Anc. Syr. Documents*, p. 25.

[4] *Can. Mur.* (*revelatum Andreae ex apostolis*), p. 17, ed. Tregelles, *Anc. Syr. Doc.* pp. 32, 34.

encounter Philip the Evangelist[1] with his daughters, and
perhaps also Philip of Bethsaida, the Apostle[2]. Here also was
settled the Apostle's namesake, John the Presbyter, also a
personal• disciple of Jesus, and one Aristion, not otherwise
known to us[3], who likewise had heard the Lord. And possibly
also other Apostles whose traditions Papias recorded, Matthew
and Thomas and James, may have had some connexion, temporary or permanent, with this district.

Thus surrounded by the surviving disciples of the Lord, by
bishops and presbyters of his own appointment, and by the
pupils who gathered about him and looked to him for instruction, St John was the focus of a large and active society of
believers[4]. In this respect he holds a unique position among
the great teachers of the new faith. St Peter and St Paul
converted disciples and organized congregations; St John alone
was the centre of a school. His life prolonged till the close of
the century, when the Church was firmly rooted and widely
extended, combined with his fixed abode in the centre of an
established community to give a certain definiteness to his
personal influence which would be wanting to the wider labours
of these strictly missionary preachers. Hence the notices of
St John have a more solid basis and claim greater attention
than stories relating to the other Apostles.

This fact is significant for the preservation of a tradition,
especially one so important as that of the authorship of the
Gospel. But there is another point, which increases the value
of the tradition itself, viz., the longevity of the principal
witnesses. Of St John himself we are told that he 'lived to
the times of Trajan[5].' His pupil Polycarp, who suffered martyr-

---

[1] Papias in Eus. *H. E.* iii. 39;
Polycrates in Eus. *H. E.* iii. 31, v. 24;
Caius in Eus. *H. E.* iii. 31; cf. Clem.
Alex. in Eus. *H. E.* iii. 30.

[2] See my *Colossians*, p. 45 sq.

[3] Papias, *l. c.*

[4] Iren. ii. 22. 5; Clem. Alex. *Quis
div. salv.* 42 (p. 958), *Can. Mur. l. c.*

(*condiscipulis et episcopis suis*); Epiph.
li. 6 (pp. 427, 8).

[5] Iren. ii. 22. 5. The date of Trajan's accession is A.D. 98. According to
the *Chronicon Paschale* St John survived
till A.D. 104; see Clinton *Fast. Rom.* I.
p. 87.

dom A.D. 155 or 156[1], speaks of himself at the time of his death as having 'served Christ fourscore and six years[2].' The expression in the original may leave some doubt whether these eighty-six years should be reckoned from his birth or from his conversion, though the former would be the more natural interpretation. But in any case he must have been born not later than A.D. 70. And as Polycarp was the disciple of St John, so Irenæus was the disciple of Polycarp. Again, of Pothinus bishop of Lyons we are told[3] that he was more than ninety years old when he suffered in the persecution of the Churches of Vienne and Lyons (A.D. 177). The date of his birth therefore cannot be later than A.D. 87. A later tradition[4] makes him a native of Asia Minor; and this would be a highly probable supposition, even if unsupported by direct evidence. But whether an Asiatic Greek or not, he must have been a lad when St John died. And Irenæus was the successor of Pothinus in the see of Lyons. Thus one link only, and that a double one, connects the life of the traditional author of the Fourth Gospel with Irenæus who preserves the tradition in writing; and two long lives, St John and Polycarp, link the personal ministry of our Lord with the latter half of the second century[5].

Of the traditions of this school, Irenæus, who had been

---

[1] [On the question of the date of Polycarp's martyrdom see *Apostolic Fathers*, Part II. vol. i. pp. 646 sq (ed. 2).]

[2] *Mart. Polyc.* 9 ὀγδοήκοντα καὶ ἓξ ἔτη ἔχω δουλεύων αὐτῷ [see the note on the passage in *Apostolic Fathers*, Part II. vol. iii. p. 379 (ed. 2)]; cf. Iren. iii. 3. 4 ἐπιπολὺ γὰρ παρέμεινε καὶ πάνυ γηραλέος...μαρτυρήσας ἐξῆλθε τοῦ βίου.

[3] Eus. *H. E.* v. 1.

[4] See the references in Tillemont *Mémoires* ii. p. 343.

[5] There was doubtless a tendency to exaggeration in this matter, e.g. in Christian Essene sources, where the age of Symeon, bishop of Jerusalem, is given as 120 years. But the in-

stances in the text are thoroughly substantiated, and can easily be paralleled. Thus three Lord Chancellors since the Reform Bill (Brougham, Lyndhurst and St Leonards) have lived to be 90. The longevity of the most distinguished German professors has been remarkable. Boeckh died at eighty-one, Humboldt at eighty-nine, Ranke [and Döllinger] at [ninety]. For the great age of the Jewish rabbi Hillel see Etheridge *Jerus. and Tiber.* p. 33. The simple life of the early Christians had probably a great deal to do with this; see Southey *Life of Wesley* ii. pp. 273 sq., 284, (1858) and compare Josephus *B. J.* ii. 8. 10, who states that the Essenes often lived ὑπὲρ ἑκατὸν ἔτη.

educated in Asia Minor, though his later life was spent in Gaul, is the principal witness. He was a pupil of St John's personal disciple Polycarp, whom he mentions more than once. He set great store on these traditions as representing most truly the primitive teaching of the Church, and appeals to them again and again with confidence. On one occasion, writing to Florinus, whom he had known in youth as a fellow-pupil of Polycarp, but who in after years had taken up heretical views, he urges that these are not the doctrines delivered to him, by the elders, who were before them, who also associated with the Apostles, and he appeals to his reminiscences of their common master in this language :

'I distinctly remember (διαμνημονεύω) the incidents of that time better than events of recent occurrence ; for the lessons received in childhood, growing with the growth of the soul, become identified with it ; so that I can describe the very place in which the blessed Polycarp used to sit when he discoursed, and his goings out and his comings in, and his manner of life (τὸν χαρακτῆρα τοῦ βίου) and his personal appearance, and the discourses which he held before the people ; and how he would describe his intercourse with John and with the rest who had seen the Lord, and how he would relate their words. And what were the accounts he had heard from them about the Lord, and about His miracles, and about His teaching, how Polycarp, as having received them from eyewitnesses of the life of the Word (τῶν αὐτοπτῶν τῆς ζωῆς τοῦ Λόγου) used to give an account harmonizing on all points with the Scriptures (πάντα σύμφωνα ταῖς γραφαῖς). To these (discourses) I used to listen at the time with attention by God's mercy which was bestowed upon me, noting them down, not on paper, but in my heart ; and by the grace of God, I constantly ruminate upon them faithfully (γνησίως)[1].'

As regards this whole extract it will suffice to notice (1) the opportunities of the witness, (2) the thoroughness of the evidence (πάντα σύμφωνα ταῖς γραφαῖς). In more than one passage also of his great work he refers to the 'Church of Ephesus[2]', or to the elders who associated with John in Asia.

It was not the object of Irenæus to defend the authorship of the Fourth Gospel, for his Valentinian antagonists not only

---

[1] Eus. H. E. v. 20.   [2] Iren. v. 33. 4.

accepted it as genuine, but even set an exclusive value on it; and therefore any testimony to its authorship from the earlier school of Asia Minor which may be gathered from his writings is incidental. But any such testimony must have the highest value.

1. It can hardly be doubted that THE ELDERS whom Irenæus quotes, and quotes for the most part anonymously, belonged to this school. Of Polycarp and Papias, of whom the former is mentioned several times by him and the latter once casually, this is certain. I shall endeavour immediately to discriminate the several persons whom he thus quotes by the topics on which they write or speak; but, before doing so, one reference to such anonymous authority deserves attention, where Irenæus refers not to individual opinion, but to the collective testimony of all the Elders who associated with St John[1]. It relates to a question of chronology. His Valentinian adversaries laid great stress on the number 'thirty.' Their celestial hierarchy comprised thirty æons, and they appealed to the thirty years' duration of our Lord's life. This computation of the Gospel chronology they derived from the notices in St Luke, interpreted by themselves[2]. At the commencement of His ministry, they contended, He was entering upon His thirtieth year, and His ministry itself lasted a twelvemonth, the 'acceptable year of the Lord' foretold by the Prophet. Irenæus in reply expresses his 'great astonishment' that persons professing to understand the deep things of God should have overlooked the commonest facts of the Gospel narrative, and points to the three passovers recorded in St John's Gospel during the term of our Lord's life (§ 3). Independently of the chronology of the Fourth Gospel, Irenæus has an a priori reason why the Saviour must have lived more than thirty years. He came to sanctify every time of life, infancy, childhood, youth, declining age. It was therefore

---

[1] Iren. ii. 22.
[2] On the chronology of the Valen-

tinians, whom Irenæus here opposes, see Epiph. Haer. li. 20 (p. 450).

necessary that He should have passed the turn of middle
life. 'From thirty to forty,' he argues, 'a man is reckoned
young, but from his fortieth and fiftieth year he is already
declining into older age, which was the case with our Lord
when He taught, as the Gospel and all the Elders who
associated with John the disciple of the Lord testify that
John delivered his account. For he remained with them
(περιέμεινεν αὐτοῖς) till the times of Trajan. Some of them
saw not only John but other disciples also, and heard these very
things from their own life (*ab ipsis*), and bear testimony to
such an account (*de huiusmodi relatione*)' (§ 4). Irenæus goes on
to argue that the same may be inferred from the language of our
Lord's Jewish opponents, who asked, 'Thou art not yet fifty
years old, and hast thou seen Abraham?' (John viii. 57). This
he contends, is properly said to one who had already lived
more than forty years, but had not yet reached his fiftieth year,
though not far off his fiftieth year (§ 6).

On this passage two points are to be remarked. (1) The
Valentinian chronology was derived from an obvious, though
not a necessary, interpretation of the synoptic narrative, more
especially of St Luke[1], while, on the other hand, the Asiatic
reckoning, which Irenæus maintains, was, or might have been,
founded on the Fourth Gospel, whereas it could not possibly
have been suggested or elicited from the first three independently of the fourth, whether reconcilable with them or not[2].
(2) Irenæus does not commit the elders of the Asiatic School to
his own interpretation of the passage quoted from St John's
Gospel, nor to his own view that our Lord was close upon fifty
years old. He only asserts that the Gospel and the testimony
of all the elders together support the view that our Lord was

---

[1] St Luke iii. 1, 23; iv. 19.

[2] St John is our authority for the
chronology of our Lord's ministry.
In the Synoptic Gospels it is highly
probable that the sequence of events
is not strictly chronological, but that
in places incidents are grouped according to subject and treatment. But
still, though the Synoptic Gospels are
consistent with a more lengthened
ministry, they do not suggest it, and
thus the argument given above, that a
knowledge by the Elders of the Fourth
Gospel may be assumed, is justified.

past middle life; and the vagueness of his language at this
point may suggest the inference that he had their testimony
distinctly on his side as against the Valentinian chronology, but
that it did not go beyond this[1]. (3) So far as the chronology of
the Asiatic School is known from other sources, the statement
of Irenæus is confirmed; for the Asiatic reckoning was distinctly based on the narrative of the Fourth Gospel. This is
the case with the duration of our Lord's ministry[2] as given by
Melito, and the time of the Crucifixion as given by Claudius
Apollinaris, to both which writers I shall have to refer hereafter[3].

From this general notice of the Asiatic Elders I turn to the
opinions of individuals belonging to this school, as reported by
Irenæus. As these opinions are given anonymously and scattered throughout his work, we can only separate one authority
from another by considering the subject-matter and treatment.

---

[1] The argument from John viii. 57
is clearly Irenæus' own, and is not
justified by the passage itself. And
this suggests the probability that much
besides is his. We cannot safely assume that the *a priori* argument is
taken from the Elders, or that the term
of years was extended by them beyond
forty. Irenæus classes together *evangelium et omnes seniores*. It is a legitimate assumption that the testimony
of the Elders went as far as the *evangelium* and no further.

[2] It may be interesting to consider
what was the term of our Lord's life.
The chief *data* are as follows: (a)
Matt. ii. 16, 22—the death of Herod
which occurred March B.C. 4, see Clinton *Fast. Hell. sub anno*. Thus the
Nativity might have taken place in
the year B.C. 5 or B.C. 6. (b) Luke
iii. 1, 23—our Lord's Baptism, and the
commencement of His ministry, stated
to have been 'in the fifteenth year of
the reign of Tiberius Cæsar' when
our Lord was 'about thirty years old
(ὡσεὶ ἐτῶν τριάκοντα).' As Sept. A.D.

28 was the beginning of the fifteenth
year of Tiberius, our Lord would be
32 or 33 years old, which does not
conflict with St Luke's statement.
(c) Matt. xxvii. 2—the Passion under
Pontius Pilate. We learn from Josephus *Ant.* XVIII. 4. 3 that Pilate was
sent to Rome by Vitellius to answer
charges made against him, and that
before he arrived Tiberius had died,
and Caius (Caligula) had succeeded.
Now Tiberius died March A.D. 37.
Therefore the passover of the Passion
might have been as late as Easter A.D.
36, but could not be later. Thus it is
possible that our Lord did live to be
over forty years of age; for we have
no right to assume that St John gives
all the passovers which occurred during
the ministry. On the whole, however,
a ministry of not more than three or
four years seems the more probable
view.

[3] See below, p. 72 sq. For the references to Melito and Claudius Apollinaris see Routh *Reliq. Sacr.* I. pp. 121,
124, 160.

This criterion of course may be fallacious; and allowance must be made for the possibility of separating one authority into two or more, or again of counting two or more authorities as one. But the argument will not be materially affected by allowance made for errors which may occur on either side. Judging then by the subject-matter, I find that the following authorities are referred to :—

(1) A person quoted with great respect as ' one better than us' [ὁ κρείσσων ἡμῶν (i. præf. 2 sq., i. 13. 3) *superior nobis* (iii. 17. 4)], in another as 'the divine old man and herald of the truth, the old man beloved of God (i. 15. 6).' Any one who will compare these references together cannot hesitate, I think, to see that they allude to one and the same person. He is a writer, as may be inferred both from the manner and from the subject of the references. His style is epigrammatic and tell-ing, full of quaint metaphors and pointed sayings, and on one occasion he runs off into iambic verse which is more vigorous than rhythmical. The work which Irenæus quotes is directed against heresies of the magico-gnostic school, and more especi-ally against Marcus.

(2) An 'Elder of a bygone generation' (*de antiquis presbyter*) a ' primitive character' (iv. 31. 1) an 'elder and disciple of the Apostles' (iv. 32. 1), or, as he is elsewhere more precisely de-scribed, 'an elder who had heard from those who had seen the Apostles and from those who had learnt' [*ab his qui didicerunt* i. e. from personal disciples of the Lord (iv. 27. 1)]. Irenæus quotes at some length the opinion of this presbyter. From the form of quotation it appears that he is relating oral discourses (perhaps from his own lecture-notes), and not any written treatise of this elder (*audivi a quodam presbytero. Huiusmodi quoque disputabat*). The subject of these discourses is the re-lation of the two covenants, and the Elder defends the Old Testament Saints, describing the office of the patriarchs as witnesses of Christ.

(3) A single saying is quoted as from 'one of the ancients'
(*quidam ex veteribus ait*), apparently from a written treatise,
that God cursed not Adam but the earth in (or through) his
works (iii. 23. 3).

(4) Irenæus, in explaining the expression 'sons of God,'
'sons of the devil,' refers to a distinction made by one of these
Elders. 'A son, as also one before us said (*dixit*, or 'has said,' ἔφη
or εἴρηκεν), is understood in two senses: one is a son according to
nature, because he is born a son, another is reputed a son
according to what he has been made, though there is a difference between the one who is born such, and the one who is
made such (iv. 41. 2).'

(5) Irenæus twice refers to some writing or writings, in
which the opinions of 'the Elders, the disciples of the Apostles,'
on eschatological subjects are given. In one passage it is
declared that the Old Testament Saints have been transferred
to Paradise and there await the coming of the Lord (v. 5. 1).
The second, which is of considerable importance, runs as
follows:—

> As the Elders say, then also shall they which have been deemed
> worthy of the abode in heaven go thither, while others shall enjoy 'the
> delight of paradise,' and others again shall possess the brightness of
> the city (i. e. the New Jerusalem); for in every place the Saviour
> shall be seen, according as they shall be worthy who see him.   (They
> say) moreover that this is the meaning of the distinction between the
> habitation of them that bring forth a hundred-fold, and them that
> bring forth sixty-fold, and them that bring forth thirty-fold ; of whom
> the first shall be taken up into the heavens, and the second shall
> dwell in paradise, and the third shall inherit the city ; and that there-
> fore our Lord has said, 'In My Father's abode are many mansions'
> (St John xiv. 2) ; for all things are of God, Who giveth to all their
> appropriate dwelling, according as His Word saith that allotment is
> made unto all by the Father, according as each man is, or shall be,
> worthy.   And this is the banqueting-table, at which those are seated
> who are called to the marriage and take part in the feast.   The Elders,
> the disciples of the Apostles, say that this is the arrangement and
> disposal of them that are saved, and that they advance by such stages,
> and ascend through the Spirit to the Son, and through the Son to the

Father, the Son at length yielding His work to the Father, as it is said also by the Apostle, 'For He must reign until He putteth all enemies under His feet, etc.' (v. 36. 1, 2)[1].

Of these five Elders (assuming them to be distinct persons) no coincidence with St John's Gospel can be traced in notices of the first and third. Of the first, indeed, though he is appealed to four times, only epigrammatic sentences against his heretical antagonists are adduced, and these naturally do not give room for any quotations either from the Old Testament or the New. The third is represented by a single short sentence relating to Adam's transgression, which from its brevity admits of no such reference. The remaining three, the second, fourth and fifth, all present more or less distinct coincidences with St John's Gospel. Of the second Irenæus reports that he was wont to say that the patriarchs and prophets gave thanks and gloried in our salvation, where there is an obscure parallel to our Lord's words in the Fourth Gospel, 'Your father Abraham rejoiced to see my day, and he saw it and was glad (John viii. 56).' The fourth is adduced to explain an expression especially character- istic of St John 'sons of the devil[2].' It is not certain indeed from the language of Irenæus that this Elder actually used this expression; but it is at least more probable than not that the distinction, which Irenæus quotes, was quoted by this father i.e. to explain the words 'sons of the devil.' I shall presently sug- gest a probable source from which this reference is taken[3]. And, lastly, the fifth Elder distinctly quotes and explains a saying of our Lord peculiar to the Fourth Gospel (xiv. 2). I shall have something to say shortly about the name of this Elder also[4]. At present it is sufficient to remark two things: first,

---

[1] The references in Irenæus to the five elders are as follows: (1) Iren. i. praef. 2, i. 13. 3, i. 15. 6, iii. 17. 4 (written: εἴρηται, ἔφη, εἴπων, dixit); (2) iv. 27. 1 sq., iv. 30. 1 sq., iv. 31. 1, iv. 32. 1, v. 17. 4 (oral: audivi, dice- bat, reficiebat nos et dicebat, dispu- tabat, ἔφη); (3) iii. 23. 3 (written: ait); (4) iv. 41. 2 (doubtful: dixit,

which may represent either ἔφη or εἴρηκεν); (5) v. 5. 1, v. 36. 1, 2 (written: λέγουσιν, λέγουσιν).

[2] See John viii. 44, 1 Joh. iii. 8, 10; cf. Acts xiii. 10. The expression is peculiar to St John among the Evangelists.

[3] See below, p. 68.

[4] See below, p. 67 sq.

the form of the sentence shows that the quotation is given as
part of the Elder's own saying, and not of an after-comment of
Irenæus; and, secondly, as Irenæus uses the present tense 'the
elders *say*,' and yet the persons referred to belonged to a past
generation and were no longer living when he wrote, he must
be quoting from some written record, and therefore we cannot
suppose that he has unconsciously fused his own after-thought
with the original saying.

These references are anonymous. But Irenæus likewise
mentions by name two of these Asiatic Elders who had conversed
with Apostles or personal disciples of the Lord, and of whom
something is also known from other sources, Polycarp and
Papias.

2.   Of POLYCARP and his reminiscences of St John, as
recounted by his own pupil Irenæus, I have already spoken[1].
It is worth while to observe in passing that in the single
sentence in which he describes the conversation of Polycarp,
he represents him as retailing lessons which he professed to
have learnt 'from eyewitnesses of the life of the Word (παρὰ
τῶν αὐτοπτῶν τῆς ζωῆς τοῦ Λόγου[2]),' an expression characteristic
of the writings of St John and suggesting that Irenæus' recollec-
tions of Polycarp were intimately connected with those writings.
Of the many letters which Polycarp himself wrote, as Irenæus
(in Eus. *H. E.* v. 20) tells us, 'either to the neighbouring
Churches to confirm them, or to individual brethren, to ad-
monish or encourage them,' only one remains. The extant
Epistle to the Philippians was written after the death of

---

[1] See above, p. 54 sq.

[2] See above, p. 55. We might be
tempted to translate the passage 'from
the eyewitnesses of the Word of Life
(cf. 1 Joh. i. 1)', but the Greek order
makes this impossible. Moreover the
expression αὐτόπτης τοῦ Λόγου occurs
in Luke i. 2. On the other hand the
rendering 'from the eyewitnesses of
the life (the earthly career) of the
Word' would require τοῦ βίου for τῆς
ζωῆς. Possibly there is an accidental
transposition in the text of Irenæus
and we should read τοῦ Λόγου τῆς ζωῆς,
cf. Ign. *Polyc.* 5 εἰς τιμὴν τῆς σαρκὸς
τοῦ κυρίου (*v. l.* τοῦ κυρίου τῆς σαρκός).
But it matters little for our immediate
purpose. The personal use of ὁ Λόγος
is Johannine in either case. The
Syriac translator has 'those who saw
with their eyes the living Word.'

Ignatius, but so soon after that Polycarp had not yet heard the particulars. It may therefore be placed about the year A.D. 110. The Epistle is not long and contains very few direct references to the New Testament writings; but numerous passages, more or less exactly quoted, are embedded in it. For the most part they are taken from the Epistles, as more suited to the hortatory and didactic character of the letter, and the references to the Gospels are very few. With the Fourth Gospel no distinct coincidence is found; but Polycarp was evidently well acquainted with the First Epistle of St John, for he writes (§ 7); 'Every one that confesseth not that Jesus Christ has come in the flesh, is Antichrist[1]; and whosoever confesseth not the testimony of the Cross, is of the devil' (1 Joh. iv. 3 compare 2 Joh. 7, and shortly after (§ 8)), 'but He endured all for our sakes, that we might live through Him' (1 Joh. iv. 9). It will be shown hereafter that this First Epistle was in all likelihood written at the same time with and attached to the Gospel. At present I will assume that it proceeds from the same author. There is a presumption therefore that the Gospel also was known to this writer. At all events, the quotations show that the writer of the Gospel flourished before Polycarp wrote. And he is cited by this father, in the same way in which our canonical writings, more especially the Epistles of St Paul and St Peter, are cited.

3. PAPIAS of Hierapolis was a contemporary and a friend of Polycarp. Whether he was a personal disciple of the Apostle St John, as asserted by Irenæus, or only of a namesake of the Apostle, the presbyter John, as Eusebius supposes, I will not stop to enquire[2]. It is certain that he lived on the confines of

---

[1] πᾶς γὰρ ὃς ἂν μὴ ὁμολογῇ Ἰησοῦν Χριστὸν ἐν σαρκὶ ἐληλυθέναι ἀντίχριστός ἐστι (§ 7). [On the genuineness of Polycarp's Epistle see *Apostolic Fathers* (Part II), I. p. 578 sq. (ed. 2).]

[2] Irenæus speaks of Papias as 'a hearer of John' (Ἰωάννου ἀκουστής v.

33. 4). On the other hand Eusebius, who mentions this statement of Irenæus, remarks; 'Yet Papias himself, in the preface to his discourses certainly does not declare that he himself was a hearer and an eyewitness of the holy Apostles, but he shows, by

the apostolic age, that he was acquainted with the daughters
of Philip, and that he conversed with two personal disciples of
the Lord, Aristion and John. He wrote an 'Exposition of our
Lord's Oracles' in five books, which he illustrated by oral
traditions. Its date is somewhat uncertain, but on the whole
it would appear to have been written in his old age, towards
the middle of the second century, not before 130 to 140. Of
this work only the most meagre fragments remain; but it is
distinctly stated by Eusebius, that he 'made use of testimonies
from the First (προτέρας) Epistle of John' (*H. E.* iii. 39)[1]. We
cannot indeed assume from this notice that he mentioned the
Apostle *by name* as the author, or that the quotations were
given as quotations (for Eusebius uses this same expression of
the quotations from St Peter in Polycarp, where St Peter is
not so mentioned and the passages are *indirectly* quoted); but
it is a fair inference from the procedure of Eusebius elsewhere
that the passages were obvious quotations (otherwise he would
not have noticed them), and that the coincidence was not so
slight as to be accidental, but clearer than the quotation from
St John in Polycarp's epistle, which Eusebius does not mention.
In carrying over the evidence from the Epistle to the Gospel,
the same remark will apply, as in Polycarp's case.

But great stress has been laid on the silence of Eusebius,
as though it were inconsistent with the supposition that Papias
was acquainted with the Gospel. The historian quotes a few
lines from Papias, preserving some traditions respecting the
Gospels of St Matthew and St Mark which he related on the
authority of John the presbyter, but says nothing about the
Fourth Gospel. And the negative argument appears stronger,

the language which he uses, that he
received the matters of the faith from
those who were his friends (*H. E.* iii.
39).' It is, however, not stated by
Irenæus that he derived his knowledge
from this preface, and from his frequent intercourse with Polycarp Irenæus doubtless had sources of infor-

mation which were closed to Eusebius.
Still Eusebius may have been right.
[See *Essays on Supernatural Reli-
gion* p. 142 sq.]

[1] κέχρηται δ' αὐτὸς μαρτυρίαις ἀπὸ τῆς
Ἰωάννου προτέρας ἐπιστολῆς, *H. E.* iii.
39.

when it is remembered that Eusebius elsewhere[1] declares his intention of extracting from early writers such notices as bear on the formation of the Canon.

Before accepting this hasty conclusion however, we must answer two preliminary questions, the one following from the other: (1) What is the practice of Eusebius elsewhere? Does he, or does he not, fulfil to the letter the intention thus expressed relative to the Canon? (2) If he does not, what principle of selection, if any, does he follow here or elsewhere in omitting or recording such notices?

To the first of these questions the answer is decisive. The Epistle of Clement besides many embedded quotations from St Peter, St James, and St Paul, and a few from the Gospels and Acts, refers by name to St Paul's First Epistle to the Corinthians. Yet Eusebius says nothing of all this. He mentions only its coincidences with the Epistle to the Hebrews (*H. E.* iii. 38). The Epistle of Polycarp again, besides the references to the Gospels mentioned above, is replete with the most obvious quotations from St Paul, and in two passages refers to his Epistles by name (§§ 3, 11). But Eusebius omits all mention of these and simply says 'he employs some testimonies from the first Epistle of Peter,' not mentioning even the coincidences with St John's first Epistle (*H. E.* iv. 14). His account of Irenæus is equally defective. Excepting one or two of the Catholic Epistles, Irenæus, as is well known, quotes by name all the canonical books of the New Testament, and most of them repeatedly; yet Eusebius, after giving one passage containing an account of the origin of the four Gospels, and another referring to the Apocalypse, adds 'he makes mention also of the First Epistle of John, adducing very many testimonies from it, and in like manner of the First Epistle of Peter' (*H. E.* v. 8). If Irenæus had been known to us only from the account of Eusebius, it would doubtless have been inferred of him (as even cautious writers have drawn this inference respecting

---

[1] Eus. *H. E.* iii. 3.

Papias), that he ignored or repudiated the Acts of the Apostles and all St Paul's Epistles.

It will then be seen that the mere silence of Eusebius justifies no such inference. And, when we come to enquire the grounds on which he has omitted or recorded notices, I think it is impossible altogether to acquit him of a certain carelessness or caprice. Yet, so far as he is guided by any principle, it appears to be this. The four Gospels, the Acts of the Apostles, the thirteen Epistles of St Paul were universally allowed as canonical. He therefore records no references to, or quotations from, these, except such as contain some interesting tradition respecting their origin or history, as e.g. in Papias the account of the Hebrew original of St Matthew or the Petrine authority of St Mark. On the other hand the authority of the Apocalypse and of the Epistle to the Hebrews was doubted; and the limits of the Catholic Epistles also (e.g. how many Epistles of St John or St Peter should be received) were an open question. On these points therefore he is more full; and, though the First Epistle of St John and the First Epistle of St Peter were not themselves questioned, yet their relation to the others leads him to note where they are quoted as authoritative[1]. There is no reason therefore to suppose that, though Papias might have quoted the Gospel of St John a score of times, Eusebius would have cared to note the fact, unless the notices contained some interesting particulars respecting its origin and history.

And in his account of Papias there is less completeness than usual in repeating the traditions of his author. The five books of the *Expositions* were largely interspersed with such traditions, which it would have been tedious to reproduce in full. The millennarian views of Papias were repulsive to Eusebius; and the historian's impatience is very evident when he is dealing with this author. He mentions the fact that

[1] But even this rule he fails to observe strictly, e.g. we know that Papias commented on the Apocalypse, yet in his account of Papias Eusebius does not mention the Apocalypse at all.

Papias records 'other narratives of the aforesaid Aristion of our Lord's discourses, and also traditions of the Elder John' which he does not repeat, and he contents himself with 'referring (ἀναπέμψαι) the studious readers (τοὺς φιλομαθεῖς)' to the book itself, professing to give what the exigencies of the case demand and nothing more (ἀναγκαίως) on this head (*H. E.* iii. 39)[1].

But there is also positive evidence very strong, though not absolutely conclusive, that Papias did quote from this Gospel. I have already mentioned the reference in the Asiatic Elder cited by Irenæus to our Lord saying 'In My father's house are many mansions'. If anyone will take the pains to read with care from the thirty-third to the thirty-sixth chapter of the fifth book of Irenæus continuously, he can hardly fail (I think) to arrive at the conclusion that the Elder in question is none other than Papias. In the thirty-third chapter he gives a passage from Papias, and in the thirty-fifth comes this passage from 'the Elders,' with which we are immediately concerned. That they are taken from the same book, appears in the highest degree probable from the following considerations. (1) Both passages treat of the future kingdom of Christ, and both regard it from the same point of view, as a visible and external kingdom, in which the enjoyments are enjoyments of the senses. (2) The subject is continuous, the matter which intervenes between the two quotations extending over some pages but all having reference to the same topic. (3) The authority in the first quotation is 'the Elders who saw John the disciple of the Lord' (33 § 3); in the second 'the Elders' (36 § 1) simply, and

[1] But why should he mention St Matthew and St Mark, without St John? The answer is probably as follows. Papias related curious facts of the two former. These are retailed. If Papias simply quoted the Gospel of St John (whether he mentioned John's name or not), or if he only related what was known to everyone, there is no reason why Eusebius should state it. Early references to a Gospel which was universally acknowledged had no interest for anyone, unless they contained some curious or important fact. If we are at a loss to say why Eusebius singled out 1 Peter and 1 John in the case of Papias, we are equally at a loss to say why he should single out 1 Peter in the case of Polycarp, except on the theory given above.

at the end 'the Elders, the disciples of the Apostles' (36 § 2).
At the close of the first quotation Irenæus adds, 'But these
things Papias also ... testifies in writing in the fourth of his
books, for there are five books composed by him.' Papias
therefore reports the statements of these Elders as we know
from Eusebius that he did on several occasions, and there is no
difficulty about the authority in the first passage. But in the
second passage Irenæus fails to explain whom he meant by
'the Elders,' unless they are the same who have been mentioned
shortly before. Only on this supposition is the reference plain.
(4) I have pointed out before[1] that the manner of quotation
obliges us to suppose that Irenæus refers to a *written* document,
and not a mere oral tradition. This limits the possibilities of
the case: for (so far as we know) Polycarp and Papias are the
only *writers* who could satisfy the description. (5) The tenour
of the passage accords entirely with the known subject of
Papias' work, as described by its title 'Expositions of Oracles of
the Lord.' We have here one of these explanations[2].

It seems fairly probable too, that not only our fifth Elder,
but the fourth also, must be identified with Papias. His explanation of 'sonship' would be framed to explain our Lord's
words addressed to the Jews: 'ye are of your father the devil.'
Gnostic dualists would interpret these words to mean that the
old covenant was directly opposed to the new, and was the
work of the evil principle. To meet this argument the Elder
makes the distinction between sons by nature and sons by
habit. In the latter sense only the Jews were sons of the
devil. The explanation at all events is a close parallel to an
extant fragment of Papias, where he explains that 'those who
practised a godly innocence were called children' by the early
Christians[3].

[1] See above, p. 61 sq.

[2] It is curious that Eusebius (*H. E.*
v. 8), describing the work of the Elder
whom Irenæus quotes, calls it unconsciously ἐξηγήσεις θείων γραφῶν, an
expression almost identical with the
title of Papias' work.

[3] τοὺς κατὰ θεὸν ἀκακίαν ἀσκοῦντας
παῖδας ἐκάλουν, ὡς καὶ Παπίας δηλοῖ
βιβλίῳ πρώτῳ τῶν κυριακῶν ἐξηγήσεων.
The extract is preserved in Maximus
Confessor's scholia to the work of

Lastly; in the few lines which Eusebius quotes from the preface of Papias, it is worth observing, *first*, that the names which he places at the head of the list of authorities are those of the Apostles known to us from the Fourth Gospel and from this alone, Andrew, Philip, Thomas[1]: and *secondly*, that he speaks of 'the truth itself[2],' meaning our Lord, in accordance with the characteristic phraseology of this Gospel[3].

But indeed, though the evidence is late and confused, we are not without direct testimony that Papias was acquainted with this Gospel. 'The Gospel of John was revealed (*manifestatum*) and given to the Churches,' says an old Latin argument to this Gospel[4], 'by John while he still remained in the body, as one named Papias, of Hierapolis, a beloved disciple of John, related in his five books (or in his fifth book) of Expositions[5]'.

Dionysius Areopagiticus *de eccl. hierarch.* c. 2, and is given in Routh *Reliq. Sac.* I. p. 8, Fragm. 2.

[1] Τί 'Ανδρέας ἢ τί Πέτρος εἶπεν ἢ τί Φίλιππος ἢ τί Θωμᾶς (Papias in Eus. *H. E.* iii. 29). Andrew, Peter and Philip are mentioned together in St John's Gospel as belonging to the same place (John i. 44). Of Philip nothing is recorded except in the Fourth Gospel. The last remark applies also to Thomas.

[2] ἀπ' αὐτῆς τῆς ἀληθείας Eus. *l. c.*; cf. John v. 33, viii. 32, xiv. 6.

[3] The story of the woman taken in adultery (John vii. 53–viii. 11) may also be an extract from Papias' work. It is certain that it is an interpolation where it stands. It is wanting in all Greek MSS. before the sixth century; it was originally absent from all the oldest versions—Latin, Syriac, Egyptian, Gothic: it is not referred to, as part of St John's Gospel, before the latter half of the fourth century. It is expressed in language quite foreign to St John's style, and it interrupts the tenour of his narrative. Eusebius

tells us that Papias 'relates also another story concerning a woman accused of many sins before the Lord' and adds that it is 'contained in the Gospel according to the Hebrews.' It may very well be an illustration given by Papias of our Lord's saying in John viii. 15 'I judge no man.' [See *Essays on Supernatural Religion*, p. 203.]

[4] The argument is contained in a Vatican MS. of the ninth century first published by Cardinal Thomasius (Op. I. p. 344).

[5] The MS. has *in exotericis, id est, in extremis quinque libris.* Overbeck in Hilgenfeld's *Zeitschr. f. Wissensch. Theol.* x. p. 68 sq. (1867), contends that some one had forged five additional works in the name of Papias, and had entitled them *Exoterica*, attaching them to the genuine books. Hilgenfeld adopts this view. But it is simpler to suppose that *exegeticis* should be read for *exotericis*, and *externis* (a gloss on *exotericis*) for *extremis*. The passage then presents no difficulties. [See *Essays on Supernatural Religion*, p. 210 sq.]

If the corruption of the context and the uncertainty of the source of the statement forbid us to lay much stress upon it, we are nevertheless not justified in setting it aside as wholly valueless.

4.   About the year 165 Polycarp suffered martyrdom at a very advanced age. An account of the death of Polycarp is extant in a LETTER OF THE CHRISTIANS AT SMYRNA addressed to a neighbouring Church at the time. In this document the brethren draw a parallel between the sufferings of their martyred friend and the Passion of the Lord, which is suggested to them by some remarkable coincidences. 'Nearly all the incidents which happened before his death,' it is said at the outset, 'came to pass, that the Lord from heaven might exhibit to us a martyrdom after the pattern of the Gospel; for Polycarp remained that he might be betrayed, just as the Lord did' (§ 1). This account is the earliest instance of the type of hagiology which sees the sufferings of Christ visibly reflected and imaged in detail in the servants of Christ, of which in the middle ages the lives of the great monastic founders St Francis and St Dominic, of Anselm and of Becket, are an example, and which has been unconsciously reproduced in more or less distinct lineaments in the biographies of the Wesleyan heroes in very recent times. This idea of literal conformity to the sufferings of Christ runs through the letter. Some of the coincidences are really striking, but in other cases the parallelism is more or less artificial. The name of the convicting magistrate is Herod (§ 6); the time of the martyrdom is the passover, 'the great sabbath' (§ 21); Polycarp's conviction is obtained by a confession elicited by torture from a youth in his employ, and thus he is 'betrayed by them of his own household' (§ 6); he is put upon an ass and so carried before the magistrate, and of course this is a parallel to the triumphal entry at Jerusalem (§ 8); his pursuers come on horseback and in arms as 'against a robber' (§ 7); when he is apprehended, he prays 'The will of God be done' (§ 7), and so forth.

Most of these incidents have their parallels in the circumstances of the Passion as recorded in the Synoptic Gospels, or recorded by these in common with St John. This is natural; for they refer mainly to external incidents, in which the Synoptic account is rich. But there are one or two exceptions. Thus we are told, at the crisis of Polycarp's trial, that a voice came from heaven, 'Be strong and play the man, Polycarp[1]. And the speaker no one saw, but the voice those of our company that were present heard' (§ 9). This corresponds to the voice which St John records as speaking from heaven to our Lord, and as imperfectly apprehended by the bystanders (John xii. 28, 29).

In §§ 5, 12 a change of circumstances brings with it the fulfilment of his prophecy as to the manner of his death (cf. John xii. 33, xviii. 32). Again we are told, when the fire would not consume the body of the Saint, his persecutors 'ordered an executioner (*confector*) to go up to him and thrust a dagger into him. And when he had done this, there came forth a dove and[2] a quantity of blood, so that it extinguished the fire; and all the multitude marvelled that there was so great a difference between the unbelievers and the elect' (§ 16). The parallel to the incident recorded in St John's account (xix. 34) of the crucifixion alone is obvious; and just as the Evangelist lays stress on his own presence as an eyewitness of the scenes (xix. 35) so also have these hagiologers done; 'we saw a great marvel,' they say, 'we to whom it was given to see; and we were preserved that we might relate it to the rest' (§ 15). And, lastly, as St John emphasizes the fact that everything was fulfilled in the death of Jesus (xix. 28, 30), so also they declare of Polycarp that 'every word which he uttered out of his mouth hath been, and shall be, accomplished' (§ 16). To these facts it should be added that the dying prayer of Polycarp contains one or two coincidences with the characteristic phraseology of the Fourth Gospel, such

---

[1] The expression itself is probably from Deut. xxxi. 7, 23, Josh. i. 6, 7, 9.

[2] The parallel is not affected by the question whether the words περιστερὰ καὶ are genuine or not.

as 'the resurrection of life,' 'the true God' (§ 14; cf. John
v. 29, xvii. 3)[1].

5. Of all the Asiatic school, exclusive of its great Gallic
representative, MELITO of Sardis appears to have been the
ablest. He possessed some slight knowledge at least of Oriental
tongues; he had travelled to the East to obtain certain information about the Old Testament Canon; he was at once learned,
thoughtful and eloquent. He moreover won deep respect by
his ascetic earnestness. His writings were very various,
embracing alike questions of speculative theology, of scriptural
exegesis, of practical duty, of ecclesiastical order.

Those works, of whose date any record is preserved, appear
to have been written between the years 165–175. When
Polycrates of Ephesus wrote in the last decade of the century
he was no longer living; and it may perhaps be inferred, from
the language there used of him[2], that his death was not very
recent[3]. These facts will fix his epoch approximately. Though
he is not likely to have conversed with St John or other
personal disciples of the Lord, he belonged to the generation
immediately following, and must have had large opportunities of
intercourse with men like Polycarp and Papias; for he was a
flourishing and apparently an influential and prolific writer
about the time of their death.

Of his numerous works only a few fragments remain; but
these are quite sufficient to attest the influence of the Fourth
Gospel on his teaching and language. It has been already
mentioned[4], that the chronology of the Saviour's life, adopted

---

[1] Perhaps too the closing words of
§ 16 ἐτελειώθη καὶ τελειωθήσεται are a
reminiscence of the τετέλεσται of St
John xix. 30.

[2] See Polycrates in Eus. *H. E.* v. 24.

[3] His treatise 'On the Paschal Festival,' he himself tells us, was written
while Sergius Paulus was proconsul of
Asia (A. D. 164–166; see Waddington
Fastes des Provinces Asiatiques, p. 731

in Le Bas and Waddington's *Voyage
Archéologique* etc.). Again we are informed that he addressed his Apology to M. Antoninus (A.D. 161–180).
From an extant fragment we learn
that L. Verus, the colleague of M.
Antoninus, was no longer living: this
places the date after the spring of A.D.
169.

[4] See above, p. 56 sq.

in the Asiatic School, was derived from this Gospel. Of this fact Melito is an illustration. Of our Lord he thus writes: 'Being at the same time both perfect God and perfect Man, He convinced us of His two natures, of His Godhead through His miracles in the three years after His baptism, and of His manhood in the thirty years which passed before His baptism[1].' If the thirty years before the baptism are taken from St Luke, the three years after the baptism cannot be derived from any other canonical Gospel but St John.

The largest extant fragment is taken from his Apology to M. Antoninus. In a treatise of this kind direct quotation is not usual; and accordingly we find no passage of either the Old or the New Testament cited in Melito's work. But the language and ideas are throughout coloured by the influence of the Fourth Gospel. 'Neither can any sight see Him, nor any thought comprehend Him, nor any word express Him' (p. xxxix.)[2]. 'Behold a light is given to us all, that in it we may see. They dare to make an image of God, Whom they have not seen' (p. xl.). 'What is God? He that is Truth, and His Word is Truth' (p. lxv.; cf. John xvii. 17). 'What then is Truth?' (cf. John xviii. 38). 'If then a man adoreth that which is made by hands, he adoreth not the Truth nor the Word of Truth. But I have many things to say concerning this matter' (p. xlv.; cf. John viii. 26, xvi. 12). 'Wherefore I give thee counsel, that thou know thyself and know God' (p. xlvii.; cf. John xvii. 3). 'Worship Him with thy whole heart; then will He grant thee to know His will' (p. xlvii.; cf. John vii. 17). 'To know God is Truth' (p. xlix.). 'To know the true God' (*ib.*; cf. John xvii. 3). 'The word of Truth reproacheth thee' (p. l.). 'If thou canst not know God, at least think that He is' (p. li.). 'It is impossible for a mutable creature to see the immutable' (p. lii.; cf. John i. 18, 1 John iv. 12). 'Then shall they who know not God, vanish away' (p. lii.). 'According as thou shalt have known God here, so

---

[1] Quoted by Anastatius of Sinai (Migne *P. G.* xxxix. p. 228 sq.).

[2] The references are to Pitra's *Spicileg. Solesm.* i.

will He know thee there' (p. liii.). 'We worship the only
God, Who is before all and above all; and we worship also His
Christ, being God the Word from eternity' (p. lvi.).

In like manner in one of the homiletic fragments which
remain[1], he speaks of our Lord as the 'Word of God and
begotten before the light, the Creator with the Father the
fashioner of man; all things in all, the Son in the Father, God
in God, King unto all eternity[2]' (p. lix.); and in another,
using the images of St John he says: 'He appeared as a lamb,
but He abode as a shepherd. He wanted food, in so far as He
was man, yet He ceaseth not, in so far as He is God, to give
food wherewith He feedeth the world[3]' (p. lviii.).

6.   CLAUDIUS APOLLINARIS was a contemporary of Melito;
the two being coupled together by Eusebius, Jerome and others.
He was a successor, if not the immediate successor, of Papias, as
bishop of Hierapolis.   The ascertainable dates of his life are: (1)
He presented an apology to M. Antoninus, who died in A.D. 180.
(2) He mentioned the incident of the thundering legion, which
occurred A.D. 174.   (3) Eusebius in his *Chronicle* seems to place
his accession to the episcopate A.D. 171[4].   (4) He is no longer
living in the last decade of the century, when Serapion[5] alludes
to him (Eus. *H. E.* v. 19).

---

[1] The fragment is extant in a Syriac
version; it is given in Pitra's *Spicileg.
Solesm.* II. p. lix. sq., in Cureton's
Spicileg. Syr. p. 53 sq., and in Otto
Corp. Apol. Christ. p. 420.

[2] There is an Armenian extract
(*Spicileg. Solesm.* I. p. 4), which gives
this passage with some alterations and
a different commencement, assigning
it to Irenæus.   There is also a Syriac
abridgment of the Armenian.   It is
probable that Irenæus introduced this
passage from Melito either anonymously or otherwise, into one of his
writings.   Another Armenian fragment
(*Spicileg. Solesm.* I. p. 1) gives as
Irenæus what is really an extract from
Papias quoted by Irenæus. [See *Essays on Supernatural Religion*, pp.
232 sq., 236 sq.]

[3] Cf. John i. 36, x. 1 sq.   The so-
called Clavis of Melito may contain a
residuum of genuine matter, but as the
amount of this is not ascertainable
with any degree of certainty, its evidence must be left out of the question.

[4] See Clinton *Fast. Rom.* I. p. 167.

[5] Eusebius *Chron.* and Jerome place
the accession of Serapion to the episcopate in the eleventh year of Commodus, i.e. A.D. 190 or 191 (Clinton,
I. p. 187), and he died apparently about
A.D. 203 (Clem. Alex. in Eus. *H. E.*
vi. 11), though Eusebius himself says
A.D. 212.   See Clinton, I. p. 211.

Of several works known to have been written by this father, the scanty fragments which remain occupy something less than half an octavo page. They contain however two or three undeniable references to the narrative of the Fourth Gospel. Thus Claudius speaks of our Lord as 'pierced in His holy side,' and 'pouring forth from His side the two purifying elements, water and blood, word and spirit' (Routh *Reliq. Sac.* I. p. 160, cf. John xix. 34). Thus too, he says, that the 14th was the true Passover of the Lord, the day on which He suffered, finding fault with those who maintain He ate the Paschal lamb with His disciples on the 14th and was crucified on the 15th, on the ground that 'according to their view the Gospels appear to be at variance.' Thus he himself takes the Fourth Gospel as the chronological standard, and interprets the others by it; and here again, as in the case of Melito, we have a confirmation of the statement of Irenæus, that the reckoning of the Asiatic School was founded thereupon or accorded therewith. It is only necessary to add that his allusions to the Gospels seem to imply that they had long been received as authoritative, but that the discussions on the Paschal question had at length awakened criticism, and started difficulties in harmonizing them which hitherto had not been perceived.

7. POLYCRATES of Ephesus closes the list of authorities belonging to the Asiatic School. In the last decade of the second century he writes to Victor, Bishop of Rome (A.D. 190–202), on the Paschal question; and having occasion to mention the practice of St John describes him in the language of the Fourth Gospel, as the disciple that 'reclined on the bosom of the Lord[1].' Nothing like this occurs in the other Gospels. It must be borne in mind also that Polycrates states that seven of

---

[1] ὁ ἐπὶ τὸ στῆθος τοῦ Κυρίου ἀναπεσών (Polycrates in Eus. *H. E.* v. 24), the very expression which occurs in John xiii. 25 ἀναπεσὼν ἐκεῖνος ἐπὶ τὸ στῆθος τοῦ Ἰησοῦ (the correct reading); comp. Iren. iii. 1 Ἰωάννης ὁ μαθητὴς τοῦ Κυρίου ὁ καὶ ἐπὶ τὸ στῆθος αὐτοῦ ἀναπεσών, where this resemblance is important, when coupled with the fact that Irenæus and Polycrates were allied on the question of the Paschal controversy.

his relatives before him had been bishops; that he carefully observes their traditions; and that he has 'gone diligently through every holy scripture' (Polycrates in Eus. *H. E.* v. 24).

8.　But to complete the evidence, before passing away from the Asiatic Church to her Gallic colony, let me direct attention to one fact.　MONTANISM, which took its rise about or soon after the middle of the second century, was strictly an offspring of the Christianity of Asia Minor.　As might have been expected, the two main props on which it relied for support were the two great writings ascribed to the Apostle St John.　As its picture of the earthly metropolis of Christ's kingdom, the New Jerusalem, was drawn from the Apocalypse, so also the prophetic mission of its founder was held to be the realisation of the promise recorded in the Fourth Gospel of the Paraclete, Who should lead the faithful into all truth.

On this subject I shall have more to say when I come to discuss the extreme view, into which the more extravagant opponents of Montanism were driven, of rejecting the writings of St John wholly[1].

II.　THE CHURCHES OF GAUL.

Intimately connected with the Churches of Asia Minor were the Christian brotherhoods established in the south of Gaul. The close alliance existing between these communities as early as the middle of the second century of the Christian era is a striking testimony to the power of the new faith in cementing the bonds of union between far-distant peoples.　As, centuries before, the districts of Gaul lying on the seashore and along the banks of the Rhine had been civilised by colonists from the Greek peoples of Asia Minor, so now it would appear that these regions were indebted to the same country for the higher knowledge of the Gospel.　However this may be, the intercourse between the two Churches during the second century was close

---

[1] See below, pp. 115 sqq.

and uninterrupted. More than one instance is recorded in
which they corresponded with each other on matters of common
or individual interest. On one occasion the Christians of Vienne
and Lyons write to their brethren in Phrygia and Asia, giving
them an account of the last hours of the martyrs who had
suffered under M. Aurelius, and among these are mentioned at
least two who were Asiatics by birth, Alexander, a physician
from Phrygia (§ 13), and Attalus of Pergamum (§ 17). On
another, the Gallican brotherhoods write to the same communities to express their opinion on the recent heresies of
Montanus, Alcibiades, Theodotus, and others, an opinion which
Eusebius describes as 'circumspect and most orthodox' (Eus.
H. E. v. 3). This opinion was appended, he tells us, to a
collection of letters written severally by the martyrs from their
prisons, and addressed to the brethren in Phrygia and Asia
(Eus. *l. c.*).

Though all these documents were known to Eusebius,
he has only preserved fragments (though very considerable
fragments) of the first mentioned (*H. E.* v. 1). Its date is fixed
as A.D. 177. In this letter the Gospel of St John is once
distinctly quoted (§ 4), 'So was fulfilled the saying of our Lord,
"The time shall come, in which every one that killeth you shall
think to do service to God" (John xvi. 2)': while elsewhere its
language is indirectly borrowed. Thus one of the martyrs is
described as 'having the Comforter in himself, the Spirit, which
he showed in the fulness (πληρώματος) of love, having been
well-pleased to lay down even his own life in defence of the
brethren (§ 3; cf. John xiv. 26, xv. 13): for he was and is indeed
a genuine disciple of Christ, following the Lamb whithersoever
He goeth' (*ib.*; Rev. xiv. 4); and another as being 'sprinkled
and strengthened from the heavenly fountain of the water of
life, that goeth forth from the body (νηδύος) of Christ' (§ 22;
cf. John iv. 14, vii. 38).

The persecution which was fatal to these martyrs placed
IRENÆUS in the vacant see of Lyons. His testimony is important, not only because a close connexion existed between the

Churches of Gaul and Asia generally, but because he was himself by birth and education an Asiatic. It is important also for another reason. He was directly connected with the Apostolic age by two remarkable instances of longevity[1]. Polycarp, his early instructor in his Asiatic home, declared himself to have been 'eighty-six years in the Lord' at the time of his martyrdom. Pothinus, his immediate predecessor in the see of Lyons, his late abode, was close upon ninety when he too died under the hands of the persecutor. Polycarp was a disciple of St John, and is said to have been placed by him in the see of Smyrna. Pothinus was a growing boy when the Apostle died, and it seems probable (though of this there is no direct evidence) that he, like his successor at Lyons, was of Asiatic birth and parentage. Irenæus, as we have seen, lays great stress on the teaching of the former, which he professes to follow implicitly; and we may suppose with much probability that among the anonymous presbyters whose authority he quotes as having associated with the Apostles and their immediate successors the latter held a prominent place. We are therefore greatly interested in enquiring what language Irenæus holds with respect to the Fourth Gospel.

The answer is decisive. He not only mentions or quotes it many times, as the work of the beloved disciple, but gives many particulars respecting it. He states in one place that it was written at Ephesus (iii. 1. 1), in another that its object was to counteract the heresies of the Nicolaitans and Cerinthians (iii. 11. 1). He uses it freely[2], not only to establish his own position, but also to confute his Gnostic opponents. To them and to him alike, as to the universal Church, it is a recognised authority. In short, a Fourth Gospel is to Irenæus not only a historical fact, but a foreordained necessity. He ransacks heaven and earth for reasons why the evangelical record should thus be foursquared. In analogies from the physical world, in types from Old Testament prophecy, in the successive developments of

---

[1] See above, p. 53 sq.

[2] He quotes it between seventy and   eighty times.

God's revelation to men, he finds evidence that this number alone is consonant with the Divine order of things (iii. 11. 8).

The extant work of Irenæus on heresies, from which these references are taken, was written during the episcopate of Eleutherus[1], who held the see of Rome from about A.D. 175 to A.D. 190. The exact date is of little or no importance. The point to be kept in view is this; that in youth he had lived in familiar intercourse with Polycarp, and had heard his aged master speak again and again of the Apostle St John, that he professed to have a very vivid remembrance of those early days[2], and that on every occasion he appealed to the traditions of the Asiatic School as authoritative in matters of Christian faith and history.

Of his honesty and good faith I think no reasonable doubt can be entertained. Eager partisanship may occasionally have blinded his judgment as to the value of the evidence before him. Close and searching criticism was not the characteristic either of his age or of his class. A tradition may here and there have been confused or exaggerated in the course of transmission; a metaphor translated into a fact; a categorical statement substituted for an individual opinion; an early date replaced by a later or conversely. Let all reasonable allowance be made for these possibilities. The fact still remains, that he firmly believed himself, and received as the tradition of St John's personal disciples, that the Fourth Gospel was written by none other than the beloved Apostle himself. On this point he does not betray a shadow of a misgiving.

On reviewing the evidence of the Asiatic school, which thus culminates in Irenæus, we cannot fail to be struck with the solidarity of the body through which it is transmitted. Polycarp

---

[1] Eleutherus is mentioned as still living (Iren. iii. 3, 3). On the other hand, a reference occurs to Theodotion's version of the LXX (iii. 21, 1), and Theodotion's version is stated not to have been published until the reign of Commodus (A.D. 182–190). But Epiphanius, our authority for Theodotion's date, is guilty of such startling confusions in the passage (de pond. et mens. 16, 17) that his trustworthiness is much discredited. [See Essays on Supernatural Religion, p. 260.]

[2] See above, p. 55.

and Papias, Melito and Claudius Apollinaris, Polycrates and
Irenæus, the martyrs of Asia and the martyrs of Gaul,
are not isolated individuals, nor is church-membership their
only bond of union; but within the Church itself they
belong to a more or less compact community, of which the
members are in constant mutual intercourse, and consult and
advise each other on very diverse matters of interest.

This fact is a strong safeguard for the continuity of transmission where a tradition so important is concerned: but in the
case before us the disputes of the age and country afford an
additional security. As soon as we bring the original theory of
the Tübingen school, which dated the Fourth Gospel about
A.D. 170, or even the modified hypothesis of some recent
antagonists, which places it close upon the middle of the
second century, face to face with these controversies, we at
once see what enormous improbabilities are involved in either
supposition. The forgery (for professing, as it evidently does,
to emanate from the beloved disciple, the Fourth Gospel must
be called by this hard name, unless it be genuine), the forgery
is almost contemporary with, or even subsequent to, the rise of
Montanism and the first outburst of the Quartodeciman controversy. It has a very direct bearing on Montanism, for it
supplies a basis for the prophetic theory of this sect; and yet it
is received by Catholics and Montanists alike. It raises
questions connected with the celebration of Easter (though it
does not touch the main subject of dispute); and yet it is
accepted without misgiving equally by the Quartodecimans
and their opponents. Yet, if the hypothesis were true, that it
first saw the light during the lifetime of the very generation
which was most actively engaged in both these controversies,
must we not believe that its authenticity would have been most
fiercely contested, and that the clearest traces of this contest
would have been stamped on the extant literature of the
period?

III. THE CHURCHES OF ANTIOCH.

1. From the Churches of Asia Minor and their Gallic colonies it is natural to turn to the neighbouring and allied Church of Antioch; and here the apostolical father IGNATIUS first claims attention. His testimony is the more important, because he is historically connected with the two principal Churches in which the influence of St John prevailed, Ephesus and Smyrna. The genuine Epistles of Ignatius were written A.D. 110, very few years after the probable date of St John's Gospel. They are brief, abrupt and epigrammatic, being chiefly occupied with personal explanations and instructions. An aged disciple on his way to martyrdom writes a few hurried lines to the Christian congregations with whom he has been brought into contact on his journey. Though they reflect the teaching, and in many places echo the language, of the New Testament—especially of St Paul—the letters contain only two direct quotations, as such, from Holy Scripture[1].

Under these circumstances it is sufficient if we are able to trace the influence of the Fourth Gospel in individual thoughts and phrases. Nor are such traces wanting. When in his Epistle to the Philadelphians Ignatius writes (§ 7), 'The Spirit is not deceived, being from God; for it knoweth whence it cometh and whither it goeth (οἶδεν γὰρ πόθεν ἔρχεται καὶ

---

[1] *Magn.* 12, *Eph.* 5. In *Eph.* 5, γέγραπται γάρ· ὑπερηφάνοις ὁ Θεὸς ἀντιτάσσεται, the quotation may have been taken direct from Prov. iii. 34, but the substitution of ὁ Θεὸς for ὁ Κύριος inclines me to suppose that Ignatius got it through 1 Pet. v. 5 or James iv. 6. The same substitution is found in Clem. Rom. 30. The following are the most striking coincidences in the Ignatian Epistles (1) with the Gospel narrative: *Eph.* 14 φανερὸν τὸ δένδρον ἀπὸ τοῦ καρποῦ αὐτοῦ (cf. Matt. xii. 33), *Smyrn.* 1 ἵνα πληρωθῇ πᾶσα δικαιοσύνη (of our Lord's baptism; cf. Matt. iii. 15), *Smyrn.* 6 ὁ χωρῶν χωρείτω (cf. Matt. xix. 12), *Polyc.* 2 φρόνιμος γίνου ὡς ὁ ὄφις ἐν πᾶσιν καὶ ἀκέραιος εἰσαεὶ ὡς ἡ περιστερά (cf. Matt. x. 16); (2) with the Pauline Epistles: *Eph.* 10 ἑδραῖοι τῇ πίστει (cf. Col. i. 23), *ib.* 16 οἱ οἰκοφθόροι βασιλείαν Θεοῦ οὐ κληρονομήσουσιν (cf. 1 Cor. vi. 9); and *ib.* 18 ποῦ σοφός; ποῦ συζητητής; (cf. 1 Cor. i. 20), *Rom.* 5 ἀλλ' οὐ παρὰ τοῦτο δεδικαίωμαι (cf. 1 Cor. iv. 4), *Polyc.* 5 ἀγαπᾶν τὰς συμβίους, ὡς ὁ Κύριος τὴν ἐκκλησίαν (cf. Eph. v. 29).

πού ὑπάγει), and it searcheth out the hidden things,' we recognise at once our Lord's description of the Spirit in His conversation with Nicodemus as related in John iii. 8. Other reminiscences, not so obvious but equally real, of Johannine language are traceable elsewhere. Thus the sentence, 'The prince of this world is abolished' (*Trall.* 4) is an echo, almost a repetition, of our Lord's language (John xii. 31, xvi. 11). Again, the contrast of the 'corruptible food' with the 'bread of God, which is the flesh of Christ and the draught of His blood,' (*Rom.* 7) is an adaptation of the characteristic discourse related in the sixth chapter of the same Gospel. So too in other passages he echoes the same expressions, 'the flesh of the Lord,' 'the blood of Jesus Christ' (*Trall.* 8; cf. *Philad.* 4), 'the bread of God' (*Eph.* 5). And elsewhere the coincidences with St John are equally patent; 'we ought so to receive him (the bishop), as Him that sent him' (*Eph.* 6; cf. John xiii. 20); 'where the shepherd is, there follow ye, as sheep, for many fair-seeming wolves make captive those that run the race of God' (*Philad.* 2; cf. John x. 4, 12); 'to Him alone (Christ) are committed the hidden things of God, He Himself being the door of the Father' (*Philad.* 9; cf. John x. 7); 'Jesus Christ, His Son, Who is His Word, coming forth from silence, Who in all things pleased Him that sent Him' (*Magn.* 8; cf. John vi. 38)[1].

2.   Following the succession of the Antiochene bishops we

---

[1] The silence of Ignatius respecting St John has been urged on the other side, especially in *Rom.* 4 (οὐχ ὡς Πέτρος καὶ Παῦλος διατάσσομαι ὑμῖν), where, it is contended, the introduction of the names of St Peter and St Paul makes the omission of St John's name more remarkable. But there is a good reason for this omission. Ignatius is addressing the Roman Church, and therefore appeals to the two Apostles to whose precepts that Church had listened. Again in *Eph.* 12, where St Paul is again mentioned, reference has been already made in the previous section to other Apostles with whom the Ephesian Church was in harmony. Moreover, Ignatius singles out St Paul on account of the parallel to himself. The Ephesian converts had sheltered St Paul as he passed through; and now Ignatius is passing through Ephesus on his way to martyrdom. Besides these two passages no Apostle is mentioned by name in the Ignatian Epistles, except St Peter in *Smyrn.* 3, where there is a reference to an incident in our Lord's life.

arrive at THEOPHILUS—the sixth bishop according to Eusebius
(*H. E.* iv. 20), the seventh according to Jerome (*Ep. ad Algas.*
quaest. 6), who commences his list of Antiochene bishops with
St Peter.   In his extant *Apologia ad Autolycum*, an undoubtedly genuine work, Theophilus quotes the beginning of
the Fourth Gospel and mentions St John as its author.   The
passage runs as follows: 'whence the Holy Scriptures and all
the inspired men (πνευματοφόροι) teach us, one of whom, John,
says, "In the beginning was the Word, and the Word was with
God," showing that at the first God was alone, and the Word in
Him.   Then he says, "And the Word was God.   All things were
made through Him, and without Him was not anything made"'
(*ad Autol.* ii. 22).   This direct and precise reference is the
more conspicuous, because it is the solitary instance in which
Theophilus quotes directly and by name any book of the New
Testament.   To this undoubted quotation should be added the
following coincidences.   'How can one fail to notice the pangs
which women suffer in child-bearing, and after that they forget
their trouble?' (*ad Autol.* ii. 23; cf. John xvi. 21); 'A corn of
wheat, or of the other seeds, when it is cast into the earth, first
dieth and is dissolved, then it riseth and becometh an ear
(στάχυς)' (*ad Autol.* i. 13).   Here the language of Theophilus
combines expressions in John xii. 24 and 1 Cor. xv. 36, 37.
Lastly, in *ad Autol.* i. 14 occurs the following expression, 'Do
not therefore disbelieve, but believe,' a reminiscence of John
xx. 27, 'Be not faithless, but believing.'

The date of these notices may be fixed with tolerable
accuracy.   Eusebius in his *Chronicon* gives A.D. 177 as the year
of Theophilus's death.   But it is almost certain that he has
antedated the event by six or more years at the lowest computation.   For in his *Apology* Theophilus mentions the death of
M. Aurelius, and he carries his chronological calculations down
to this epoch (iii. 28).   These calculations indeed are confessedly
taken from Chryseros 'the nomenclator' (ii. 27), a freedman
of Aurelius, who stopped at this point; but as the object of
Theophilus is to calculate the age of the world at the time

when he writes, it is a tolerably safe conclusion that the third book, in which these calculations occur, must date not long after the death of the Stoic emperor, i.e. not long after A.D. 180. The three books were written and despatched separately, so that the first and second, in which the quotations are found, may be placed a little earlier than the third book.

Besides the direct evidence which the *Apologia ad Autolycum* supplies to the authorship of the Fourth Gospel, Theophilus is in another way an indirect witness to the wide acceptance of four Gospels in the Canon of the New Testament. Jerome speaks in more than one passage of a work of Theophilus, now lost, which he calls his 'commentaries[1].' In one reference indeed he appears to throw doubt upon the authenticity of this work. Speaking of Theophilus in *Vir. Illustr.* 25 he says, 'I have read commentaries written in his name on the Gospel and on the Proverbs of Solomon, which in my opinion do not appear to agree with the elegance and style of the volumes mentioned above' (i.e. the *ad Autolycum* and other works). But elsewhere he quotes the work without the slightest misgiving. In the preface to his own commentary on St Matthew's Gospel (*in Matth.* praef. *Op.* VII. p. 7) he confesses 'to have read many years before the commentaries on Matthew...of Theophilus, bishop of the city of Antioch.' In his epistle to Algasia (Ep. cxxi. *Op.* I. p. 866), written in A.D. 407, he throws further light upon the character of this lost writing. He speaks of it as a harmony of the four Gospels and as a lasting monument of the writer's genius (Theophilus...qui quattuor Evangelistarum in

---

[1] The four books of *commentarii*, extant in Latin and ascribed to Theophilus, cannot represent the genuine work alluded to by Jerome. The theology is evidently post-Nicene; passages are found nearly word for word in S. Ambrose (i. § 120, p. 295, *ed.* Otto; cf. Ambrose *Comm. in Luc.* iii. § 2), in Cyprian (i. § 153, p. 301; cf. Cyprian *Epist.* lviii. § 5), and in Jerome (i. § 4, p. 280; cf. Jerome *Comm. in Matt.* i. *Op.* VII. p. 12); and the work is evidently not a translation from the Greek, but originally written in Latin, see *e.g.* i. p. 283 apex (= κεραία) autem quatuor literas habens per evangelium quadruplex testamentum indicat novum.

unum opus dicta compingens ingenii sui nobis monumenta
dimisit). It is needless to point out the importance and
significance of a harmony of the four Gospels constructed in
the second century, in its relation to the genuineness of
St John's Gospel, and to the *Diatessaron* of Tatian.

IV. THE CHURCHES OF PALESTINE.

Contemporaneously with the Ignatian Epistles and the
treatise of Theophilus, we have the evidence of writers in the
neighbouring region of Palestine.

1. The date of the writings of JUSTIN MARTYR is of some
importance. The two Apologies were written in the reign of
Antoninus Pius, i.e. between July, 138, and March, 161. If we
can trust the present text, the first (the longer) *Apology* was
composed before M. Aurelius became Cæsar, i.e. before A.D. 140.
Against this early date, however, it is urged (1) that L. Verus,
who is there styled ἐραστὴς παιδείας, was only ten years old
at this time; (2) that Justin (*Apol.* i. 46) speaks of our Lord
as born 150 years before, (3) that Marcion is mentioned as
already influential (*Apol.* i. 26). I do not think that much
stress can be laid on these arguments. The expression ἐραστὴς
παιδείας was a very fit one to apply to an imperial boy, who
was, or was presumed to be, studious and intelligent, and to
whom owing to his youth no other compliment could be paid.
As regards the question of the chronology of our Lord's life,
if Justin followed the ordinary computation (which is probably
the case), he would place the Crucifixion in A.D. 29; and,
allowing about thirty-three years for the interval between the
Nativity and the Crucifixion, Justin's 150 years would bring
the date of the work to A.D. 146. The third objection, the
allusion to Marcion, is more difficult to meet, but the dates
of his life are very uncertain. Happily, however, we can escape
these difficulties altogether. By a very plausible emendation
(see Hort in the *Journal of Philology*, III. pp. 163, 165, 1857),
which reads και καισαρι for καισαρι και in the opening words

of the *Apology*[1], M. Aurelius has already become Cæsar before the date of the work. If we accept this conjecture, the passage itself affords no posterior limit except the martyrdom of Justin, and the death of Antoninus Pius in A.D. 161. The second *Apology* is a sort of appendix or postscript to the first, written at the same time or soon after.

The *Dialogue with Trypho* was written after the longer *Apology*, to which it contains a clear allusion[2], and therefore probably after both Apologies. It is represented as held at Ephesus, where Justin had stayed (Eus. *H. E.* iv. 18). Justin's testimony therefore becomes in some sense the testimony of the Asiatic school. The time of the dialogue is stated to be during the war of Barcochba[3] A.D. 132–135, i.e. when Polycarp and Papias were scarcely advanced beyond middle age, and while Melito and Apollinaris were yet young men. From the allusion to the first *Apology* given above, it is evident that if we accept the later date for the *Apology*, the dialogue cannot have been published until several years after it actually took place.

Eusebius and others after him place Justin's martyrdom in the reign of M. Aurelius, and the *Paschal Chronicle* fixes it at A.D. 165[4]. On the other hand, Epiphanius[5] apparently and others

---

[1] The *Apology* opens as follows: Αὐτοκράτορι Τίτῳ Αἰλίῳ Ἀδριανῷ Ἀντωνίνῳ Εὐσεβεῖ Σεβαστῷ Καίσαρι καὶ Οὐηρισσίμῳ υἱῷ φιλοσόφῳ καὶ Λουκίῳ †φιλοσόφου† Καίσαρος φύσει υἱῷ καὶ Εὐσεβοῦς εἰσποιητῷ, ἐραστῇ παιδείας, κ.τ.λ. Over and above the question of date involved, it is unnatural to describe Antoninus' titles in a descending scale from Imperator to Cæsar.

[2] οὐδὲ γὰρ ἀπὸ τοῦ γένους τοῦ ἐμοῦ... τινὸς φροντίδα ποιούμενος, ἐγγράφως Καίσαρι προσομιλῶν εἶπον πλανᾶσθαι αὐτοὺς κ.τ.λ. *Dial.* § 120.

[3] φυγὼν τὸν νῦν γενόμενον πόλεμον *Dial.* § 1.

[4] Eus. *H. E.* iv. 15; *Chron. Pasch.* p. 481 sq. (ed. Bonn).

[5] Epiphanius (391 A; II. p. 411 *ed.*

Dindorf) makes Justin thirty years at the time of his martyrdom, which he places ἐπὶ Ῥωστικοῦ ἡγεμόνος καὶ Ἀδριανοῦ βασιλέως. The name Rusticus is too common at this period to give us much assistance, and the text of Epiphanius is so corrupt that we may without hesitation read Ἀντωνίνου for Ἀδριανοῦ in this passage, especially as a few lines lower down Epiphanius speaks of Tatian as setting up his heretical school about the twelfth year of Antoninus (περὶ τὸ δωδέκατον ἔτος Ἀντωνίνου τοῦ εὐσεβοῦς Καίσαρος). He had already described Tatian as a contemporary of Justin (συνακμάζει Ἰουστίνῳ) who lapsed into heresy after Justin's death.

place it in the reign of Antoninus Pius, and, as far as we can judge, before A.D. 150. If we adopt with Hort A.D. 149 as the date (*l. c.* p. 180), and leave time for the *Dialogue*, we may place the extant works of our author between A.D. 145–149.

We now turn to the evidence which Justin affords as to the Fourth Gospel. He does not quote it by name, but he shows more than one striking coincidence with its language. Thus speaking of the sacrament of baptism he says (*Apol.* I. 61), 'For Christ also said, "Unless ye be born again (ἀναγεννηθῆτε), ye cannot enter into the kingdom of heaven", for that it is quite impossible for those that are once born to enter into their mother's womb is manifest to all' (cf. John iii. 3–5). If any doubt could be entertained whence this saying was derived, it will appear from a passage in the chapter immediately preceding (§ 60) that the Fourth Gospel was present to his mind. Applying the incident of the brazen serpent as an image of the Crucifixion, he reports Moses as erecting the serpent and saying, 'If ye look on this image (τῷ τύπῳ τούτῳ), and believe, ye shall be saved in Him.' This is a very wide departure from the account in Numbers (xxi. 7–9), where there is nothing about a type or about the necessity of belief; but the writer obviously had in his mind John iii. 14, 15, 'as Moses lifted up the serpent in the wilderness, even so must the Son of man be lifted up, that whosoever believeth in Him...should have eternal life'[1]. Again, in the sixth chapter of the same *Apology*, Justin says: 'The prophetic spirit we reverence and worship, honouring (it) in reason and in truth,' where we are reminded of John iv. 24. Speaking of the holy eucharist, 'We have been (or were) taught (ἐδιδάχθημεν),' he writes (§ 66), 'that the bread and wine are both the flesh and the blood of that Jesus Who became flesh,' an expression founded upon John vi. 54. 'For,' he adds, 'the Apostles, in the memoirs left by them, which are called Gospels, have recorded that it was so enjoined on them' etc. This passage alone however would be far from conclusive. It can only be taken to strengthen a position already established.

[1] Compare the treatment of this incident in *Dial.* § 94.

One other coincidence from the same work will suffice. Speaking of the prophecy in Isaiah of the miraculous conception of the Messiah, Justin remarks that God by the Spirit of prophecy foretold what was incredible, 'so that, when it came to pass, it might not be disbelieved, but might be believed from its having been foretold' (*Apol.* I. 33), where we are at once reminded of John xiv. 29.

Turning now to the *Dialogue with Trypho* we find numerous expressions, which cannot well be explained except on the supposition that John had the Fourth Gospel before him. Our Lord is described as 'the only spotless and righteous light, that was sent from God to men' (*Dial.* 17; cf. John i. 9); He is the 'only-begotten of the Father of the universe, His Word and Power sprung in a special way (ἰδίως) from Him, as we have learnt from the memoirs (ὡς ἀπὸ τῶν ἀπομνημονευμάτων ἐμάθομεν)' (*Dial.* 105; cf. John i. 14). An allusion to the imagery of Genesis xlix. 11 is explained of Christ because 'His blood sprung not of man's seed, but of the will of God' (*Dial.* 63; cf. John i. 13). We are informed (*Dial.* 69) that the Jews 'dared to call Him a magician and a deceiver of the people (λαοπλάνον),' where the last word seems to have been suggested by John vii. 12 'Nay, but he deceiveth the people (πλανᾷ τὸν ὄχλον).' Speaking of himself and of his brother Christians, Justin says, 'We are called, and are, the true children of God, who keep His commandments (*Dial.* 123; cf. John i. 12, 1 Joh. iii. 1, 2)'; 'to us it is given both to hear, and to be with, and to be saved through this Christ, and to know all the things of the Father' (*Dial.* 121; cf. John xiv. 7); 'who are instructed in all the truth' (*Dial.* 39; cf. John xvi. 13). 'He that knoweth not Him (i. e. Christ), knoweth not the counsel of God, and he that insulteth and hateth Him, manifestly hateth and insulteth Him that sent Him; and if any man believeth not on Him, he believeth not the preaching of the prophets, who announced the glad tidings of Him, and preached them unto all' (*Dial.* 136, a reminiscence of John v. 23, 45, 46). Again, in the description of John the Baptist given in *Dial.* 88, an account which is chiefly taken from the Synoptic Gospels, unmistakeable proofs are given of Justin's acquaintance with the Fourth Gospel also.   Thus the repudiation of the Baptist's own claim to the Messiahship is closely associated with the announcement of the presence of the 'one stronger,' whose shoes John proclaims himself unworthy to bear, in a way which presupposes Justin's knowledge of John i. 19–27. Lastly, in *Dial.* 57 occurs an expression which reminds us very forcibly of John vi. 31, 'Of the manna, on which your fathers were nourished in the wilderness, the scripture saith, that they ate angels' food.'

A work of Justin earlier than any extant is his treatise against Marcion. A few lines of this lost work are preserved in Irenæus (iv. 6. 2). The passage is very short, not more than half a dozen lines, and does not give much scope for quotations from the New Testament, but in it occurs an expression suggested by St John, 'The only-begotten Son came to us, gathering up His own creation in Himself.' The latter part of the clause is based on Ephes. i. 10, the former on John i. 18.

2. We now turn from the master to the scholar, from Justin Martyr to TATIAN. The facts of Tatian's life are soon told. An Assyrian by birth, as he himself distinctly says, and a heathen, he exercised the profession of a sophist, in which capacity he travelled far and wide. His mind was first turned towards Christianity by reading the Scriptures, which impressed him greatly. He was converted, and became a disciple of Justin Martyr, doubtless at Rome, and after the death of his master appears to have remained some time in the metropolis teaching. Subsequently he left Rome, and seems to have spent the remainder of his life in the East, more especially in Syria and the neighbouring countries. After Justin's death—how soon after we do not know—his opinions underwent a change. He separated himself from the Church, and espoused views closely allied to those of the Encratites. When Irenæus wrote his first book, Tatian was no longer living, as may be inferred from the language of this father (Iren. i. 28, 1); and this book must

have been written before A.D. 190, and may have been written
as early as A.D. 178[1]. On the whole, we shall perhaps not be
far wrong if we place the period of his literary activity at about
A.D. 155–170[2].

Of several writings of Tatian mentioned by the ancients,
only one has come down to us[3], his *Address to the Greeks*, a
work composed before Tatian's separation from the Church,
apparently not long after the death of Justin.

This *Oratio ad Graecos* is an Apology, addressed to Gentiles.
We do not therefore expect to find in it quotations from the
sacred books, with which Gentile readers would as a matter of
course have no acquaintance, and to which they would attribute
no authority. But the following passages place beyond the
reach of any reasonable doubt what was at least an *a priori*
presumption, that the pupil of Justin knew and accepted the
Fourth Gospel, to which his master's extant writings have
been shown to give testimony.

§ 4. 'God is a Spirit (cf. John iv. 24).'

§ 13. 'And this then is the saying (τὸ εἰρημένον), "The
darkness comprehendeth not (οὐ καταλαμβάνει) the light"
(cf. John i. 5).'

§ 19. 'Follow ye the only God. All things have been
made by Him, and apart from Him hath been made no thing
(cf. John i. 3).'

These passages are conclusive, for they are characteristic
passages of the Fourth Gospel. There are other coincidences
with Johannine language, such as § 5 'God was in the beginning,' which, taken by themselves, cannot be pressed, but in the

---

[1] See above, p. 79. Clement of Alexandria *Strom.* i. 1. 11 (p. 322) mentions an 'Assyrian' as one of his earlier
teachers, and the identification of this
Assyrian with Tatian is highly probable; see below, p. 92.

[2] [On the whole subject of Tatian
see *Essays on Supernatural Religion*,
p. 272 sq.]

[3] [The discovery and publication in

1888 by Ciasca of Tatian's *Diatessaron*
in an Arabic version has set at rest for
ever the question whether or no Tatian
knew the Fourth Gospel. The *Diatessaron* is, as its name implies, a
Harmony of the Four Gospels; and
as Dr Lightfoot had surmised, consists
of our four canonical Gospels, and
commences with the opening words of
St John's Gospel.]

light of the extracts given above are probably derived from the same source.

V. THE CHURCH OF ALEXANDRIA.

1.   In all probability, the Epistle of Barnabas is to be considered the earliest piece of extant Christian literature, outside the Canon, which emanates from Alexandria.   Whoever is its author—and it is noticeable that he nowhere claims to be the Apostle Barnabas—in his general style and his interpretation of the Old Testament, he represents Alexandrian thought.   He gives us moreover a picture of feuds between Jews and Christians, which is in keeping with what we know from other sources of the character of the population of that great city. For reasons which cannot be entered into here, but which bear upon the interpretation of a passage in § 4, I am inclined to place the date of the Epistle in the reign of Vespasian, after that emperor's association with himself of his sons Titus and Domitian in the supreme power (A.D. 70–79).   In this case, it was written before the Fourth Gospel; we must therefore look elsewhere for the evidence of which we are in search.   We shall find, if I mistake not, that the earliest quotations from the Fourth Gospel (and these very important) which proceed from Alexandria, are contained in the works of Gnostic writers, as Basilides, Valentinus etc.; and these will be considered later on[1].   At present we will confine ourselves to orthodox writings. With one possible exception there is no orthodox literature extant which comes from the Alexandrian Church between the Epistle of Barnabas and the writings of Clement of Alexandria. That exception is the latter part (§§ 11, 12) of the EPISTLE TO DIOGNETUS.   In our solitary authority for this Epistle, the Strassburg MS., now no longer extant, the beginning of one treatise and the conclusion of another have been accidentally attached together so as to form in appearance one work.   The writer of the latter part is clearly an Alexandrian, and indulges

[1] See below, p. 104 sq.

in the allegorical interpretations of the Old Testament which are characteristic of that school. He calls himself ' a disciple of the Apostles and a teacher of the Gentiles.' The whole tone of thought of the fragment is second-century. These indications appear to point to Pantænus, the master of Clement, and the Apostle of the Indies (c. A.D. 180–210), as the author of the treatise. The account given of him in Eusebius (*H. E.* v. 10) would seem to imply that his journey to India[1] preceded his appointment as head of the Catechetical school of Alexandria; and Anastatius of Sinai speaks of him as one of those early exegetes, who understood all the narrative of the Hexaemeron as referring to Christ and the Church, a view which harmonizes in a remarkable degree with the allegorical interpretation of the garden of Eden preserved in this fragment.

The influence of St John is very manifest in this treatise, though there is no direct quotation from his Gospel. The Word who is called 'the Life' ($\dot{\eta}$ $\zeta\omega\dot{\eta}$ § 12 ; cf. John i. 4), ' who was from the beginning' ($\dot{o}$ $\dot{a}\pi$' $\dot{a}\rho\chi\hat{\eta}s$ § 11 ; cf. John i. 2), 'through whom the Father is glorified' ($\delta\iota$' $o\hat{\upsilon}$ $\Pi a\tau\dot{\eta}\rho$ $\delta o\xi\dot{a}\zeta\epsilon\tau a\iota$ § 12; cf. John xiii. 31, xiv. 13), 'has revealed Himself' to His disciples ($o\hat{\iota}s$ $\dot{\epsilon}\phi a\nu\dot{\epsilon}\rho\omega\sigma\epsilon\nu$ $\dot{o}$ $\Lambda\dot{o}\gamma os$ $\phi a\nu\epsilon\dot{\iota}s$ § 11 ; cf. John ii. 11). These and other coincidences with the Fourth Gospel, occurring in a fragment which occupies less than two octavo pages, are sufficient to indicate that the writer's mind was imbued with Johannine teaching and phraseology.

2. CLEMENT OF ALEXANDRIA in his *Stromateis*[2] (i. 1. 11) describes one of his instructors in Greece as ' the Ionian' ($\dot{o}$ $\mu\dot{\epsilon}\nu$

---

[1] Jerome *Vir. Ill.* 36, *Ep.* 70 (p. 428) states that he was sent to India by Demetrius (bishop of Alexandria A.D. 189-231). But Eusebius (*l.c.*) represents him as head of the catechetical school ten years before the accession of Demetrius. We must conclude that Jerome places the visit to India too late.

[2] The *Stromateis* was written A.D. 194 or 195 under Severus. Clement's other extant works are earlier. He

enumerates his teachers as follows, giving the country in which he was their pupil, (1) *in Greece*, 'the Ionian,' (2) *in Magna Græcia*, (*a*) one from Cœlo-Syria, (*b*) another from Egypt, (3) *in the East*, (*a*) one from Assyria, (*b*) another, in Palestine, a Hebrew, (4) *in Alexandria*, the last and greatest *i.e.* Pantænus. I am inclined to identify 'the Ionian' with Melito.

ἐπὶ τῆς Ἑλλάδος ὁ Ἰωνικός), and places him first on the list of his teachers, as though he were the earliest.

Thus he is connected with Asia Minor, and probably with the school of St John. Consequently his testimony is of great importance for our purpose. To Clement we owe several traditions of St John[1]. He speaks[2] of a certain statement as 'not occurring in the four Gospels handed down to us (ἐν τοῖς παραδεδομένοις ἡμῖν τέτταρσιν εὐαγγελίοις) but only in the Gospel according to the Egyptians,' thus showing that in his time the number of the Gospels was definitely fixed at four. In another passage[3] he appeals to the tradition of the presbyters of a former generation (παράδοσις τῶν ἀνέκαθεν πρεσβυτέρων) as to the order in which the Gospels were written, saying that after the other Gospels had been written, 'John, last of all, observing that the external (bodily) facts (τὰ σωματικὰ) had been set forth in the existing Gospels, at the urgent request of his friends and by the divine guidance of the Spirit, composed a spiritual Gospel (πνευματικὸν ποιῆσαι εὐαγγέλιον).' The value of this tradition may be great or it may be small; but his whole language bears testimony to the fact that the Gospel of St John had long been recognised as authoritative, and that traditions had grown up about it[4].

3. ORIGEN was born in A.D. 185, and began to teach at eighteen. Of him it is sufficient to say that he wrote a commentary on St John's Gospel, and that he betrays no knowledge that the authenticity of the Gospel had ever been called in question[5].

---

[1] e.g. the story of St John and the young robber (*Quis div. salv.* 42, p. 958), quoted in Eus. *H. E.* iii. 23.

[2] *Strom.* iii. 13, p. 553.

[3] Cited in Eus. *H. E.* vi. 14.

[4] In his book on the Paschal Festival Clement makes the 14th the day of the Crucifixion (*Fragm.* p. 1017 *ed.* Potter), thus following out the tradition of the Asiatic School. Of this work only two short fragments survive, but Eusebius informs us (*H. E.* vi. 13) that in it he mentioned 'the traditions which he had heard from the elders.' This is another indirect link with the School of St John.

[5] See Lücke, p. 78. His commentary on St John was written about the year 222. In it he controverts Heracleon.

VI. The Churches of Greece and Macedonia.

1. The extant remains belonging to this branch of the Church in the second century are very slight indeed. In the few lines of Dionysius of Corinth that survive, no quotation could have been introduced naturally. Perhaps however the EPISTLE TO DIOGNETUS §§ 1–10 may belong to this Church. It certainly shows evidence of Hellenic culture both in diction and matter. This however is a very slight presumption in favour of its ascription to Greece proper; and I only include it here because some place must be found for a document which is undoubtedly very early, and cannot well be assigned to a later date than the middle of the second century[1].

The Epistle is full of indications of the influence of St John's writings. 'Christians dwell in the world, but are not of the world (§ 6; cf. John xvii. 11, 14, 16).' The doctrine of the Word is drawn out fully in § 7. He is described as 'the artificer and creator of the universe, by Whom God made the heavens, by Whom He enclosed the sea in its proper bounds (cf. John i. 3, Heb. i. 2)': 'God sent Him as saving...He sent Him as loving and not as judging (cf. John iii. 17).' In a later passage (§ 10), in language which is an echo of John iii. 16, we are told, 'For God loved men...to whom He sent His only-begotten Son, to whom He promised the kingdom in heaven and will give it to those that love Him (cf. 1 John iv. 9).' 'How then,' the writer goes on, 'shalt thou (worthily) love Him that before loved thee so (cf. 1 John iv. 10, 11)?'

2. That ATHENAGORAS should be considered a representative of the Church of Greece is evident from the heading of his

---

[1] Westcott (*Canon of the N. T.* p. 88, *ed.* 4) places it c. A.D. 117, Bunsen (*Hippolytus* I. p. 170) A.D. 135. I am inclined to date it somewhat later. The Diognetus addressed is not improbably the tutor of Marcus Aurelius, and the reference to 'a King sending his son as a King' (ὡς βασιλεὺς πέμπων υἱὸν βασιλέα § 7), as illustrating the Incarnation, may very well have been suggested by the adoption of M. Aurelius by Antoninus Pius in A.D. 147. On the other hand the simplicity of the theological teaching will not allow us to bring the date down much later.

extant Apology, in which he describes himself as an 'Athenian.' Thus the account of him given by Philippus Sidetes and preserved by Nicephorus Callistus[1], which makes him the first leader of the Catechetical school at Alexandria, must be inaccurate. But Philip of Side, who lived in the fifth century and was ordained deacon by Chrysostom, was a notoriously pretentious and careless writer. For instance, in his short account of Athenagoras he makes Pantænus the pupil of Clement, and asserts that Athenagoras' Apology was addressed to Hadrian and Antoninus, whereas its title shows it to have been dedicated to the emperors Aurelius and Commodus, and therefore written after Commodus was associated in the government (autumn of A.D. 176). From other indications it seems possible to fix the date more precisely between the end of A.D. 176 and the end of A.D. 177[2].

The absence of all appeal to Holy Scripture, which is characteristic of apologies addressed to the heathen, is noticeable in Athenagoras also. But this does not prevent him from exhibiting correspondences with the thought and teaching of the Fourth Gospel. Thus God the Father 'hath made all things by the Word that proceedeth from Him ($\delta\iota\grave{\alpha}$ $\tau o\hat{v}$ $\pi a\rho'$ $a\vec{v}\tau o\hat{v}$ $\Lambda\acute{o}\gamma o\nu$ § 4; cf. John i. 3).' Again, 'the Son of God is (the) Word of the Father in form and in energy; for of Him and by Him were all things made, the Father and the Son being one, the Son being in the Father, and the Father in the Son (§ 10 ; cf. John i. 3, xvii. 21 sq.).' 'To know God and the Word that proceedeth from Him, what is the union of the Son with the Father, what the communion ($\kappa o\iota\nu\omega\nu\acute{\iota}a$) of the Father with the Son' is the Christian's life (§ 12; cf. John xvii. 3).

---

[1] See Dodwell *Dissert. in Iren.*

[2] The $\beta a\theta\epsilon\hat{\iota}a$ $\epsilon\iota\rho\acute{\eta}\nu\eta$ (§ 2) is only applicable to the years 176—178 in the reign of M. Aurelius. This peace intervened between the close of the insurrection of Avidius Crassus and the outbreak of the Marcomannic War. On the other hand to place the Apology after the outbreak of the persecution of the Christians of Vienne and Lyons (A.D. 177) raises a difficulty. Athenagoras declares (§ 35) that no slaves had ever accused their Christian masters of the infamous crimes attributed to them. This statement ceased to be true after the commencement of the persecution in question.

The later Church of Greece proper is almost a blank as regards any literary activity.

VII. THE CHURCH OF ROME.

The genuine Epistle of Clement has been assigned with great probability to A.D. 95 or 96, during the reign of Domitian, when St John was still in banishment in the island of Patmos. It was almost certainly composed before St John wrote his Gospel. Accordingly, in this, the first contribution to Christian extra-canonical literature which emanated from Rome, no quotation from the Fourth Gospel is possible.

1. We therefore pass on to the SHEPHERD OF HERMAS, the author of which is described in the *Muratorian Canon*, in a well-known passage, to have composed his work during the episcopate of his brother Pius (c. A.D. 141–156) in Rome[1]. It is the earliest Christian allegory, written probably by a slave[2], and is noticeable for its absence of quotations from Holy Scripture. This applies not merely to the New Testament but to the Old Testament likewise. There are numerous passages which recall the language of the psalms and prophetical books in the one case, and of the Synoptic Gospels and Epistles—especially the Epistle of St James—in the other, but the coincidences are embedded in the narrative itself, and have to be carefully disentangled from it. The only quotation which is avowedly such, is taken from an apocryphal work, the book of Eldad and Modad[3]. In spite however of this characteristic feature, the treatise contains indications that the author was influenced by the writings of St John. The very title *The Shepherd* recalls the parable of the Good Shepherd in John x., and the sixth Similitude is an elaboration of the metaphor employed in that

---

[1] *Sedente cathedra urbis Romae ecclesiae Pio episcopo fratre eius.* Can. Murator. p. 58 sq. (*ed.* Tregelles).

[2] *Vis.* i. 1, unless indeed he is assuming a fictitious character. His mention of Arcadia (*Sim.* ix.) makes it probable that he came originally from Southern Greece.

[3] Ἐγγὺς Κύριος τοῖς ἐπιστρεφομένοις, ὡς γέγραπται ἐν τῷ Ἐλδὰδ καὶ Μωδάτ *Vis.* ii. 3.

parable. The same chapter in the Fourth Gospel affords a more remarkable coincidence. In the ninth Similitude the Son of God is called 'the Gate[1],' and it is added that 'no man can enter into the kingdom of God otherwise than through the name of His Son Who is beloved by Him (*Sim.* ix. 12; cf. John x. 9, xiv. 6).' In the same section the Son of God is said to be 'begotten prior ($\pi\rho o\gamma\epsilon\nu\acute{\epsilon}\sigma\tau\epsilon\rho o\varsigma$) to all His Creation, so that He became His Father's adviser in His creation.' These correspondences occurring together seem to indicate the influence of the Fourth Gospel. Elsewhere St John's teaching on 'the Truth' underlies Hermas' words as in *Mand.* iii., 'Love the truth, and let nothing but truth proceed out of your mouth ...and thus shall the Lord, Who dwelleth in thee, be glorified, for the Lord is true in every word, and with Him is no lie,' a clear allusion to 1 John ii. 27. Lastly, another passage recalls expressions in John x. 18, the Son 'having Himself cleansed the sins of His people, showed them the paths of life, giving them the law which He received from His Father (*Sim.* v. 6).'

2. The reasons for assigning the MURATORIAN CANON to Rome are briefly as follows : (1) the mention of 'urbs', implying that the writer was familiar with Rome and probably wrote at Rome, (2) the translation of the work into Latin and its preservation in the Western Church, (3) the fact that the Canon which it presents is substantially the Canon of the Western Church[2], (4) the knowledge which the writer displays of the Roman authorship of the Pastor of Hermas, (5) the prominent position assigned to the Epistle to the Romans, which he explains more fully than usual, promising an exposition of the Epistle itself[3]. I will not discuss the

---

[1] The word is θύρα in St John, πύλη in Hermas; but the passage in St John is loosely quoted at least three times by the early heretics given in Hippolytus with πύλη instead of θύρα; and so also in the Clementine Homilies; see below, p. 114.

[2] There is however an obscure allusion to some (quidam ex nostris) who

refuse to allow the public reading of the Apocalypse of Peter, as though implying that the majority accepted this work as canonical.

[3] Romanis autem ordine (? ordinem) scripturarum sed et principium earum esse Christum intimans prolixius scripsit, de quibus singulis necesse est a nobis disputari.

question of the authorship of this interesting fragment. It
has been assigned to Gaius, the Roman presbyter, to He-
gesippus, to Hippolytus. It was obviously written in Greek
originally, and Greek was for the first two centuries the
language of the Roman Church. The data for ascertaining the
age of the writing are two, (1) the notice of an event occurring
in the episcopate of Pius (A.D. 141–156) as having taken place
nuperrime temporibus nostris, (2) the mention in a passage
manifestly corrupt of Arsinous, Valentinus, Miltiades[1], Basilides
and the founder of the Montanists. We have thus the inferior
and the superior limits within which the work is to be assigned;
and, though the problem presents considerable difficulties, we
may provisionally place the date at A.D. 170 or thereabouts.

The fragment opens with an account of the Four Gospels.
It is mutilated at the beginning, and the description of
St Matthew's Gospel is wanting. This is the case too with the
notice of St Mark's Gospel, which is lost all but the conclusion
of the last sentence—'at which however he was present and so
he set them down[2].' But the account given of St Luke throws
light upon the writer's meaning. St Luke, he tells us, was
a physician who after the Ascension became a follower of
St Paul and compiled his Gospel in his own name. 'But
neither did he (*nec ipse* i.e. any more than St Mark) see the
Lord in the flesh,' that is to say, he was not an eyewitness.
'He wrote from hearsay (*ex opinione ἐξ ἀκοῆς*).' The writer
then continues, 'The Fourth Gospel is (the work) of John one
of the (personal) disciples (of Christ) (*ex discipulis ἐκ τῶν
μαθητῶν*).' This expression is significant. St John's position
is here contrasted with that of St Mark and St Luke, who were
not eyewitnesses. The word μαθητής implies a personal disciple of the Lord, and it is so used in Papias and Irenæus[3].
Moreover in this place it is peculiarly appropriate, inasmuch as
St John uses this expression of himself (John xviii. 15, 16,

---

[1] For speculations as to Arsinous
and Miltiades see Bunsen *Anal. Anten.*
I. p. 134 sq., and Credner *Canon*, p. 82.

[2] Quibus tamen interfuit et ita posuit.

[3] Irenæus always calls John ὁ τοῦ
Κυρίου μαθητής; e.g. above, p. 57.

xix. 26, 27, xxi. 20, 23, 24)[1]; and his example doubtless fixed the usage of the Asiatic School. A little lower down, after quoting 1 John i. 1, he draws attention to the fact that St John 'not only claimed to have seen and heard' the Lord (read *non solum visorem se esse et auditorem*), 'but to have written all the marvels of the Lord in order (*sed et scriptorem omnium mirabilium Domini per ordinem profitetur*).' This statement is emphatic. As distinct from the arrangement of events in the second and third (perhaps also in the first) Gospel, the eyewitness is declared to preserve the true chronology.

The references to the writings of St John in the Muratorian Canon are full and explicit. (1) The circumstances under which the Gospel was written are first described; (2) incidentally the opening words in the first Epistle are quoted, 'What wonder then if John so boldly puts forward each statement in his Epistle (*in epistolis suis* ταῖς ἐπιστολαῖς[2]) also saying of himself, "What we have seen with our eyes and heard with our ears and our hands have handled, these things we have written unto you"'; (3) The mention of the number of St Paul's Epistles introduces an allusion to the Apocalypse, 'for John likewise in the Apocalypse, although he writes to seven Churches, yet speaks to all.' (4) Next the Catholic Epistles are discussed[3], and we are told that 'two Epistles of the before-mentioned John are considered canonical[4],' (5) lastly, the Apocalypse is mentioned again in conjunction with the Apocalypse of St Peter, and an unqualified testimony is given to its acceptance in the Church. Thus there is a continuous chain of

---

[1] See Westcott *Canon of the N. T.* p. 211 (ed. 4).

[2] The plural is here probably used to describe one epistle. This is not uncommon, cf. the Epistle of Polycarp (§ 3); Euseb. *H. E.* vi. 1; vi. 43; Joseph. *Ant.* xii. 4. 10; and in classical writers Thuc. i. 132; iv. 50; viii. 51; Polyb. v. 43. 5 etc. It is common in the LXX; cf. Esth. iii. 14; 1 Macc. v. 14, etc. See my *Philippians*, p. 140 sq.

[3] There is evidently a lacuna in the MS. hereabouts, for the First Epistle of St Peter is not mentioned.

[4] Superscripti Iohannis duas (*l.* duae) in catholica (*l.* catholicis) habentur. The two Epistles meant are probably the *Second* and *Third* Epistles, the first being considered as a kind of prologue to the Gospel, detached from the shorter pair, and treated with the Gospel.

notices, and the absence of the faintest hint to the contrary
renders it unquestionable that the same John is meant from
beginning to end as the author of the Gospel, of the First
Epistle, of the two shorter Epistles, and of the Apocalypse.

But is not the account of the Gospels in this fragment
founded upon Papias? And if so, what account did Papias
give? We have found that the Muratorian writer lays stress
on the secondary character of St Mark's account, with apparent
reference to his chronology. Papias also[1] informs us concerning
St Mark, that, though strictly accurate, he ' did not write in order
(οὐ μέντοι τάξει), for he was not himself a hearer or follower of
the Lord (οὔτε γὰρ ἤκουσε τοῦ Κυρίου οὔτε παρηκολούθησεν
αὐτῷ).' Again, we notice that the Muratorian writer quotes
from the First Epistle of St John in evidence. Papias likewise
does the same. We are not told with what object Papias
adduced this testimony from the Epistles; but it is at least a
plausible hypothesis that he had the same end in view as the
Muratorian writer. May it not then be inferred with some
degree of probability that the writer of the Muratorian Canon
borrowed in some degree from Papias? The use of the term
ex discipulis seems to point to such a source of information.

3. It might have been unnecessary to carry the history of
the Canon in the Roman Church further; but doubts have been
thrown[2] of the view of HIPPOLYTUS upon this question. It
has been maintained that he shows no knowledge of the Gospel
as the work of St John. It would indeed have been marvellous
if Hippolytus, the pupil of Irenæus, and the friend of Origen,
both of whom bear such unmistakeable testimony to the reception of the Fourth Gospel, had entertained any doubts on this
subject. But the answer to the objection is evident. (1) When
Hippolytus expounds his own views, he is addressing heathens.
He therefore does not appeal to any scripture, because it would
not carry authority with his hearers. (2) It is perfectly evident

---

[1] Papias in Eus. *H. E.* iii. 39.   *character of the Fourth Gospel*, pp. 57,
[2] Tayler *An attempt to ascertain the*   77, 87.

when he refers to the quotations from St John in Gnostic writings[1], that he and they alike received as authoritative the documents which are quoted.   (3) He does not mention by name St Matthew or St Luke.   He mentions St Peter and St James indeed, but without any connexion with their writings in the New Testament.   The only Pauline Epistles which he connects with the name of St Paul are Romans, 2 Corinthians, 1 Timothy and perhaps Galatians[2], though he quotes these and most of the other Epistles of St Paul repeatedly.   (4) In the work against Noetus (§§ 12, 14, 15 etc.) and in a fragment preserved by Lagarde (p. 52) he distinctly quotes the Fourth Gospel and attributes it to 'John, the beloved disciple[3].'   (5) Among the list of works ascribed to him on his statue is a 'Defence of the Gospel and Apocalypse of St John.'   The work is lost, but there is reason to suppose that it was known to, and used by, Epiphanius[4].   These reasons seem to me amply to justify our claim to reckon Hippolytus among the witnesses for the Johannine authorship.

Hippolytus is the last and most famous representative of the Greek Church of Rome.   Henceforward Rome becomes the focus of Latin Christendom.

VIII.   THE CHURCHES OF AFRICA.

Meanwhile Latin Christianity has had its headquarters in Africa and especially at Carthage.   And it is here that we must seek the opinion of the early Latin Church on the question of the Canon.   The Roman Church, Greek in nation and Latin in soil, was the natural link between Greek and Latin Christendom. Carthage and Africa were converted from Rome.   The Canon

---

[1] See below, p. 105 sq.

[2] Romans, 2 Corinthians, Galatians once only, 1 Timothy twice.

[3] The quotations are as follows: John i. 1 (by name), 1-3 (by name), 10, 14, 18, 20, 29 (twice, once by name), 30, ii. 19, iii. 6, 13 (twice and by name), 31, iv. 34, v. 25 (twice), 36, vi. 27, 35, 45, viii. 12, x. 18, 30, xi. 35, 52, xiv. 6, 8 sq. 12; xvi. 28, xix. 14, 37, xx. 1, 17.

[4] On this work see below, p. 118.

of the African Church therefore may be supposed, in all the more important points, to reproduce the Canon of the Church of Rome.

1. TERTULLIAN is the first known writer of the African Church; as to his own individual opinion on the authority of the Fourth Gospel no doubt can be entertained. He quotes it some two hundred times or more without the slightest misgiving. It is more important to trace the evidence, which his language affords, to the traditional testimony to its use. Thus in his treatise against Marcion (iv. 2, 5), after mentioning the four Evangelists together by name, he appeals to the Churches founded by St John and the succession of bishops derived from St John, as evidence for the reception of the Gospels by the Catholic Church. Making all allowance for his rhetoric, such an appeal cannot be considered unmeaning. Of the Gospel of St John especially he speaks (*adv. Prax.* § 5) as though it had long worked itself into the phraseology and the teaching of Christianity.

2. Another document, contemporary with, or rather earlier than, Tertullian, THE ACTS OF MARTYRDOM OF SS. PERPETUA AND FELICITAS (Ruinart, p. 80 sq.) shows what deep hold the writings of St John had taken on the African Church at this time. At the outset, we meet in the preface with two obvious coincidences with Johannine phraseology. The courage of the martyrs is instanced as a proof of the power of God, 'Who worketh always the works which He hath promised, for a testimony to them that believe not, for a support to them that believe' (*quae repromisit non credentibus in testimonium, credentibus in beneficium*—a reference to John x. 38). The passage then proceeds, 'accordingly in our case too, that which we have heard and handled declare we unto you also, brothers and sons, that ye also may...recount the glory of God (*et nos itaque quod audivimus et contrectavimus annuntiamus et vobis, fratres et filioli, ut et vos...rememoremini gloriae Domini*)', an ex-

pression based upon the opening words of St John's First Epistle[1]. Less stress can be laid on the fact that in her vision Perpetua sees (§ 4) sitting in the midst of a garden *hominem canum in habitu Pastoris*, for this favourite idea of Christ as the Good Shepherd may have been derived from the Pastor of Hermas, though its original source was doubtless John x. But towards the close of the document occurs an allusion to the Fourth Gospel, which is interesting because it is not apparent on the surface. The only direct quotation from the New Testament found in this martyrology runs as follows: 'But He who had said, "Ask and ye shall receive" (*qui dixerat Petite et accipietis*), gave (to the martyrs) at their prayer that form of death which each had desired (§ 19).' Now, though the passage quoted occurs in three of the four Gospels (Matt. vii. 7, Luke xi. 9, John xvi. 24), yet the exact form in which it is couched[2] shows that it was derived, not from the Synoptic narrative, but from the Fourth Gospel. In short, with the exception of the Apocalypse (*e. g.* especially § 12), there are no such coincidences with any other part of the New Testament as are afforded to the language of the Fourth Evangelist.

The Montanist, or rather Montanizing[3], tendencies of this Martyrology bear testimony to its early date. Indeed, there is every reason to believe that it was contemporary with the events which it records. Tertullian refers to the document in his *de anima* § 55, and the date usually assigned to this treatise is c. A.D. 208. The date of the martyrdom of S. Perpetua and her companions is fixed by a reference in the Martyrology itself to the birthday of Geta Cæsar[4], thus placing it between A.D. 198, when Geta became Cæsar, and A.D. 209, when he was created Augustus. It is highly probable that the actual year was A.D. 202, during the persecution of Severus.

---

[1] The passage quoted is probably verse 3. Notice however the variation quod audivimus et contrectavimus for quod vidimus et audivimus.

[2] St Matthew and St Luke have αἰτεῖσθε καὶ δοθήσεται ὑμῖν, St John alone αἰτεῖσθε καὶ λήμψεσθε.

[3] The allusion to 'cheese' in § 4 can, I think, hardly be taken to show that the writer or the martyrs were Artotyrites.

[4] Natale tunc Getae Caesaris § 7.

IX. The Churches of Syria.

There is no early Syrian writer of importance until Bardesanes. He flourished at the close of the second century, or at the beginning of the third century, according as we consider the emperor Antoninus mentioned in connexion with him (Epiph. i. 477 A, Eus. *H. E.* iv. 20, Jerome *Vir. Ill.* etc.) to have been M. Aurelius or Caracalla. Bardesanes was a voluminous writer, but of the various works assigned to him only one has survived, *The Book of the Laws of Countries,* which was discovered by Cureton among the Nitrian MSS., and published by him in his *Spicilegium Syriacum* in 1855. When examined, however, this treatise appears to have emanated from the disciples of Bardesanes rather than from Bardesanes himself, and its date is too late to be of assistance in determining the tradition of the Syrian Church on the question of the Fourth Gospel. Among the *Ancient Syriac Documents* discovered by Cureton in 1848 and published in 1864, is one entitled *The Doctrine of the Apostles,* in which Simon Peter is represented (Cureton *l. c.* p. 25) as quoting the promise of the Comforter in the language of John xiv. 26 ; and in another document, *The Doctrine of Simon Cephas,* the same quotation in a shorter form is again put into St Peter's mouth (Cureton *l. c.* p. 36). But here again, the value of this evidence is lessened by the uncertainty of the date which is to be assigned to these ancient documents.

X. The Testimony of Heretical Writers.

We now pass from the evidence of orthodox writers to the testimony of heretics, and when we begin to look into it we are surprised at its extent and at its early date. The numerous controversies which the early fathers held with the multiform systems to which Christianity gave rise, has resulted in our possessing, embedded in the works of the defenders of the faith, large extracts from the writers who assailed it. This mine of unorthodox literature has been largely increased by the acquisition in recent years of Hippolytus' great work the *Refutation of all Heresies*.   From this newly-discovered work I shall draw the greater part of the evidence which I hope to bring before you.   The evidence itself I shall state as briefly as I can.   We will begin with the Gnostics.

A. The Gnostics.

1.   Simon Magus is credited with a work called *The Great Revelation* (ἡ μεγάλη ἀπόφασις), of which Hippolytus has preserved considerable extracts (*Ref.* vi. 9–18).   There is however reason to believe that the treatise was mainly written by his disciples.   In a quotation from this book given by Hippolytus (*l. c.* vi. 9), where man is described as 'born of blood' (τὸν ἐξ αἱμάτων γεγεννημένον), some have found an allusion to John i. 13 (οἳ οὐκ ἐξ αἱμάτων...ἐγεννήθησαν).   This seems to me very doubtful.   Indeed the book was probably composed somewhere about the close of the first century, perhaps before the Gospel of St John was written, or at least circulated.

2.   The Ophites or Naassenes.   This was a very early sect, almost pre-Christian in its origin, which broke up into several distinct branches, as it adopted diverse extraneous elements. But its assimilative character makes it next to impossible for us to separate the more ancient features of its teaching from the more recent developments.   Thus we have no means of ascertaining the exact date of the writings quoted by Hippolytus. But Hippolytus himself composed his *Refutation* some time early in the third century[1], and he intimates that when he wrote the Ophite system was already on the wane.   There is good reason therefore for assigning an early period in the second century for the document which he had before him.   It abounds with quotations from the Fourth Gospel.   I will not weary you

---

[1] The limits of date for the composition are the death of Callistus A.D. 220, of whom an account is given (*Haer.* ix. 11 sq.), and Hippolytus' own death, which took place somewhere between A.D. 235 and 238 (*Liber Pontificalis* I. pp. 64, 145, Duchesne).

by detailing them at length, but will content myself with giving the references to the Gospel and to the pages in Duncker and Schneidewin's edition (1859) of the *Refutatio*, merely premising that the quotations are clear and explicit.

John i. 3.	*Refutatio*	v. 8 (p. 150), v. 9 (166).
i. 9.		v. 9 (p. 172).
iii. 5.		v. 8 (p. 162).
iii. 6.		v. 7 (p. 148).
iv. 10, 14.		v. 9 (p. 172).
iv. 21.		v. 9 (p. 166).
v. 37.		v. 8 (p. 154).
vi. 44.		v. 8 (p. 158).
vi. 53.		v. 8 (p. 152).
viii. 21.		v. 8 (p. 154).
x. 9.		v. 8 (p. 156).
xiii. 33.		v. 8 (p. 152).

There are also undoubted allusions to the marriage of Cana in Galilee (John ii. 1–11; cf. *Ref.* v. 8 p. 152) and to the man born blind (John ix. 1; cf. *Ref.* v. 9 p. 172), which are evidently taken from the same source. And this list might be enlarged without difficulty.

3.   The distinction between the PERATÆ and the Naassenes is not very clearly defined, and the two bodies seem to have held many tenets in common; but Hippolytus treats them as separate sects, and it is evident therefore that he considered the Peratæ, as a body, to have a real and independent existence. I tabulate as before the obvious quotations from the Fourth Gospel, which occur in the account of them taken by Hippolytus from one of their own documents.

John i. 1–4.	*Refutatio*	v. 16 (p. 194).
iii. 14.		v. 16 (p. 192).
iii. 17.		v. 12 (p. 178).
viii. 44.		v. 17 (p. 196).
x. 7.		v. 17 (p. 198).

4. We pass on to another Ophite sect, which is treated next in order in the *Refutatio*—the SETHIANI. As far as we can judge from the extracts which Hippolytus gives us, the formularies of this sect do not indulge in scriptural phraseology to any great extent. But here again we meet with traces of the use of St John's language, *e.g. Ref.* v. 19 (p. 206), where the Logos is said to have 'drunk the cup of the living water which springeth up,' an expression which recalls John iv. 10, 14; and *Ref.* v. 21 (p. 212), where true believers are spoken of as those 'who are born again of the Spirit, not of the flesh,' words which remind us of John iii. 6.

5. JUSTINUS, whom Hippolytus quotes as another Ophite heresiarch, elaborated a system which combined heathen mythology and the book of Genesis into a fantastic theory of the universe. The *Book of Baruch*, from which Hippolytus quotes, presents few correspondences with the New Testament, but the same coincidence is found with John iv. 10, 14, which we have noticed already; and Jesus, as he leaves his body on the cross, says to his mother Eden, 'Woman, thou hast to the full thy son' (Γύναι, ἀπέχεις σου τὸν υἱόν), words which, though with a wholly different application, betray an acquaintance with John xix. 26.

6. The evidence which the Ophite system affords can be supplemented from the PISTIS SOPHIA, one of the few remains of the old Gnostic literature which have come down to us. This work is preserved in a Coptic version. It is in four books, the fourth probably by a different author, and containing a simpler form of teaching than the other three. The date usually assigned to the composition is the middle of the third century. I give from Petermann's edition the correspondences which it presents with the Fourth Gospel.

John i. 20.	*Pistis Sophia* p. 9.
vii. 33.	p. 11.
xii. 35.	p. 11.
xiv. 3.	p. 145.

John xv. 15.   *Pistis Sophia* p. 145.

xv. 19.   pp. 8, 145.

xvii. 14, 16.   pp. 8, 145.

xvii. 23.   p. 145.

xvii. 25.   pp. 120, 175.

The Johannine expression 'Verily, verily' ('Αμὴν ἀμήν) occurs very frequently (pp. 23, 55, 117, 197) in this treatise.

7. BASILIDES, Gnostic teacher of Alexandria, flourished in the reign of Hadrian (A.D. 117–138). He professed to have been instructed by Glaucias, a follower of St Peter. Clement of Alexandria, to whom we owe this information (*Strom.* vii. 17 p. 898), classes him in a loose way with those heretics 'who arose about the times of Hadrian, and who reached until the period of the elder Antoninus[1].' Though Clement was interested in placing his date as low as possible[2], there is no serious difference of opinion in this respect. Within a few years the limit must lie. Now Hippolytus gives an abstract of a work, or portion of a work, by Basilides; and in it one or two passages of St John are quoted and gnostically explained: 'And this,' says he, 'is what is called in the Gospels, "That was the true light that lighteth every man who cometh (or coming) into the world"' ('Ην τὸ φῶς τὸ ἀληθινόν, ὃ φωτίζει πάντα ἄνθρωπον ἐρχόμενον εἰς τὸν κόσμον *Ref.* vii. 22 p. 360; cf. John i. 9). And again: 'But that every thing,' says he, 'has its own proper times (καιρούς), the Saviour states explicitly, saying, "My time is not yet come"' (οὔπω ἥκει ἡ ὥρα μου *Ref.* vii. 27 p. 376; cf. John ii. 4). It is said, however, that these quotations are taken not from Basilides himself, but from some other Basilidean writer. But what are the facts? The general form in which the quotations are introduced—the word φησίν— cannot be urged as an argument one way or the other; for the expression is often used impersonally, and may mean 'he says'

---

[1] Our chief authorities for the life of Basilides are Clem. *l.c.*, Iren. i. 24, 3 sq., Eus. *H. E.* iv. 7, Epiph. *Haer.* xxiv. 1. (p. 68 c), Theodoret *H. F.* i. 2.

[2] He is contending that the Catholic Church is older than the sects.

or 'they say.' The question must be decided by an examination
of the passages themselves. Hippolytus begins by stating
(p. 356 l. 64), that Basilides and Isidore his son and disciple
declare that Matthew delivered to them certain secret truths
which he had heard from the Saviour. Then follows a series of
quotations, extending over many pages and ushered in (p. 356
l. 69) by φησίν. This connecting particle is repeated again and
again, but it links together a continuous argument from which
it is patent that Hippolytus is quoting some one book and
some one representative of the school. When he comments on
the statements made, he occasionally speaks of his opponents in
the plural[1], but the narrative quoted exhibits more than once the
writer's personality, e.g. '"I do not admit", says he' (οὐ δέχομαι,
φησίν p. 356 l. 79); '"By willed, I mean," says he' (τὸ δὲ
ἠθέλησε λέγω, φησί p. 358 l. 97), clearly showing that the
writer was a single individual who delivered his opinions with
authority. Who then was this writer? The answer is obvious.
None other than Basilides himself. No other name is
mentioned[2] by Hippolytus. After the first introduction Isidore
is tacitly dropped, and Basilides is treated as the solitary
antagonist. But it may be contended that this was a later
work written by a disciple in the name of Basilides. To this
contention we may reply, (1) that no such work was ever heard
of, (2) that Basilides differed herein from other heresiarchs, as
Simon Magus for example, in that his followers had no interest in
forging documents in his name. For unlike the Ophites and the
Valentinians, the Basilideans were not a large and spreading sect.
They soon dwindled away, leaving by a natural selection the
Ophites and Valentinians masters of the Gnostic field. On the
other hand, the abstract which Hippolytus gives shows the
influence of a master mind. Now it is known that Basilides
wrote twenty-four books upon the Gospel[3]—a work which is

---

[1] e.g. p. 356 ll. 84, 86, p. 360 ll. 45,
49, p. 366 l. 36, p. 368 l. 69, p. 376
l. 7, p. 378 l. 12.

[2] e.g. p. 356 l. 85, p. 360 l. 27
(φεύγει γὰρ ὁ B.), p. 362 l. 67 καλεῖ τὸ

τοιοῦτο B.), p. 364 l. 8 (διῄρηται γὰρ
ὑπὸ B.), p. 366 l. 46 (B....διασαφεῖ), cf.
p. 366 l. 47, p. 368 l. 50 etc.

[3] See Agrippa Castor in Eus. *H. E.*
iv. 7.

quoted by Clement of Alexandria[1], and which therefore was very likely to be in the hands of Hippolytus. And part of the abstract in Hippolytus is taken up with explaining what is meant by the term 'the Gospel'[2]; while the whole is closed with the significant sentence, 'These then are the fables which Basilides utters, who taught throughout Egypt, and such were the fruits which he produced who was instructed in so great wisdom (p. 378 ll. 40 sq.).' And then Basilides is dismissed, and Hippolytus goes on to combat his contemporary Saturninus[3]. The extreme probability therefore that we have in the *Refutation* the very words of Basilides himself falls little short of demonstration; and thus we have a passage from St John quoted, as contained 'in the Gospels', by one outside the Church who ranks in antiquity between Clement of Rome and Polycarp[4].

8.   VALENTINUS came to Rome, we are told, in the episcopate of Hyginus (A.D. 138–141) and was in his full vigour in the episcopate of Pius (c. A.D. 141–156)[5]. He professed to have received his instruction from Theodas, a disciple of St Paul[6]. Tertullian informs us[7] that he adopted the Canon of the New Testament complete, and the fact that the whole phraseology of the Valentinian system is built upon the opening verses of St John's Gospel[8] is conclusive evidence that he recognised our Fourth Evangelist. Indeed, we have Irenæus' authority (iii. 11, 7) for saying that the Valentinians especially affected the Gospel of St John. But the matter is set at rest once for all by a distinct quotation from St John (x. 8) which Hippolytus records of him (διὰ τοῦτο, φησί, λέγει ὁ Σωτήρ· Πάντες οἱ

---

[1] Clem. Alex. *Strom.* iv. 12, 83 sq. (p. 599 sq.)

[2] e.g. p. 370 l. 97 sq., p. 372 ll. 12 sq., 32, 37, 40, p. 378 l. 10 sq., and especially p. 376 l. 6 sq.

[3] ταῦτα μὲν οὖν ἐστιν ἃ καὶ B. μυθεύει ...Σατορνεῖλος δέ τις συνακμάσας τῷ B. κ.τ.λ. *Ref.* vii. 27, p. 378 l. 40 sq.

[4] See Westcott *Canon of the N. T.* p. 290, ed. 4.

[5] Irenæus iii. 4, 3.

[6] Clem. Alex. *Strom.* vii. 17, p. 898.

[7] Tert. *de praescr.* 38, si Valentinus integro instrumento uti videtur, non callidiore ingenio quam Marcion manus intulit veritati; cf. *de carne Chr.* 19, Iren. iii. 14, 4.

[8] πλήρωμα, μονογενής, φῶς, σκότος, λόγος, ζωή, ἀλήθεια are Valentinian terms, so also is παράκλητος.

πρὸ ἐμοῦ ἐληλυθότες κλέπται καὶ λῃσταὶ εἰσί Ref. vi. 35 p. 284 l. 77 sq.).

9. The Valentinians were divided into two schools (1) Western and (2) Eastern (Hipp. Ref. vi. 35 p. 286). Of the Western Valentinians the most noticeable names are Heracleon, Ptolemæus and Marcus. Now HERACLEON[1] wrote a commentary on St John, which is quoted frequently by Origen[2]. Origen informs us that Heracleon was reported to have been a familiar friend of Valentinus (Comm. in Joan. Tom. II. § 8). The rise of commentaries shows an advanced stage in the history of the text of the Fourth Gospel. PTOLEMÆUS, like Heracleon, was a direct disciple of Valentinus. His letter to his sister Flora is preserved in Epiphanius (Haer. xxxiii. 3 p. 216 sq.); and in it John i. 3 is quoted (§ 3) as the statement of ὁ ἀπόστολος. Again, in Iren. i. 8, 2 a Valentinian writer quotes John xii. 27 (τί εἴπω οὐκ οἶδα), and a little later on (§ 5) follows a direct quotation from the same or another writer, commencing, 'John the disciple of the Lord', and explaining from a Valentinian stand-point the prologue of the Fourth Gospel. From the clause added at the end of the section in the Latin version (et Ptolemaeus quidem etc.) it appears that the anonymous writer was Ptolemæus. MARCUS himself must have been of early date, inasmuch as 'the Elder who lived before' Irenæus wrote against him (Iren. i. 15, 6). From the account which Irenæus preserves of him, he appears to have used our Four Gospels, and the extracts from his teaching which survive in the works of this father contain an illustration of the mystical number ten, founded on a reference to the appearance of our Lord after His resurrection 'when Thomas was not present' (Iren. i. 18, 3; cf. John xx. 24).

It is doubtful whether Marcus should be included among the Western, and not rather among the Eastern Valentinians. Our information as regards these last is very scanty, but a ray

---

[1] For his date see Hilgenfeld Zeit-schr. x. p. 75, and Westcott Canon p. 299 sq. ed. 4.

[2] He is also quoted by Clem. Alex. Strom. iv. 73, p. 595.

of light is thrown upon them by a collection of extracts appended to the works of Clement of Alexandria and according to Bunsen (*Analect. Antenic.* p. 203) taken from the first book of the *Hypotyposeis*. The collection is entitled ἐκ τῶν Θεοδότου καὶ τῆς ἀνατολικῆς καλουμένης διδασκαλίας κατὰ τοὺς Οὐαλεντίνου χρόνους ἐπιτομαί. It abounds in quotations from the Fourth Gospel, explained in a Valentinian sense. I tabulate the most striking, giving the pages from Potter's edition of Clement :—

John i. 1.	Clem. Alex.	§§ 6, 18 pp. 968, 973.
i. 3.		§ 45 p. 979.
i. 4.		§§ 6, 18 pp. 968, 973.
i. 9.		§ 41 p. 979.
i. 14, 18.		§ 6 p. 968.
ii. 16.		§ 9 p. 969.
iii. 8.		§ 17 p. 972.
iv. 24.		§ 17 p. 972.
viii. 12.		§ 35 p. 978.
viii. 56.		§ 18 p. 973.
x. 7.		§ 26 p. 975.
xi. 25.		§ 6 p. 968.
xiv. 6.		§ 6 p. 968.

10.   MARCION elaborated his system about A.D. 150. At first he accepted all the Four Gospels (Tert. *de carne Chr.* §§ 2, 3), but afterwards he became 'ultra-Pauline,' rejecting all but mutilations of the writings of St Luke and St Paul. The ground on which he would reject the authority of the three 'pillar-Apostles[1]' is evident from Tertullian (*adv. Marcion.* v. 3), who tells us that he appealed to St Paul's references in the Epistle to the Galatians to certain false apostles who had perverted the Gospel of Christ, and especially to St Peter, as not walking uprightly after the truth of the Gospel. Thus he would consider them plunged in the blackness of intellectual darkness and incapable of imparting any teaching to a Gnostic like himself, while his

[1] Galat. ii. 9 οἱ δοκοῦντες στύλοι εἶναι.

condemnation of the Fourth Gospel would be pointed by the consideration that St John was an Apostle of the circumcision. His silence therefore with respect to the Fourth Gospel becomes an argument in favour of its genuineness; had Marcion quoted it with approval, the fact would have been, so far as it went, evidence against the Johannine authorship. Apelles, his disciple, was certainly aware of its existence, for he tells us[1] that after His resurrection our Lord showed His disciples 'the marks of the nails and in (of) His side,' an incident which is mentioned by St John alone (xx. 25).

11.   The DOCETÆ doubted the reality of the Incarnation, saying that our Lord's humanity was an appearance and nothing more. Their language was founded upon St John's phraseology—λόγος, μονογενής, πλήρωμα occurring constantly in their formularies (Hipp. *Ref.* viii. 9, 10, pp. 416, 418, 420). John iii. 5, 6 is adduced in support of their opinions in a Docetic document given us by Hippolytus (*Ref.* viii. 10 p. 422).

12.   The JUDAIZING CHRISTIANS in the primitive Church separated off into two main divisions, according to the view that they adopted of the obligation of the Mosaic Law. The Nazarenes, while recognising the binding nature of the law upon themselves, were in the main orthodox. On the other hand the Ebionites considered the old dispensation permanent and for everyone, and repudiated the authority and Apostleship of St Paul. In considering the testimony which these two early Judaizing sects afford to the Fourth Gospel, we are fortunate in being able to appeal at first hand to extant works emanating from representatives of both schools of thought.

The CLEMENTINE HOMILIES represent the views of Gnostic Ebionism[2]. The exact date of the work is uncertain, but it may be placed with confidence between A.D. 100—180. I am myself inclined to fix it at c. A.D. 150. Formerly our knowledge of the treatise was derived from a manuscript mutilated

---

[1] In Hipp. *Ref.* vii. 38, p. 410.   my *Galatians*, pp. 327 sq., 340 sq.
[2] On the Clementine literature see   [*Dissertations*, pp. 83 sq., 98 sq.]

at the end, and some alleged correspondences with the Fourth
Gospel, which it contained, were hotly disputed by the Tübingen
school, who made this document the keystone of their elaborate
theory of the alleged antagonism between St Paul and St Peter in
the early Church. In 1853, however, Dressel published the missing conclusion from a Vatican MS., and it was found to contain
an obvious allusion to the story of the man born blind[1]. From
that time the acquaintance of the Clementine writer with the
Fourth Gospel has not been denied. Though this passage in
the 19th homily is decisive, it may be of interest to give
other coincidences from the earlier portions of this work; e.g.
Clem. Hom. iii. 25 'He was a murderer and a liar' (φονεὺς γὰρ
ἦν καὶ ψεύστης, cf. John viii. 44); *Clem. Hom.* iii. 52 'I am
the gate (ἡ πύλη)[2] of life, he that entereth through me entereth
into life' (cf. John x. 27); *ib.* 'My sheep hear my voice' (cf.
John x. 9); *Clem. Hom.* xi. 26 'Verily I say unto you, except
ye be born again of living water in the name of the Father,
Son and Holy Spirit, ye shall not enter into the kingdom of
heaven' (cf. John iii. 5).

The book entitled THE TESTAMENTS OF THE TWELVE
PATRIARCHS is a product of Nazarene, as the *Clementine
Homilies* of Ebionite, Judaism. It was written after the
capture of Jerusalem by Titus, and probably before the
rebellion of Barcochba (A.D. 132—135)[3]. It professes to be a
prophecy of the Messiah, and it could not therefore without
loss of dramatic propriety quote from the Evangelical record,

---

[1] ὅθεν καὶ διδάσκαλος ἡμῶν περὶ τοῦ
ἐκ γενετῆς πηροῦ καὶ ἀναβλέψαντος παρ'
αὐτοῦ ἐξετά[ζων ἐρωτήσασιν] εἰ οὗτος
ἥμαρτεν ἢ οἱ γονεῖς αὐτοῦ ἵνα τυφλὸς
γεννηθῇ, ἀπεκρίνατο, Οὔτε οὗτός τι ἥμαρτεν οὔτε οἱ γονεῖς αὐτοῦ, ἀλλ' ἵνα δι' αὐτοῦ
φανερωθῇ ἡ δύναμις τοῦ Θεοῦ *Clem.
Hom.* xix. § 22; cf. John ix. 2, 3.

[2] For πύλη see above, p. 97.

[3] For the various dates assigned to
this work see on *Galatians*, p. 320,
[*Dissertations*, p. 76]. It is directly

named by Origen (*Hom. in Jos.* xv. 6),
and probably was known to Tertullian
(c. *Marc.* v. 1, *Scorpiace* 13), and (as I
believe) even earlier to Irenæus (*Fragm.*
17, p. 836 sq. Stieren). Had it been
written after the suppression of Barcochba's rebellion, it is next to impossible that no mention should have
been made of an event so important
to the Judaizing Christians as the
second destruction of Jerusalem by
Hadrian.

but it contains many expressions which are characteristic of the Fourth Gospel, as μονογενής (*Test. Benj.* 9), ὁ ἀμνὸς τοῦ Θεοῦ (*Test. Jos.* 19, *Benj.* 3), ὁ σωτὴρ τοῦ κόσμου[1] (*Test. Levi* 14, *Benj.* 3), ἡ πηγὴ εἰς ζωὴν πάσης σαρκός (*Test. Jud.* 24). Other longer sentences are apparently due to the same source; thus *Test. Levi* 14 τὸ φῶς τοῦ κόσμου τὸ δοθὲν ἐν ὑμῖν εἰς φωτισμὸν παντὸς ἀνθρώπου (cf. John i. 9, viii. 12), *ib.* § 18 αὐτὸς ποιήσει κρίσιν ἀληθείας ἐπὶ τῆς γῆς (cf. John v. 27); *ib.* τότε ἀγαλ- λιάσεται Ἀβραάμ (cf. John viii. 56); *Test. Jud.* 20 τὸ πνεῦμα τῆς ἀληθείας μαρτυρεῖ πάντα καὶ κατηγορεῖ πάντων (cf. John xv. 26); *Test. Benj.* 9 ἐπὶ ξύλου ὑψωθήσεται...καὶ...ἔσται ἀναβαίνων ἀπὸ γῆς εἰς οὐρανόν (cf. John iii. 13, 14, vi. 62).

Hitherto the voice of antiquity, whether uttered by the early fathers of the Church or by those who stood outside her pale, has been unanimous, as far as we can follow it, in testifying to the genuineness and authenticity of the Fourth Gospel. To this universal tradition, however, there is one exception, and one only, and we will conclude our examination of the external evidence by a consideration of this solitary exception to the chorus of universal attestation.

After speaking of Marcion's mutilation of the Canon, Irenæus (iii. 11, 9) goes on to mention 'others also, who, in order that they may frustrate the gift of the Spirit, do not admit that type of Church teaching (*illam speciem*), which is in accordance with St John's Gospel, in which the Lord promised that He would send the Paraclete; but at one and the same time reject both the Gospel and the spirit of prophecy. Unhappy men in very truth, who desire false prophets to exist (*pseudo-prophetae*—read *pseudo-prophetas—quidem esse volunt*), but yet banish from the Church the grace of prophecy... Accordingly they ought not to acknowledge the Apostle Paul either...because he testifies to men and women prophesying in the Church[2].'

---

[1] This expression occurs only in John iv. 42 and 1 John iv. 14.

[2] A reference to 1 Cor. xi. 4, 5.

Now from Irenæus' argument, of which I have given only a part, it is clear (1) that these objectors repudiate the Gospel of St John, because it contains a special promise of spiritual gifts, (2) that they confess the existence of false prophets, and yet deny the existence of a true prophecy, (3) hence, Irenæus argues, they are as unreasonable as those who refuse to associate with the brethren for fear there should be hypocrites among them, (4) on this ground they ought not only to reject the Gospel of St John, but also the Epistles of St Paul, for St Paul has spoken very emphatically about spiritual gifts, and recognises both men and women as prophesying in the Church[1]. Irenæus goes on in the next chapter to show at great length that there is a Spirit.

It is evident therefore that the persons spoken of are strong anti-Montanists; they took offence at the claims of the Montanists to spiritual gifts, more especially at the prophesyings of women. We must therefore read *pseudo-prophetas* in the passage given above[2]. For Montanism was spiritualism considered as a reaction against formalism and intellectualism. The Montanists laid great stress upon the writings of St John, especially the Apocalypse, hence these opponents of Montanism cut the knot by denying the authority of the Fourth Gospel[3]. And they did more than this. Irenæus speaks only of their rejection of the Gospel of St John. He is dwelling only on the Gospels; and therefore he would naturally not say anything

---

[1] See a similar argument used against these same persons by Epiphanius (li. 32 p. 106 ed. Oehler).

[2] The alternative correction of Lücke (p. 65) *nolunt* for *volunt* seems to interfere with the sense.

[3] Considerable light is thrown on Irenæus' attitude upon this matter by the letter of the Gallican Churches to the Asiatic Churches quoted in Eus. *H. E.* v. 3 on this very subject of Montanism. The letter is an attempt at mediation; it was written avowedly εἰρήνης ἕνεκεν, and it was penned by the martyrs 'while yet in bonds' to the brethren in Asia and Phrygia. At the same time the martyrs sent Irenæus, then a presbyter, as their delegate with letters of recommendation to Eleutherus, bishop of Rome (Eus. *H. E.* v. 4) for the sake of conferring with him on this same question. Irenæus therefore is not a strong anti-Montanist. He mentions the pseudo-prophetae in another passage (*Haer.* iv. 33, 6) with, again, a probable reference to Montanism.

about their position with respect to other canonical books. It
appears however from other sources that they rejected also the
Apocalypse. For Epiphanius (who wrote after A.D. 350) describes
a sect of heretics, whom he dubs Ἄλογοι, or irrationalists. It is
a play on the word, for they rejected the testimony of John, who
taught the doctrine of the Logos. He says, 'I put upon
them this nickname; from henceforth they shall be so called,
and therefore, my beloved, let us give them this name' (Epiph.
Haer. li. 3). He seems to have succeeded in affixing this
opprobrious title upon them, for Augustine so calls them
afterwards (*Haer.* 30, Oehler I. p. 202). Of these Alogi Epiphanius relates that they sprang up after the Cataphrygians,
and he evidently considers that they originated in the same
neighbourhood (*l. c.* esp. § 33). He begins by describing them
(§ 1) as ἐπιγεῖοι 'material,' 'sensual,' in their views, and as
gainsaying the Holy Spirit and the wonderful sequence of the
Gospels (§ 16). He closes a full account of them with a passage
commencing (§ 35) 'And these not receiving the Holy Spirit
are convicted by the Spirit etc.' Thus his account begins and
ends with an allusion to their attitude towards the doctrine o
the Holy Spirit, and his expressions are meaningless unless he
is describing an anti-Spiritualist, anti-Montanist movement.
We may therefore take it for granted that Irenæus and
Epiphanius are referring to one and the same body of people.
Epiphanius goes on to say that they rejected the Gospel and
the Apocalypse, and attributed these writings to Cerinthus.
He supposes that they also rejected the Epistles of St John
likewise, 'for these,' he says, 'agree in character with the
Gospel and the Apocalypse' (§ 34), but he evidently knows
nothing definite about this last point.

In every other respect the Alogi seem to have been orthodox
(Epiph. li. § 4 δοκοῦσι γὰρ καὶ αὐτοὶ τὰ ἴσα ἡμῖν πιστεύειν[1]). It
does not appear that they rejected the doctrine of St John's
Gospel. The silence of Epiphanius on this point is speaking.

[1] Compare Prædestinatus *Haer.* I. 30 omnia nobiscum sapiunt (Oehler I.
p. 243).

Certainly this energetic champion of orthodoxy does not detect any mark of Ebionism in them. They may, however, have repudiated the Johannine form under which the Divinity of our Lord was taught, though even this is doubtful.

Very similar is the brief notice of the Alogi in Philastrius (Oehler I. p. 61). He mentions those who reject both the Gospel and the Apocalypse; but he seems to restrict to the Apocalypse their attribution of the authorship to Cerinthus. And this was perhaps really the case. For Dionysius of Alexandria (Eus. *H. E.* vii. 25, comp. iii. 28) speaks of some before him who attributed this book to Cerinthus and the Cerinthians, because they thought that they saw in it a gross and material picture of an earthly kingdom of Christ. This ascription would suit very well the fragment of Gaius written against the Montanists and preserved in Eusebius (*H. E.* iii. 28), and it is possible that Dionysius alludes to Gaius; but it is strange that, if this was the view of Gaius, Eusebius should not have told us so distinctly. Certainly Theodoret interpreted it differently (*Haer. Fab.* ii. 3; see Routh *R. S.* ii. 139).

But whence did Epiphanius draw his information? We can make a shrewd guess. Hippolytus of Portus wrote a book ὑπὲρ τοῦ κατὰ ᾽Ιωάννην εὐαγγελίου καὶ ἀποκαλύψεως[1]. This fact is recorded on his statue (Fabricius *Hippol.* pp. 36 sq., Bunsen *Hippol.* I. p. 460). That this book was known in the East appears from the Catalogue of Ebed-Jesu (Assemani *Bibl. Or.* III. p. 15), where it occurs in the list of Hippolytus' works as *Apologia pro Apocalypsi et Evangelio Ioannis Apostoli et Evangelistae.* It is probable also that this is the same work of which the title is given by other writers, *e. g. de Apocalypsi* (Jerome *Vir. Ill.* 61), περὶ ἀποκαλύψεως (Andreas of Cæsarea in *Apocal. Synops.,* Syncellus *Chron.* p. 674 ed. Bonn). At all events, Epiphanius is borrowing largely from some earlier writer[2]. Here then and elsewhere Epiphanius may have consulted Hip-

---

[1] See above, p. 101.

[2] The common source underlying the works of Epiphanius, Philastrius and the pseudo-Tertullian on heresies is an interesting problem, which cannot be entered upon here.

polytus. Now twice in the immediate context (li. §§ 6, 7) is an allusion to a Merinthus who is mentioned side by side with Cerinthus; and from another passage[1] it is clear that Epiphanius was uncertain whether they were not after all one and the same person. The passage is interesting. 'Whether the same Cerinthus was afterwards called Merinthus, or there was a separate person by name Merinthus, a fellow-worker of his, is known to God (alone).' Now Μήρινθος means a 'noose,' and was doubtless, as Fabricius shrewdly suggested (*Cod. Apoc. N. T.* 344), nothing more nor less than an opprobrious nickname given by an earlier writer, whose work was in Epiphanius' hands, and who may have written thus 'Cerinthus, or had we not better say Merinthus' (ὁ δὲ Κήρινθος οὗτος, εἴτε Μήρινθον δεῖ λέγειν), and in this way misled his copyist. Such pleasantries were by no means uncommon as applied to antagonists. Thus Democritus is called by Epicurus Lenocritus (Zeller *Stoics* iii. 1 p. 429), Photinus of Pirmium in the *Macrostich* Skotinus[2], Manes (Μανῆς) by Eusebius[3] and others Maneis (Μανεὶς). This habit of playing upon names is quite characteristic of Hippolytus. Thus in his treatise against Noetus, he turns his antagonist's name to ridicule, Νοητὸς μὴ νοῶν τὴν ἀλήθειαν (*c. Noet.* 8), and in his *Refutation*, when dealing with the Docetæ, he plays upon the words δοκεῖν 'to seem' and δοκός 'a beam,' contending that they are so named[4], not because they 'seemed to be of importance' (Gal. ii. 6), but because of 'the beam in their eye' (Matt. vii. 3). For these reasons we are tempted to infer that, though Epiphanius claims for himself the invention of the term Alogi, he may have borrowed the name and the account which he gives from his more fanciful predecessor[5].

---

[1] Epiph. *Haer.* xxviii. 8, p. 1150.

[2] See Bright's *Church History* (1860), p. 52, who gives instances from Eusebius *H. E.* v. 23, vi. 41, vii. 10, 31.

[3] See Bright *l.c.* and Cotelier *Patr. Apost.* i. p. 543.

[4] Δοκητὰς ἑαυτοὺς προσηγόρευσαν, ὧν οὐ τὸ δοκεῖν εἶναι τινὰς κατανοοῦμεν ματαΐζοντας, ἀλλὰ τὴν ἐκ τοσαύτης ὕλης δοκὸν ἐν ὀφθαλμῷ φερομένην διελέγχομεν, Hipp. *Ref.* viii. 11.

[5] Two additional sources of testimony have been omitted in the above account, viz. that (1) of heathen writers, (2) of Apocryphal documents. In the former class, *Celsus* (c. A.D. 150) treats the Gospel of St John as a record considered authoritative by the

In looking back over the subject which has been occupying us, we cannot fail to be struck with the variety and the fulness of the evidence which has been adduced. Within the Catholic Church that evidence springs in the first instance direct from the fountain-head, the band of disciples which in Asia Minor gathered round the person of the aged Apostle of Love. From Polycarp and Papias it is handed down to the next link in the chain in Irenæus, the great scholar and traveller, whose life is associated with three distinct and important Churches— Churches in constant intercommunication—Asia Minor, Rome, Gaul. These three great centres we are able to test by independent extant documents, the *Apology* of Theophilus, the

Christians (Origen *c. Celsum* i. 67, ii. 18, x. 24). He speaks of Christians calling our Lord αὐτόλογον (*c. Cels.* ii. 31), he refers to our Lord sitting thirsty by Jacob's well (*c. Cels.* i. 70; cf. John iv. 6), and to the piercing of His side and the result (*c. Cels.* ii. 36; cf. John xix. 34). Therefore we conclude that by the middle of the second century this Gospel was so well known amongst Christians that Celsus could appeal to it as an accredited witness. Again *Lucian* (c. A.D. 165—170), in his account of Peregrinus Proteus (§ 11), gives indications of acquaintanceship with the Fourth Evangelist (see Zahn *Ignatius* p. 593), and so does *Amelius* in Eusebius *Praep. Euang.* xi. 19. The last-named was a disciple of Plotinus, and flourished c. A.D. 250. Prominent in the latter class are the *Acta Pilati* (given in Tischendorf *Evangelia Apocrypha*), which form the first sixteen chapters of the *Evangelium Nicodemi*, and appear not only in Greek but in Coptic and in Latin. This is a very early work, and in its Latin form exists in a Vienna palimpsest of the 5th or 6th century. There is little doubt that it is the composition referred to by Justin Martyr (*Apol.* i. 35, 48) and Tertullian (*Apolo-*

geticus 21), for it answers in all particulars to the books described by these writers. Apocryphal Gospels are notoriously liable to interpolations; we cannot therefore lay much stress upon the evidence in this case, but as the document stands, with whatever uncertainty hanging over it, the incidents are again and again taken from St John's Gospel. Lastly the *Sibyllist* lends her voice to the general attestation. The eighth book of the *Oracula Sibyllina* is the work of a Christian who wrote during the reign of Antoninus Pius (A.D. 138—161). Speaking of the resurrection, the poet declares that those shall rise with the risen Lord 'who have washed away their former sins in the waters of the eternal fount (πηγῆς), having been born again from above (ἀναγεννηθέντες ἄνωθεν)...For the Lord will exhibit Himself first to His own, in bodily shape as He was before, and will show them His hands and His feet and the marks printed upon His limbs, four in number, east and west, south and north (χερσίν τε ποσίν τ' ἐπιδείξει Τέσσαρα τοῖς ἰδίοις ἴχνη πηχθέντα μέλεσσιν Ἀντολίην δύσιν τε, μεσημβρίαν τε καὶ ἄρκτον (*Orac. Sib.* viii. 316 sq.; cf. John iii. 3, xx. 20).

Muratorian Canon, the *Letter of the Gallican Churches*, and we
find an unhesitating response to our enquiry. We pass over to
other Churches of the East, to Palestine and Alexandria, to
Greece and Macedonia, with equally satisfactory results. We
cross the Mediterranean southwards to Carthage, and the earliest
extant writings of the Latin Church of Africa show unmistakeable acquaintance with St John. And now we take a new
departure. We leave the apologists and fathers of the orthodox
Church, and we turn to the representatives of those multifarious
heresies whose rank growth seemed likely to stifle the infant
Church of the second century. And here we are startled at
once by the variety and the unanimity of the evidence presented.
Differing in almost every other particular, heterodoxy unites in
bearing testimony to St John's Gospel. Gnosticism, the out-
come of Gentile license of speculation and practice, Ebionism,
the offspring of Judaizing tendencies, Montanism, the expression of spiritual excitement—they all presuppose, and to some
extent build upon, the Fourth Gospel. Fresh discoveries, which
have added considerably to our stock of heretical treatises, have
only served to give new weight and force to this testimony.
Making every allowance for the possibility that in some cases
zealous disciples may have interpolated documents already
existing, or have perpetrated forgeries in their masters' names,
yet more than enough of unorthodox literature can be tested
to throw back the date of the general acceptance outside the
Church of St John's Gospel as genuine to a very early period in
the second century. The solitary exception to this chorus of
attestation is found to proceed from an insignificant sect, which,
having a special doctrine to inculcate, seeks to effect its end by
impugning the documents which strike at the root of its theory.
When we pass to the consideration of heathen writers in
the opponents of Christianity, or of Apocryphal literature, the
supplementary evidence which we are able to collect, though
necessarily scanty, still bears out the results to which our
previous investigations have already pointed us.

Lastly, so far from considering that the general subject is in any way exhausted, we rise from our review with the consciousness that it has been most inadequately treated, and with the confident persuasion, that a little more patient investigation bestowed on the literature of the first two centuries of the Christian era, as it has come down to us, would enable us to add very materially indeed to the weight of external evidence which with fresh force from year to year tends to the conviction that this most divine of all divine books was indeed the work of 'the disciple whom Jesus loved.'

[1867—1872.]

III.

INTERNAL EVIDENCE FOR THE AUTHENTICITY AND GENUINENESS OF ST JOHN'S GOSPEL.

Printed from Lecture-notes.

III.

INTERNAL EVIDENCE FOR THE AUTHENTICITY AND GENUINENESS OF ST JOHN'S GOSPEL.

IN considering this question three points will be taken in succession. I shall endeavour to show:—

I. That the writer was intimately acquainted with the language, customs, ideas, geography and history of Palestine at the time which he describes.

Inference. He was not only a Jew, but a Palestinian Jew; not a Hellenist, but a Hebrew. And most probably too he was a contemporary. For the double destruction of Jerusalem— by Titus and by Hadrian—had caused a dislocation, a discontinuity, in the history of the Jews, which it would be difficult to bridge over by one writing after the occurrence of the second of these events.

II. That the narrative bears on its face the credentials of its authenticity. It is precise, circumstantial, natural in the highest degree.

Inference. It is the work of an eyewitness.

III. That it contains indications—the more convincing because they are unobtrusive—(*a*) that the author was the Apostle St John; (*β*) that the book was written at the time and under the circumstances, under which tradition reports it to have been written, i.e. at Ephesus, towards the close of the first century after Christ.

These, then, are the three stages in the argument:—

(1)   The writer was a Hebrew, probably a contemporary.

(2)   The writer was an eyewitness.

(3)   The writer was St John (and as a subsidiary matter, St John writing under peculiar circumstances).

I.

THE WRITER WAS A HEBREW, PROBABLY A CONTEMPORARY.

The main heads of this division of the argument are as follows:—

1.   His knowledge of the Jewish language.

2.   His knowledge of Jewish ideas, traditions, expectations, modes of thought, etc.

3.   His knowledge of external facts, the history, geography, names and customs of the Jewish people.

1. *THE WRITER'S KNOWLEDGE OF THE JEWISH LANGUAGE.*

This is shown (i) *indirectly*, by his own Greek style; (ii) *directly*, by his interpretation of Hebrew words and his quotations from Hebrew Scriptures.

(i)   *The writer's indirect knowledge of Hebrew shown by his Greek style.*

I spoke of the Jewish language; but what is meant by this? There are two languages with which a Palestinian Jew might be familiar:—

(1)   The *Hebrew*—the sacred language, the language of the Old Testament.

(2)   The *Aramaic*—the colloquial language, the language of common life.

He would necessarily know the second, not necessarily know the first.

The *Hebrew* of the New Testament is Aramaic. This is the meaning of Ἑβραϊστὶ in such passages as John v. 2 ; xix. 13, 17 ; xx. 16. The forms quoted as Hebrew (*Talitha cumi, Maran atha*) are Aramaic. This is no doubt the language of the inscription on the cross (John xix. 20), and of St Paul's speech on the temple-stairs (Acts xxi. 40).

It is a common error to suppose that Aramaic is a corrupt form of Hebrew. This is quite wrong. The Shemitic family of languages has three main languages, one of which—Arabic—may be neglected for our purpose, leaving Hebrew and Aramaic. Of these, *Aramaic*, the language of Aram (Syria) [the highland ?], has, as its dialects, Syriac, Chaldee, Assyrian (the cuneiform inscriptions). On the other hand, *Hebrew*, the language of Canaan [the low-lands ?], was originally the language of Phœnicians and Canaanites, the people on the coast.

Which then was the language of the Jewish nation at the beginning of the Christian era ?

Abraham comes from Ur of the Chaldees, and therefore would naturally speak an *Aramaic* language. But he settles in Palestine among the Canaanites, adopts a Canaanite language, and speaks what we call *Hebrew*. Hence the incident in Gen. xxxi. 47, 48. The 'heap of witness' is called by Laban 'Jegar-Sahadutha,' by Jacob 'Galeed.' Thus the descendants of Terah in the third generation speak two languages. The grandson of Nahor retains his Aramaic, while the grandson of Abraham has adopted Hebrew. This is what we should expect, and is an incidental testimony to the credibility of the Mosaic narrative. After the return from the Babylonian captivity the Jews gradually merged their own *Hebrew* language in *Aramaic*, but the name 'Hebrew' was transferred to the adopted language. Thus the Jews returned apparently to what was the language of their ancestors. How they came by this Aramaic—whether it was the dialect of their Chaldean masters, or the dialect of the people who overran their land during their absence, or a mixture of both—we need not stop to enquire.

At the time of our Lord the natives of Palestine were

bilingual; they spoke Greek and Aramaic. At least this was the case in a great part of the country, more especially in the towns and populous districts, the centres of commerce[1], such as the lake of Galilee and Jerusalem. In this respect the Palestinian Jew resembled a Welshman on the border-land, a Fleming in the neighbourhood of the half-French towns of Flanders, a Bohemian in Prague.

Now apply this to the case of the Apostle St John. John was not a man of the lowest class socially. He was a native of Bethsaida, and had connexions or friends in high quarters at Jerusalem (xviii. 16). He would be able to understand and speak Greek from his boyhood, possibly even to write it. But he would think in Aramaic. Aramaic would mould the form of his thoughts[2].

Take the case of a person writing in a language which was not the common language of his daily life, not his mother-tongue. What would be the phenomena, which his style would present? The two parts of a language, in which a person writing in a foreign tongue is apt to be at fault, are the *vocabulary* and the *syntax*. As regards *vocabulary*, we should not expect great luxuriance of words, a copious command of synonyms for instance. In the matter of *syntax*, we should not look for a mastery of complex and involved syntax, or of sustained and elaborate periods.

Now apply this to the Fourth Gospel.

1. *The Vocabulary.* The words in this Gospel are very few; probably much fewer than in any other portion of the New Testament of the same length.

(*a*) We meet with constant repetition of the same words: e.g. γινώσκειν (57 times), κόσμος (79 times), πίστις, πιστεύειν (99 times), ζωή, ζῆν, ζωοποιεῖν (55 times), μαρτυρία,

---

[1] See Roberts, *Dissertations on the Gospels*, whose view however is perhaps somewhat exaggerated.

[2] The incident given in John xii. 20—22, relating to his friends and fellow townsmen Andrew and Philip, is strictly in accordance with probabilities. It is a significant fact that they both bear Greek names.

μαρτυρεῖν (47 times); πρόβατον occurs in the tenth chapter alone 15 times; κόσμος occurs in the seventeenth chapter alone 18 times[1].

(b) We find not only the same words, but the same phrases: e.g. ἔρχεσθαι, ὁ πέμψας με, ἀποστέλλειν, καταβαίνειν ἐκ (ἀπὸ) τοῦ οὐρανοῦ—all used of Christ's Incarnation, etc.[2].

2. *The Syntax.* On the extreme simplicity of the Fourth Gospel in this respect, I shall have to speak later. This characteristic of the writer is well expressed by Heinsius, who describes him thus, *In sermone ἀφέλεια: in sensibus est ὕψος*[3]. The absence of periods is particularly noticeable, and is without a parallel in the New Testament.

Thus much, generally, of one writing in another language than his mother tongue. Now to come to the special case of one accustomed to speak in a Shemitic tongue, and obliged to write in an Aryan; of one familiar with (say) Aramaic, the conversational, spoken language, and Hebrew, the sacred language; but writing in Greek. Both these languages present striking contrasts with Greek. In these Shemitic tongues there is little or no *syntax.* This is due partly to

(1) The absence of moods, inflexions, etc.

(2) The paucity of connecting particles.

On this last point, which is of special importance, one example will suffice.

(1) *Paucity of connecting particles.*

The ן is used equally for opposition and for simple connexion; in Hebrew and Aramaic it stands for 'but' as well as 'and.' The extent of this use is best shown by the variety of particles which are employed under it in the Authorised Version of the Old Testament.

Thus in Deut. i. (taken at hap-hazard) ן is translated 'so'

---

[1] These calculations are based upon Luthardt *Das Johanneische Evangelium* I. p. 27 (1852).

[2] See Luthardt I. p. 31 sq.

[3] Quoted by Luthardt I. p. 28.

vv. 15, 43, 46; 'then' v. 29; 'yet' v. 32; 'but' v. 40; and with אֹל, 'notwithstanding' v. 26.

Again in 1 Kings xii. (again taken at hap-hazard) it is rendered 'but' vv. 8, 17, 22; 'so' vv. 12, 33; 'so when' v. 16; 'wherefore' vv. 15, 19; 'then' vv. 18, 25; 'whereupon' v. 28; 'that' v. 3. There are thirty-three verses in this chapter, and all the verses but vv. 4, 23, 27 (i.e. thirty verses out of thirty-three), begin with ١. Of the remaining three, two are be-ginnings of speeches, and therefore necessarily are *asyndeta*.

Indeed in the later Aramaic, Greek particles (ἀλλά, δέ, and afterwards μέν) were deliberately introduced to supply the deficiency[1].

Consequently, in these languages sentences are not subordi-nated, but coordinated; 'hence,' as Winer describes it[2], 'the very limited use of conjunctions (in which classical Greek is so rich), the uniformity in the use of the tenses, the want of the periodic compactness which results from the fusion of several sentences into one principal sentence, and along with this the sparing use of participial constructions, so numerous and diversified in classical Greek.' The result is an entire absence of periods, producing a monotony of expression, which however is most impressive.

The character of the Greek language was quite different. Greek writers distinguished two styles:

(1) The periodic (κατεστραμμένη);

(2) The disjointed (διῃρημένη), or 'jointed' (εἰρομένη). See Aristot. *Rhet.* iii. 9, τὴν λέξιν ἀνάγκη εἶναι ἢ εἰρομένην καὶ τῷ συνδέσμῳ μίαν...ἢ κατεστραμμένην....λέγω δὲ εἰρομένην ἢ οὐδὲν ἔχει τέλος καθ᾽ αὑτὴν, ἂν μὴ τὸ πρᾶγμα λεγόμενον τελειω-θῇ...κατεστραμμένη δὲ ἡ ἐν περιόδοις· λέγω δὲ περίοδον λέξιν ἔχουσαν ἀρχὴν καὶ τελευτὴν αὐτὴν καθ᾽ αὑτὴν καὶ μέγεθος εὐσύνοπτον.

---

[1] This strange lack of particles, which seem to us indispensable to express our simplest thoughts, is illus-trated likewise by Coptic.

[2] Winer *Grammar of N. T. Greek* p. 33 (Moulton's translation).

In the infancy of the language the earlier prose writers Hecatæus and Herodotus exhibit the εἰρομένη; the later, when a mastery over the language had been attained, the κατεστραμμένη. Now, Hebrew and Aramaic do not lend themselves to the κατεστραμμένη, the genius of the languages necessitating the εἰρομένη. Hence, as a rule, the general simplicity of the New Testament writers, who either spoke Aramaic, or derived their materials from Aramaic sources. The exceptions are the cases of those who commonly spoke Greek, and did not speak Aramaic at all, as St Luke in the prologue to his Gospel (for where he is using documents, the case is different), and the author of the Epistle to the Hebrews.

This simple, jointed style, is seen in its extreme form in St John. In fact, no greater contrast can be exhibited in this respect than the prologue of St John when compared with the prologue of St Luke. The sentences are strung together, where they are not altogether *asyndeta*. There is no attempt at periodicity. The καὶ takes the place of the ו, and has almost as wide a range, connecting together not only independent, but dependent, and even opposite and contrasted clauses[1]. I give a few examples of this:

John i. 1, 4, 5, 10, 14, 19, 20, 21, 24, 25, 34; ii. 1, 3, 4, 8, 12–16; iii. 11, 12, 13, 14; iv. 11, 40, 41; vi. 17; vii. 26, 28, 33, 34; ix. 18, 19; x. 3, 9, 12, 14–16, 22, 27, 28, 39–41; xiv. 23, 24; xv. 6; xvi. 22, 32; xvii. 1, 8, 10, 11 (six times in three lines); xix. 34, 35.

For instances where καὶ introduces an opposition, with the meaning of 'and yet,' 'nevertheless,' see John i. 5, 10; iii. 10, 11, 19, 32; iv. 20; v. 40; vi. 70; vii. 4, 19, 26, 30; viii. 49, 55; ix. 30, 34 etc.

A single instance would occur here and there in classical Greek as in any other language; but it is the frequency of occurrence in the Fourth Gospel which betrays the Hebræo-Aramaic mould in which the diction is cast.

---

[1] See the references in Wilkii *Clavis N. T.* (ed. Grimm, 1868, *s. v.* καὶ p. 215).

(2) *Hebraic parallelism of sentences.*

Instances of this characteristic can be found in almost every part of the Fourth Gospel. The prologue especially presents a succession of parallel clauses. I content myself with drawing attention to some special phenomena of this parallelism.

(a) Repetition of words and phrases in parallel and opposed clauses, e.g. iii. 6 (τὸ γεγεννημένον ἐκ τῆς σαρκὸς σάρξ ἐστιν καὶ τὸ γεγεννημένον ἐκ τοῦ πνεύματος πνεῦμά ἐστιν); iii. 31 (ὁ ὢν ἐκ τῆς γῆς ἐκ τῆς γῆς ἐστίν...ὁ ἐκ τοῦ οὐρανοῦ ἐρχόμενος ἐπάνω πάντων ἐστίν); cf. vii. 6, 7, 8, viii. 14, 23, x. 18, xi. 9, 10 etc. etc.

(b) Repetition of words and phrases in parallel, but not opposed clauses, e.g. ix. 21, 22 (πῶς δὲ νῦν βλέπει οὐκ οἴδαμεν, ἢ τίς ἤνοιξεν αὐτοῦ τοὺς ὀφθαλμοὺς ἡμεῖς οὐκ οἴδαμεν); xvii. 16 (ἐκ τοῦ κόσμου οὐκ εἰσὶν καθὼς ἐγὼ οὐκ εἰμὶ ἐκ τοῦ κόσμου); cf. xviii. 18, xix. 10 etc. etc.

(c) Strengthening of a statement by the negation of its opposite, e.g. i. 3 (πάντα δι' αὐτοῦ ἐγένετο καὶ χωρὶς αὐτοῦ ἐγένετο οὐδὲ ἕν); i. 20 (ὡμολόγησεν καὶ οὐκ ἠρνήσατο); cf. iii. 18, x. 28, xi. 25, 26, xx. 27 etc. etc.

(3) *Oriental definiteness of expression by the repetition of the same word or phrase.*

(a) Repetition of the name, instead of using a personal pronoun, e.g. i. 43 sq. (εὑρίσκει Φίλιππον...ἦν δὲ ὁ Φίλιππος ...εὑρίσκει Φίλιππος τὸν Ναθαναήλ...καὶ εἶπεν αὐτῷ Ναθαναήλ ...λέγει αὐτῷ ὁ Φίλιππος); cf. iii. 23 sq., xii. 21 sq. etc. etc.

(b) Repetition of the nominative pronoun, where the Greek does not require it, e.g. i. 42 (σὺ εἶ Σίμων ὁ υἱὸς Ἰωάνου, σὺ κληθήσῃ Κηφᾶς); cf. i. 25, 31, iv. 10, 19 etc. etc.

(c) Repetition of the noun, e.g. vii. 6 (ὁ καιρὸς ὁ ἐμὸς οὔπω πάρεστιν, ὁ δὲ καιρὸς ὁ ὑμέτερος πάντοτέ ἐστιν ἕτοιμος); cf. vii. 8, 19, xii. 43, 47 etc. etc.

(d) Repetition of the verb, e.g. v. 17 (ὁ πατήρ μου ἕως ἄρτι ἐργάζεται, κἀγὼ ἐργάζομαι); cf. vi. 63, vii. 24, 28, viii. 53, x. 10, xiii. 43 etc. etc.

(e) Repetition of the same phrase in successive clauses, e.g. iii. 31 (ὁ ὢν ἐκ τῆς γῆς ἐκ τῆς γῆς ἐστιν καὶ ἐκ τῆς γῆς λαλεῖ); cf. viii. 14, 23, 24, x. 18, xi. 9 sq. etc. etc.

(f) Taking up a word or expression from the preceding sentence; e.g. x. 11 (ἐγώ εἰμι ὁ ποιμὴν ὁ καλός· ὁ ποιμὴν ὁ καλὸς τὴν ψυχὴν αὐτοῦ τίθησιν κ.τ.λ.); cf. i. 1, iii. 32, 33, xvii. 2, 3 etc. etc.

(4) *Preference of the direct over the oblique narrative in relating the words of another.*

In some instances these will be the precise words themselves; in others only an approximation, and in this latter case the direct narrative is only a different way of expressing what we express by the oblique. Thus we find the narrator himself relating the words or surmises of a crowd, where from the nature of the case the exact words cannot be reproduced; or we find persons referring back to their own words or the words of another, and not always reproducing the exact expressions. Examples of all these varieties are very common, see the narrative of the Samaritan woman in ch. iv. (esp. vv. 17, 27, 33); of the sick man healed in ch. v. (esp. vv. 11, 12); the conversation in ch. vi. (esp. vv. 41, 42); cf. vii. 11 sq., 35, 36, 40 sq., viii. 22, ix. 8 sq., 23 sq., 40 sq., x. 20, 36, 41, xi. 31, 36, 37, xii. 19 sq. etc. etc.

(5) *The arrangement of words in the sentence*, especially the precedence of the verb, e.g. i. 40—47 (ἦν Ἀνδρέας...εὑρίσκει οὗτος...ἤγαγεν αὐτόν...ἐμβλέψας αὐτῷ...λέγει αὐτῷ ὁ Ἰησοῦς ...ἦν δὲ ὁ Φίλιππος...εὑρίσκει Φίλιππος...καὶ εἶπεν αὐτῷ Ναθαναήλ...λέγει αὐτῷ ὁ Φίλιππος...εἶδεν Ἰησοῦς). This is noticeably the case with the expression λέγει αὐτῷ, e.g. iv. 7—26, xi. 34, 35, 39 sq. etc. etc.

(6) *Other grammatical and lexical peculiarities.*

(a) The superfluous pronoun (1) after a relative, representing the Heb. אֲשֶׁר which is indeclinable, e.g. i. 12 (ὅσοι δὲ ἔλαβον αὐτόν, ἔδωκεν αὐτοῖς); v. 38 (ὃν ἀπέστειλεν ἐκεῖνος

τούτῳ ὑμεῖς οὐ πιστεύετε); cf. i. 33, vii. 38, xvii. 2, xviii. 9, 11
etc. etc. (2) after nouns or participles, e.g. i. 18 (μονογενὴς θεὸς
ὁ ὢν εἰς τὸν κόλπον τοῦ πατρὸς ἐκεῖνος ἐξηγήσατο); v. 11 (ὁ
ποιήσας με ὑγιῆ ἐκεῖνός μοι εἶπεν Ἆρον τὸν κράβαττόν σου);
cf. vi. 46, vii. 18, 38, x. 1, xiv. 21, 26, xv. 5, etc. etc. This construction, it is true, occurs in classical Greek, but the point to
be noticed is the extreme frequency of the usage in the Fourth
Gospel.

(b) The characteristic Hebraism πᾶς...οὐ (μὴ) occurs
three times in this gospel; iii. 16, vi. 39, xii. 46.

(c) The frequent use of ἵνα in St John, especially as
the complement of a demonstrative pronoun, is probably to be
explained by the flexibility of the Aramaic כְּ.   Instances are
i. 27, iv. 34, vi. 29, 40, viii. 56, xi. 50, xiii. 34, xv. 8, 12, 13, 17,
xvi. 7, 33, xvii. 3, 24 (see Winer § xliv. p. 425 ed. Moulton).
In every one of these passages a Greek would probably have
expressed himself differently.

(d) The use of ἄνθρωπος for τις, e.g. v. 7. Κύριε,
ἄνθρωπον οὐκ ἔχω), vii. 22, 23 (ἐν σαββάτῳ περιτέμνετε
ἄνθρωπον· εἰ περιτομὴν λαμβάνει ἄνθρωπος κ.τ.λ.); cf. viii. 40,
ix. 16 etc. This represents a thoroughly characteristic use of
אִישׁ, see Gesenius s. v.

(e) The transition from the dependent to the independent clause, e.g. i. 32 (τεθέαμαι τὸ πνεῦμα καταβαῖνον...καὶ
ἔμεινεν ἐπ᾽ αὐτόν); cf. xi. 44 (Winer § lxiii. p. 717 ed. Moulton).
This transition however appears in other New Testament
writers also, and cannot be pressed into an argument.

(f) The frequent recurrence of the expressions εἰς τὸν
αἰῶνα, especially with a negative, e.g, iv. 14, vi. 51, 58, viii. 35,
51, 52, x. 26, xi. 28, xii. 34, xiii. 8, xiv. 16; and the use of
ἐκ τοῦ αἰῶνος ix. 32.

(g) Other Hebraisms are: i. 13 (αἱμάτων), 15, 30 (πρῶτός
μου, cf. xv. 18), iii. 29 (χαρᾷ χαίρει), vii. 33, xii. 35, xiv. 19
(ἔτι μικρόν, cf. xvi. 16, 17, 19), iv. 23 (ἔρχεται ὥρα καὶ νῦν
ἐστίν), xi. 4 (οὐκ ἔστιν πρὸς θάνατον, cf. xvi. 20), iv. 26, viii.

24, 28, xiii. 19, xviii. 5, 6 (ἐγώ εἰμι), x. 24 (ἕως πότε), xviii. 37 (σὺ λέγεις).

(7) *Imagery, secondary senses of words etc.*

This displays a thoroughly Hebrew, or at least Oriental, colouring. The simple facts in life are used to convey deep spiritual truths. Nature and history become signs (σημεῖα) of the heavenly and the eternal. Instances of this figurative treatment are to be found in the Evangelist's use of the following words and phrases; ἀλήθεια i. 14, 17, iii. 21; δόξα i. 14, ii. 11, xii. 41; ὕδωρ ζῶν iv. 10, 13; κοιλία vii. 38; ζωή v. 24; τὸ μάννα vi. 31; ἄρτος vi. 32; τὸ ποτήριον xviii. 11; ὑψωθῶ, ἑλκύσω xii. 32.

If the special Hebraisms, or Aramaisms, are few, this is unimportant: for the whole casting of the sentences, the whole colouring of the language, is Hebrew.

In short, it is the most Hebraic book in the New Testament, except perhaps the Apocalypse. The Greek is not ungrammatical Greek, but it is cast in a Hebrew mould. It is what no native Greek would have written. As Grotius puts it, *Sermo Graecus quidem, sed plane adumbratus ex Syriaco illius saeculi* (quoted in Lücke[1] I. p. 172). On the general accord of recent writers on this point, see Sanday *Authorship of the Fourth Gospel*, p. 28[2].

On the other hand, there are no classicisms; not a single sentence, I believe, from first to last which suggests in the smallest degree acquaintance with classical literature.

In this respect the writer presents a great contrast to St Luke, and even to St Paul, e.g. Luke i. 1 sq.; 2 Cor. vi. 14 sq.

(ii) *The writer's direct knowledge of Hebrew.*

1. *The quotations from the Old Testament.*

The quotations are a valuable criterion of the position of a writer.

---

[1] *Commentar über das Evangelium des Johannes* (1840).

[2] Mr Sanday (*l. c.*) says 'The Greek is purer than that of the Synoptists.' If purer in one sense, yet it is more Hebraic.

The quotations in St Paul show a knowledge of the Old Testament in Hebrew. He frequently quotes the LXX, but in other passages he is as plainly indebted to the original. On the other hand, the quotations in the Epistle to the Hebrews are all derived from the LXX. There are no distinct traces of a knowledge of the original.

What are the facts in St John's case?[1] The quotations in St John are not very numerous. Moreover they are often free quotations; so free that we cannot say whether they were taken from the Hebrew or the Greek. But there is a residuum of passages, which are decisive, and certainly cannot have been borrowed from the Greek.

(a) Passages certainly taken from the Hebrew.

(1) Zech. ix. 9 quoted in John xii. 14, 15 (see Turpie, p. 222).

The quotation is loose. Two points are noticeable. St John has ὁ βασιλεύς σου ἔρχεται. The LXX ὁ βασιλεὺς ἔρχεταί σοι (but some edd. insert σου). The Heb. represents ὁ βασιλεύς σου ἔρχεταί σοι, as in Matth. xxi. 5.

The other point is more important. St John has πῶλον ὄνου, which comes from the Hebrew, the LXX having πῶλον νέον, while St Matthew quotes the Hebrew still more literally, ἐπὶ πῶλον υἱὸν ὑποζυγίου.

(2) Zech. xii. 10 quoted in John xix. 37, ὄψονται εἰς ὃν ἐξεκέντησαν (Turpie, p. 131).

This agrees with the Heb. 'They shall look upon me whom they have pierced.' But the LXX is quite different, καὶ ἐπιβλέψονται πρὸς μὲ ἀνθ' ὧν κατωρχήσαντο, i.e. they shall look on me, because they have derided. The LXX evidently read רקרו for דקרו, and this reading is actually found in some MSS. of Kennicott and de Rossi. The LXX has not a single word in common with St John.

---

[1] My investigation was made before I saw Bleek's *Beiträge*, and agrees almost entirely with his results (p. 244 sq). I have derived much help from Turpie *The Old Testament in the New* (1868).

On the reading אֵלַי 'unto me' and אֵלָיו 'unto him,' which
is read by many MSS., see de Rossi III. p. 217.   Aquila, at
least, of the other versions, seems to point to this reading.   He
renders σὺν ᾧ.   The Evangelist however, if he had אֵלַי, would
not unnaturally change the person from the first to the third to
suit the connexion.   Comp. Apoc. i. 7.

(3)   Ps. xl. 10 quoted in John xiii. 18 (Turpie, p. 55).

St John has ὁ τρώγων μου τὸν ἄρτον ἐπῆρεν ἐπ' ἐμὲ τὴν
πτέρναν αὐτοῦ.   The LXX ὁ ἐσθίων ἄρτους μου ἐμεγάλυνεν ἐπ'
ἐμὲ πτερνισμόν.

Here again there is hardly a word the same in the two
translations.   St John's is evidently a loose quotation taken
from the Hebrew.   The LXX translation has lost the meaning
in endeavouring to render הִגְדִּיל.   St John gives the more
correct, though free, rendering.   So Gesenius takes it (p. 266,
ed. 1829); but Perowne *ad loc.* seems to think either interpretation admissible.

(4)   Is. vi. 10 quoted in John xii. 40 (Turpie, p. 233).

It is a very free quotation.   The LXX is quite different.

The point to be observed is the use of the *active* in St John
τετύφλωκεν αὐτῶν τοὺς ὀφθαλμοὺς καὶ ἐπώρωσεν αὐτῶν τὴν
καρδίαν.   God Himself is represented as blinding, as hardening.
This points to the Hebrew, which has also the active.   But
there it is imperative; and the change to the indicative is
intelligible.   As Symmachus translates הַכְבֵּד, הַשְׁמֵן ἐβάρυνε,
ἔμυσε, it is quite possible that St John translated the same words
τετύφλωκεν, ἐπώρωσεν, perhaps from a mixture of Aramaic
with Hebrew forms.   In the Syriac the imperative and 3rd
pers. pret. are the same.

On the other hand, the LXX has adopted a precise form of
the sentence, ἐπαχύνθη ἡ καρδία κ.τ.λ., evidently to get rid of a
doctrine which was a stumbling-block.   Symmachus seems likewise to have surmounted the difficulty, though in another way.

He takes הַעָם הַזֶּה as the nominative, ὁ λαὸς οὗτος τὰ ὦτα ἐβάρυνεν καὶ τοὺς ὀφθαλμοὺς αὐτοῦ ἔμυσε κ.τ.λ.

Now it is quite inconceivable that the writer of the Fourth Gospel, having only the LXX before him, should accidentally have reconverted it, and thus reintroduced the perplexity. The chances are a thousand-fold against it; and he would surely have shrunk from it.

It is noticeable too, that the other New Testament writers who quote the sentence (Matt. xiii. 14, 15 ; Acts xxviii. 26, 27), quote it from the LXX. In Mark iv. 12, Luke viii. 10, this part of the quotation is omitted.

(5) Is. liv. 13 quoted in John vi. 45 (Turpie, p. 198).

This is a doubtful case. The Hebrew has 'And all thy sons (are) disciples of God,' St John καὶ ἔσονται πάντες διδακτοὶ Θεοῦ. The LXX however attaches the sentence to what goes before, καὶ πάντας τοὺς υἱούς σου διδακτοὺς Θεοῦ. St John treats it as independent—so do the Targum, Ewald, Gesenius, in interpreting the Hebrew.

These passages then, except perhaps the last (5), are decisive. In no case could they be derived from the LXX.

But, it may be said, they came perhaps not from the original Hebrew, but from a Targum.

This admission is sufficient for my purpose, which is to show the direct acquaintance of the Evangelist with Hebrew writings.

(β) *Passages which may have come from either the Hebrew or the Septuagint.*

In many cases it is doubtful whether a quotation was taken from the LXX or the Hebrew.

These instances divide themselves into three classes:—

(1) Where the *Greek and Hebrew differ*, but the quotation is too loose to allow of any inference. Examples of this are:

(a) Deut. xix. 15 quoted in John viii. 17 (Turpie, p. 49). Here the LXX inserts πᾶν; but St John paraphrases the

whole sentence δύο ἀνθρώπων ἡ μαρτυρία. Thus the crucial
point of difference is evaded.

(β)   Exod. xii. 46 (Numb. ix. 12) quoted in John xix. 36
(Turpie, p. 31).

Here St John follows neither the Hebrew nor the LXX.
But the passage intended to be quoted may be Ps. xxxiii. 21;
in which case the Hebrew and LXX agree, and no inference
can be drawn.   Or St John may have had all three passages
in his mind, and combined them in a loose way.

(2) Where the *Greek and Hebrew agree*, but the Greek
is the obvious, or an obvious, rendering of the Hebrew; and no
conclusion can be drawn.   Examples:

(a)   Ps. xxxiv. (xxxv.) 19, lxviii. (lxix.) 5 οἱ μισοῦντές
με δωρεάν.   Comp. Ps. cviii. (cix.) 3, in John xv. 25 (Turpie,
p. 30).

(β)   Ps. lxix. (lxviii.) 10 quoted in John ii. 17 (Turpie, p.
29), where the Evangelist substitutes καταφάγεται for κατέ-
φαγεν.

(γ)   Ps. lxxxii. (lxxxi.) 6 quoted in John x. 34 (Turpie,
p. 4).

Or again, (3) The Greek and Hebrew agree, but the Greek
is not an obvious rendering.   Yet the Evangelist's quotation is
not exact enough to warrant an inference.   Examples:—

(a)   Ps. lxxviii. (lxxvii.) 24 quoted in John vi. 31 (Turpie,
p. 60).

The use of ἄρτον however here in St John seems to show
that he had the LXX rendering in mind, for this is apparently
the only passage in the Old Testament where דָּגָן is rendered
by ἄρτος.

(β)   Is. xl. 3 quoted in John i. 23 (Turpie, p. 219).

Yet εὐθύνατε (St John) for εὐθείας ποιεῖτε (LXX) looks like
a direct derivation from the Hebrew, which has one word יַשְּׁרוּ,
not two, in the original.   All the other Evangelists have
εὐθείας ποιεῖτε (Matt. iii. 3; Mark i. 3; Luke iii. 4); and this
makes the probability stronger.

(γ) *Passages almost certainly, or most probably, taken from the LXX.*

(1) Ps. xxi. 19 quoted in John xix. 24 (Turpie, p. 4).

The LXX is a literal translation of the Hebrew; but the probabilities are greatly against the Evangelist stumbling upon the same rendering word for word, more especially the opposition of ἱμάτια and ἱματισμός.

(2) Is. liii. 1 quoted in John xii. 38 (Turpie, p. 106).

Again the LXX is a literal rendering of the Hebrew, for τίνι as a rendering of עָל־מִי can hardly be regarded as an exception. But the probabilities are against the whole combination of words being the same.

These are all the quotations from the Old Testament in St John, and the result at which we arrive is as follows:—

The writer certainly derived several of his quotations from the Hebrew, or from an Aramaic Targum, not from the LXX.

On the other hand, he most probably took one or two from the LXX, though the evidence for the LXX is not so decisive as for the Hebrew. The majority of the passages prove nothing either way.

2. *The writer's interpretation of Hebrew words.*

(a) Rabbi, Rabbouni, i. 38 (῾Ραββεί, ὃ λέγεται μεθερμηνευόμενον Διδάσκαλε), xx. 16 (῾Ραββουνεί, ὃ λέγεται Διδάσκαλε). The longer form is the more impressive, the higher title; hence it is peculiarly adapted to the solemnity of the circumstances of Mary's recognition of the risen Lord. In this respect compare Mark x. 51, where again the circumstances are exceptional. These are the only two passages in the New Testament in which the form occurs; see Keim iii. p. 560, Buxtorf p. 2177 sq., Levy p. 401. The omission by St John of the interpretation of the pronoun '*my* master' is to be explained by the fact that it had got attached to the word, as in Rabbi, and had ceased to have any distinct force: just as, by the reverse principle, ὁ κύριος is rendered in Syriac 'our Lord.'

(b) Messias, i. 41 (εὑρήκαμεν τὸν Μεσσίαν, ὅ ἐστιν μεθερμηνευόμενον Χριστός), iv. 25. The word does not occur in the New Testament save in these two places.

(c) Cephas, i. 42 (Κηφᾶς, ὁ ἑρμηνεύεται Πέτρος). This title is only used by John and St Paul. Elsewhere, when the appellation is employed, the Greek form is preferred.

(d) Thomas, xx. 24, xxi. 2 (Θωμᾶς, ὁ λεγόμενος Δίδυμος). Thus St John takes care to let us know that the familiar name of this Apostle was merely a surname, 'twin.' There was an early tradition in the Syrian Church that Thomas' real name was Judas, e.g. Eus. H. E. i. 13 Ἰούδας ὁ καὶ Θωμᾶς, Acta Thomae I. Ἰούδα Θωμᾷ τῷ καὶ Διδύμῳ (ed. Tisch. p. 190), see Assemani Bibl. Orient. I. pp. 100, 318, Cureton's Syriac Gospels p. l., Anc. Syr. Documents p. 32. In the Curetonian Syriac of John xiv. 22 'Judas Thomas' is substituted for 'Judas, not Iscariot.' As there were two other Apostles of this same name, some distinction would be necessary; and this we find was the case, one being called Lebbæus, another Thomas, the third Iscariot.

(e) Siloam, ix. 7 (εἰς τὴν κολυμβήθραν τοῦ Σιλωάμ, ὁ ἑρμηνεύεται Ἀπεσταλμένος). The word occurs in Isaiah viii. 6 שִׁלֹחַ (A. V. Shiloah), and signifies a 'conduit,' 'emissary,' 'aqueduct,' from the root שָׁלַח 'send,' which is used of water in Ps. civ. 10, Ezek. xxxi. 4 (Gesenius p. 1415). בֵּית־הַשִּׁלֹחִים occurs in the Talmud, meaning either 'a conduit for irrigation' or field needing artificial irrigation' (Buxtorf p. 2412 sq). Another form שֶׁלַח (A. V. Siloah) is found as a proper name in Neh. iii. 15, if indeed the Masoretic pointing may be trusted. That two forms should exist side by side is very conceivable, for the word is not strictly speaking a proper name. In Greek the forms vary: Σιλωάμ (LXX Luke xiii. 4, Josephus frequently), Σιλωᾶς (Josephus elsewhere), Σιλωά (Aquila, Symmachus,

Theodotion). The geographical and symbolical bearing of the notice will be considered hereafter[1]. At present I am only concerned with the etymology. This the Evangelist has explained rightly. Two further points deserve attention. He has given the correct meaning, notwithstanding that it is somewhat obscured by the Greek form. Again he has added the definite article 'the Siloam.' This is in accordance with Jewish usage. In the Old Testament, and generally in the Targums and the Rabbinic passages, as well as in St Luke *l. c.*, the definite article occurs. With this compare Acts ix. 35 'the Sharon' (τὸν Σαρῶνα).

(*f*) Golgotha, xix. 17 (εἰς τὸν λεγόμενον Κρανίου Τόπον, ὃ λέγεται Ἑβραϊστὶ Γολγοθά); cf. Matt. xxvii. 33, Mark xv. 22 (Luke xxiii. 33). As the interpretation occurs in the Synoptic narrative also, no argument can be drawn from it.

(*g*) Gabbatha, xix. 13 (εἰς τόπον λεγόμενον Λιθόστρωτον· Ἑβραϊστὶ δὲ Γαββαθά). Pliny (*H. N.* xxxvi. 28) tells us that the pavements called *lithostrota* were first introduced by Sulla, and that in the temple of Fortune at Præneste one could be seen in his day which Sulla had placed there. Again, Suetonius (*Jul.* 46) states that Julius Caesar was accustomed to carry tesselated pavements about with him for his own use in his expeditions (*in expeditionibus tesselata et sectilia pavimenta circumtulisse*). This last notice however does not help us much, for evidently St John's account speaks of some fixed locality. It shows, however, that such a flooring would seem necessary for a Roman magistrate's tribunal. A fixed place at Amathus was so called, Boeckh *C. I. G.* 2643 ἀπὸ τοῦ Ἡραίου ἕως τοῦ Λιθοστρώτου.

But what is the meaning of the Hebrew Gabbatha? It is commonly connected with גב from גבה or גבע 'to be high,' meaning a 'prominence' or 'hill,' compare *gibbus*. The word would then represent גבעתא; see Levy, I. p. 123, Lücke, Hengstenberg *ad. loc.*, Keim iii. p. 365. This theory receives further

---

[1] See below, p. 171.

support from the fact that Josephus (*Ant.* v. 1. 29, vi. 4, 2 and
elsewhere) uses Γαβαθά for Gibeah, 'a hill.' And it is a very possible solution, for the Evangelist does not say that the Hebrew
represents the meaning of the Greek equivalent. But this
interpretation labours under the disadvantage that it does not
account for the doubling of the β. Accordingly Ewald (*Johan.
Schr.* I. p. 408) suggests as the derivation קבע ,גבע 'to collect
together,' and thus the word would imply 'a mosaic.' This
appears to me highly probable, for I find this word קבע used
of studding or inlaying with jewels or precious stones, e.g.
Ex. xxv. 7, of the jewels of the high-priest's ephod, and
Deut. xxxiii. 21, where the *Targum Ben Uzziel* has 'a place
inlaid (מקבע) with precious stones and jewels'; see Levy *s. v.*
II. p. 342. Thus here again St John shows his intimate knowledge
of the derivation of an obscure Hebrew term.

(*h*) Iscariot. The phenomena which St John's Gospel
presents in the use of this name are somewhat remarkable. As
soon as the false readings are swept away which obscure the
true text, we find (1) that the designation is attached to the
father's name (vi. 71, xiii. 26) as well as to the son's (xii. 4,
xiii. 2, xiv. 22), (2) that in more than one place (xii. 4, xiv. 22)
the definite article should precede the name. We gather therefore that the word is not strictly speaking a proper name at
all, but merely describes the native-place of the traitor. This
solution is suggested by St John's Gospel, but there is no hint
of it given by the Synoptists. Yet it is rendered highly probable
by other considerations also. The word Ἰσκαριώτης is איש
קריות 'the man of Kerioth.' Now in 2 Sam. x. 6, 8 among the
mercenaries hired by the children of Ammon to attack David
are mentioned 'of Ishtob twelve thousand men,' or, as it almost
certainly should be rendered, 'of the men of Tob twelve
thousand men,' Tob being a district mentioned in Judges
xi. 3–5. This word becomes in Josephus *Ant.* vii. 6, 1 a proper
name, Ἴστοβος. The interpretation of Josephus may be right or
wrong; but we are only concerned with the representation of
the Hebrew form in Greek; and, so far as it goes, it is an

adequate illustration of the way in which איש קריות would appear in a Greek dress. Again, the tradition of Judas' birth-place is preserved in some MSS. of the New Testament. Thus in Matt. x. 4, xxvi. 14 some old Latin MSS. have *Carioth*, while other authorities have intermediate readings, *Scarioth*, Σκαριωτης; in Mark iii. 19 the correct reading (א B C L) is Ισκαριωθ, the termination not having been interfered with, *e* has *Cariotha*, and there are other variations. In Mark xiv. 10 א B L C* have Ισκαριωθ, while Ισκαριωτης is found in A and the majority of authorities. Here again *Scarioth* is read by some Latin MSS. On the whole it seems probable that Ἰσκαριὼθ is consistently St Mark's form of the appellation. In Luke vi. 16 Ισκαριωθ is the right reading (א B L); on the other hand in xxii. 3 Ισκαριωτην seems to be correct, though here again the alternative form has supporters. St Luke therefore appears to vary, and this we might expect from the manner in which his Gospel was composed. Turning now to St John's Gospel we find that D has απο Καρυωτου in four out of the five verses in which the name occurs, and (followed by three Latin MSS.) Σκαριωθ in the fifth passage (vi. 71), where, on the other hand, απο Καρυωτου receives the support of א¹ 69, 124, and of the margin of the Harclean Syriac. Thus the trace of the original meaning of the word seems to linger in the Western text of the Fourth Gospel.

Καριωθ is the LXX rendering of קריות. The word signi-fies 'cities,' i.e. a conjunction of small towns. Hence it is of frequent occurrence. Thus a place of the name was situated in Moab (Jer. xlviii. 24, 41, Amos ii. 2, see Merx *Arch. f. Wissensch. Erf. der Alt. Test.* p. 320), another in Judah (Joshua xv. 25). This latter is perhaps the birth-place of Judas who, like Perugino, Correggio, Veronese and others, has merged his per-sonal name in that of his native town.

2. *THE WRITER'S KNOWLEDGE OF JEWISH IDEAS, TRADITIONS, EXPECTATIONS, MODES OF THOUGHT.*

(i) *The Messiah.* Occasion has been taken elsewhere to point out that, in the Fourth Gospel, 'the narrative and the discourses alike are thoroughly saturated with the Messianic ideas of the time[1].' In discussing this subject attention was drawn to two facts as especially worthy of notice : (1) that though the writer's point of view is twofold, the Word as the theological, the subjective, centre, no less than the Messiah as the historical, the objective, centre, yet, with a true insight which is the best evidence for his veracity, he keeps these two points of view separate. The topic of our Lord's discourses with the Jews is not the doctrine of the Logos, for which His auditors would feel neither predilection nor interest, but the Messianic expectation, in which they were thoroughly absorbed. (2) It was shown that the Messianic conceptions are not the ideas as corrected by the facts, but the ideas in their original form, not yet spiritualised, but coarse and materialistic still, reflecting the sentiments not of the second century but of the early years of the first ; in a word, Jewish, not Christian. This Messianic idea is turned about on all sides. We learn very much more about it from the Fourth Gospel than from all the other three Gospels together. This is a fact which we do not sufficiently realise, and it is a characteristic, though an accidental, token to this fact that the Hebrew equivalent for Χριστός—the word Μεσσίας—is found only in this Gospel. The prevalence, nay, the ubiquity, of the Messianic idea is the key to the motive of the narrative. Does Jesus work a miracle ? It is a sign of His Messianic office. Does He suffer an indignity ? It is fatal to His claims as the triumphant King and Avenger of His people. Does He utter an unpalatable truth, or a seemingly unpatriotic sentiment ? Such language is inconsistent with the office of the long-expected Saviour of the Jewish nation. Does He exhibit in His person the common associations and relationships

---

[1] [See above, p. 23 sq., where this part of the argument is treated fully.]

of life? This again is not compatible with His Messianic character.

Moreover, He is only one in a long line of claimants who have arrogated to themselves this high office. Before Him many thieves and robbers have entered into the fold by stealth and violence (x. 8). This last passage has been attacked as fatal to the authority of the Gospel, and this on two grounds. First, we are told[1] that it is a thoroughly Gnostic sentiment, directed against the lawgiver and the prophets. They are the thieves and the robbers. Thus it is inconsistent not only with our Lord's own position, but also with the position of St John as a 'pillar-apostle' of the Circumcision. Secondly, we are informed[2] that the statement is historically incorrect; for as a matter of fact we do not hear of false Messiahs before Christ. I give this as a sample of the attacks which are made in certain quarters upon the genuineness of the Fourth Gospel. In reply it is sufficient to state (1) that the interpretation, which sees in the thieves and robbers a reference to Moses and the prophets, is quite untenable. It contradicts the whole teaching of the Gospel. Our Lord constantly refers to the Old Testament Scriptures as authoritative, and as foretelling Himself. Thus Abraham rejoiced to see Christ's day, and he saw it and was glad. The Jews are Abraham's seed, yet they seek to kill Him (viii. 37, 56). Moses will accuse them to the Father; for had they believed Moses, they would have believed Christ, for Moses wrote of Him (v. 45 sq.). And the Evangelist sees in the persistent unbelief of the Jewish race a fulfilment of a prophecy of Isaiah uttered when he saw Christ's glory and spake of Him (xii. 37 sq.). The interpretation therefore may safely be dismissed. Curiously enough it is a view borrowed from Valentinus, who states that 'all the prophets and the law spake from the Demiurge, a foolish God, and were foolish themselves and ignorant' (Hippol. *Haer.* vi. 35 p. 194), and then proceeds to quote this passage: and it is echoed by the Manicheans

---

[1] By Hilgenfeld.   [2] By Baur and Scholten.

(August. *c. Faust.* xvi. 12, VIII. p. 288 F., 289 A.) and probably by other dualistic sects.   Such at least would appear from Clem. Alex. *Strom.* i. 17 pp. 366 sq. (*ed.* Potter).   Further, the consciousness of the misuse that was made of the text would account for the omission of the words πρὸ ἐμοῦ by some authorities[1].   (2) The expression need not necessarily be confined to false Messiahs.   'Shepherds' are teachers (Jer. xxiii. 1, Ezek. xxxiv. 2, 3), and thus the Scribes and Pharisees, the leaders of religious thought, would naturally be included in the category.   In other passages our Lord refers to them as robbers, as wolves in sheep's clothing (Matt. vii. 15), as devouring widows' houses (Matt. xxiii. 14, Mark xii. 40, Luke xx. 47). And the beginning of this corrupt state of teaching did not synchronize with the time of our Lord's life upon earth.   For some generations past the whole tendency of religious education had been thoroughly vicious[2].

But after all there is no sufficient reason for denying the appearance of false Messiahs before the Christian era.   On the contrary, everything points to the fact of such appearances. And if these earlier false Messiahs do not come forward so prominently in Josephus as those who flourished afterwards, this is only what was to be expected; for they did not fall within his own lifetime.   Gamaliel, at all events, in his speech as recorded by St Luke (Acts v. 35 sq.), mentions two of these impostors, Theudas and Judas the Galilean, the latter of whom is described as having revolted 'in the days of the taxing.'   In the case of the former, there is a well-known chronological difficulty, Josephus (*Ant.* xx. 5. 1) speaking of a Theudas who headed a rebellion in the procuratorship of Cuspius Fadus after A.D. 44; but the occasion of the revolt of Judas the Gaulanite is given by him in detail (*Ant.* xviii. 1. 1 sq.), and his language shows evidently that the rising took a theocratic

---

[1] The words are omitted in אֲ*, in most Latin MSS., in the Syriac, Sahidic and Gothic versions, and by Cyril,   Chrysostom and Augustine.

[2] See Ewald, *Jahrb. der Bibl. Wissenschaft* ix. 43.

character[1]. In another place Josephus, referring to the time of the death of Herod the Great (*Ant.* xvii. 10. 8), tells us that 'Judæa was infested with robbers (λῃστηρίων ἡ Ἰουδαία πλέως ἦν), and as the bands of the seditious found anyone to head them, he was created a king at once, in order to do damage to the community.' He mentions several of these adventurers by name, beginning (*Ant.* xvii. 10. 5) with Judas the son of a certain Hezekiah, whom he calls the 'brigand-chief' (ὁ ἀρχι-λῃστής). Now it is quite impossible to separate all these uprisings from Messianic anticipations, even if the contrary was not directly stated in some cases by the historian. For the air was full of rumours, and echoes of the Messianic expectations had penetrated as far as Rome, and found expression in the pages of Suetonius (*Vesp.* 4), and in the Fourth Eclogue of Virgil. By some the Herod-family was looked to as the embodiment of the national hope, Antipas (Vict. Ant. *ap.* Cramer *Cat. in Marc.* p. 400), Agrippa (Philastrius *Haer.* xxviii.), and Herod the Great (Epiphanius *Haer.* xx. p. 45) being at different times regarded as the Messiah by their partisans[2].

But it is not only the prevalence of the Messianic idea exhibited in this Gospel, it is the minuteness and variety of detail displayed which arrests our attention, and is so powerful a testimony to the authenticity of the narrative. This phenomenon can be conveniently illustrated by the designations which the Evangelist applies to the Messiah. I give some of the most striking.

(a) *The Lamb of God* (i. 29, 36). The reference is to Isaiah liii. 4, a passage which was commonly interpreted of the Messiah, apparently before the Christian era (see Bishop Harold Browne, *Sermons*[3] p. 92 sq., and cf. Sanday, *Authorship of the Fourth Gospel* p. 39 sq), and is interpreted of our Lord directly by Philip the Evangelist (Acts viii. 32), and indirectly

---

[1] Joseph. *Ant.* xviii. 1. 6 δυσνίκητος δὲ τοῦ ἐλευθέρου ἔρως ἐστὶν αὐτοῖς μόνον ἡγεμόνα καὶ δεσπότην τὸν Θεὸν ὑπειλη-φόσιν.

[2] See the article *Herodians* in Smith's

Dictionary of the Bible; and compare Keim i. p. 244 sq.

[3] *Messiah as foretold and expected* Cambridge (1862).

by St Peter (1 Pet. i. 19).   This idea of the lamb as typifying
the Messiah is not found in the other three Evangelists.   It is
introduced however by St John naturally and without comment:
the meaning is only explained by recalling the Messianic
expectations of the time, and in fact is lost sight of by many
commentators.   With the substitution of another Greek word
(ἀρνίον for ἀμνός) the same metaphor occurs in the Apocalypse
nearly thirty times.

(b) *The Son of God, the King of Israel* (i. 49).   The
naturalness of this outburst on the part of Nathanael is
deserving of notice.   The titles with which he hails the Messiah
are introduced in a way which is absolutely free from artifici-
ality.   The first designation, the ' Son of God,' is derived from
Ps. ii. 7.   It occurs again in the Fourth Gospel, i. 34, iii. 18, ix. 35
and especially xi. 27, in the last passage coupled expressly with
the title ' the Christ,' a combination which we find elsewhere
(Matt. xxvi. 63 in the mouth of the High Priest, and Matt. xvi.
16 in the confession of St Peter).   Even when it stands
alone, as in Luke iv. 41, xxii. 70, it is at once recognised as
applying to the Christ.   The second title, ' the King of Israel,'
is a favourite appellation in the Fourth Gospel (xii. 13, cf. xviii.
36, 37, xix. 3, 5, 12, 14, 19).   As Mr Sanday appositely remarks
(*Authorship of the Fourth Gospel* p. 35), ' the phrase is especially
important, because it breathes those politico-theocratic hopes,
which, since the taking of Jerusalem, Christians, at least, if not
Jews, must have entirely laid aside.   It belongs to the lowest
stratification of Christian ideas, before Christianity was separated
from Judaism; and there is but one generation of Christians,
to whom it would have any meaning.'

Other Messianic titles which are found in our Evangelist are
(c) *He that is coming* (ὁ ἐρχόμενος) vi. 14, xi. 27, cf. Matt. xi. 3,
Luke vii. 19, 20, derived from the well-known Messianic psalm
(Ps. cxviii.), which is quoted in this sense by all the four Evangelists (Matt. xxiii. 39, Mark xi. 9, Luke xiii. 35, John xii. 13);
(d) *The Holy One of God* (ὁ ἅγιος τοῦ Θεοῦ) vi. 69, cf. Mark i.
24 and other passages; (e) *the Son of Man*, i. 51 etc., the most

familiar of all designations of the Christ, especially in St Luke's
Gospel ; (*f*) *the Light*, i. 7, 8, viii. 12, xii. 46, cf. Luke ii. 32 ; an
idea found in Messianic passages like Is. ix. 2, xlii. 6, 7, Mal. iv.
2, 3, and expressly interpreted of Christ by the Talmud—'Light
is the name of Messiah' (see Lightfoot *Hor. Heb.* p. 564 quoted
by Sanday, p. 152); (*g*) *He that hath been sent* (ὁ ἀπεσταλμένος),
ix. 7, where the interpretation of the name Siloam connects the
pool with Christ (see x. 36, xvii. 3, 8, 18, 21, 23, 25 etc., cf. Is. lxi.
1) rather than with the man (see Wetstein *ad loc.*), but where
the allusion to the title, so far from appearing on the surface,
is inserted in the most unobtrusive manner possible. These
instances show the perfect ease and familiarity with which the
writer of the Fourth Gospel moves among the Messianic expectations and the national feelings of the period which he depicts.

(ii) *The companions of the Messiah.* Attention has been
drawn elsewhere[1] to the significant references to 'the prophet'
which occur in four places in St John (i. 21, 25, vi. 14, vii. 40).
It has been pointed out that the form which the conception
takes is strictly Jewish, not Christian. While Christian teachers
identified the prophet foretold by Moses (Deut. xviii. 15) with
our Lord Himself (Acts iii. 22, vii. 37, cf. John i. 46)[2], the Jews
in St John's Gospel conceive of 'the Christ' and 'the prophet'
as two different persons. If He is not the Christ, they adopt
the alternative that He may be 'the prophet' (i. 21, 25); if
not 'the prophet,' then 'the Christ' (vii. 40). But this brings
us to another point, which is worthy of consideration. Springing out of the phrase employed by Moses in the passage quoted
above ('a prophet like unto me') came the Jewish idea of the
parallelism of the lawgiver and the Messiah. In part this idea
was justified by the prophecy, and finds its proper place in the
language of the New Testament. Thus, as the writer of the
Epistle to the Hebrews shows, Moses and Christ are the two

---

[1] See above, p. 25.
[2] This identification is a commonplace in patristic writers, see Tertull.
adv. Marcion. iv. 22, *Apost. Const.* v.
20, *Clem. Recogn.* i. 43, Origen *in
Johan.* vi. 4, Eusebius *Demonstr.
Evang.* i. 7, p. 26 sq. (*ed.* Paris 1628).

mediators of the two covenants (Heb. viii. 5, 6). Thus again, in
a well-known passage (1 Cor. x. 1—11), St Paul works out the
parallel in his record of the wanderings of the children of Israel.
The crossing of the Red Sea is a baptism by Moses. The rock
smitten in the wilderness is Christ. Thus again, St John in
the Apocalypse (xv. 3) sets in the mouth of the redeemed a
twofold song, 'the song of Moses the servant of God, and the
song of the Lamb.' And lastly, our Lord Himself instances
the action of Moses in lifting up the serpent in the wilderness
as emblematic of Himself (John iii. 14). But the Rabbis
carried out the parallelism into the most minute details, so
that the career of the Messiah became in effect a reproduction
of the career of Moses. Of this belief adventurers, who wished
to pose as the Messiah, were not slow to take advantage. For
instance Theudas, to whom allusion has already been made[1],
undertakes to divide the Jordan (Jos. *Ant.* xx. 5. 1), in imitation
probably as much of Moses as of Joshua and Elijah. Again,
other nameless adventurers, to whom Josephus makes reference
a little later on (*Ant.* xx. 8. 6), 'urged the multitude to follow
them into the wilderness, and pretended that they would
exhibit manifest wonders and signs that should be performed
by the providence of God (κατὰ τὴν τοῦ Θεοῦ πρόνοιαν).'
Gfrörer, who has worked out this subject in his *Jahrhundert
des Heils* (ii. p. 318 sq), tells us that Micah vii. 15 was quoted
to prove that the passover was the time in which this manifestation of Messianic power should be exhibited. In fulfilment
of the prophecy of Zechariah (ix. 9), the King should appear
riding an ass (Gfrörer p. 339). The miracles which he was
expected to perform were to include the two mighty works of
his prototype, the smiting of the waters as suggested by
Zechariah (x. 11), and the giving of the manna. We have seen
how the first of these symbolical acts was promised by Theudas.
To the general expectation of the second miracle rabbinic
literature furnishes full and explicit testimony. Thus in
Coheleth Rabba, 9 fol. 86. 4, we read *Dixit P. Berachia nomine*

---

[1] See above, p. 147.

R. Isaaci; qualis fuit redemptor primus, talis erit redemptor ultimus....Sicut redemptor primus fecit descendere manna, ita redemptor posterior faciet descendere manna. Again, in *Shir Rabba,* fol. 16, *Redemptor posterior revelabitur iis...et quonam illos ducet? Sunt qui dicunt in desertum Judae, sunt qui dicunt in desertum Sichoris et Ogi et descendere faciet pro iis manna* (see Lightfoot *Hor. Heb.* II. pp. 552, 557 ; cf. *Shemoth Rabba* XXV.). In the light of these notices we can imagine the ferment which would be occasioned by the feeding of the five thousand, and we can now understand the full significance of the challenge thrown out to Him on the part of the unbelieving crowd, 'What dost thou work? Our fathers did eat manna in the wilderness (vi. 30, 31),' which in St John's narrative occurs in so abrupt and unexplained a manner[1]. The key to the understanding of the whole situation is an acquaintance with the national expectation of the greater Moses. But this knowledge is not obtruded upon us by the Evangelist. It is tacitly assumed. In fact, the meaning is unintelligible, except to one who is brought up among the ideas of the time, or to one who, like a modern critic, has made them his special study.

And so we might pass in review the various details of the Messianic conception, and show how marvellously they correspond with the account given so naturally and incidentally by the Evangelist. The birth and generation of the Christ who, in accordance with Micah v. 2, should be a descendant of David, born in Bethlehem (vii. 42), and yet at the same time the mystery and uncertainty of that birth (vii. 27) based upon the wellknown passage in Isaiah 'who shall declare His generation?' (Is. liii. 8)[2], the apparent discrepancies of the two accounts being explained by the rabbis on the analogy of Moses who was born and then hidden[3]; His manifestation 'to Israel'

---

[1] See this matter treated more fully above, p. 24.

[2] See Sanday p. 146, Gfrörer, pp. 203, 307, Wetstein and Lightfoot on John vi. 27.

[3] The Gemarists (*Hieros. Berachoth*

fol. 5. 1) alleged that the Messiah had been born at Bethlehem a good while before their own times but had been snatched away. The same idea is found in *Midrash Sair* fol. 1, 16. 4 (on *Canticles* ii. 9) Caprea apparet et oc-

(i. 31 a passage with which Sanday, p. 33, compares Luke i. 80 spoken of John the Baptist; cf. xiv. 22, xvii. 6 sq), an event which Jewish tradition decided would take place at the Passover (*Shemoth Rabb.* xv. 150, *Jerusalem Targum* on Ex. xii. 42, *Mechilta* on Ex. xii. 42, R. Bechai in *Kad Hakkemach* 49)[1] —doubtless another element in the excitement of the crowds after the Feeding of the Five Thousand which took place at Passover-tide (John vi. 2); lastly, His eternal continuance (xii. 34), a point much discussed among the rabbis[2].

One of the accompaniments of the Messiah in Jewish anticipations was the return of the Shechinah, the symbol of that visible divine presence, the loss of which after the captivity had been so universally deplored. This confident hope was based on such prophecies as Ezekiel xxxvii. 27, xliii. 7, Zechariah ii. 10 sq, viii. 3, Isaiah viii. 8, and on the language of Ecclesiasticus xxiv. 8 sq 'He that created me caused my tabernacle to rest (κατέπαυσε τὴν σκηνήν μου), and said, Let thy dwelling be in Jacob (ἐν 'Ιακὼβ κατασκήνωσον)...in the holy tabernacle I served before him (ἐν σκηνῇ ἁγίᾳ ἐνώπιον αὐτοῦ ἐλειτούργησα).' It finds expression in more than one passage in the Apocalypse (vii. 15, xiii. 6, xv. 5, xxi. 3). It remains however for St John in his Gospel, in words which are replete with local colouring, to point with a quiet triumph to the fulfilment of this expectation in the person of Jesus Christ, 'The Word became flesh, and tabernacled (ἐσκήνωσεν) among us, and we beheld His glory

---

cultatur, apparet et occultatur. Sic redemptor primus (Moses) apparuit et fuit occultatus, et tandem apparuit iterum...Sic redemptor posterior (Messias) revelabitur iis atque iterum abscondetur ab iis...In fine quadraginta quinque dierum revelabitur iterum iis et descendere faciet pro iis manna.

[1] And at midnight; Traditio Judaeorum est Christum media nocte venturum in similitudinem Aegyptii temporis, quando Pascha celebratum est et exterminator venit et Dominus super tabernacula transiit et sanguine agni

postes nostrarum frontium consecrati sunt. Hieron. *Comm. in Matth.* IV. 25. 6, Op. VII. 203 (*ed.* Vallarsi). For the Christian counterpart of this Jewish expectation see Justin *Dial. c. Tryph.* § 8, p. 34, § 110, p. 368 (*ed.* Otto).

[2] See these various speculations given in Gfrörer pp. 252 sq, 296, 315—317. The passages referred to by the multitude (ἡμεῖς ἠκούσαμεν ἐκ τοῦ νόμου) were probably Is. ix. 6, Dan. vii. 13, 14, and the Targums on these texts will repay study.

(τὴν δόξαν αὐτοῦ), the glory as of the only-begotten from the
Father, full of grace and truth (i. 14).'

(iii)   *The Messianic expectation among the Samaritans.*

It has been denied[1] that the Samaritans had any Messianic
anticipations at all.   But, firstly, they had the prophecy referred
to above (Deut. xviii. 15), which, as forming part of the Penta-
teuch, they would accept as authoritative.   This was sufficient
in itself to suggest such expectations, and the fact that they were
under the same stimulating influences as the Jews, influences
arising from the political troubles of the times, would encourage
presentiments of a Deliverer.   Secondly, as a matter of fact,
there is sufficient evidence to show that Messianic hopes were
as rife among them at the time of our Lord, as they are now at
the present day.   Thus Josephus informs us (*Ant.* xviii. 4. 1)
that in the procuratorship of Pilate a disturbance arose among
the Samaritans in consequence of an impostor who 'bade them
assemble on Mount Gerizim' under promise that he 'would
show them the sacred vessels (δείξειν τὰ ἱερὰ σκεύη) which
were buried there, because Moses had put them there.'   All
this is distinctly Messianic in character, and has an obvious
reference to the narrative of 2 Maccabees (ii. 1—8), where
Jeremiah is related to have buried the tabernacle, the ark and
the altar of incense on the mountain 'where Moses climbed up
and saw the heritage of God,' and to have declared that the
secret of the hiding place should not be revealed 'until the
time that God should gather His people again together, and
receive them unto mercy.'   And this view finds confirmation
from a passage in the *Joma Babl.* (fol. 526, quoted by Gfrörer
p. 350), and explains the reference in Apoc. ii. 17 to the 'hidden
manna,' which was one of the treasures contained in the ark
(Ex. xvi. 33, 34, Heb. ix. 4).   These disturbances among the
Samaritans took place A.D. 34, 35, and are connected by Keim
(I. p. 518) with the preaching of John the Baptist.   Further
light is thrown on these Samaritan aspirations in the *Clementine*

---

[1] *e.g.* by the author of *The Jesus of History* (1869).

Recognitions. Here Simon Magus and Dositheus are both mentioned as Samaritans who professed themselves to be Messiahs[1], and the Samaritans are described as 'rightly looking forward to one true Prophet in accordance with the foretelling of Moses, but prevented by the perverse teaching of Dositheus from believing that Jesus was He whom they expected (*Recogn.* i. 54; cf. vii. 33).' For the later communications with the Samaritans held by Scaliger, Ludolf, and de Sacy see Westcott, *Introduction to the Study of the Gospels* p. 148. Petermann likewise, who resided two months at Nablous, gives the results of his visit and investigations in Herzog's *Real-Encyklop.* xiii. p. 372 sq. All these authorities agree that the Samaritans found their hopes upon the appearance of the prophet like unto Moses. All agree too that they expect the discovery of the furniture of the Sanctuary, *e.g.* the ark, the manna and the tables of the commandments, a fact which leaves the interpretation of the passage in Josephus beyond a doubt. With them the Messiah is represented under two aspects, first as the *Hashab* or *Hathab* (התב) the Converter, Restorer, Buyer-back (Westcott and Petermann *l.c.*), secondly as the *El Muhdi* the Guide (Robinson, *Biblical Researches* II. 278[2]). Thus we see how the confident aspirations placed by St John in the mouth of the Samaritan woman, 'I know that Messias cometh, which is called Christ; when he is come, he will tell us all things' (iv. 25, cf. *vv.* 29, 42), are not the invention of a later generation, but reflect the contemporary national feelings of this interesting people.

(iv) *Jewish beliefs, and sentiments on other points.*

(a) *The relation of the Jews to Abraham* exemplified in John viii. 33 sq. is worthy of notice, as illustrating the writer's acquaintance with the Jewish ideas of his time. The boast,

---

[1] *Recogn.* ii. 7, Simon hic...gente Samaraeus...gloriae ac jactantiae supra omne genus hominum cupidus ita ut excelsam virtutem...credi se velit et Christum putari (cf. *Hom.* ii. 22);

Recogn. i. 54 magistrum suum (i.e. Dositheum) velut Christum praedicarunt; cf. Origen *c. Cels.* i. 57 (i. 372).

[2] *ed.* 1867.

' We are Abraham's seed,' is an evidence of a justifiable pride of
birth (cf. *v.* 53), but the latter part of the sentence 'and we
have never been in bondage to any man' has given much
difficulty to the commentators. Certainly it is not what a
stranger would have said of the Jewish people. The opinion
felt by the Romans for the Jews is well expressed by Cicero,
who contemptuously classes together the Jews and the Syrians
as nations born to slavery (*Judaeis et Syris nationibus natis
servituti*, Cic. *Prov. Cons.* 5). And Apion casts in the teeth of
Josephus the fact that, so far from ruling the Gentiles, the
chosen people were as a fact subject to them (τὸ μὴ ἄρχειν
δουλεύειν δὲ μᾶλλον ἔθνεσι Jos. *c. Apion.* ii. 11). Yet this
proud assertion of liberty is exactly what the Jews would make
on their own behalf, whatever wresting of facts might be
necessary to maintain it. The answer of Josephus to Apion
at the end of the section is quite characteristic. 'At a time
when even the Egyptians,' he contends, 'were servants to the
Persians and the Macedonians, we (the Jews) enjoyed liberty,
and moreover had the dominion of the cities round about us
for about a hundred and twenty years, until Pompey the Great.
And when all nations were conquered by the Romans, who are
kings everywhere, our ancestors were the only people who
continued to be esteemed their allies and friends because of
their fidelity.' And in a certain sense the claim was true.
The national spirit of the Jews had never been thoroughly
enslaved. But externally it would appear to be the reverse of
the truth, and it is difficult to conceive how words such as the
Evangelist records could have found a place in a narrative
written in the middle of the second century, after the twofold
destruction of Jerusalem by Titus and by Hadrian had stamped
out the last spark of national liberty.

(*b*) *The authority assigned to Moses* is another graphic
touch which shows a minute acquaintance with Jewish thought.
The assertion 'We are Moses' disciples' (ix. 28) is illustrated
by Lightfoot (*Hor. Heb.* II. p. 572) from *Joma* fol. 4. I., where the
same expression occurs, and the favourite title of Moses in

vogue among the Jews was 'Moses, our master' (quoted by
Schöltz on this verse). Associated with this idea is the
prestige which attached to the rabbinical schools. The
surprise expressed that our Lord should set up for a teacher
(vii. 15), the contemptuous disregard for the opinion of the
people (vii. 49), the very form of address (Σὺ εἶ ὁ διδάσκαλος
τοῦ Ἰσραήλ; iii. 10), which was apparently a formula of
remonstrance among the Jews[1]—all these features can be
readily illustrated from rabbinical literature.

(c) The jealousy and contempt with which the Palestinian
Jews viewed the Greek dispersion is strikingly evidenced by
the sarcastic comment of the Jews—'Will he go unto the
dispersed among the Gentiles (Μὴ εἰς τὴν διασπορὰν τῶν
Ἑλλήνων μέλλει πορεύεσθαι), and teach the Gentiles?' (vii. 35.)
Contemporary Jewish opinion drew a hard and fast line
between their brethren of the Babylonian dispersion, i.e. those
who preferred to remain in the land of their captivity, and the
Greek dispersion in Asia Minor, the result of the wholesale de-
portations of Seleucus Nicator and Antiochus Epiphanes. The
former were held in high honour. The land of Babylon was
considered to be as holy as that of Palestine (Rabbi Solomon in
Gittin fol. 2. 1), and the descendants of the Jews there even
purer than those in Judæa itself (*Kiddush* fol. 69. 2). Even
Gamaliel deigned to hold correspondence with the 'sons of
the Dispersion of Babylonia' (Frankel *Monatsschrift*, p. 413,
1853). Hence, as Lightfoot remarks (*Hor. Heb. ad loc.*), 'for a
Palestine Jew to go to the Babylonish dispersion was to go to
a people and country equal, if not superior, to his own : but to
go to the dispersion among the Greeks was to go into unclean
regions, to an inferior race of Jews, and into nations most
heathenized.'

(d) Lastly (to confine ourselves to one further instance),
the question put to our Lord concerning the man born blind,
'Master, who did sin, this man, or his parents, that he was

---

[1] See the story told in Lightfoot, from *Echah Rabbathi*, fol. 66. 2.
Hor. Heb. II. p. 534, of Rabbi Joshua

born blind[1]?' reflects with a faithful accuracy the popular teaching of the day as regards the consequences of sin. It was a received doctrine in the Jewish schools that physical defect in children was the punishment of sin committed by their parents; and though the Jewish doctrine of metempsychosis was confined to the souls of the righteous (Jos. *B. J.* ii. 12), and thus a man brought no taint of sins with him from his previous existence, yet it is clear from many curious Rabbinic passages which Lightfoot quotes (*ad loc.*) that even in the womb the infant, from the moment of his first quickening, was considered capable of incurring stain of sin.

3. *THE WRITER'S KNOWLEDGE OF EXTERNAL FACTS, THE HISTORY, GEOGRAPHY, NAMES AND CUSTOMS OF THE JEWISH PEOPLE.*

(i) *The relations of the Jews with those around them.*

(a) *The Galileans.* Owing to the fact that St John lays special stress on the Judæan ministry, the references to the Galileans in his Gospel are less numerous than in the Synoptic narrative. But the notices, though few, are highly significant, and the touches with which St John depicts them, singularly vivid. Thus we cannot fail to observe the contempt which the Jews of the metropolis display for them. 'Shall Christ come out of Galilee?' 'Out of Galilee ariseth no prophet' (vii. 41, 52). 'Can there any good thing come out of Nazareth?' (i. 46). Such is the objection, which rises unpremeditatedly to the lips of speakers, when the northern province is indicated as the home of the Messiah. This disparagement of the Galileans is reflected more than once in the rabbinic literature of the period. 'Foolish Galilean' seems to have been the inevitable form of address when a Galilean appears as a character in a dialogue[2]. This contempt arose in great measure from the admixture of foreign blood in the Galilean people. The Sea of

---

[1] John ix. 2.   [2] *e.g.* see Lightfoot, *Hor. Heb.* ii. pp. 78, 543.

Galilee was an important commercial centre, and as a natural consequence strangers—Phœnicians, Syrians, Greeks and Romans —settled in the district, and intermarried with the Jewish inhabitants, to the prejudice of the race in the eyes of a strict Jew of the capital (see Keim I. p. 309). The distinction thus inaugurated by the taint of foreign blood was further emphasized by a difference of pronunciation. The rough dialect of the northerners, which was a subject of comment in the case of St Peter (Mark xiv. 70), is a favourite theme likewise in rabbinical writers[1]. Thus in one story[2] a Judæan professes himself unable to distinguish between אִמַּר 'a lamb,' עֲמַר 'wool,' חֲמַר 'wine' and חֲמֹר 'an ass,' as pronounced by a Galilean when the latter wants to make a purchase, an illustration which shows that the divergence consisted largely in a careless confusion of gutturals on the part of the Galileans. The bad name, from which the Galileans suffered generally, seems to have attached itself more particularly to their city Nazareth (John i. 46). Certainly the account which we have of them from other passages in the Gospels (Luke iv. 16—29, Matth. xiii. 54—58) conveys the impression that the Nazarenes were a violent, unscrupulous, irreligious people. They may therefore have fully justified their invidious reputation. That this reputation was widespread appears from the irony in the superscription on the cross, 'Jesus *of Nazareth*, the King of the Jews,' (John xix. 19). We pass on to notice the Evangelist's accurate knowledge of other traits in the Galilean character. In John iv. 45 occurs a brief and incidental mention of the welcome accorded to our Lord by the Galileans in consequence of His doings at Jerusalem at the feast, 'for they also went to the feast.' Now it is worthy of record that Josephus (*Ant.* xx. 6. 1) relates that serious troubles arose owing to collisions between the Samaritans and the Galileans while the latter were on their way to keep the feasts at Jerusalem[3]. The

---

[1] See the instances given by Lightfoot, II. p. 78 sq, and cf. Fürst *Aram. Idiom.* § 15.

[2] See my *Galatians*, p. 197 (*ed.* 6).

[3] This notice illustrates John iv. 4 compared with Luke ix. 51 sq.

natural turbulence of the Galileans, to which Josephus calls attention[1], was on these occasions aggravated by their intense religious enthusiasm[2]. It is therefore quite what we should expect when we find a reference in St Luke (xiii. 1) to certain Galileans 'whose blood Pilate had mingled with their sacrifices,' and the portrait which St John gives us of St Peter is, as Keim truly observes (I. p. 315), of 'a genuine Galilean type.'

(b) *The Romans.* St John's consummate skill does not fail him as he sketches the relations of the Jews with their Roman masters. We notice on the one hand the cringing political deference exhibited in the words of the chief priests, 'The Romans shall come and take away both our place and nation (xi. 48),' 'We have no king but Cæsar (xix. 15),' 'If thou let this man go, thou art not Cæsar's friend (xix. 12);' on the other, the religious horror of the pollution attaching to contact with the Romans, which even at the height of their frenzied hatred of their prisoner kept the Jews outside the judgment hall, 'lest they should be defiled (xviii. 28).' He then proceeds to give us details which reveal an accurate acquaintance with the Roman customs and military arrangements of the time. Twice over is reference made to 'the band' (ἡ σπεῖρα xviii. 3, 12), once to 'the captain' (ὁ χιλίαρχος xviii. 12). Now, we learn from Polybius[3] and Suidas[4] that σπεῖρα and χιλίαρχος were technical terms, the recognised Greek renderings of *cohors* and

---

[1] πρὸς πᾶσαν ἀεὶ πολέμου πεῖραν ἀντέσχον· μάχιμοί τε γὰρ ἐκ νηπίων κ.τ.λ. Jos. *B. J.* iii. 3. 2; cf. *Vit.* 17 νεωτέρων ἐπιθυμοῦντες ἀεὶ πραγμάτων.

[2] Many of the false Messiahs were Galileans, e.g. Ἰούδας ὁ Γαλιλαῖος (Acts v. 37).

[3] τρεῖς σπείρας· τοῦτο δὲ καλεῖται τὸ σύνταγμα τῶν πεζῶν παρὰ Ῥωμαίοις κοόρτις Polybius xi. 23. Schweighäuser in his note (*ad loc.*) contends that σπεῖρα here means *manipulus*, and that the term *cohors* is applied to the complement of three maniples; but Livy in the parallel passage (xxviii. 14) has *ternis peditum cohortibus*, and the

expression καλεῖται shows that he is merely giving the Latin equivalent (κόρτις) for the Greek expression (σπεῖρα). A little later on (xi. 33. 1) Polybius has again ἐπὶ τέτταρας κοόρτις· τοῦτο δ' ἔστι σπεῖρα, where Casaubon has struck out the last four words, though they occur in all the manuscripts.

[4] Suidas (*s. v.*) states that χιλίαρχοι came into office at Rome three hundred and fifteen years after the foundation of the city. This coincides with the institution of military tribunes with consular power at the close of the Decemvirate.

tribunus respectively.   Accordingly the use of the definite
article by St John in both cases, '*the* cohort' '*the* tribune[1],'
shows that he was aware of a fact, which we learn from
Josephus also (*B. J.* ii. 12. 1), that a Roman cohort was
quartered in the Turris Antonia at Jerusalem to prevent
disturbances at the great festivals[2].   A few years later we find
soldiers from this Roman garrison employed in rescuing St Paul
from the hands of the Jewish mob during the feast of the
Passover[3].

Again, the scene of the Crucifixion furnishes St John with
another opportunity of showing his intimate knowledge of
Roman military customs.   A quaternion ($\tau\epsilon\tau\rho\acute{a}\delta\iota o\nu$ Acts xii. 4)
of soldiers, as we learn from Vegetius and others[4], was usually
employed as a watch on night duty, or for purpose of escort.
Now, it is noticeable that, when the other Evangelists speak
of the guard which attended at the Crucifixion, no number is
given.   It is simply stated (Matt. xxvii. 35, Mark xv. 26,
Luke xxiii. 34), that the soldiers divided the Saviour's garments
among them.   St John however gives the actual number.   But
observe how incidentally the fact comes out.   He makes no
mention of a quaternion : he merely says, 'Then the soldiers,
when they had crucified Jesus, took His garments, and made
four parts, to every soldier a part.'   The information is not
paraded in any way ; it is involved in the narrative.   One more

---

[1] On the other hand, though 'the
band' is mentioned by the Synoptists
(Matt. xxvii. 27, Mark xv. 16) at a
later stage in the proceedings, the
definite article, as used in the Fourth
Evangelist, is more decisive.

[2] When Cumanus was procurator,
the insolent conduct of a Roman
soldier at the Passover resulted in a
riot (*B. J. l.c.*, cf. *Ant.* xx. 5. 3) in
which ten thousand (*B. J. l.c.*, twenty
thousand *Ant. l.c.*) Jews perished.
For the disturbances at the great
festivals see *B. J.* i. 4. 3.   Whiston
instances the cautious procedure of

the chief priests (Matt. xxvi. 5) as evidence to these disturbances.

[3] Acts xxi. 31 sq, where again the
same technical terms are used with
the definite article $\acute{a}\nu\acute{\epsilon}\beta\eta$ $\phi\acute{a}\sigma\iota\varsigma$ $\tau\hat{\omega}$ $\chi\iota\lambda\iota$-
$\acute{a}\rho\chi\omega$ $\tau\hat{\eta}\varsigma$ $\sigma\pi\epsilon\acute{\iota}\rho\eta\varsigma$ $\kappa.\tau.\lambda$.   This account,
like that in the Fourth Gospel, is pro-
bably the narrative of an eye-witness.

[4] De singulis centuriis quaterni equi-
tes et quaterni pedites excubitum
noctibus faciunt, Vegetius *de re militari* iii. 8 ; cf. Philo *in Flacc.* 13, II. p.
533 $\sigma\tau\rho\alpha\tau\iota\acute{\omega}\tau\eta\nu$ $\tau\iota\nu\grave{a}$ $\tau\hat{\omega}\nu$ $\grave{\epsilon}\nu$ $\tauo\hat{\iota}\varsigma$ $\tau\epsilon\tau\rho\alpha\delta\acute{\iota}o\iota\varsigma$
$\phi\upsilon\lambda\acute{a}\kappa\omega\nu$ $\kappa\alpha\theta'$ $\acute{o}\delta\grave{o}\nu$ $\epsilon\acute{\upsilon}\rho\acute{\omega}\nu$, Polyb. vi. 33
$\tau\grave{o}$ $\phi\upsilon\lambda\acute{a}\kappa\epsilon\iota\acute{o}\nu$ $\grave{\epsilon}\sigma\tau\iota\nu$ $\grave{\epsilon}\kappa$ $\tau\epsilon\tau\tau\acute{a}\rho\omega\nu$ $\grave{a}\nu\delta\rho\hat{\omega}\nu$.

instance, and I leave this part of the subject. 'The Jews,' we read, 'besought Pilate that their legs might be broken....Then came the soldiers, and brake the legs of the first, and of the other which was crucified with Him (xix. 31, 32).' This again is a detail added by St John, which a forger would not have cared to risk. For *crurifragium* formed no part of a crucifixion. It was a separate punishment[1], to which slaves could be subjected at the caprice of their masters, and it was abolished together with crucifixion at the command of Constantine (Lipsius *de Cruce* III. 14). But there is some reason to suppose that it was used to hasten death in the case of Jewish criminals (Lactant. *Inst.* iv. 26), in order that the ends of justice might not be defeated by the Mosaic enactment which required the bodies to be taken down on the day of execution (Deut. xxi. 23 quoted by Tertull. *adv. Judaeos* 10).

(ii) *The writer's acquaintance with Jewish Institutions.*

1. *The High-Priesthood.*

The relative positions of Annas and Caiaphas at the time of the Crucifixion have been a source of some perplexity. Annas the high-priest had been deposed by Gratus the predecessor of Pilate, and after intermediate appointments Gratus had nominated Caiaphas to the office. The date of Caiaphas' succession is probably A.D. 25, one year before Pilate became procurator, and he was deposed apparently about the passover of A.D. 37; whereupon there followed a series of changes, as many as seven high-priests holding office in the next ten years. These facts we learn from a comparison of certain passages in Josephus (esp. *Ant.* xviii. 2. 2 compared with xviii. 4. 3). Thus at the time of our Lord's Passion Caiaphas was the actual high-priest, while Annas had been high-priest a few years before. Turning now to the New Testament, we find a certain vagueness in the description of the two by the Synoptists, a vagueness due partly

---

[1] See Plaut. *Asinar*. ii. 4. 68, *Paen.* iv. 2. 64, Sen. *de Ira* iii. 32; Suet. *Aug.* 67, *Tib.* 44, passages quoted with others by Lipsius *de Cruce* II. 14.

to the wide use of the word ἀρχιερεύς, but not altogether explained thereby. Thus, in his Gospel St Luke dates the first year of our Lord's ministry ἐπὶ ἀρχιερέως ʺΑννα καὶ Καιάφα (Luke iii. 2), but in the Acts he mentions as present at the meeting of the Sanhedrin shortly after the day of Pentecost ʺΑννας ὁ ἀρχιερεὺς καὶ Καιάφας (Acts iv. 6). He would seem therefore either to have consulted documents which did not recognise the validity of Caiaphas' appointment, or to have had himself no very clear conception of the relative positions of the two. The account in the Fourth Gospel is much more precise. St John is aware that Caiaphas is the high-priest (xi. 49, xviii. 13, 24), but he assigns an important position to Annas also, whom in some sense he recognises likewise as ἀρχιερεύς (xviii. 15, 16, 19, 22)[1]. On these facts we may remark, first that this unguarded, and to us unintelligible, way of speaking betokens a genuine author, who does not feel the necessity of explaining what to himself is a familiar fact. As was natural with one who was 'known unto the high-priest' (γνωστὸς τῷ ἀρχιερεῖ xviii. 15, 16), he evidently has a very clear conception of the relation of the two persons, though he has not definitely put it on paper. Secondly, so far as we are able to test the accuracy of his facts, they satisfy the test, i.e. Caiaphas is the actual high-priest. Thirdly, his account serves as a connecting link between scattered and apparently divergent notices in the New Testament[2]. Yet this episode about Annas in the history of the Passion is peculiar to St John[3].

The use of ὁ ἀρχιερεύς as applied to two different persons in St John is admirably illustrated by a passage in Josephus (*Ant.* xx. 9. 2). The high-priest Ananias (the Ananias of the Acts) has been deposed, and Ishmael the son of Phabi has succeeded (*Ant.* xx. 8. 8). Ishmael again has been set aside, and his place given to Joseph, surnamed Kabi (xx. 8. 11).

---

[1] The A. V. has taken unwarrantable liberties with ἀπέστειλεν in xviii. 24. It should be 'sent him' not 'had sent him.' The events are related in strict chronological order.

[2] e.g. Matt. xxvi. 3, 57 compared with Acts iv. 6.

[3] Keim's attempt (iii. p. 322) to set this episode of Annas aside is quite futile.

Shortly after, Joseph is deposed, and the office conferred upon
the younger Annas or Ananus, son of the Annas of the Gospels
(xx. 9. 1). A period of three months however witnesses the
fall of Ananus, and Jesus (Joshua) the son of Damnæus is
appointed (*ib.*). In spite of this, however, after these four
changes in the high-priestly office, when Ananias reappears
upon the scene, he is still called 'the high-priest' (ὁ ἀρχιερεύς
xx. 9. 2), and this title is applied to him, even as late as the
breaking out of the Judaic war (*B. J.* ii. 17. 6. 9), though in the
meantime there has been a fifth change[1] in the actual holder of
the high-priesthood. And this is not all. Ananias is designated 'the high-priest' in describing his dealings with the
actual high-priest even in the same sentence (*Ant.* xx. 9. 2
ὁ δὲ ἀρχιερεὺς 'Ανανίας καθ' ἑκάστην κ.τ.λ. ἦν γὰρ χρημάτων
ποριστικός· καθ' ἡμέραν γοῦν τὸν 'Αλβῖνον καὶ τὸν ἀρχιερέα
δώροις ἐθεράπευεν). This is at least as great an intermingling
of the use as in John xviii.; and is exactly of the same kind[2].
Again, the passage in Josephus gives an example of the employment of the plural (οἵ τε ἀρχιερεῖς ὅμοια κ.τ.λ.), a sufficiently
striking phenomenon. All this is perfectly natural in Josephus,
a contemporary and eye-witness, perfectly natural also in the
Fourth Evangelist, supposing him to be a contemporary and
eye-witness; but incredible in a forger, who could not have
failed to betray himself by some slip when treading upon such
delicate ground. Lastly, the prominence assigned by Josephus
to Ananias is a parallel to the case of Annas in the Gospel
and the Acts. If we had only a chapter or two of Josephus
detached from the sequence of the narrative, and read of
'Ananias the high-priest,' we should certainly suppose him to
have been the actual holder of the office at the time. It is
conceivable that some such mistaken inference has resulted in

---

[1] Jesus the son of Gamaliel appointed in place of Jesus the son of
Damnæus (*Ant.* xx. 9. 4).

[2] It is evident that the references in
vv. 13, 24 are to Caiaphas, those in
vv. 19, 22 to Annas, while *vv.* 15, 16

may be considered doubtful. On the
other hand Mr Sanday (p. 245) considers the title to apply to Caiaphas
throughout, a view which compels him
to regard the aorist ἀπέστειλεν in *v.*
24 as a pluperfect.

the expression 'Annas the high-priest and Caiaphas' in Acts
iv. 6.   Indeed it is quite possible that St Luke himself did not
know the precise facts, but had copied an authentic document,
in which an especially leading part had been assigned to
Annas[1].

2.   *The Jewish Festivals.*

We cannot fail to notice the large place which religious
festivals occupy in this Gospel.   They are much more prominent than in the Synoptic narrative.   The main incidents are
connected with them, and this applies not merely to the
Passover, but to the other feasts likewise.

(*a*)   *The Feast of Tabernacles* is described in John vii.   It
is introduced by a remarkable expression (ἦν δὲ ἐγγὺς ἡ ἑορτὴ
τῶν Ἰουδαίων ἡ σκηνοπηγία v. 2).   '*The* feast of the Jews'
was not in itself an unnatural way of designating the Feast of
Tabernacles.   For it was called by the rabbis גח 'the festival
par excellence[2],' and Josephus (*Ant.* viii. 4. 1) speaks of it as
'a feast of the utmost sanctity and importance among the
Hebrews' (ἑορτῆς σφόδρα παρὰ τοῖς Ἑβραίοις ἁγιωτάτης καὶ

---

[1] For the popular idea that the high-
priest had a sort of inspiration (John
xi. 51 'And this spake he not of himself, but being high-priest that year he
prophesied') comp. Josephus *B. J.* iii. 8.
3 περὶ κρίσεις ὀνείρων ἱκανὸς...αὐτὸς ὢν
ἱερεύς, and Philo *de Creat. Princ.* § 8 (II.
p. 367) ὁ πρὸς ἀλήθειαν ἱερεὺς εὐθύς
ἐστι προφήτης, the gift however being
in both passages extended to the
priesthood generally.   Other minor
references which show St John's acquaintance with Jewish rites and customs are (1) viii. 17, the necessity for
two witnesses (cf. Deut. xvii. 6, xix.
15, Matt. xviii. 16, 2 Cor. xiii. 1, Heb.
x. 28, 1 John v. 7 sq); (2) viii. 44, the
allusion to Cain (cf. 1 John iii. 12):
the argument appealed to certain ideas
prominent at the time which would
not have occurred to any writer of a
later date; (3) iv. 27, talking with a

woman, on which see above, p. 35;
(4) ii. 6, the purificatory rites on which
see Lightfoot, *ad loc.*; (5) marriage
customs, especially 'the friend of the
bridegroom' (iii. 29), a metaphor instinct with meaning, but it is only
when we enter into the Jewish practice
that this meaning comes out; (6)
funeral ceremonies, especially the form
of the grave (xi. 38, 41), and the mode
of burial (xii. 7, xix. 39, 40, xx. 1, 5,
7, 11), on which last point compare
Tacitus *Ann.* xvi. 6, where we read of
Poppæa, a Jewish proselyte, 'corpus
non igni abolitum, ut Romanus mos;
sed regum externorum consuetudine
differtum odoribus conditur.'   Most of
these passages are well illustrated from
rabbinical sources in Lightfoot's *Horae
Hebraicae.*

[2] See Smith's *Dictionary of the
Bible, s. v.*

μεγίστης). It was sufficiently prominent to attract the notice of the heathen, as Plutarch (*Symp.* iv. 6, *Op. Mor.* p. 671 sq.), who regards it as a sort of Dionysiac festival. Still, if the words ἡ ἑορτὴ τῶν Ἰουδαίων alone had been used, the Passover would probably have been meant. Hence the words ἡ σκηνοπηγία are added. A little later on (*v.* 37) St John speaks of the 'last, the great day of the feast' (ἐν τῇ ἐσχάτῃ ἡμέρᾳ τῇ μεγάλῃ τῆς ἑορτῆς), language which may mean either the last of the seven days, i.e. strictly speaking the last of the feast, or the eighth day, the holy convocation, which followed upon the seven. There seems however to have been no special sanctity about the seventh day[1]. The first was apparently much more important than the seventh. On the other hand it is urged that the eighth day did not properly belong to the feast, which lasted only seven days. But though the feast is sometimes spoken of as a seven days' feast, and the eighth day is not regarded (Deut. xvi. 13 sq., Ezek. xlv. 25), yet elsewhere the eighth day is reckoned as part of the feast, and a special prominence attached to it. This is the case in Numb. xxix. 35, in Neh. viii. 18, in 2 Macc. x. 6[2], in Philo and Josephus[3] and in Jewish writers generally[4]. I need not dwell upon the fact, to which attention has been frequently drawn, that on this occasion our Lord bases His discourse (vii. 37 sq., viii. 12 sq.) upon the two most prominent features in the ceremonial of the day, the pouring out of the water of Siloam upon the altar, and the illumination of the city by flaming torches lighted in the Temple area[5]. It will be sufficient to notice, first, that as in

---

[1] Buxtorf, *Syn. Jud.* xvi. p. 327, gives a certain prominence to it in his description of the modern Jewish celebrations of the tabernacles: see too Groddeke in Ugol. xviii. p. 534.

[2] μετ' εὐφροσύνης ἦγον ἡμέρας ὀκτὼ σκηνωμάτων τρόπον, 2 Macc. x. 6.

[3] ἑπτὰ δὲ ἡμέραις ὀγδόην ἐπισφραγίζεται, καλέσας ἐξόδιον αὐτήν, οὐκ ἐκείνης ὡς ἔοικε μόνον τῆς ἑορτῆς ἀλλὰ πασῶν τῶν ἐτησίων ὅσας κατηριθμήσαμεν, Philo *Septen.* §24, p. 298 M.; ἐφ' ἡμέρας

ὀκτὼ ἑορτὴν ἄγοντας, Jos. *Ant.* iii. 10. 4, and so a little lower down ἀνίενται δὲ ἀπὸ παντὸς ἔργου κατὰ τὴν ὀγδόην ἡμέραν.

[4] *Succah* iv. 4 (hymnus et gaudium octo dies), iv. 9 (omnes octo dies), v. 6 (octavo die redibant ad sortes); cf. Gem. *Hieros.* in Ugol. xviii. p. 492.

[5] On the ceremonies of the eighth day see esp. Ewald *Alterth.* p. 404. The people broke up their tents and repaired to the Temple. As the dwelling

our Lord's discourse, so in the ceremonial itself, the lighting of
the lamps followed the pouring out of the water, and was
intimately connected therewith; secondly, that it took place in
the court of the women where the treasury (γαζοφυλάκιον)
stood[1], and where our Lord was speaking at the time (viii. 20).
Thus He would be able to point to the candelabra. Thirdly,
it is worthy of remark that Philo also incidentally connects the
same two images with the Feast of Tabernacles[2].

(b)   *The Feast of Dedication.*   This festival (τὰ ἐγκαίνια) is
mentioned by St John alone, and it is remarkable how thorough
and confident a knowledge of it is implied in his narrative.
Here, again, the mode in which it is introduced deserves notice,
'At that time the feast of dedication was held at Jerusalem'
(x. 22 ἐγένετο τότε τὰ ἐγκαίνια ἐν τοῖς Ἱεροσολύμοις). There
is no mention made, as in the case of other feasts (e.g. ii. 13,
iv. 45, v. 1, vii. 8), of going up to Jerusalem. For the ἐγκαίνια,
unlike the Passover, Tabernacles and Pentecost, might be
celebrated anywhere (see Lightfoot *ad loc.*). 'It was winter,'
we are told. Now the festival was held to commemorate the
purification and dedication of the altar and temple after pollution by Antiochus Epiphanes B.C. 167. This event and the
institution of the annual festival are described in 1 Macc. iv.
36 sq., where Judas Maccabæus directs that the commemoration
should take place 'from year to year by the space of eight days,
from the five and twentieth day of the month Chisleu (*v.* 59).'
Now the month Chisleu falls in November and December,
coinciding more nearly with December, and the Jewish winter
is reckoned to commence on the fifteenth of Chisleu. Hence
the notice of the season of the year in St John is strictly
accurate. Yet it is introduced quite incidentally, apparently to

in tents symbolized the wilderness life,
itself a deliverance from bondage, so
the eighth day would be taken to
signify the end of their wanderings
when they settled in the land of
promise.

[1] See below, p. 169.

[2] ἡ μὲν γὰρ δικαιοσύνης ἐστὶν ἡ δὲ
ἀδικίας ἀρχή τε καὶ πηγή, καὶ ἡ μὲν
ἀσκίου φωτός, ἡ δὲ σκοτοῦς συγγενής,
Philo *Septen.* § 24, not as read in the
ordinary texts, but as given in Tisch.
Philonea.

explain the fact that Jesus was not teaching in the open air but under cover. 'It was winter, and Jesus was walking in the Temple in Solomon's porch.'

(c) *The Feast of the Passover.* Graphic touches which illustrate St John's acquaintance with the details of this feast are his references to the paschal victim (xix. 36), to the danger of ceremonial pollution (xviii. 28), and to the Preparation (παρασκευή xix. 14, 31, 42), a term which he employs in common with the Synoptists (Matt. xxvii. 62, Mark xv. 42, Luke xxiii. 54), but, unlike St Matthew, uses twice without the article, and in one case defines more accurately by the addition of the words τοῦ πάσχα (xix. 14), implying that the term was not restricted to the Passover[1]. Lastly, the parenthetical remark on xix. 31, 'For the day of that sabbath was a high day' (ἦν γὰρ μεγάλη ἡ ἡμέρα ἐκείνου τοῦ σαββάτου) points to the special sanctity of the day as a double sabbath, the sabbath alike of the week and of the festival, hebdomadal as well as Paschal.

(iii) *The Topography of Jerusalem.*

From this review of the festivals we pass on to consider the localities mentioned in the Fourth Gospel, merely premising that the complete destruction of Jerusalem by Titus and Hadrian would have gone far to obliterate traces of the actual sites, and would thus have rendered the work of a subsequent forger more than usually exposed to danger of errors.

(a) *The Temple.* We start with the Temple. Observe the familiarity with which the Evangelist moves about among the sacred precincts. He mentions the Porch of Solomon, 'the east portico,' as Josephus describes it to us (*Ant.* xx. 9. 7), 'on the outer part of the Temple, lying in a deep valley with walls four hundred cubits (long), built of square and very white stones' of enormous size. It was the work of Solomon, and was left

---

[1] This was apparently the case (Lightfoot, *Hor. Heb.* on Mark xv. 42).

untouched in Herod's restoration[1]. A covered portico of so
vast an extent was doubtless a favourite place of resort and
shelter in winter time, to which its eastern aspect, catching the
warmth of the morning sun, would not be a disadvantage, and
thus it was a natural scene for our Lord's teaching. Another
spot where our Lord is stated to have taught is the treasury,
the γαζοφυλάκιον (viii. 20). This word St John employs in
common with the Synoptists (Mark xii. 41 sq., Luke xxi. 1), but
with characteristic exactness, he gives us additional information.
The other Evangelists merely speak of casting money 'into the
treasury,' confining the term apparently to the corban-chests,
and this is probably the use in Josephus also, when he says
(*Ant.* xix. 6. 1) that Herod Agrippa hung up a certain golden
chain which Caligula had given him 'within the temple-pre-
cincts over the treasury (ὑπὲρ τοῦ γαζοφυλακίου).' St John
however shows that the expression was extended to embrace
the chamber in which the chests were placed. This chamber
was situated in the outer front of the Temple in the court of
the women. Thus it would be a frequented spot, since women
could penetrate no further, and St Luke (*l. c.*) calls special
attention to the crowd of people which passed to and fro (ἐθεώρει
πῶς ὁ ὄχλος βάλλει χαλκὸν εἰς τὸ γαζοφυλάκιον). How
natural to take advantage of this concourse, and how significant
the addition 'and no man laid hands on him (viii. 20),' when we
recollect that the Sanhedrin held its meetings[2] hard by between
the court of the women and the inner court, within a stone's
throw of the speaker.

(b)   *The Watercourses of Jerusalem.*

(1)   *Bethesda, Bethsaida,* or *Bethzatha* (v. 2). The Evangelist describes this as 'a pool near the sheep (gate)[3]' (ἐπὶ τῇ
προβατικῇ κολυμβήθρα). The 'sheep gate' is mentioned more

---

[1] Herod's restoration of the Temple
was so complete, that it is unlikely
that in the second century a distinction would have been preserved between what was, and what was not,
included in it.

[2] In a hall called Gazzith (Lightfoot, I. p. 2005).

[3] A.V. 'sheep market.'

than once by Nehemiah (iii. 1, 32, xii. 39 ἡ πύλη ἡ λεγομένη προβατική), but it is difficult to fix its exact position.   It was this uncertainty of locality, doubtless, which led to the omission of the words ἐπὶ τῇ προβατικῇ in the Curetonian and Peschito Syriac, and to the reading of the Codex Vaticanus ἐν τοῖς Ἱεροσολύμοις προβατικὴ κολυμβήθρα, which understands the two descriptions as defining one and the same spot.   However it is clear that others also, besides the scribe of א, explained προβατική as an adjective describing κολυμβήθρα. Thus Eusebius in his *Onomasticon* makes the following statement : Βηζαθὰ κολυμβήθρα ἐν Ἱερουσαλήμ, ἥτις ἐστὶν ἡ προβατική[1], and goes on to derive the name from the animal sacrifices which used to take place there (παρ᾽ ὃ καὶ προβατικὴ καλεῖται διὰ τὰ θύματα).   And this interpretation may have produced the reading which we find in א.   It is possible, however, that Eusebius may have got hold of the rabbinical word פריבטאות or פרובטיא (Buxtorf p. 1796), which seems to mean 'a bath,' unless indeed this word has come from προβατική, the bath as well as the gate bearing the name.   But it does not follow that Eusebius and the Bordeaux Pilgrims were right in their locality.   Where then must we place the pool ?   The question would be answered if we could fix the position of the 'sheep gate.'   This however is only roughly possible.   From the notices in Nehemiah we draw the conclusion that the gate was situated somewhere near the Temple, on the east side of the city.   The traditional site identifies it with St Stephen's gate, north of the Temple area, but there is no sufficient ground for

---

[1] He proceeds τὸ παλαιὸν πέντε στοὰς ἔχουσα· καὶ νῦν δείκνυται ἐν ταῖς αὐτόθι λίμναις διδύμοις, ὧν ἑκατέρα ἐκ τῶν κατ᾽ ἔτος ὑετῶν πληροῦται, θατέρα δὲ παραδόξως πεφοινιγμένον δείκνυσι τὸ ὕδωρ, ἴχνος, ὥς φασι, φέρουσα τῶν πάλαι καθαιρομένων ἐν αὐτῇ ἱερείων. Jerome, knowing the locality better, says quae vocabatur προβατική, Hier. *de situ et nom.* (op. III. p. 182 *ed.* Vallarsi). The curious red colour of the waters to which Eusebius draws attention is mentioned by the Bordeaux Pilgrims in their description : Interius vero civitatis sunt piscinae gemellares, quinque porticus habentes, quae appellantur Betsaida. Ibi aegri multorum annorum sanabantur : aquam autem habent eae piscinae in modum coccini turbatam, quoted by Wesseling, *Itineraria* (1735), p. 589.

this; and Robinson's conjecture (I. p. 342) that Bethesda is the intermittent spring in the Upper Pool known as the ' Fountain of the Virgin[1]' at all events accords with the uninterpolated[2] account of St John, which implies nothing miraculous in the water itself, but describes what was evidently an intermittent and medicinal, perhaps (from the allusions quoted above to the redness of the water) a chalybeate spring.   However we need not pursue the enquiry further.   Enough has been said to show that from early times much uncertainty was felt as to the actual site.   What forger then would have ventured to introduce, or if he introduced, to localise, so obscure and contested a spot ?   Who but one thoroughly familiar with the scene would have been content to describe the position by so elliptical and ambiguous a phrase as ἐπὶ τῇ προβατικῇ, employing an adjective without a qualifying noun, a phrase which, as we have seen, has been interpreted to mean 'sheep market,' 'sheep gate,' ' sheep pool'?   The naturalness of this vague allusion is the best guarantee for the authenticity of the narrative.

(2)   *Siloam* (ix. 7).   Attention has been drawn already[3] to the derivation of this word, and the symbolical use which St John makes of this derivation.   The topographical question however requires a separate treatment.   Fortunately the situation, unlike that of Bethesda, can hardly be considered doubtful. Siloam is frequently mentioned and described by Josephus, and the tradition of its position is tolerably continuous.   It bears the same name now, *Silwân*, as in our Lord's time.   It lies at the mouth of the Tyropœon valley, close to its junction with the valley of Hinnom, and is fed by a stream issuing somewhere from the heart of the rocks of Jerusalem.   Its proximity to Jerusalem is evidenced by the well-attested tradition that water was brought from it for the libations customary at the Feast of Tabernacles, and by the name which it gave to one of the gates

---

[1] It was connected by an underground passage with the pool of Siloam.

[2] Textual criticism compels us to omit the words ἐκδεχομένων...νοσήματι (*vv.* 3, 4), which are found in the Textus Receptus.

[3] See above, pp. 141, 150.

of Jerusalem, ' the water gate.'   It was both a fountain and a
pool.   The fountain (πηγή) is mentioned by Josephus (B. J. v.
12. 2), the pool or tank by Nehemiah (iii. 15, ברכה) and St John
(κολυμβήθρα)[1].   The derivation of the name, which means an
'aqueduct' or 'conduit' (from שלח to send) seems to imply
that the Siloah properly so-called was not the pool, but the
stream which feeds it or which flows from it.   The points on
which the Evangelist incidentally displays his exact knowledge
are two : first, he apparently places the pool near the Temple,
for it is improbable that a blind man would be sent on a long
journey ; secondly, he is aware of, and draws a lesson from, the
Hebrew meaning of the name, in which he sees a spiritual
significance.   Long ago these very waters had been invested by
Isaiah (viii. 6) with a symbolical interpretation.   The contrast
between the 'waters of Shiloah that go softly' and the 'waters
of the River (i.e. the Euphrates), strong and many' typified the
contrast between Judah and Assyria, between the quiet dwelling
in Jerusalem under Jehovah and the overwhelming of a foreign
conquest.   This idea of an indigenous stream, the possession of
the favoured people, 'the river, the streams whereof shall make
glad the city of God' (Ps. xlvi. 4 ; cf. Isaiah xxxiii. 21), bespoke
the Messianic hope.   It foretold the stream of running,
life-giving waters, which should issue from the temple-rock,
and revive the nations.   It recalled and renewed the type of
the waters flowing from the rock smitten by Moses, which rock
was understood by St Paul to be the Christ (1 Cor. x. 4).   Thus
St John seizes upon the current thought, and extends its
application.   The Healer who sends the blind man is Himself
'the sent[2].'

(3)   *Cedron* (xviii. 1).   This is undoubtedly the Kidron of

---

[1] Isaiah (viii. 6) has simply מי השלח
(LXX τὸ ὕδωρ τοῦ Σιλωάμ).

[2] Epiphanius rightly connects the
two passages. After quoting Isaiah viii.
6, he continues ὕδωρ γὰρ Σιλωάμ ἐστι
διδασκαλία τοῦ ἀπεσταλμένου· τίς δ' ἂν
εἴη οὗτος ἀλλ' ἢ ὁ Κύριος ἡμῶν Ἰησοῦς, ὁ

ἀπὸ τοῦ θεοῦ πατρὸς αὐτοῦ ἀπεσταλμένος;
Haer. xxxv. 3.   So the ps.-Basil on
Isaiah viii. 6, τίς οὖν ὁ ἀπεσταλμένος
καὶ ἀψοφητὶ ῥέων ἢ περὶ οὗ εἴρηται ὁ
Κύριος ἀπέστειλέν με; Basil, op. I. p.
536 A.

the Old Testament (2 Sam. xv. 23 etc.), and is mentioned by St John alone of the Evangelists. The common text runs πέραν τοῦ χειμάρρου τῶν Κέδρων ('the torrent of the Cedars'), and the passage has a peculiar interest because it has furnished the text for an elaborate attack upon the personality of the Evangelist. Baur and Hilgenfeld after him (see Ewald *Jahrbuch*, vi. p. 118) have pointed triumphantly to the undoubted fact that Κέδρων is the Hebrew word קדרון 'dark,' so called probably from its turbid stream[1], and have proceeded to argue that the Evangelist in his ignorance has imagined it to be the genitive plural of κέδρος 'a cedar.' The writer therefore, they conclude, cannot have been the Apostle St John, who, as a Jew, must have been aware of the true derivation of the name.

Before admitting this conclusion, let us look the facts fairly in the face. In Josephus the form Κέδρων occurs frequently (*B. J.* v. 2. 3, v. 6. 1, v. 12. 2; *Ant.* vii. 1. 5, viii. 1. 5, ix. 7. 3) used as a declinable noun. This is quite after Josephus' manner in dealing with Hebrew substantives. In the LXX the expression ὁ χειμάρρους Κέδρων is employed without an article, e.g. 2 Sam. xv. 23 (its second occurrence in this verse); 2 Kings xxiii. 6, 12; 2 Chron. xv. 16, xxix. 16, xxx. 14; Jer. xxxi. 40. But in two passages it is found with the plural article—2 Sam. xv. 23 (on the first occurrence), and 1 Kings xv. 13 ἐν τῷ χειμάρρῳ τῶν Κέδρων. This is the reading of AB in both passages. Now it is quite clear that the LXX translators did not mistake the meaning of the word. Otherwise they could not have written, as they generally do, ὁ χειμάρρους Κέδρων, a solecism on this supposition; but we should have had in every case ὁ χειμάρρους τῶν Κέδρων. Therefore either there is a corruption in the best manuscripts of the LXX, or ὁ χειμάρρους τῶν Κέδρων was considered a legitimate Greek rendering of the Hebrew phrase 'the brook Kidron.' Turning now to the passage in St John, we find that there is great uncertainty as to the actual reading, authorities varying between τῶν Κέδρων, τοῦ Κέδρου and τοῦ

[1] Compare Ps. cxx. 5 'the tents of Kedar' i.e. the dark-skinned folk.

Κέδρων[1], and that the preponderance of evidence is either for τῶν Κέδρων or τοῦ Κέδρου. But the necessity for making a selection suggests another view. What then is the probability? I believe the true account to be that the original reading was τοῦ Κέδρων; and this for two reasons. First, it is the intermediate reading, the reading which explains the other two, whereas neither of the other two will explain either this or each other[2]. Secondly, it is much more probable that τοῦ Κέδρων would be changed into τῶν Κέδρων and τοῦ Κέδρου, than conversely. Indeed the converse change in either case is hardly conceivable, the tendency being to assimilate terminations. And unless τῶν Κέδρων be a legitimate rendering of 'the brook Kidron,' the corruption has taken place, and has still more completely obliterated the original reading, in the LXX. This solution was adopted by Griesbach and Lachmann, even before the discovery of ℵ, and recommends itself to Renan, Meyer and Sanday. Tregelles gives it as an alternative. On the other hand Tischendorf reads τοῦ Κέδρου.

But suppose τῶν Κέδρων is after all, as Westcott considers, the right reading, what then? The Septuagint shows that it was held to be an adequate rendering of the Hebrew נחל קדרון. We must suppose therefore that it was the equivalent familiar to Greek ears, and that St John writing to Greeks would not hesitate to employ it. In confirmation of this view we may notice the general tendency to assimilate Hebrew terminations to Greek forms, which has coined the Greek plural σάββατα out of the Hebrew noun שבתון as though σάββατον. As Κέδρων was only used with χειμάρρους, the change to the genitive would be natural[3]. Again, the temptation to extract

[1] BCL, with the bulk of the Greek manuscripts and the Gothic Version, have των κεδρων; AΔS, the Vulgate and certain manuscripts (c, (e) f, g) of the Old Latin, the Peschito and the Philoxenian Syriac and the Armenian have του κεδρων.

[2] A good instance of the application of this test is the celebrated passage 1 Tim. iii. 16, where ὅς is to be preferred as accounting for both the variants θεός and ὅ.

[3] In Ps. lxxxii. 10 ℵAB read εν τω χειμμαρρω κεισων (κισσων A) anarthrous, but some inferior manuscripts have των κισσων.

a Greek sense out of Hebrew names is exemplified in the derivations given to Jerusalem and Essene[1]. If by an accident
there were any cedars in the valley, the adoption of this
Grecised form would be facilitated.

(c)   Scenes illustrating our Lord's Passion.

Bethany is mentioned by the Synoptists in connexion with
the triumphal entry into Jerusalem (Mark xi. 1, Luke xix. 29),
with our Lord's retirement during Holy Week (Matt. xxi. 17,
Mark xi. 11, 12), especially the feast at the house of Simon the
leper (Matt. xxvi. 6, Mark xiv. 3; cf. John xii. 1), and with the
Ascension (Luke xxiv. 50). It occurs in St John's narrative
likewise as the scene of the raising of Lazarus (John xi. 1, 18),
and he exhibits his acquaintance with the place in a characteristic way by mentioning that it was distant fifteen furlongs
from Jerusalem (xi. 18, Ἦν δὲ Βηθανία ἐγγὺς τῶν Ἱεροσολύμων
ὡς ἀπὸ σταδίων δεκαπέντε[2]). This statement exactly accords
with the account which a modern writer gives of its situation.
'We reached it in three-quarters of an hour from the Damascus
gate. This gives a distance of a little less than two Roman
miles from the eastern part of the city' (Robinson I. p. 431).

Gethsemane is not named in the Fourth Gospel, but this
does not prevent St John from adding to our stock of knowledge regarding the scene of the Agony, which he describes
more precisely than the Synoptists, calling it 'a garden' (κῆπος

---

[1] Jos. *B. J.* vi. 10. 1, διὰ τοῦτο
ἱεράσατο τῷ θεῷ πρῶτος καὶ τὸ ἱερὸν
πρῶτος δειξάμενος Ἱεροσόλυμα τὴν πόλιν
προσηγόρευσε, Σόλυμα καλουμένην πρότε
ρον, Philo *quod omn. prob.* 12, II. p. 457
Ἐσσαῖοι...διαλέκτου ἑλληνικῆς παρωνύ
μοι ὁσιότητος; cf. § 13, p. 459, and
fragm. II. p. 632 (*ed.* Mangey). The
same tendency is to be seen in English
in the forms Charterhouse, Barmouth
etc.

[2] No inference can be drawn as to
the date of the composition of the
Gospel from the use of the imperfect

tense. The Evangelist sometimes uses
the imperfect (xviii. 1, xix. 41, 42),
sometimes the present (v. 2), occasionally both tenses together (iv. 6. 9).
Similarly St Luke uses the imperfect
(Luke iv. 29), and we may compare
Kinglake's *Crimea* III. pp. 38, 117, 118,
122, 286, which is unquestionably the
narrative of one who was an eyewitness of the events he relates, and
who writes not half a century later,
but within a very few years of the
occurrences.

xviii. 1) instead of simply 'an enclosure' (χωρίον Matt. xxvi. 36, Mark xiv. 32), and defining its position as 'over the brook Cedron.' Can we wonder if the events of that evening were burnt into the memory of the beloved disciple in letters of fire?

Again, he alone of the Evangelists informs us that the Crucifixion took place outside the city-walls (xix. 20). This statement is thrown out quite naturally, and no point is made of it, but it is borne out by the author of the Epistle to the Hebrews (xiii. 11 sq.), who sees in it a deep moral lesson. And no one denies that this Epistle was written at some time or other in the first century after Christ.

(iv) *The Topography of Palestine generally.*

As far therefore as knowledge of the locality of the Holy City is concerned, our author has ably stood the test applied to him. Let us now take a wider sweep and investigate his acquaintance with the geography of Palestine at large.

(*a*) *Galilee.* As is well known, the Fourth Evangelist directs his attention chiefly to our Lord's ministry in Jerusalem. We do not therefore expect him to give us many fresh details about the topography of Galilee. However he mentions Cana in Galilee[1] (ii. 1, 11, iv. 46, xxi. 2), and he gives a new designation to the Lake of Gennesareth, which he calls 'the sea of Tiberias[2]' (vi. 1, xxi. 1). Again, in describing the events which clustered round the Feeding of the Five Thousand, his varying use of πέραν 'on the other side,' now for the west, now again for the east shore of the lake, bespeaks the eye-

---

[1] Cana is named several times by Josephus (*Vit.* 16, *B. J.* i. 17. 5, *Ant.* xiii. 15. 1), but the references do not throw much light on its position. The traditional site is *Kefr Kenna*, about four miles north-east of Nazareth, and this identification is as old as S. Willibald in the eighth century. Robinson however prefers a village, *Kana el-Jelil*, some five miles further north, and the spelling of the name (with a *Koph* instead of a *Caph*) is more closely allied to the representative in the Curetonian and Peschito *Katna*, though the *t* is not represented.

[2] The city of Tiberias also occurs (vi. 23). As it was built by Herod Antipas (Jos. *Ant.* xviii. 2. 3, *B. J.* ii. 9. 1), it could hardly have given its name to the lake as early as the date of our Lord's ministry. The designation however 'sea of Tiberias' is found in Josephus (*B. J.* iii. 3. 5), before St John wrote his Gospel.

witness, who, as he records the miracle, fancies himself enacting
the scene once more, and speaks as if he were himself first here,
then there.

(b)   *Judæa.*

(1)   *Ephraim.*   In xi 54 St John describes our Lord's
retirement 'into the country near the desert, into a city called
Ephraim' (ἐγγὺς τῆς ἐρήμου, εἰς 'Εφραὶμ λεγομένην πόλιν).
This 'desert of Judah' seems to mean the broad mountain
pasture lands near Jerusalem, which were sparsely inhabited, for
in the Gospel narrative 'the desert' (ἡ ἔρημος) is generally
associated with 'the mountain district' (τὸ ὄρος).   This city
Ephraim (or Ephrem) is noticed here only in the New Testament.   But it is mentioned by Josephus (B. J. iv. 9. 9) in
connexion with the mountain district (ἡ ὀρεινή) north of
Judæa, as a small fort (πολίχνιον) captured and garrisoned by
Vespasian when on his way westward to fight against Vitellius.
Josephus couples it with Bethel, and it is a coincidence that,
where it occurs in 2 Chron. xiii. 19, Bethel is named with it.
The two places were probably not far apart.   Mr Robinson
(I. p. 447) identifies it with *El-Tayibeh,* some eight miles north
of Jerusalem.   In the passage in the Chronicles referred to,
the Kthib has *Ephron* עֶפְרוֹן, but the Qri *Ephraim* עֶפְרִין,
perhaps a dual form like Mizraim, the Upper and Lower Egypt.
It is mentioned also in the Talmud (Neubauer p. 155).   The
Ephraim of St John must not be confused with the wood of
Ephraim of 2 Sam. xviii. 6, or the Ephraim of 2 Sam. xiii. 23,
both of which are spelt with an *Aleph* like the patriarch
Ephraim; or with the district called Apherema in 1 Macc. xi.
34.   Mr Robinson (*l. c.*) identifies it with Ophrah עָפְרָה of
Benjamin (1 Sam. xiii. 17, Josh. xviii. 23).   This may or may
not be the case[1].   The Qri of 2 Chron. *l. c.* and the passage in

[1] It is noticeable that in the Codex
Alexandrinus Εφραιμ is the LXX rendering of the other Ophrah, the birth-
place of Gideon, in Judges viii. 27, ix. 5.
Eus. *Onom. s. v.* says καὶ ἐστι καὶ νῦν
κώμη 'Εφραὶμ μεγίστη περὶ τὰ ὅρια

Αἰλίας ὡς ἀπὸ σημείων κ'; cf. Hier.
Op. III. p. 203, who repeats the same
statement.   But if Mr Robinson's
identification is correct, the Ephraim
of St John is the Aphra of Eus. *Onom.*
s. v.

Josephus are sufficient for my purpose. Whether the Qri be
the right reading or not, it shows that such a place existed just
in the region where, from St John's account, we should expect
it to be.

(2) *Bethany* (i. 28). This is certainly the correct reading
in this passage, and accordingly St John has been charged[1]
with gross ignorance as not being aware that Bethany was near
Jerusalem. In the light of the accurate and minute acquaintance with topography elsewhere displayed by the Apostle, such
an accusation is hardly worth the trouble of refutation.

We may however briefly reply, first, that the writer carefully
distinguished the two places, speaking of one as 'Bethany
beyond Jordan' (i. 28), of the other as 'Bethany the town of
Mary and her sister Martha' (xi. 1); secondly, that he accurately described the Bethany of chapter xi. as 'nigh unto
Jerusalem about fifteen furlongs off[2]'; thirdly, that if we assume
with most commentators the identification of Bethany beyond
Jordan with 'the place where John was at first baptizing'
(x. 40), our Lord is represented at the time as out of
Judæa (xi. 7, ἄγωμεν εἰς τὴν Ἰουδαίαν πάλιν), as journeying
from the one Bethany to the other, a journey which occupies
three days (xi. 39, τεταρταῖος γάρ ἐστι), which takes Him into
Judæa once more (xi. 7, ἄγωμεν εἰς τὴν Ἰουδαίαν πάλιν), and
into danger from a position of security (xi. 8). Personally I
prefer to keep these scenes of St John's baptism distinct, and
to place the Bethany of chapter i. somewhere in the Upper
Jordan[3]. It was probably an obscure place. 'In any case,' as
Mr Sanday truly says (p. 45), 'the distinction between two
places having the same name is a mark of local knowledge
which is unlike fiction[4].'

(3) *Ænon near to Salim* (iii. 23). Here again we are

---

[1] By Paulus and Bolten; see Lücke
I. p. 394.

[2] See above, p. 175.

[3] This is the view of Dr Caspari,
quoted by Sanday, p. 45.

[4] In Mark viii. 22 there is a well-
supported variant Βηθανιαν for Βηθ-
σαιδαν, which may contain some underlying foundation of fact, pointing to a
Bethany in the north-east of Galilee.

introduced by the Evangelist to fresh names.   It is true that
in Joshua xv. 32 mention is made in the tribe of Judah of
שׁלחים ועין (Cod. A, Σελεείμ, A.V. 'Shilhim and Ain'); but
neither name corresponds exactly to the notice in St John.
Moreover the places mentioned in the Old Testament lie in the
arid country south of Judæa (see Grove in Smith's *Dictionary
of the Bible, s. v.* Salim).   The most probable site of the
Salim of the Fourth Gospel is that assigned to it by Eusebius
and Jerome near the Jordan, eight Roman miles south of
Scythopolis.   In Jerome's time it was called Salimias.   A
Salim has been discovered by Van de Velde (*Memoir* p. 345 sq.)
exactly in this position, six English miles south of Beisân
(Bethshan), and two miles west of Jordan.   The name Ænon
fully bears out St John's description of the place, 'there
was much water (πολλὰ ὕδατα) there,' the plural noun indicating 'many fountains' or 'springs.'   Evidently therefore
Ænon was not situated on the Jordan itself.

These last two notices are especially interesting as showing
how carefully the successive stages of John the Baptist's
preaching are brought out in the Fourth Gospel.   We find
him first at the lower fords of Jericho 'beyond Jordan,' ὅπου
ἦν Ἰωάννης τὸ πρῶτον βαπτίζων (x. 40; cf. Matt. iii. 1).   We
meet with him next at Bethany (i. 28, A.V. 'Bethabara')
'beyond Jordan,' probably at the upper fords.   Lastly, his
headquarters are at Ænon, near Salim (iii. 23).   Thus we seem
able to trace his course northward, and the successive changes
of scene bear out what we gather from the more general
account with which St Luke supplies us.   Though John's
native town is in the hill country of Judæa (Luke i. 39), yet
he is apprehended and put to death by Herod, the tetrarch of
Galilee (Luke iii. 19, 20), and therefore must, before his arrest,
have passed within Herod's jurisdiction.   The minuteness of
detail which in the Fourth Gospel characterizes the episodes in
which John the Baptist takes part, becomes doubly significant
when we consider the great probability that John the Apostle
had been in his early days a disciple of the Baptist.

II.

The Writer was an Eye-witness of the Events recorded.

In a striking passage in one of his works[1] Auguste Sabatier draws attention to two characteristics of this Gospel which run side by side: that though in its teaching it is the most dogmatic, yet at the same time in its narrative it is the most vivid of the Four Gospels. We are apt to forget this latter point in the absorbing eagerness with which we fix our attention upon the sublimity of the doctrines inculcated. Yet this vividness of description is the best guarantee for the conclusion that the writer was not merely a Palestinian Jew, but an actual eye-witness of the events which he records. We shall be compelled to treat this part of our subject in a very cursory and incomplete manner.

(i) *The minuteness and exactness of detail which he exhibits.*

Sometimes these minute notices stand more or less closely in connexion with the progress of the story; sometimes they are detached personal reminiscences which apparently struck the writer at the time, and have dwelt in his memory since. Such a reminiscence, introduced *apropos* of nothing, is the incident recorded by St Mark (xiv. 51 sq.) of the young man clad with the linen cloth, which has been generally interpreted as an allusion to the history of the Evangelist himself. I shall divide what I have to say on this subject under the following heads: (1) Time, (2) Place, (3) Persons, (4) Incidents.

(1) *Time.* The chronology of our Lord's life can be gathered from St John's Gospel alone. In the other Evangelists the incidents are often grouped together with little or no reference to their chronology. This is especially the case with St Luke, who, having neither been present himself at the events, nor, like St Mark, especially attached to one who was himself

---

[1] A. Sabatier, *Essai sur les sources de la vie de Jésus* (1866), p. 34.

present, is of the four the farthest removed from the position of
an eye-witness. The minute exactness of St John's chronology
shows itself most particularly in his record of the first (i. 29,
35, 43, ii. 1) and of the last week (xii. 1, 12 etc.) of the narrative,
but it is present throughout (iv. 40, 43, vi. 22, vii. 14, 37, x. 22,
xi. 6, 17). It arises in great measure from the part which he
himself has in the drama. It extends even to the hour of the
day (i. 39, iv. 6, 52, xix. 14), or, if not the hour, the time
approximately (iii. 2, vi. 16, xiii. 30, xviii. 28, xx. 19, xxi. 3, 4).

(2) *Place.* We have had occasion already to allude to the
increased definiteness to be observed in the Fourth Gospel in
this respect[1]. All the incidents are referred to their locality.
Compare this feature with the other Gospels, e.g. St Luke's
account of Martha and Mary, Luke x. 38, εἰς κώμην τινά, with
John xi. 1, ἀπὸ Βηθανίας ἐκ τῆς κώμης Μαρίας καὶ Μάρθας
τῆς ἀδελφῆς αὐτῆς. It runs through the whole narrative, e.g.
vi. 59, ἐν συναγωγῇ διδάσκων ἐν Καφαρναούμ, viii. 20, ἐν τῷ
γαζοφυλακίῳ, x. 22, ἐν τῷ ἱερῷ ἐν τῇ στοᾷ τοῦ Σολομῶνος.
Notice the precision with which on two occasions the distance
of the boat from the shore is recorded, measured by the
practised eye of the fisherman, vi. 19, ὡς σταδίους εἴκοσι πέντε ἢ
τριάκοντα, xxi. 8, ὡς ἀπὸ πηχῶν διακοσίων, and for his greater
chronological accuracy contrast the Fourth Evangelist with
St Luke in the scenes of St Peter's denial (xviii. 15 sq.),
remembering that the narrator is 'the other disciple who was
known unto the high-priest,' himself a spectator throughout
the terrible tragedy.

In all these details we recognise the hand of the personal
disciple, and it would be strange indeed if an author with such
opportunities did not produce more exact and precise results
than one who, like St Luke, was the disciple of one who was not
even himself a personal disciple.

(3) *Persons.* Sayings, instead of being left vaguely general,
are attributed to the speakers by name, e.g. i. 41, 45, 46

[1] See above, p. 168 sq.

(bis), 48, 49 of Andrew, Philip and Nathanael, vi. 7, 8 Andrew
and Philip, 68 Peter, xi. 16 Thomas, xii. 4 Judas Iscariot,
21 Andrew and Philip again, xiii. 8, 9 Peter, 24, 25 Peter and
John, 36, 37 Peter again, xiv. 8 Philip, 22 Judas not Iscariot,
xx. 25 sq. Thomas, xxi. 3 Peter, 7 Peter and John, 15 sq.,
20 sq. Peter.   This exactness is more noticeable when we have
an opportunity of comparing the incidents with the Synoptic
records, as in the miracle of the feeding of the Five Thousand,
where the objection on the part of the disciples is left general
(Mark vi. 37 λέγουσι) instead of being placed in the mouth of
Philip (John vi. 7), or the feast at Bethany, where the loving
ministrations of Mary (John xii. 3) are vaguely assigned to
'a woman' (Matt. xxvi. 7, Mark xiv. 3 γύνη), and where the
expressed discontent of Judas (John xii. 4) is robbed of half its
force by being generalised (Matt. xxvi. 8 οἱ μαθηταί, Mark xiv.
4 τινες).   Or again take the scene of the betrayal, where a
flood of light is thrown upon that part of the drama when we
learn from St John that it was St Peter (John xviii. 10) who
with characteristic impulsiveness drew his sword in his Master's
defence[1].

(4) *Incidents.* The Fourth Evangelist acquaints us with
a number of details, which, though in some cases unimportant
in themselves, add greatly to the life-like character of his
portraiture of events.   The six waterpots of water containing
two or three firkins apiece (ii. 6), the thirty and eight years
during which the man lying at the pool of Bethesda had been
afflicted (v. 5), the bag in which our Lord and His disciples
kept their common fund (xii. 6), the sop given to Judas
(xiii. 26), the three languages of the title on the cross (xix. 20)[2],
the four parts into which the tunic (χιτών) and the cloak
(ἱμάτια) were divided (xix. 23), the water and the blood which
issued from the Saviour's side (xix. 34), the weight of the

---

[1] The Synoptists are perhaps de-
signedly vague (Matt. xxvi. 51, εἰς
τῶν μετὰ Ἰησοῦ, Mark xiv. 47, εἰς τῶν
παρεστηκότων, Luke xxii. 50, εἰς τις ἐξ

αὐτῶν).   The name of the servant
Malchus is also given by St John.

[2] The corresponding notice in St
Luke xxiii. 38 is an interpolation.

myrrh and aloes used for the embalming (xix. 39), the
orderly folding of the napkin which had been about
His head (xx. 7), and, in the last chapter, the side of the
ship on which the net was to be thrown (xxi. 6) and the
number of the fish which were drawn up (xxi. 11)—all these
are instances of the miniature painting which is noticeable in
this Gospel.   What is the inference from all this?   Minuteness
is not in itself an evidence of authenticity.   But taken in
conjunction with the other arguments which have been adduced,
this fact is important, pointing as it does to an author who,
as he wrote, had all the scenes clearly and vividly before his
eyes.

(ii)   *The naturalness of the record.*

This is exhibited in two ways, (1) by the development of
the characters depicted, and (2) by the progress of the incidents
related.

(1)   *The characters.*   Some of these appear also in the Synoptic Gospels; others are new.   Of the former class are Martha and
Mary, Mary Magdalene, Peter, Judas, Pontius Pilate, Caiaphas;
of the latter, Andrew, Philip, Thomas, Nathanael, the woman
of Samaria, Nicodemus[1].   In the first group of instances we
have an opportunity of testing the Fourth Gospel by other
independent accounts.   The Evangelist therefore must be found
true to his fellow-Evangelists.   In the second group we have
no such external criterion to guide us; but the Evangelist must
be found true to himself.   We will select an example or two
from each of the two classes.

(a)   *St Peter.*   His character is sketched for us in clear
outlines in the Synoptic narrative.   We cannot fail to notice
his eager, forward, impetuous nature.   He is the self-constituted
spokesman of the disciples.   His eagerness to learn, his curiosity,
his love of definiteness shows itself in the type of question
which from time to time he puts before his Master.   He will

[1] [The characters of Martha and   in the first Essay (p. 37 sq.); they are
Mary and of Thomas are given above   therefore omitted here.]

know the precise point at which forgiveness ceases to be a duty
('Lord, how oft shall my brother sin against me and I forgive
him?' Matt. xviii. 21); the exact reward which those who
follow Jesus should obtain ('Behold, we have forsaken all, and
followed thee; what shall we have therefore?' Matt. xix. 27).
He will have one mysterious parable explained ('Declare unto
us this parable' Matt. xv. 15), and he will know the exact
range of the application of another ('Lord, speakest thou this
parable unto us, or even to all?' Luke xii. 41). Notice his
eagerness to remark upon what is going on around him,
whether it be the evidence of Christ's power ('Master, behold,
the figtree which thou cursedst is withered away' Mark xi. 21),
or the current of popular opinion ('All men seek for thee'
Mark i. 37). His impetuosity leads him on two occasions to
administer rebuke to the Lord Jesus Christ Himself, either
alone ('Then Peter took Him, and began to rebuke Him, saying,
Be it far from thee, Lord: this shall not be unto thee' Matt.
xvi. 22), or with others ('Peter and they that were with Him
said, Master, the multitude throng thee and press thee, and
sayest thou, Who touched me?' Luke viii. 45). His eagerness
of faith and assurance is discernible throughout the whole
course of the Gospel narrative. It prompts his confession at
Cæsarea Philippi ('Thou art the Christ, the Son of the living
God' Matt. xvi. 16), his proposal on the Mount of Transfigura-
tion ('Lord, it is good for us to be here: if thou wilt, let us
make three tabernacles' Matt. xvii. 4), his confidence on the
Sea of Galilee ('Lord, if it be thou, bid me come unto thee on
the water' Matt. xiv. 28), his protestation on the night of the
betrayal ('Though all men shall be offended because of thee,
yet will I never be offended' Matt. xxvi. 33). After the arrest,
with a characteristic mixture of courage and of curiosity, he
follows Jesus into the high priest's palace 'to see the end'
(Matt. xxvi. 58). On the other side, we notice sudden revul-
sions of feeling, resulting, now in lack of faith ('Lord, save me'
Matt. xiv. 30), now in lack of courage (the three denials
Matt. xxvi. 69 sq.), now again in unexpected self-abasement

('Depart from me, for I am a sinful man, O Lord' Luke v. 8).
Accordingly we find our Lord in the Garden rebuking Peter
specially and by name (Matt. xxvi. 40, Mark xiv. 37), as though
implying that his actions had in the most signal way belied his
professions.

Such is St Peter's character as delineated in the Synoptic
Gospels. Before proceeding to test the record of the Fourth
Gospel, we must turn aside to notice a charge brought against
St John by M. Renan (*Vie de Jésus* p. xxviii. and p. 159) and
reiterated by other critics (e.g. Lampe iii. p. 510). It is to the
effect that St John was jealous of St Peter's reputation and
endeavoured to undermine it in his Gospel. The charge is
false in every way. Compare St John's account of the third
denial (xviii. 27) with that of St Matthew (xxvi. 74) or of
St Mark (xiv. 71), the one Synoptist writing for the Jewish
Christians among whom St Peter was especially honoured, the
other 'the interpreter' of St Peter. Or again, remember that
the rebuke 'Get thee behind me, Satan,' is confined to St
Matthew (xvi. 23) and St Mark (viii. 33), and is not recorded
by St John. These facts will show how gratuitous this offensive
insinuation is. On the other hand, another antagonistic critic
(Köstlin in *Theol. Jahrb.* for 1850–2, p. 293) has supposed
that the object of the twenty-first chapter is to glorify St Peter
and St Peter's see. Thus one criticism serves to neutralise the
other[1].

We return to St Peter's character, as portrayed by St
John. It is in thorough accord with what we have already
gathered from the other Evangelists. His curiosity comes out
in the eager question with which he interrupts his Master's
discourse in the upper room 'Lord, whither goest thou?'
(xiii. 36), in the expedient by which he endeavours to obtain
through the medium of the beloved disciple the traitor's name

[1] M. Renan accepts the latter criticism, but supposes this last chapter to
be a later addition by some other hand,
in which amends are made to St Peter.
But the internal evidence of style
proves chap. xxi. (though probably
a postscript) to have been written by
the author of chaps. i–xx. (see the
additional note at the end of this
Essay).

(xiii. 24 sq.), in the anxiety which he shows to learn his brother apostle's destiny ('Lord, what shall this man do?' xxi. 21). He will not rest content with dark forebodings and mysterious intimations; he will know the facts, and know them definitely. Again, his ready profession of faith, which makes him now the mouthpiece of the apostolic band ('Lord, to whom shall we go? Thou hast the words of eternal life' vi. 68), now the revealer of his own deepest heart-utterances ('Lord, thou knowest all things; thou knowest that I love thee' xxi. 17), is in perfect keeping with what the Synoptic narrative has led us to expect. His impetuosity shines out in every action which is recorded of him. In Gethsemane, without a thought for the consequences, he draws his sword and smites the high-priest's servant (xviii. 10 sq.); at the tomb, while the younger disciple stands awestruck and uncertain, he enters in without a moment's hesitation (xx. 6); at the sea of Galilee, he plunges into the lake (xxi. 7), he drags the net to land (xxi. 11). And the sudden revulsion of sentiment, of which such striking examples are recorded in the first three Gospels, has its complete parallel in an incident peculiar to the Fourth Evangelist— the washing of the disciples' feet ('Thou shalt never wash my feet.' 'Lord, not my feet only, but also my hands and my head' xiii. 8, 9).

(b) *Pontius Pilate.* In the portraiture of the Roman pro-curator there is much in common between the Synoptists and St John. Thus in all we see the abstract love of justice, inherent in a Roman magistrate, overborne by the desire of securing popularity, natural to a provincial governor. But his personal characteristics appear especially in the Fourth Gospel, and it is not too much to say that we should not have appre-hended his character as a whole without the light thrown upon it from this fresh source of evidence. Here at last we get to understand the man thoroughly in all the variety of his complex nature—his desire to purchase public favour at the expense of justice and yet his unwillingness to condemn Jesus, his cynical contempt of the subject-people, his sarcasm, his scepticism and yet his fear.   It is only when, fresh from studying him in the Fourth Gospel, we turn once more to the pages of the Synoptists, that his scorn for the Jews as a nation is clearly discerned. However, when once we have found the clue, that scorn is evident enough.   It appears in the form of his questions ' Art thou the King of the Jews?' (Matt. xxvii. 11), ' What will ye that I should do unto him whom ye call the King of the Jews ?' (Mark xv. 12)[1]; and especially in the title placed over the cross[2].   Apparently he could not lose the opportunity of insulting the Jewish rulers, whom he was obliged to gratify nevertheless.   But when we read St John's account, we see these lurid features of Pilate's character emphasized and lighted up under the glow which issues from the narrator's master-pen.   With what persistency does Pilate evince his desire to shirk the responsibility of condemnation!   'Take ye him, and judge him according to your law' (xviii. 31).   Baffled here by the logic of facts, the inability of the Jews to condemn to death, he tries another loophole to escape from his dilemma.   'Ye have a custom, that I should release unto you one at the passover; will ye therefore that I release unto you the King of the Jews?' (xviii. 39). Foiled again by the malignant hostility of the crowd, he seeks to appeal to their pity by exhibiting his prisoner scourged and mocked.   In vain.   He is met by the cry, 'Crucify him.' Once more he would shift the responsibility on the shoulders of the chief-priests, 'Take ye him and crucify him, for I find no fault in him.'   From the furious, raging mob he turns to meet the calm, impassive countenance of Jesus Christ.   The sight only increases his perplexity.   'From henceforth Pilate sought to release him.'   The struggle is ended by the twice-repeated name of Cæsar (xix. 12), and the dread image thus called up before his mind of the suspicious, vindictive emperor prevails at last over his sense of justice and of awe.   He tries one last

---

[1] The scorn is lost in the form in which the question appears in St Matthew (xxvii. 22).

[2] Though here again the climax of contempt is found in St John's version, ' Jesus *of Nazareth*, the King of the Jews'; see above, p. 159.

appeal, 'Behold, your King,' and then delivers Him unto them
to be crucified.   And if the wavering, vacillating temper of the
governor is drawn in clearer outline by St John than by the
Synoptists, no less is his cynicism, his sarcasm and unbelief
painted in deeper colours.   'Am I a Jew?' (the English fails to
convey the withering scorn of the Greek original μήτι ἐγὼ
Ἰουδαῖός εἰμι;), 'Art thou a King then?' (οὐκοῦν βασιλεὺς εἶ
σύ ;—we can imagine the intonation of the voice upon the final
word σύ, as Pilate amuses himself with what he considered the
fanaticism of his prisoner), 'What is truth?' And so the
conversation ends, Pilate no doubt thinking that he had had
the best of it, had secured the last word.   Notice too how he
repeats the expression 'the King of the Jews,' harping on the
title which he knows to be offensive to his Jewish audience
(xviii. 39, xix. 14, 15, 19, 22).   And the Roman soldiers catch
up the spirit of the Roman governor, who sets the fashion, and
cry, 'Hail, King of the Jews' (xix. 3).

(c) *Philip.* Of the characters known only from St John's
Gospel the first in importance undoubtedly is Thomas; but
there are others, which the Evangelist, with a few masterly
touches, depicts for us, and which deserve more than a passing
notice.

There is in Philip a certain cautious, business-like way of
looking at things which bespeaks much circumspectness of
disposition. We remark this at once when we are introduced to
him in the first chapter (i. 43 sq.). Unlike Andrew and the nameless disciple, he does not make the first advances himself; but
he is found and summoned by the Saviour. Yet when found, he
accepts the call without hesitation, and finds a new adherent
in his turn. But the mode in which he announces his discovery
to Nathanael is characteristic. He keeps back the name as
long as possible, and the place to the last word in the sentence,
for Nazareth would prejudice any cause. When Nathanael
demurs, he does not argue; he simply bids him try, 'Come and
see.' Philip appears again upon the scene in the sixth chapter
on the occasion of the feeding of the five thousand. Again it is

Jesus who opens the conversation: 'Whence shall we buy bread, that these may eat (*v.* 5)?' The business question is put to the business man. It is answered in a business spirit. He makes the necessary calculation. 'Two hundred pennyworth of bread is not sufficient for them that every one of them may take a little.' But he does not reply to the question. It is left for Andrew to suggest a remedy. We meet with him a third time in the twelfth chapter, when certain Greeks come to him with the request, 'Sir, we would see Jesus.' Here again he does not take the initiative. He will not act without consultation. 'Philip cometh and telleth Andrew, and again Andrew and Philip tell Jesus[1].' It has been suggested that Philip was the steward, the purveyor of the little company, that he managed the commissariat; just as Judas was the treasurer, the purser. Such a position at all events would suit his business-like character. And it would account for strangers (xii. 21) applying to him first, as they may have been brought in contact with him in this capacity[2].

(*d*) *Andrew.* In two places Andrew is associated with Philip, and on both occasions he appears not merely in contact with, but in contrast to, his brother-Apostle. He is as eager and prompt as the other is slow and cautious. While Philip is calculating the amount of bread required to feed the multitude, Andrew has hit upon an expedient (vi. 8, 9). While Philip cannot act alone in bringing the Greek strangers to Christ, Andrew, as soon as he is consulted, goes with him to tell Jesus. Thus he is quick alike to act and to speak. It is this decision of character which made him the first to join the Saviour himself, and the first to bring another to the Saviour (i. 37, 40, 41). In short, he has much of his brother Peter's eagerness, without that brother's tendency to grievous falls. It is quite in accordance with this characteristic that

---

[1] John xii. 20—22.

[2] An early tradition identified him with the disciple who requested that he might first go and bury his father (Clem. Alex. *Strom.* iii. 4. 25, p. 522). This would be in keeping with Philip's hesitating faith.

we read in the Muratorian Canon that Andrew was the Apostle
to whom it was revealed that John should write his Gospel,
and that the revelation took place on the first night of the
three days' fast[1].

(iii) *The progress of events.*

We cannot rise from the perusal of the characters as they
appear in the Fourth Gospel without the assurance that we
have been introduced to real, living persons, described by some
one who knew them well. Individuality is seen to be stamped
on every face. Exactly in the same way, as we mark the
progress of events gradually unfolded before us in the narrative,
our conviction becomes more and more settled that the guide
who conducts us has been an eyewitness of the incidents which
he records. In order to get the full effect of the extreme
naturalness of the description, we have only to read the historical portions successively, and to remark how vivid is the
sequence of the narrative as it opens out from point to point.
Or we may take a conversation like that held in the fourth
chapter between our Lord and the woman of Samaria. We
notice, first of all, the development of the conviction in the
woman's mind. Starting with a contemptuous irony (*v.* 9),
she passes by gradual stages into a growing respect mingled
with curiosity (*v.* 11), then into wonder ripening into faith
(*v.* 15). The conversation now takes another turn. There is a
direct home-thrust at the vicious part of her character (*v.* 16).
This she disingenuously parries. Convinced by this time of her
questioner's spiritual insight, she attempts to divert into a
general theological channel the conversation which was taking
so inconvenient a turn (*v.* 19). Our Lord's answer contains a
tacit reproach (*v.* 24), but she still shows her unwillingness to
appropriate the lesson (*v.* 25), and quietly ignores all particular

---

[1] Cohortantibus condiscipulis et episcopis suis dixit [Iohannes] Conieiu-
nate mihi hodie triduum, et quid
cuique fuerit revelatum alterutrum
nobis enarremus. Eadem nocte revelatum Andreae ex apostolis ut recog-
nescentibus cunctis Iohannes suo nomine cuncta describeret. *Canon Murator.* p. 33 (*ed.* Tregelles).

allusions (*v.* 25).   Observe secondly, that the spiritual teaching
of our Lord, which is so prominent throughout, arises naturally
out of the external incidents.   The presence of the woman with
the pitcher at the well (*v.* 7) leads to the subject of the living
water; the arrival of the disciples with provisions (*vv.* 8, 27, 31)
to the reference to the spiritual food.   In these two cases the
point of connexion is distinctly stated; in others it is mentally
supplied by the recollection of the eye-witness.   Thus the
mountain of Gerizim towering above them, and the expanse of
corn-fields stretched out at their feet, are each in turn taken
advantage of as opportunities for inculcating spiritual truths.
And the whole is woven together with a naturalness which
defies all separation of its component parts; for the teaching
and the incident are the woof and the web of the fabric.
Thirdly, the amount of local and special knowledge contained
in the incident is both considerable and varied.   As we glance
through the chapter, we notice that it demands a particular
acquaintance with the well of Jacob (*v.* 5), the relations of
Jews and Samaritans (*v.* 9), the depth of the well (*v.* 11), its
history (*v.* 12), the mountain and the worship on its summit
(*v.* 20), the social position of women (*v.* 27), the corn-fields and
the harvest-time (*v.* 35).   And all this intimacy with places
and customs is not an excrescence merely, but an integral and
essential part of the narrative.   You cannot remove it without
the whole structure falling to the ground[1].

Or take the scene enacted in the Judgment Hall (xviii. 28
—xix. 16).   Observe at the outset the unartificial, the unsyste-
matic, character of the narrative.   The incidents are not grouped
according to subject, but related in sequence as they actually
occurred.   Hence the history of St Peter's denials is interrupted
by other matters.   The third denial interposes between the
mention of the transfer from Annas to Caiaphas, and the
transfer from Caiaphas to Pilate.   On the other hand St Luke
(xxii. 54–62) adds force to the episode by placing all three
denials together.   With St John however dramatic propriety

---

[1] [This whole incident has been already treated above, p. 33 sq.]

is sacrificed to chronological accuracy. Notice, in the second place, the gaps in the narrative. Jesus is first examined before Annas, then He is transferred to Caiaphas; but nothing is recorded of what happened at this second examination. We may perhaps infer from the silence of the Evangelist that he was not an eye-witness of this part of the scene. Again, we cannot fail to be struck by the introduction of certain incidents which have no direct bearing on the history, but yet are not on this account excluded. A moment's consideration will explain their presence in the narrative. The fire of coals kindled in the hall (xviii. 18), the goings in and goings out of Pilate (xviii. 29, 33, 38, xix. 4, 9, 13), notes of place and of time (xviii. 28, xix. 14)—such would be just the kind of circumstances which would impress themselves indelibly upon the memory of an eye-witness, and would inevitably rise up again before him as, years after, he recalled the memorable scene. Or consider the respective attitudes of the chief-priests and of the Roman governor. How natural the representation. On the one side, the Jews, with their fear of ceremonial pollution (xviii. 28), their appeals to the law (xviii. 30, xix. 7), their inability to punish (xviii. 31), their affected loyalty (xix. 12, 15). On the other, Pilate—that masterpiece of portrait-painting to which attention has been drawn already. Surely, whether we examine the details, or regard the picture as a whole, we are constrained to admit that all this is something more than 'ben trovato': nay, we may say with confidence 'e vero.' And so we might pass in review other incidents; the calling of the disciples, the marriage at Cana, the man at the pool of Bethesda, the scene at Bethany and at the tomb of Lazarus, the washing of the disciples' feet, the declaration of the betrayal—all these bear stamped upon their face the impress of trustworthy and con-temporaneous testimony. I will conclude this part of my argument by an appeal presented from a somewhat different quarter. The writer of the Fourth Gospel often distinguishes the facts which he records from his commentary upon those facts, made when an interval of time had thrown fresh light upon their spiritual import. Is it Christ's prophetic language, 'Destroy this temple, and in three days I will raise it up'? We are told that 'when He was risen from the dead, His disciples remembered that He had said this unto them; and they believed the scripture, and the word which Jesus had said' (ii. 22). Is it the mysterious utterance, 'He that believeth on me, as the scripture hath said, out of his belly shall flow rivers of living water'? The Evangelist's comment, made subsequent to the Pentecostal gift, explains it of 'the Spirit which they that believe on Him should receive; for the Holy Ghost was not yet given, because that Jesus was not yet glorified' (vii. 39). Is it Christ's announcement of results to issue from His coming exaltation, 'I, if I be lifted up, shall draw all men unto me'? It is explained as 'signifying what death He should die' (xii. 33). The prophecy of Caiaphas (xi. 51), the triumphal entry into Jerusalem (xii. 16), Christ's appeal on behalf of His disciples in the moment of the betrayal (xviii. 9)—all form texts for the conveyance of spiritual truths viewed from the standpoint of the Evangelist's maturer experience. Some have maintained that the commentary is wrong. I do not assert this, nor do I allow it. But one thing at least is clear. If the fact or the saying had been invented for the sake of the comment, the fact or saying would in most instances have taken a different form and the correspondence would have been made more obvious. But the fact does not lead up to the comment, for the simple reason that the fact was already there, in absolute possession; and as, in the light of a fuller and clearer knowledge, the Evangelist draws out its hidden meaning, he will not venture to subserve the purpose of the application by diverging one hair's-breadth from the exact letter of the record[1].

---

[1] [For the third section of this Essay, THE WRITER WAS JOHN THE SON OF ZEBEDEE, the reader is referred to the first Essay in this volume, p. 39 sq.]

ADDITIONAL NOTES.

A. On the twenty-first Chapter.

The Gospel was originally intended to end with the twentieth chapter. The conclusion of the narrative is significant, 'Blessed are they that have not seen, and yet have believed' (xx. 29, μακάριοι οἱ μὴ ἰδόντες καὶ πιστεύσαντες), and the writer's own addition (vv. 30, 31) is evidently the original close to the whole. The twenty-first chapter therefore is an after-thought. This distinction is no refinement of modern theorists; it is as old as the time of Tertullian[1]. But did it emanate from the same author or not? Clearly yes. The style is essentially Johannine. There is the same historic οὖν, so characteristic of St John's narrative, and of his alone (vv. 5, 6, 7 (bis), 9, 11, 15, 21, 23); the same comparative absence in the narrative part of δὲ (which is wrongly inserted by the scribes in v. 12); the same tendency to place the verb first (vv. 1, 2, 3, 4, 5, 7, 10, 11, 12, 13, 23, 25), especially with λέγει (v. 15 sq.); the same abruptness of diction, the result of the avoidance of connecting particles (vv. 3, 12, 13, 16, 17). Again such sentences as ὑπάγω ἁλιεύειν...ἐρχόμεθα καὶ ἡμεῖς σὺν σοί (v. 3), δεῦτε ἀριστήσατε...σὺ τίς εἶ; (v. 12), ἀκολούθει μοι (v. 19), Κύριε, οὗτος δὲ τί; (v. 21), τί πρὸς σέ; σύ μοι ἀκολούθει (v. 22) etc. are features which are familiar to us from previous chapters, and should be compared with e.g. the narrative of i. 35 sq. or xx. 11 sq. We find the same fondness for ἐκεῖνος (vv. 3, 7, 23), the same love of definiteness, e.g. τὰ δεξιὰ μέρη (v. 6), ἀπὸ πηχῶν διακοσίων (v. 8), ἑκατὸν πεντήκοντα τριῶν (v. 11), τοῦτο ἤδη τρίτον (v. 14), to which we have already drawn attention; the same vivid painting (e.g. vv. 7, 9 etc.), the same use of a parenthetic explanation (vv. 7, 8, with which compare vi. 23). Favourite Johannine expressions are found, as the doubled ἀμὴν (v. 18), which is peculiar to this Gospel, τοῦτο εἶπεν σημαίνων ποίῳ θανάτῳ κ.τ.λ. (v. 19; cf. xii. 33, xviii. 32), καὶ τὸ ὀψάριον ὁμοίως (v. 13; cf. vi. 11 ὁμοίως καὶ ἐκ τῶν ὀψαρίων, which last is a word only used by the Fourth Evangelist). We notice the

---

[1] Ipsa quoque clausula evangelii propter quid consignat haec scripta, nisi Ut credatis, inquit, Iesum Christum filium Dei? Tert. adv. Prax. 25. He refers however in three places to the twenty-first chapter (see Rönsch, p. 290).

characteristic mode of designating places, τῆς θαλάσσης τῆς Τιβεριάδος (v. 1 ; cf. vi. 1), and of describing disciples, 'Thomas called Didymus' (v. 2 ; cf. xi. 16), 'Nathanael from Cana of Galilee' (*ib.*, his abode specified as in the case of Philip xii. 21), 'Simon, son of John' (v. 15 sq. ; cf. i. 42), 'the disciple whom Jesus loved' (vv. 7, 20 ; cf. xiii. 23, xix. 26, xx. 2)[1]. Again there is the suppression of the author's own name, which would most certainly have been mentioned by a continuator of the narrative. Lastly, the delineation of the character of St Peter, and of his relation to St John, has all the refinement of our Evangelist. This is the case in the two scenes in which they appear in contact. The spiritual insight of St John (v. 7) is matched by the impetuosity (vv. 3, 7, 11) and the curiosity (v. 21) of St Peter[2].

Thus, though an after-thought, this chapter was certainly written by the author of the Gospel. How soon after, it is impossible to say ; but there is nothing in the style which requires us to postulate more than a few weeks or a few days. As all the manuscripts without exception contain the chapter, and there is no trace of its ever having been wanting from any copies, the probable conclusion is that it was added before the Gospel was actually published. After the Gospel was written and submitted to his friends, the Apostle may have heard that some misapprehension was abroad respecting himself, or that some disappointment had been expressed because no mention had been made of an incident which they had heard him relate, and which would naturally be interesting to his admirers. He may have then consented to add it as a postscript. Apart from the identity of style, it is hardly likely that the chapter was written after the Apostle's death, for in that case an event which

---

[1] The Evangelist is fond of marking his characters by some striking circumstance which serves as a label. Examples are the designation of Nicodemus (xix. 39, vii. 50 from iii. 2), and of Caiaphas (xviii. 14 from xi. 49). From a different spirit and with a different aim Carlyle exhibits the same tendency.

[2] Against such indications of identity of authorship, the objections commonly alleged (e.g. by Lücke) are powerless, e.g. the use of new expressions, as ἐφανέρωσεν δὲ οὕτως (v. 1)

and ἐξετάσαι (v. 12). Any writing or portion of a writing might be set aside on the same grounds. Thus, to take ch. xx. 30, μὲν οὖν is a ἅπαξ λεγόμενον in St John, so is βίβλιον, so is ἐνώπιον. Indeed the first and third phrases are rather characteristic of St Luke; but the endeavour to press such arguments would justly be scouted as fatal to all fair criticism. The chronological difficulty of τοῦτο ἤδη τρίτον (v. 14) remains unaffected by the question of authorship.

threw so much light upon our Lord's mysterious utterance respecting the beloved disciple would scarcely have been passed over in silence.

The question of the integrity of the last two verses of the chapter is an issue which has to be treated separately. The twenty-fourth verse is a confirmation or attestation of the truth of the narrative on the part of his friends and disciples, and it bears out the traditional account, given in the Muratorian Canon, of the origin of the Fourth Gospel[1]. The last verse is evidently a scholium. Tischendorf declares that in the Sinaitic manuscript ($\aleph$) it is written in a different hand from the rest of the Gospel, by the διορθωτής of the whole, and it is perhaps omitted in a valuable cursive (63)[2]. However, as it occurs in all the other copies, and

---

[1] See above, p. 190.

[2] [Dr Gwynn kindly supplies (Oct. 4, 1892) the following information respecting this manuscript. 'I think there is no room for doubt that Cod. 63 has lost a leaf (or more) at the end, and that it when complete contained John xxi. 25. At first sight, one might be led to form an opposite opinion. For the last page of the MS., as it now is, is the last of a complete quaternion, and in it the text ends καὶ οἴδαμεν ὅτι ἀληθής ἐστιν ἡ μαρ | τυρία αὐτοῦ· (the last ten letters being arranged in the middle of a new line). The final stop looks like a colon, but may be a period ; and one might suppose that the scribe's reason for placing τυρία αὐτοῦ thus, was because his text was at an end. But on looking through the MS., one would find this supposition to be unfounded. It frequently happens that he ends a page with an incomplete line, longer or shorter, not ranging with the previous lines, either at its beginning or its end. Comparing the place with the ends of the three preceding Gospels, one finds a small bit of negative evidence. Each of them has, after its last word, the marks :— These do not appear after τυρία αὐτοῦ. None

of them has any subscription, or even τέλος subjoined.

So much for the text; but when we look at the surrounding scholia all doubt is removed. The MS. has in every page a body of continuous scholia, some half-dozen lines in the top margin, a pretty long column (in continuation) all down the outer margin, and six or eight more lines at the foot. As the scholia proceed, the scribe denotes change of subject commented on, by a numeral letter (sometimes), and always by beginning the new matter with a capital letter, in red. The last two lines of these scholia run as follows: ἐξετάζειν ͵τὰ γεγραμμένα· Δ΄Ὑπερβολικῶς τοῦτο φησίν· ἐκ μυρίων γὰρ | θαυμάτων· τὰ μόνα πρὸς πίστην (sic) καὶ ἀρετὴν. Here you will observe (1) that the scholium breaks off in the middle of a sentence, shewing that there ought to be another leaf : (2) that this broken scholium referred to verse 25, as is proved by the word ὑπερβολικῶς, the μύρια θαύματα being the ἄλλα πολλά of St John. These facts seem to settle the question'. Compare Scrivener, *Collatio Cod. Sinait.* p. lix., C. R. Gregory's *prolegomena* to Tischendorf, *N. T.* (ed. 8) p. 479.]

these come from very various sources, we may safely infer that, if an addition, it was written by St John himself, or by one of his immediate disciples.

B.   *On the conversational character of the Gospel.*

The Fourth Gospel was addressed to an immediate circle of hearers.   In this respect it differs from the other three, St Luke's Gospel approaching most nearly to it in this respect.   But Theophilus, if a real person, and not a *nom de guerre*, the type of a God-loving or God-beloved Christian, soon disappears out of sight. On the other hand, the Fourth Evangelist keeps his disciples before his mind.   He has to correct misapprehensions, to answer questions, to guide and instruct a definite class of persons, and those persons his immediate circle of acquaintance.   Hence he assumes a knowledge of himself in the case of those for whom he writes.   He does not give his own name, because his hearers already know his personal history.

For the most part however the reference to these disciples is indirect.   They are before the Evangelist, but he does not address them in the second person.   Instances of allusions to misapprehensions or to questionings rife in those about him are i. 41 '*He* was the first to find' etc., ii. 11 '*This* was the beginning of his miracles,' iii. 24 'John was *not yet* cast into prison,' iv. 54 'This again was the second miracle which Jesus did,' xviii. 13 'He (Annas) was father-in-law to Caiaphas, who was high-priest of that year,' xix. 34 sq. 'There came out water and blood.'   Great stress is laid upon this last point, doubtless in allusion to some symbolism which is not explained, because they would understand it.   So xxi. 14 'This was now the third time that Jesus manifested Himself,' xxi. 23 'The saying therefore went abroad among the brethren that that disciple should not die.   Yet Jesus said not unto him, He shall not die' etc.   Thus we find the Evangelist clearing up matters which the current tradition had left doubtful, or on which the popular mind wished to be further informed.   Through the main part of the narrative we see these parenthetical additions, these conversational comments. At length (xix. 35, xx. 31) there is a direct appeal to these disciples, for whom the whole has been written.   'He knoweth that he saith true, that ye might believe.'   'These things are written that ye might believe that Jesus is the Christ, the Son of God; and that believing ye might have life through His name.'

The Gospel however does not stand alone. Its connexion with the First Epistle is both intimate and important. Its authenticity and genuineness are still further confirmed by this consideration, which brings out in clearer colours the circumstances under which the Gospel was written, and sets more vividly before us the relation of the Evangelist to his band of hearers. The Muratorian Canon points to this connexion[1]. The close association of the two Johannine writings warrants the inference that the author of the Canon treated the First Epistle as an epilogue to the Gospel. And this in fact is its true character. The Epistle was intended to be circulated with the Gospel. This accounts for its abrupt commencement, which is to be explained as a reference to the Gospel which in one sense preceded it. This accounts likewise for the allusion to the water and the blood (1 John v. 6 sq.) as the witnesses to the reality of Christ's human nature, the counterpart of the statement in the Gospel narrative (xix. 35).

The evidential value of all this cannot be over-estimated. It presents us with a combination of circumstances which a forger would not have had the ingenuity to invent; nor, if he had invented it, would he have commanded all the circumstances necessary to carry out to a successful issue so stupendous an undertaking.

[1867, 1868].

---

[1] See above, p. 99.

IV.

ST PAUL'S PREPARATION FOR THE MINISTRY.

Printed from Lecture-notes.

IV.

ST PAUL'S PREPARATION FOR THE MINISTRY.

ST Paul dates the commencement of his preparation for the ministry as far back as the day of his birth. He describes himself as set apart for the Gospel of God, set apart from his mother's womb (Rom. i. 1, Gal. i. 15). In his social position, in his intellectual training, in his religious creed—in all the influences which wrought upon his childhood and youth—there was a schooling which eminently adapted him to fill the part for which he was designed—to gather the Gentiles into the fold of Christ, to preach the universality of the new dispensation. This was especially his work—his Gospel.

And, when we come to piece together the notices preserved of his early life, we find that this training was in itself very remarkable, that it did in a way forecast his future destination, furnishing him with a large store of varied experiences, idle and unfruitful in Saul the Persecutor, but quickened suddenly into life in Paul the Apostle of Jesus Christ, the Preacher to the Gentiles, by the lightning flash which struck him on the way to Damascus.

We are accustomed to look to three countries especially as the great teachers of the modern world—Rome, Greece, Judæa. Rome, the foremost of all nations in the science of government, has handed down to us the principles of law and order. Greece, setting before us her rich treasures of thought and imagination, has been a schoolmistress in art and literature. Above all, from Palestine we have learnt our true relation to God, which gives higher significance to art and literature and an eternal

value to the principles of law and order.   If Rome supplied the
bone and sinew to our colossal man, while Greece clothed him
with flesh and gave him grace and beauty, it was Judæa that
breathed the breath of life into him.   Now all these three
influences were combined in the great Apostle of the Gentiles.
He was a citizen of Rome.   His native place, Tarsus, was the
great university of Greece.   He was brought up in the Jew's
religion in its most rigorous and most typical form.

We are accustomed to dwell solely on the Jewish education
of St Paul when considering his preparation for the ministry,
not only as the most important, but also as the most prominent
in the notices preserved of his early history.   But the other
elements in his training must not be neglected.   It is not
probable that one whose maxim it was to 'become all things to
all men,' whose nature was eminently sensitive and impressible,
could have failed to be moved by these powerful influences, and
the traces of their working are sufficiently distinct in his life and
writings.   On the other hand, exaggeration must be avoided.
It would be a grave mistake to picture to ourselves the Apostle
as an active politician, or an erudite philosopher and man of
letters.   The sphere of his thought was far different.   His life
was far otherwise spent.   But he must have received from his
political status as a Roman citizen and from his residence in the
heart of a great Greek University impressions which enlarged his
sympathies and his views, and thus, enabling him to enter more
deeply into the thoughts and strivings of others, and to contemplate the Gospel from different points of view, rendered him a
fitter instrument in the hands of God for the special work for
which he was destined.

1.   Let us consider St Paul as *a citizen of Rome*.   The
extension of the franchise was the keystone of the Roman
system[1].   By this means a connexion and sympathy was kept
up in the remotest parts of the Empire.   The blood of the
political body thus circulated freely by veins and arteries
through the great heart of the republic to its extreme

[1] Cic. *pro Balb.* 13; Becker *Handbuch der römischen Alterthümer* II. (1), p. 91.

members, and any injury done to one limb was an injury done to the whole. The metaphor which I have employed is not my own: I am only expanding the image used by Cicero[1] to express these relations. To the Roman his citizenship was his passport in distant lands, his talisman in seasons of difficulty and danger. It shielded him alike from the caprice of municipal law and the injustice of local magistrates. In Syria, in Asia, in Greece—wherever he went—he bore about with him this safeguard of his liberties. How valuable such a protection must have been to St Paul, how often he must have invoked its aid in a life spent in travel and in the midst of enemies, we can well imagine. He had never known what it was to be without this citizenship, for he had been born a citizen of Rome[2]. It procured him an honourable discharge from the prison at Philippi[3]; it loosed his fetters in the tower of Antonia[4]; it rescued him from the lawlessness of a zealot mob, and sped him on his way under escort to Cæsarea[5]; it transferred him from the hearing of a provincial governor to the court of Cæsar himself[6]. As he lived, so he died—a citizen of Rome. It is recorded that, while his brother-Apostle St Peter suffered the punishment of a common malefactor on the cross, St Paul was allowed to die by the sword, as the last recognition of his civic rights conceded by the law, when everything besides had been forfeited[7].

In this way St Paul's position as a citizen must have been of essential service in the spread of the Gospel. But this is not exactly the point on which I wish to dwell. I am anxious rather to point out that, having been so constantly in requisition, it must have impressed itself upon his mind with a corresponding force. And thus he must have been led to appreciate, as far as it was necessary for him to appreciate, the position which Rome occupied as a teacher of the world. I

[1] Cic. *Verr.* v. 67; Becker, II. (1), p. 98.
[2] Acts xxii. 28.
[3] Acts xvi. 37 sq.
[4] Acts xxii. 25 sq.
[5] Acts xxiii. 27.
[6] Acts xxv. 12.
[7] Tertull. *Scorpiace* § 15, *de Praescr. Heret.* 36, etc. See Wieseler *Chron.* p. 542.

think there are very clear indications of this. It was no vulgar pride or idle self-assertion, but a true political instinct, which led St Paul to demand a practical apology from the magistrates at Philippi. It is clear from his language on this occasion, as on others, that he valued his position as a citizen of Rome. It was something to be connected with that gigantic Empire, whose presence he had felt everywhere, and which, in the restraints it placed on the lawless opposition of his adversaries, presented itself to him as a type and manifestation of that letting power which keeps Antichrist in check till the last day (2 Thess. ii. 7).

Nay, so strong is the impression left in his mind, that he chooses the Roman franchise as the fittest image of the position of the believer in his heavenly kingdom. I have already referred to the language of Cicero in which he compares the connexion of the different parts of the Roman empire by this political tie to the circulation of the blood, language which reminds us of the Apostle's own image of the Church as the body knit together by its joints and ligatures (Col. ii. 19). Another passage of the same writer suggests still more striking points of comparison. 'I maintain it as a universal principle,' says Cicero (*pro Balbo* c. 13), 'that there is no nation any-where so hostile or disaffected to the Roman people, none so united by ties of faith and friendship, that we are debarred from admitting them to the right of citizens[1].' What wonder then if the Apostle saw a peculiar fitness in this image ? In the guarantee it offered to individual freedom, in its independence of circumstances of time and place, in its superiority over inferior obligations, in the sympathy which it established between all the members of the community, in the universality of its application, lying as it did within the reach of all, far or near, friend or foe—in all these points it expressed, as no other earthly institution could do, the eternal relations of the king-dom of Christ. Hence the language of St Paul, ' Our citizen-ship is in heaven' (Phil. iii. 20). ' Only perform your duties as

---

[1] Becker II. (1), p. 93, note (18).

citizens in a manner worthy of the Gospel of Christ' (Phil. i. 27).
And in a third passage, where the image reappears, his
language seems to be coloured by the legal distinction of *cives*
and *peregrini*. 'Ye are no longer strangers and foreigners, but
fellow-citizens of the saints,' οὐκέτι ἐστὲ ξένοι (the recognised
Greek equivalent of *peregrini*[1]) καὶ πάροικοι, ἀλλὰ συμπολῖται
τῶν ἁγίων (Ephes. ii. 19). They were once *peregrini*, they
have been enrolled in the *civitas coelitum*.

All this shows the deep impression which the Roman
institutions had made on St Paul. And this being so, we
cannot be wrong in recognising here a special training for the
Apostleship of the Gentiles, opening out this wider view of
social life, and suggesting to him the true relation between the
ordinances of men and the Gospel of Christ.

2. But secondly, he was *a native of Tarsus*, the capital of
Cilicia, 'no mean city,' as he himself styles it[2]. We have it on
the authority of Strabo[3], a contemporary of St Paul, that
Tarsus surpassed all other universities, such as Alexandria and
Athens, in the study of philosophy and educational literature
in general. 'Its great pre-eminence,' he adds, 'consists in this
that the men of learning here are all natives.' Accordingly he
and others[4] have made up a long catalogue of distinguished
men who flourished at Tarsus in the late autumn of Greek
learning: philosophers—of the Academy, of the Epicurean and
Stoic schools—poets, grammarians, physicians. At Tarsus, one
might say, you breathed the atmosphere of learning. How far
St Paul may have availed himself of these opportunities of
cultivating a knowledge of Greek literature, how much of his
boyhood and youth was spent here and how much at Jerusalem, we cannot say. His Jewish teacher Gamaliel, who was
distinguished for his liberality in this respect, would at least
have encouraged him not to neglect this culture. It has been
the tendency of recent writers to underrate St Paul's attain-

---

[1] Plaut. *Rudens*, Prol. v. 2.
[2] Acts xxi. 39, οὐκ ἀσήμου πόλεως
πολίτης.

[3] Strabo xiv. p. 673.
[4] Pauly *Real-Encycl. der class. Alterthümer s.v.* Tarsus.

ments. The extravagant language of older writers has produced
a natural reaction. A treatise was even published 'On the
stupendous erudition of St Paul'[1]. Such exaggerations would
be ludicrous if they were not painful. The majesty of the
Gospel is not glorified by such means. St Paul's strength lay
in a widely-different direction. It was 'not with enticing
words of wisdom or philosophy (οὐκ ἐν πειθοῖς σοφίας λόγοις),
but in the demonstration of the Spirit and of power' (1 Cor. ii. 4),
that he won his way. There is no ground for saying that
St Paul was a very erudite or highly-cultivated man. An
obvious maxim of practical life from Menander (1 Cor. xv. 33),
a religious sentiment of Cleanthes repeated by Aratus, himself
a native of Tarsus (Acts xvii. 28), a pungent satire of
Epimenides (Tit. i. 12), with possibly a passage here and
there which dimly reflects some classical writer, these are very
slender grounds on which to build the supposition of vast
learning. His style certainly does not conform to classical
models : his logic savours little of the dialectics of the schools.
But on the other hand he did get directly or indirectly from
contact with Greek thought and learning lessons far wider
and far more useful for his work than a perfect style or a
familiar acquaintance with the classical writers of antiquity.
Whoever will study carefully the picture of the gradual degra-
dation of the heathen world in the opening chapters to the
Romans, or, still better, the address to the philosophical
Athenians from the Areopagus, will see how thoroughly St
Paul entered into the moral and religious position of the
heathen world, and with what deep insight he traced its
relations, whether of contact or of contrast, with the great
message of which he was the bearer. These are only samples[2].
If we recognise in such passages the voice of inspiration, in
union with that instinctive quickness of moral apprehension
which a tender love always inspires, we have still to look to
external influences to supply the material on which inspiration

---

[1] Schramm *De Stupenda Eruditione*
Pauli (1710).

[2] See Jowett *The Epistles of St Paul*
I. p. 352 sq. (1859).

might work. And foremost among these must be reckoned the lessons derived from his residence in early life in the centre of a great school—the greatest of its day—of Greek thought and learning.

We are disposed indeed to think lightly of the literary efforts of the Greeks at this late date: but though Greek literature had now lost the freshness and beauty of the spring and early summer of its existence, it had in the decline of its autumn still a glory of its own. We must not forget that the later schools of Greek philosophy exhibited a much greater earnestness of moral purpose, whether for good or evil, and achieved in consequence a much wider influence than the earlier. And if later Greek literature was rather critical and reproductive than original and imaginative, as the earlier had been, this only rendered it a fitter handmaid for the diffusion of the Gospel. It was required that the great Apostle of the Gentiles should be able to understand the bearings of the moral and religious life of Greece as expressed in her literature, and this lesson he could learn more impartially and more fully at Tarsus in the days of her decline, than at Athens in the freshness of her glory. Greece in her old age was now summing up, as it were, the experiences of her past life.

3. I have dwelt hitherto on the Gentile side of St Paul's training. The most important feature in his education has still to be considered. He was a Jew in the strictest sense of the term. Let us take his account of himself. περιτομῇ ὀκταήμερος, ἐκ γένους Ἰσραήλ, φυλῆς Βενιαμείν, Ἑβραῖος ἐξ Ἑβραίων (Phil. iii. 5). 'I was not admitted to the privileges of the covenant late in life, as a proselyte. I was circumcised on the earliest day sanctioned by the law. I was not even the son of proselyte parents, but of the race of Israel—Israel the chosen of God. I was not descended from the rebellious Ephraim, who had played fast and loose with the covenant, as many Jews are, but from the select tribe of Benjamin, always faithful to Jehovah. I had no admixture of alien blood in my veins, for my ancestors from first to last were Hebrews.' Thus

in respect of these four points, (1) the covenant, (2) race, (3) tribe, (4) lineage, he was identified most closely and narrowly with the chosen people of God. He includes himself in the inmost circle of Judaism.

And not only this, but in sect, education and conduct nothing was wanting to identify him fully with Jewish feeling and Jewish life in its most rigid and trenchant form[1]. He was a Pharisee, the son of a Pharisee. He had been instructed at Jerusalem in the strictest principles of the law by Gamaliel, one of the seven great doctors, 'the Beauty of the Law,' whom all the Jews revered. He had carried out these principles with the utmost zeal and devotion. He was surpassed by none.

And the lessons which he learnt in this way, and which he could not have learnt so well in any other way, were two-fold.

First of all, there was the negative lesson of what the law could not effect. He had borne in his own person the burden. He had felt its galling pressure, striving earnestly, with all the intensity of his nature, to meet its exactions. In propor-tion as he increased his efforts, he had to confess his weakness and inability. Who can read his pathetic description in the Epistle to the Romans of the helplessness and despair of one struggling under the weight of this load, without feeling that the Apostle is drawing from his own personal experiences, that these are the words not of a vague theorizer, but of a painful sufferer. And here too it is important to observe the influence of the sect to which he belonged. Of the three great parties who shared the empire of Jewish thought—the Essenes, the Sadducees, the Pharisees—the last alone could teach him the lesson in its completeness. On the Sadducee the law sat loosely; he could not entirely divest himself of it, for it was the national badge, but he would wear it as lightly as he could. The Essene indeed was a most strict observer of ordinances, but the law was to him the starting-point of his mystical reveries, the

---

[1] The chief passages relating to St Paul's Jewish experiences are Gal. i. 13, 14; Phil. iii. 5, 6; Acts xxii. 3, xxiii. 6, xxvi. 4, 5; 2 Cor. xi. 22.

foundation of an ascetic practice by which he hoped to extricate the soul from the defilement of matter. Thus the Essenes could abandon the law where it seemed to interfere with their aspiration after purity, e.g. in sacrifice. To the Pharisee, on the other hand, the law presented itself in a different light. He regarded it as an end, as an absolute rule of conduct. He respected it in and for itself. 'Fulfil the law and you shall live,' was his motto. His vision did not extend beyond the law— the law as laid down by Moses, and as enlarged and interpreted by tradition. It was to him a compact strictly binding on the contracting parties in its minutest details. And thus it became to him, what it could scarcely have been to the Essene, the means of righteousness ($\delta\iota\kappa\alpha\iota\sigma\sigma\acute{\nu}\nu\eta$ $\dot{\epsilon}\kappa$ $\nu\acute{o}\mu\sigma\nu$). This is just the point which St Paul seizes upon as the important feature of the law regarded as an instrument of training. It is in contrast to, and in consequence of, it that he develops the doctrine of grace, essentially the cardinal point in the Gospel of the Apostle of the Gentiles.

But secondly, the positive influence which St Paul's Jewish education exercised upon him was equally great and important. Notwithstanding the opposition he met from his countrymen, in spite of all the liberal and the awakened sympathies which he derived from his work, despite the necessity of contending daily and hourly for the freedom of the Gospel among the Gentiles, he never ceased to be a Jew. From his repeated denunciations against the Judaizers we are apt to forget this feature in the Apostle's character until we are startled to find by some passing allusion how deep-seated is this feeling in his heart. The Apostle's whole nature was made up of contrasts, and this was one. 'The strength of sin is the law,' and 'the law is holy and righteous and good,' these two maxims[1] he could hold together and repeat in one breath. The most ardent patriot could not enlarge with greater pride on the glories of the chosen race than he does in the Epistle to the Romans. His care for the poor in Judæa is a touching proof

[1] 1 Cor. xv. 56; Rom. vii. 12.

of the strength of this national feeling. His attendance at the great annual festivals in Jerusalem is still more significant. 'I *must* spend the coming feast at Jerusalem[1]' (Δεῖ με πάντως τὴν ἑορτὴν τὴν ἐρχομένην ποιῆσαι εἰς Ἱεροσόλυμα). This language becomes the more striking when we remember that he was then intending to open out a new field of missionary labour in the far West, and was bidding perhaps his last farewell to the Holy City, the joy of the whole earth.

And here again it is important to remark on his connexion with the Pharisees. Whatever may have been their faults, they, and they alone, entered into the religious feeling of the nation. Hence their influence with the people. They were the true historical link with the past, they represented the growing consciousness of the chosen people, in the two all-essential points in which it prepared the way for the Gospel—in their belief in the immortality of the soul and in the cherished expectation of the Messiah. In more senses than one they sat in Moses' seat. The pure negativism of the Sadducee lent no aid here. Even if he did entertain some faint Messianic hopes, which is more than questionable, he deprived them of all religious value by denying a future state. And so again with the Essenes. Whatever importance we may attach to the reveries of the mystic Essene recluse, as testifying to the reality of a spiritual world, when all around was frozen and stiffened into formalism, still in his isolation from the national life of the Jews he lost that true historical instinct which was the life-blood of the people, and with it the vivid anticipations of the coming of Messiah.

It is not the spirit of the Sadducee, or of the Essene, but of the Pharisee, the son of Pharisees, which breathes in these glorious words, 'And now for the hope of the promise made by God to our fathers I stand at the bar as a criminal, unto which promise our twelve tribes, instantly ministering day and night,

---

[1] Acts xviii. 21, cf. xx. 16. If St Paul's words quoted above are to be rejected as an interpolation, this does not affect the fact of his visit to Jerusalem at this crisis (Acts xviii. 22).

hope to attain: for this hope I am accused, king Agrippa, *by Jews*' (Acts xxvi. 6, 7). And whatever shadow of worldly policy may for a moment be supposed to have overclouded the Apostle's conscience, as by his timely appeal he divided the two rival sects on the question of the resurrection of the dead[1], still the appeal in itself was perfectly justifiable, because perfectly true. His cause was the cause of the Pharisees, while between them and the Sadducees a great gulf was fixed.

I have thus traced the three threads which were in-woven into the texture of the Apostle's mind, to strengthen its fabric and so to prepare him for his great work. It may be said indeed that when he is first brought before our notice, he bears no traces of any other than Jewish influences. He is a bigoted zealot, a narrow-minded persecutor. There is even a strong contrast between the cautious liberality of Gamaliel the master, and the persecuting rage of Saul the pupil. But is it not a matter of common experience, that the lessons of youth often lie for a time dormant and unnoticed, till they are suddenly kindled into flame by some electric stroke from without? The miraculous appearance on the way to Damascus produced in St Paul a change far greater indeed but analogous to that which the more striking incidents of life have produced on many another. It flashed a new light on vast stores of experience laid up unconsciously in the past. It quickened into energy influences long forgotten and seemingly dead. The atoms of his nature assumed a fresh combination. The lightning fused the Apostle's character and moulded it in a new shape, and the knife of the torturer was forged into the sword of the Spirit.

[1] Acts xxiii. 6.

[1863.]

14—2

V.

THE CHRONOLOGY OF ST PAUL'S LIFE AND EPISTLES.

Printed from Lecture-notes.

V.

THE CHRONOLOGY OF ST PAUL'S LIFE AND EPISTLES.

O N the subject of the chronology of St Paul's life originality is out of the question. Unless new documents are discovered to throw fresh light upon the period, little or nothing can be added to our present stock of knowledge. Recent writers have treated the matter with a fulness which may be considered exhaustive, and it only remains for those who are later in the field to repeat and to sift the results at which their predecessors have already arrived.

It may be as well to premise at the outset that as regards the exact dates in St Paul's life absolute certainty is unattainable. An approximation to the truth is the most that we can expect, but this approximation is all that is necessary for my main object, which is to place his Epistles in connexion with his life. This impossibility of arriving at definite chronological results arises from the fact that there are very few points of contact between the Acts of the Apostles and contemporary history, and such points of contact as exist are of a vague kind chronologically. Indeed there are only two events in secular history which help us primarily in our search, though there are other allusions of a more uncertain character which can be appealed to as secondary and corroborative evidence. The two events to which I refer are, (1) the death of Herod Agrippa, (2) the procuratorship of Felix. We will proceed to investigate them in turn.

1. The death of Herod Agrippa, which is recorded in Acts xii. 23, is known to have fallen in 44 A.D. For Josephus

says that at the time of his death he had already completed the third year of his reign over the whole of Judæa (*Ant.* xix. 8. 2). Now this dignity was conferred upon him by Claudius soon after the commencement of that Emperor's reign, which took place on January 24th, A.D. 41. He died after the Passover, for it was during that festival that St Peter was imprisoned by him, and soon after Herod left Jerusalem for the last time. Now Herod's persecution of the Church and his subsequent death are related by St Luke in connexion with St Paul's second visit to Jerusalem. The account is inserted between the notices of St Paul's journey thither and his return to Antioch. It must not be assumed however that they exactly synchronized with that visit. St Luke's language is indefinite, 'about that time,' and as his object in digressing is to describe the state of the Church at Jerusalem when St Paul arrived, the incidents which are then interpolated in the narrative may be supposed to have happened previously to that visit. In this case St Paul's second visit to Jerusalem may be placed at the end of 44, or in 45.

St Paul's object in visiting Jerusalem on this occasion was to carry relief to the Jews suffering from a dearth which extended 'over the whole land,' or, as others would translate, 'the whole world' (ἐφ' ὅλην τὴν οἰκουμένην), and happened in the reign of Claudius[1]. Unfortunately contemporaneous history does not furnish us with the exact date of this dearth: but so far as we can draw any conclusion, it is quite in accordance with the result already obtained. We read of several famines occurring at different times in different parts of the Roman Empire during this reign, but of no general dearth. Among these, one (and one only) is recorded as having happened in Judæa. Whatever interpretation therefore is to be put upon the words ἐφ' ὅλην τὴν οἰκουμένην, this must be the occasion in question, as history supplies no other.

Now Josephus states[2] that this famine in Judæa fell in the procuratorships of Cuspius Fadus and Tiberius Alexander. Cuspius Fadus was appointed soon after the death of Herod

---

[1] Acts xi. 28.   [2] Jos. *Ant.* xx. 5. 2.

Agrippa, i.e. probably in 44, and Tiberius Alexander ceased to be procurator about 48. During this period then (44–48) the famine must have raged. Cuspius Fadus was still procurator at the end of June 45, but the close of his office is uncertain. If we suppose him to have been succeeded by Alexander in 46, the famine may have broken out in 45, and spread over the following year at least.

This date is further confirmed by another incident recorded by Josephus[1]. Helena, Queen of Adiabene, having recently embraced the Jewish religion, paid a visit to Jerusalem and, finding the famine raging, purchased food for the sufferers. This incident is inserted among events of 45, and the historian immediately adds that about this time (κατὰ τοῦτον τὸν καιρόν) Fadus appeared in his province. It seems highly probable then that the famine broke out in 45, and as the Christians of Antioch had been prepared beforehand by the prophecy of Agabus, and were ready with the means of relief, it may be presumed that Paul and Barnabas would be sent to Jerusalem as soon as the pressure began to be felt, i.e. in the year 45.

2. The date of the recall of Felix and the succession of Festus to the procuratorship is not directly known, but may be ascertained with a tolerable degree of accuracy.

Pentecost had already passed when St Paul was imprisoned at Jerusalem[2], and he remained in captivity two years before Festus reached his province. Festus therefore did not arrive before Pentecost. Again, at the great fast of the same year, which fell in October, St Paul was as far as Crete on his way to Rome. Festus therefore must have entered upon his procuratorship between Pentecost and October, i.e. some time in the summer or autumn of the year. We have now to determine this year.

The following considerations show that it could not well have been earlier than A.D. 60:—

(a) St Paul pleading before Felix (Acts xxiv. 10) says: 'I know that thou hast been of many years (ἐκ πολλῶν ἐτῶν) a

---

[1] Jos. *Ant.* xx. 2. 6, xx. 5. 2.   [2] Acts xx. 16, xxi. 27.

judge unto this nation.' Now Felix entered upon his procuratorship at the close of 52, and, if we allow between five and six years for the period designated πολλὰ ἔτη, this will give 58 as the date of St Paul's imprisonment, and 60 as that of Felix' recall. We can scarcely allow less, and on the other hand, considering the rapid succession of the procurators at this time, a period of five or six years might fairly be considered a long term of office.

(b) Nero came to the Imperial throne in October 54. Now Josephus[1] mentions several incidents which happened during the procuratorship of Felix subsequent to Nero's accession, and these together must have occupied a considerable time. These events include the death of Azizus, king of Emesa, the succession of Aristobulus to the kingdom of Chalcis, and the readjustment of the dominions of the younger Agrippa. They cover the period of the 'great quarrel' between the Jewish and Syrian inhabitants of Cæsarea, which was closed by the armed intervention of the Roman procurator. Describing the jealousy which arose at this time between Felix and the high priest Jonathan, and which led to the assassination of Jonathan in the streets of Jerusalem by the governor's order, Josephus speaks of the reign of terror which, as the result of this dark deed, prevailed at festival times from the bands of assassins, who infested the capital, murdering their private enemies with impunity, even inside the sacred precincts. He devotes two long chapters to an account of the various robbers and impostors who flourished during this period of Felix's procuratorship, beginning with Eleazar, son of Dinæus, who was treacherously slain by Felix, and culminating in the formidable insurrection of the Egyptian.

(c) This last-mentioned incident, the rebellion headed by the Egyptian, is alluded to by Claudius Lysias (Acts xxi. 38), on the occasion of St Paul's imprisonment, as having happened some time before (πρὸ τούτων τῶν ἡμερῶν). We may fairly allow five or six years for the events which happened previously (as enumerated in the last paragraph), for the duration of this

[1] Jos. *Ant.* xx. 8. 1—8, *B. J.* ii. 13.

rebellion itself, and for the period which elapsed; and this again will bring the date of St Paul's imprisonment to A.D. 58.

If this consideration leads to the year 60 as the earliest probable date of the recall of Felix, there are other circumstances which show that it cannot well have been later.

(1) Felix was the brother of Pallas, the notorious favourite of the Emperor Claudius, and after he had been removed from the procuratorship to make room for Festus, was only saved from the clamours of the Jews by the intercession of his brother. As Pallas was poisoned A.D. 62 (Tac. *Ann.* xiv. 65), Felix must have been recalled before this. It might have been supposed that this incident occurred before the removal of Pallas from power, A.D. 55, related by Tacitus (*Ann.* xiii. 14), but the considerations already adduced preclude this supposition.

(2) Again St Paul, after his arrival in Rome, preaches two whole years unmolested (Acts xxviii. 30, 31). The great fire at Rome broke out in July 64, and the persecution of the Christians commenced immediately after. Thus the Apostle cannot have arrived in Rome later than 62, and Felix must have been recalled in the summer of 61 at the latest.

(3) But there are other considerations which lead to the previous year 60 as the probable date of St Paul's arrival at Rome, for in Acts xxviii. 16 his fellow-prisoners are given up to the prefect of the prætorium (τῷ στρατοπεδάρχῃ). Now Burrus held the office of prefect alone, but after his death it was shared by two, as had been the case also before his appointment. As the plural is generally used in similar cases, the singular here would seem to imply that there was but one prefect at this time, i.e. that Burrus was still living. But Burrus died early in the year 62 (in February at the latest)[1], and St Paul can scarcely have arrived in Rome before the end of March. The great fast, which fell on the 10th of Tishri (corresponding roughly to October), had already passed when the ship left Lasæa in Crete. The voyage thence to Malta occupied fourteen days, and there they stayed three months, leaving for

[1] Tac. *Ann.* xiv. 52.

Puteoli by an Alexandrian vessel, that had wintered at Malta (Acts xxviii. 11). The season at which the seas became navigable is stated by Vegetius[1] to be the sixth before the Ides of March. For long voyages Pliny[2] places it at the vernal equinox. Taking the earlier date we have to allow three days for the stay at Syracuse, one for the delay at Rhegium, two for the voyage thence to Puteoli, and seven for the stay at Puteoli (Acts xxviii. 12—14). Besides this we have to account for the voyages from Malta to Syracuse and from Syracuse to Rhegium, with the journey from Puteoli to Rome, St Luke not having stated the time occupied by these. If therefore Burrus was still living when St Paul reached the metropolis, he must have arrived in the preceding year 61, and Felix must have been recalled in the summer of 60.

(4) This date is further borne out by another consideration. Felix was succeeded by Festus, Festus by Albinus. Now Albinus was already procurator at the Feast of Tabernacles A.D. 62. For the Jewish war broke out in 66, and Albinus was at Jerusalem at the season of this festival four years before. How long he had held office at that time we are ignorant. At most however this would allow only a year and a quarter for the procuratorship of Festus, supposing him to have entered on his office in the summer of 61. But the number of incidents which Josephus records as having taken place during his procuratorship can scarcely be crowded into this short space of time; and we are thus led to the year 60 as the more probable date of his appointment.

We have thus ascertained two fixed dates in the chronology of St Paul's life—A.D. 45 for his second journey to Jerusalem and A.D. 60 for his voyage to Rome. The former of these being an isolated event in St Luke's narrative is of little value comparatively for our purpose; but from the latter the whole of the known chronology of St Paul's life is determined, by means of the notices in the Acts of the sequence of events and the

---

[1] Vegetius *de re militari* iv. 39.　　　[2] Pliny *N. H.* ii. 47.

time occupied by them, together with occasional allusions in the Epistles.

These notices in St Luke's narrative are much more exact in the latter part of the history, commencing with the third missionary journey, than in the former: and it will be seen from the following table how the dates of the Apostle's life are ascertained by a backward reckoning from the date of the procuratorship of Festus.

A.D.

34. St Paul's conversion.

Cf. Gal. i. 15 sq. Three years after his conversion he went up to Jerusalem, for (1) the point of time is obviously his conversion, for the argument depends on that, and (2) μετὰ τρία ἔτη must mean three whole years, or substantially so, for the preposition μετὰ, to say nothing of the argument, excludes the supposition of a Judaical reckoning, by which a term of a little more than a year might be so designated [1].

He visits Arabia, and returns to Damascus (Gal. i. 17, Acts ix. 20–25, 2 Cor. xi. 32, 33).

37. First visit to Jerusalem (Acts ix. 26, Gal. i. 18).

Cf. Gal. ii. 1. Between the first and third visit to Jerusalem a period of 14 years elapsed, for (1) the visit recorded in this passage of the Galatians must be identified with the third of the Acts, (2) διὰ δεκατεσσάρων ἐτῶν must be reckoned from the first visit, not from the date of the Apostle's conversion, because St Paul's object is to show how long a period elapsed without his holding communication with the Apostles of the Circumcision, (3) πάλιν ἀνέβην refers back to the previous visit.

37–44. To Cæsarea and Tarsus, visit to Syria (Acts ix. 30, Gal. i. 21).

44. St Paul brought by Barnabas to Antioch. He stays there a year (Acts xi. 26).

45. Second visit to Jerusalem with alms (Acts xi. 29, 30).

46, 47. At Antioch.

48. FIRST MISSIONARY JOURNEY (Acts xiii. 1–xiv. 26) with Barnabas.
He visits Cyprus, Antioch in Pisidia, Iconium, Lystra, Derbe, and returns to Antioch.

---

[1] [In his commentary on the Galatians, however, Dr Lightfoot adopts the Jewish reckoning, and places the conversion in A.D. 36, and the first visit to Jerusalem in A.D. 38; see note on Gal. ii. 1, 2.]

A.D.

51. Third visit to Jerusalem with Barnabas (Gal. ii. 1 sq., Acts xv. 1 sq.). The Council of Jerusalem.

Returns to Antioch.   The interview with Peter (Gal. ii. 11 sq.).

SECOND MISSIONARY JOURNEY (Acts xv. 36–xviii. 22) with Silas.

First visit to Galatia.

52. Crosses into Europe.   First visit to Philippi, Thessalonica, and Corinth.

[1 Thessalonians.]

53. At Corinth.

[2 Thessalonians.]

54. (Spring) Leaves Corinth for Ephesus.

(Summer) Fourth visit to Jerusalem at Pentecost (Acts xviii. 21, 22).

Returns to Antioch.

(Autumn) THIRD MISSIONARY JOURNEY (Acts xviii. 23–xxi. 15).

Second visit to Galatia (Acts xviii. 23, Gal. iv. 13–16).

To Ephesus again.

55. At Ephesus.

Second visit to Corinth (2 Cor. xii. 14, xiii. 1, 2).

56. At Ephesus.   Sends a letter (now lost) to the Corinthians (1 Cor. v. 9).

Reply from the Corinthians (1 Cor. vii. 1).

57. (Spring) At Ephesus.   Mission of Timotheus to Corinth (1 Cor. xvi. 10–12, Acts xix. 22).

[1 Corinthians.]

First Mission of Titus to Corinth (2 Cor. xii. 18).

St Paul leaves Ephesus, overtaking Timotheus (?).

Visits Troas and Macedonia.

Second visit to Philippi and Thessalonica.

(Autumn) Titus rejoins St Paul in Macedonia (2 Cor. vii. 6).

[2 Corinthians.]

Second Mission of Titus to Corinth.

(Winter) Third visit to Corinth (Acts xx. 2).

[Galatians [1].]

58. (Spring) At Corinth.

[Romans.]

Third visit to Philippi ; meets the elders of Ephesus at Miletus.

(Summer) Fourth visit to Jerusalem : arrested and sent to Cæsarea.

59. At Cæsarea.

60. (Autumn) Voyage to Rome, and shipwreck at Malta.

61. (Spring) Arrival at Rome.

---

[1] The Epistle to the Galatians may have been written in the early spring   of A.D. 58.

A.D.

62. (Spring) At Rome.

[Philippians.]

(Autumn)   [Colossians, Ephesians, Philemon.]

63. (Spring) Release of St Paul.

St Luke's narrative mentions 'two whole years' (Acts xxviii. 30) as the period of St Paul's sojourn at Rome. The notice implies a change at the end of this period, hence we fix the release in the spring of 63.

63–66. *First journey Eastward.*

(?) He revisits Macedonia. Fourth visit to Philippi (ταχέως ἐλεύσομαι, Phil. ii. 24).

(?) Revisits Asia and Phrygia. Visit to Colossæ (Philemon 22). *Journey Westward.*

(?) Founds the Church of Crete.

Visits Spain, Gaul (?) (2 Tim. iv. 10), and Dalmatia (?) (2 Tim. iv. 10). *Second journey Eastward.*

Revisits Asia and Phrygia (2 Tim. i. 15 sq.). Visits Ephesus (1 Tim. i. 3) ; here probably he encounters Alexander the coppersmith (1 Tim. i. 20, 2 Tim. iv. 14). Leaves Timothy in charge of the Ephesian Church.

67. Revisits Macedonia (1 Tim. i. 3). Fifth visit to Philippi.

(?) Revisits Achaia (Athens and Corinth).

[1 Timothy.]

Visits (perhaps revisits) Crete, and leaves Titus in charge of the Church there (Titus i. 5). Returns to Asia.

[Titus.]

Visits Miletus (2 Tim. iv. 20), sails to Troas (2 Tim. iv. 13), is at Corinth (2 Tim. iv. 20) on his way to Nicopolis to winter (Tit. iii. 12).

(Autumn) Arrested (probably at Corinth)[1], and carried to Rome. Titus joins him there.

[2 Timothy.]

Timothy shares his imprisonment (Heb. xiii. 23).

68 (?). (Spring) Martyrdom of St Paul (Jerome *de vir. illustr.* 5 'in the fourteenth year of Nero'[2]).

June. Death of Nero.

The table of the events of St Paul's life given above has been drawn up with the special object of presenting a record of the Apostle's association with the Churches to which he wrote

[1] Nero was in Greece from A.D. 66 to August A.D. 67 (Suet. *Nero* 19 sq.; Jos. *B. J.* ii. 20. 1).

[2] Eusebius (*Chronicon*) places it 'in the thirteenth year of Nero' i.e. before Oct. 67.

letters, and of the periods of his epistolary activity. It remains for us now to consider in their mutual relations the letters which have come down to us.

The Epistles of St Paul may be divided into four chronological groups, each group being separated from the next by an interval of about five years, each group again corresponding to a marked epoch in the Apostle's life, and representing a distinct phase in his teaching. To make my meaning clear, I give the scheme in a tabulated form:—

Period	Epistles	Dates	Characteristics
1. Second Missionary Journey	1 and 2 Thessalonians	A.D. 52, 53	Christ the Judge *or* The Tribunal
2. Third Missionary Journey	1 and 2 Corinthians Galatians Romans	57, 58	Christ the Redeemer *or* The Cross
3. First Roman Captivity	Philippians Ephesians Colossians Philemon	62, 63	Christ the Word *or* The Throne
4. After the Release, including the Second Roman Captivity.	1 Timothy Titus 2 Timothy	67, 68	Church Organisation *or* The Congregation

These dates are in some cases approximate only. Thus there is a possibility that 1 Thessalonians was written in A.D. 51, and 2 Thessalonians in A.D. 52; a possibility also that the Epistles of the First Roman Captivity should be antedated a year throughout; but upon the whole the above is the result which falls in best with the chronology of St Paul's life as given above; and the phenomenon which this result presents throws much light upon the way in which we should approach the study of Holy Scripture as the vehicle of Divine revelation.

In every inspired writing there are two elements, the human and the Divine, or, as it is sometimes expressed, the letter and the spirit; and the different views held of the doctrine of inspiration depend upon the prominence given to one or the other of these elements, and the judgment formed of their mutual relations. Hence it will be seen that no conceivable shade of opinion is excluded, and every attempt at classifying these views must be more or less fallacious. But it will be sufficiently exact for our present purpose roughly to assume a threefold division in the attitude taken by writers on this question—in the first of these the Divine element being too exclusively considered, in the second this undue prominence being assigned to the human agency, and in the third, and only adequate view of inspiration, each of these elements being recognised in its proper sphere and the two harmoniously combined. The first of these views is irrational, the second is rationalistic, the third alone is in accordance alike with the highest reason and the fullest faith.

The irrational view—that which loses sight of the human agency—is prior in time (I am speaking now of modern criticism) to the rationalistic. It refuses to recognise any peculiarities in the individual writer who is under the guidance of the Spirit; it is insensible to any varieties in style, any difference in the method of treatment in different books of Holy Scripture. It reduces the whole Bible to one uniform colour. It is needless to say that such a view must fall at once before the assaults of criticism. If this were all, it might be borne patiently, but unhappily it has dragged down the tottering faith of not a few in its fall. It may also be said that it is derogatory to the majesty of God, that it has no support from analogy in His workings elsewhere, and no authority from Holy Scripture itself.

This theory of inspiration provokes a reaction. The rationalistic view is the natural consequence of its exaggerated form. In this the human element is put so prominently forward that the Divine is obscured. The Divine agency is perhaps not actually denied, but it is so virtually. By indefinitely extending the action of inspiration, it is in fact rendered meaningless. It is allowed that Moses and David, that St Paul and St John, were inspired, but then the same privilege is claimed for Homer and Æschylus, for Pythagoras and Plato. Now I should be the last

L. E.   15

to deny that whatever is good, whatever is beautiful, whatever is true in the heathen writers is derived from the primal source of all beauty, truth and goodness. I have been taught—and I fully believe it—that every good gift and every perfect gift cometh from above. But practically there is such a vast difference between the illumination of the apostle and prophet, and the illumination of the philosopher and poet, that to call both by the same term 'inspiration,' instead of tending to clear our conceptions, does in fact leave a very erroneous impression on our minds. Inspiration is thus emptied of its significance.

The true view is a mean between these extremes, or rather it is a combination of the two. It recognises the element of truth which each contains, adopting and uniting the elements. And it recognises them too in all their fulness. It does not assign less power to the Divine agency, nor does it ignore any of the characteristics of the human instrument. The truth is one, but it has many sides. One man is more fitted than another by natural endowments to appreciate it from some particular point of view. No man is capable of seeing it from every side, else he becomes more than a man. The Holy Spirit has chosen His instruments, as Christ chose His Apostles, for their natural gifts, whether intellectual or spiritual, and has inspired them for our instruction and guidance. But He has not destroyed their individuality. Each with his special message to deliver, they become fit instruments under Divine guidance to develop a particular aspect of the truth, and we may suppose, without presumption, that they had each their part assigned them, according to their natural capabilities and acquirements, in penning the volume of Holy Scripture, as we know that they had in rearing the fabric of the Church.

To sum up and to apply what has been said. Inspiration is not a mechanical power or a magical agency. It does not use men merely as its instruments. It is a moral and spiritual power. It does not transmute its agents: it moulds them. Hence, as a natural result arising from the varied circumstances and training of the inspired writers, it is not uniform. And, for a right appreciation of the lessons of Holy Scripture, three stages in this absence of uniformity must be recognised. First, there is a growth from age to age. From the Law we advance to the prophets; from the prophets to the Gospels. Thus inspiration is developed. Secondly, there is a diversity of inspiration in different persons in the same age. One sacred writer, St Paul, views the Gospel as the abrogation of the Law; another, St James, as its fulfilment. They are not contradictory, but complementary the one to the other, for the Gospel is at once the abrogation and the fulfilment of the Law. One Evangelist, St John, dwells chiefly on the Eternal Sonship of the Saviour; another, St Luke, on His human tenderness and His sympathy with our infirmities. They are both true, for He is very God and very Man. Thus they have different functions to perform; their office is to set forth the Gospel message from different points of view, which are determined by their respective positions and characters. Thirdly, there is a diversity in the same writer in different stages in his career. When we apply this principle to St Paul, we discover on examination that he exhibits a historical development in his teaching. By the word 'development' is meant, not that St Paul added to his doctrines, but that he altered the lights in which he placed them, making one point more prominent at one time than at another. The whole doctrine is there from the first implicitly involved in the fundamental conception of the person of Christ, but the particular aspects are brought into special prominence, as they are called out at different times by the exigencies of external circumstances.

These external circumstances are twofold; first, the varying requirements of the Church at large, secondly, the altered conditions of the Apostle's own life. These are the two forces through which inspiration acts upon the development of St Paul's teaching; and the progress in his case I have endeavoured to express in the watchwords which I have attached above to the four groups of Epistles—'The Tribunal,' 'The Cross,' 'The Throne,' 'The Congregation.'

For the sake of convenience we will set aside the chronological order, and consider, at the outset, the first and the fourth group of his Epistles. The doctrine of the Epistles to the Thessalonians throughout is the Second Advent, 'Christ the Judge.' This is the one prominent idea which runs through this pair of letters from end to end. Similarly, the purpose of the Pastoral Epistles is ecclesiastical organization. In the light of the external circumstances of the Church at the two periods involved, the reasons for this striking difference between the two groups are hardly less obvious than the fact of its existence.

It is only natural that the doctrine of the Second Advent should occur early in the Pauline Epistles. And this for several reasons. The Resurrection was the central point in the teaching of the Twelve after the Day of Pentecost, and the Resurrection naturally suggested its necessary correlative, the Second Coming of Christ. Again, the doctrine of the Second Advent involved the doctrine of rewards for faithful service in the infancy of the Church. When persecution was rife, the disciples would need the necessary incentive to steadfastness under trial which such a promise brought with it. Thirdly, the expectation of the Second Advent implied the call to repentance, and therefore found its natural place in the forefront of St Paul's early teaching, just as the Baptist's cry 'Repent' preceded our Lord's ministry. Thus, in his discourse on the Areopagus, St Paul, after drawing attention to God's presence in nature, goes on to point the moral of the special doctrine of revelation as repentance resulting upon Christ's coming to judgment[1]. Lastly, Messianic hopes had to be satisfied. Hitherto, externally everything had ended in disappointment. The King had suffered a malefactor's death; and the Ascension, which followed upon the triumph of the Resurrection, was, to Jewish Christians, if not a negation, at least a deferring, of the promised kingdom of God. Thus the Second Advent became the answer to Messianic expectations.

And if the Second Advent furnished the natural theme for St Paul's earliest Epistles, not less obvious is it why his latest

---

[1] Acts xvii. 30, 31.

utterances should have been devoted to the question of the organization of the Church. A study of the history of the Church at this period shows a growing restlessness both in thought and action, synchronizing with the withdrawal of the teachers most competent to check these disorders. Schisms and heresies were starting into life within the fold, and meanwhile the apostolate was dying out. Therefore a double necessity was laid upon 'Paul the aged' to meet this danger by strengthening and developing the Church's system of government. If we look at the Pastoral Epistles, we find no new doctrine inculcated. The two notes which are struck again and again are (1) 'Hold fast the tradition' ($\tau\dot{\eta}\nu$ $\pi\alpha\rho\alpha\theta\dot{\eta}\kappa\eta\nu$ $\phi\dot{\upsilon}\lambda\alpha\xi\upsilon\nu$ 1 Tim. vi. 20, 2 Tim. i. 14), and (2) 'Preserve order in the Church.' In short, this group of Epistles constitutes St Paul's last will and testament, in which he gives his final instructions for the maintenance and continuity of the faith.

Thus the two letters to the Thessalonians and the Pastoral Epistles may be entitled the preface and the postscript respectively to the Pauline literature, its prologue and its epilogue. We have now cleared the ground, and may pass on to consider the second and third of the groups of Epistles, which contain the main substance of the Apostle's doctrine. And here a somewhat fuller explanation will be necessary. The ancient Greek Fathers divided what we call by the general name of 'Theology' into two distinct provinces, $\omega\kappa\upsilon\upsilon\upsilon\mu\dot{\iota}\alpha$ and $\theta\epsilon\upsilon\lambda\upsilon\gamma\dot{\iota}\alpha$. The first of these two terms points, as its derivation implies, to a Divine dispensation. The Church is, in effect, the household ($\dot{\upsilon}$ $\upsilon\dot{\iota}\kappa\upsilon\varsigma$) of God, and $\dot{\eta}$ $\omega\kappa\upsilon\upsilon\upsilon\mu\dot{\iota}\alpha$ is the plan by which God rules His household. It is the means whereby God ransoms from sin. It includes the dispensation of the gifts and graces of the Spirit which form part of the Divine 'household-stuff.' On the other hand, as understood by the Fathers, $\dot{\eta}$ $\theta\epsilon\upsilon\lambda\upsilon\gamma\dot{\iota}\alpha$ directed itself to the contemplation of Christ's Eternal Being—His relation to the Father and the Holy Spirit before the worlds were made. It was in this technical sense of the word that Gregory of Nazianzus and St John alike procured the title of ὁ θεολόγος. Thus the spheres in which the two sciences move are different. The one centres round the Incarnation and embraces all that flows therefrom; the other, taking for its theme the Divine attributes of Christ, pierces behind the Incarnation to the Eternal, Pre-existent Word. This twofold division in the province of Theology has its counterpart in the two groups of St Paul's Epistles with which we are now concerned. The distinctive feature of the Epistles of the Third Missionary Journey is the stress laid upon οἰκονομία; on the other hand, the Epistles of the First Roman Captivity deal mainly with θεολογία. I have therefore given as its leading characteristic to the one group, 'the Cross,' to the other, 'the Throne.'

Justification, Atonement, Sacrifice—the vast majority of passages which bear upon these doctrines are to be found in the Epistles of the second group. And if we turn to the circumstances of the Church at the period at which they were written, the reason becomes obvious. This was the time of St Paul's great conflict with Judaism on the one hand and Hellenism on the other. The Cross of Christ contains the complete answer to the error of both, to the formalism of the one and the antinomianism of the other. 'Christ died for us'—here is the reply to the legalism of the Jew, setting forth that the true ground of Christian hope is faith, not works; 'we must die with Christ'—here is the reply to the license of the Greek, exhibiting as it does the true motive of life. In short, there is a work done for us, and a work done in us. The two must not be separated. Christ's righteousness, so St Paul tells us, cannot become our righteousness, unless we become one with Christ, unless we live in Christ. It is this repose in Christ which makes sin impossible. This is St Paul's doctrine. He never sacrifices the one proposition to the other. When he dwells on the truth 'Christ died for us,' he is ever mindful of its correlative 'We must die with Christ,' i.e. die to self and to sin. He never separates the religious belief from the moral change. Nay, he cannot conceive of the two as separated. For

faith in Christ is a moral as well as an intellectual state, and
with St Paul its moral aspect is in fact the more prominent of
the two. So that not 'justification by faith' so much as 'dying
and living with Christ' 'oneness with Christ' may be regarded
as the central point of his Gospel. This is the meaning of his
constantly repeated phrase 'in the Lord,' 'in Christ' (ἐν Κυρίῳ,
ἐν Χριστῷ)[1], and this fact it is which, when once realised, makes
it impossible even to suspect an opposition between St Paul
and St James in their fundamental views, though the verbal
statement of them is at first sight different[2]. The two proposi-
tions of the antithesis contain the answer to the two fundamental
errors of the Jew and the Gentile. The Jewish error, which was
dogmatic, rested upon a false ground of hope. The Hellenic
error, which was practical, sprang from a false theory of life.
The Jewish convert said, 'We are saved by the works of the law.'
St Paul's answer is, 'No: Christ died for us. A work has been
done for us by God; and we are saved by faith in Christ'
(meaning thereby, faith in Christ, with all that the idea conveys
with it). The Gentile convert said, 'We are no longer under
the works of the law. We are free to do as we like; let us sin
that grace may abound.' 'No,' replies the Apostle, 'we must
die with Christ; Christ's work must be done in us.' Thus the
danger of the one was bondage; the danger of the other
license. These respective errors he meets separately in writing
to the Galatians and to the Corinthians. The watchword of

---

[1] Ἐν Κυρίῳ Rom. xiv. 14, xvi. 2, 8,
11, 12, 13, 22; 1 Cor. iv. 17, vii. 22, 39,
ix. 1, 2, xi. 11, xv. 58, xvi. 19; 2 Cor.
ii. 12 etc.; ἐν Χριστῷ Rom. iii. 24, vi.
11, 23, viii. 1, 2, 39, ix. 1, xii. 5, xv. 17,
xvi. 3, 7, 10; 1 Cor. i. 2, 4, 30, iii. 1,
iv. 10, 15, 17, xv. 18, 19, 31; 2 Cor. ii.
17, v. 17, xii. 2, 19 etc.

[2] Some modern teachers however,
alleging his name, have forgotten the
one proposition or the other. Taking
justification by faith and by faith alone
as their watchword, they have produced,
as an extreme result, antinomianism.

Hence Luther's saying 'Sin, and sin
boldly,' though Luther himself was
anything but antinomian. Mr M.
Arnold justly protests against this
perversion, this one-sided view, of St
Paul's doctrine, and all its dangerous
consequences, dangerous to practice
and dangerous to belief, for it has
done more than almost anything else
to repel the moral sense. On the
other hand, Mr M. Arnold himself, it
seems to me, has thrown the other
proposition 'Christ died for us' a little
too much into the background.

the one Epistle is 'Liberty, not license'; of the other 'Not license, but liberty,' though in neither is the antithetical proposition suppressed[1]. Finally in the Epistle to the Romans the composite character of the Church which he addressed compelled him to combine the two aspects, and to treat them in a full exposition.

And side by side with the special questions which were agitating the Church at large at this crisis of her history, must be set the particular circumstances of the Apostle's life. This was its most tumultuous period, a time of constant travel, of bitter personal opposition, of ceaseless activities of every kind. All this combined to fit him at this time to be the exponent of this particular side of Gospel truth.

We turn to the third group of Epistles, and at once we notice a change of subject-matter. The metaphysical, mystical, contemplative aspects of the Gospel are brought out into special prominence. In place of the lessons of soteriology and redemption which we meet with in the Epistles of the Third Missionary Journey, Christ is exhibited as the Eternal Word, as God manifest in the flesh[2], and, as the corollary upon this teaching, is set forth the union of the individual and the Church with God through Christ[3]. Christ's reign in heaven, His pre-existence, His omnipotence, form the Apostle's theme rather than His life on earth, His humiliation, the example of His perfect character. The Church militant is for the time lost in the Church triumphant. As before, the secret of this change of thought is to be found in the altered conditions of the Apostle's life and the Church's needs. A lengthened term of imprisonment, first at Cæsarea, then at Rome, had succeeded upon a period of bustling, strained activity. In God's good

---

[1] Contrast generally Gal. ii. 15 sq (vv. 19, 20 supply the corrective), iii. 2, 10 sq, v. 3—6, 11 (vv. 13 sq, 16 sq corrective), vi. 14, with 1 Cor. v. 6, 7 (v. 7 καὶ γὰρ τὸ πάσχα corrective), vi. 9 sq (v. 11 corrective), 15 sq (v. 20 corrective), vii. 19, 23, viii. 8, 9 (v. 11 corrective), ix. 19, 21, x. 14, 16, 23, 32, xi. 3, xii. 12, 27, 2 Cor. i. 5, iv. 10—12, v. 17—20 (v. 21 corrective).

[2] Cf. Eph. i. 10, 20–23, iii. 15, iv. 15, vi. 9; Phil. ii. 6 sq; Col. i. 15 sq, ii. 9 sq, iii. 1, 4, etc.

[3] Cf. Phil. iii. 20; Eph. ii. 19, etc.

providence St Paul was enjoying a season of uninterrupted rest, which gave the opportunity for a contemplation of the highest mysteries of the faith. The most tranquil period of his life supervened upon the most tumultuous. The Epistle to the Ephesians is the expression of the one period, the Second Epistle to the Corinthians is the reflection of the other. But the consideration that the Apostle's frame of mind at this time would naturally lead him to the study of metaphysical specu- lation must not blind us to the propriety of this study in relation to the altered conditions of the Church. The foe from which she had most to fear now was no longer Judaism or Hellenism, but Orientalism, that mystic, theosophic speculation with regard to angelic, intermediate beings between God and man which was afterwards known as Gnosticism and reached its climax in the fantastic systems of Basilides and Valentinus. That this was the case is evident when we consider the character of the heresy in the Colossian Church, against which St Paul argues in his Epistle to that Church. In order therefore to confront these false doctrines, it was necessary for the Apostle to show that there was only one link between God and man, Christ manifest in the flesh, and that there was no room for the successive emanations, in the creation of which his opponents delighted to indulge their elaborate fancy.

[1863.]

VI.

THE CHURCHES OF MACEDONIA.

VI.

THE CHURCHES OF MACEDONIA.

ST PAUL'S first visit to Macedonia was the dawn of a new era in the development of the Christian Church. The incidents, which ushered it in, spoke significantly to himself and his fellow-labourers; and, in St Luke's record, they stand out in bold relief. The entrance into Macedonia and the visit to Rome are the two most important stages in the Apostle's missionary life, as they are also the two most emphatic passages in the historian's narrative—the one the opening campaign of the Gospel in the West, the other its crowning triumph. It is no surprise therefore that St Paul years afterwards should speak of his labours in Macedonia, as 'the beginning of the Gospel[1],' though his missionary course was now half run. The faith of Christ had, as it were, made a fresh start.

This portion of St Luke's narrative[2] is emphasized not by any artifice of the writer, but by the progress of the incidents themselves which all converge to one point. St Paul having

---

[1] Phil. iv. 15 ἐν ἀρχῇ τοῦ εὐαγγελίου.

[2] Acts xvi. 6–10 Διελθόντες δὲ τὴν Φρυγίαν καὶ Γαλατικὴν χώραν, κωλυθέντες ὑπὸ τοῦ ἁγίου πνεύματος λαλῆσαι τὸν λόγον ἐν τῇ Ἀσίᾳ, ἐλθόντες κατὰ τὴν Μυσίαν ἐπείραζον εἰς τὴν Βιθυνίαν πορευθῆναι καὶ οὐκ εἴασεν αὐτοὺς τὸ πνεῦμα Ἰησοῦ· παρελθόντες δὲ τὴν Μυσίαν κατέβησαν εἰς Τρῳάδα κ.τ.λ. If the reading διῆλθον...ἐλθόντες δὲ... be correct, the complexion of the incident will be slightly, but not materially, altered. But, though the preponderance of authority is considerably in its favour, it is open to suspicion as an attempt to simplify the grammar of a sentence rendered awkward by the accumulation of participles.

passed through the country of Phrygia and Galatia is driven
forward under the divine guidance and in spite of his own
impulses towards the shores of the Hellespont. Attempting to
diverge on either side, he is checked and kept in the direct
path. He first looks wistfully towards the country lying on his
left, wishing to preach the Gospel in the populous district of
Proconsular Asia. 'The Holy Spirit forbids him' to do so.
He next turns his steps towards Bithynia situated on his right,
doubtless with the same purpose. This attempt is as futile as
the former. 'The Spirit of Jesus' will not permit it. Thus
hemmed in on either side, he has no choice but to go forward,
and so he arrives on the coast of the Ægæan. Here at length
the meaning of those strange hindrances, which had thwarted
his energetic purpose, becomes apparent. God's providence has
destined him for a nobler mission-field. While at Troas gazing
on the sight of the opposite shores of Europe, he receives an
intimation which decides him. He sees a vision in the night.
A man of Macedonia stands before him and entreats him:
'Come over and help us.' He considers this as an indication of
the will of God, and in obedience thereto he crosses the narrow
sea which separates Asia from Europe.

In this way St Luke forces upon our notice the importance
of this visit to Macedonia. When he comes to narrate the
visit itself, he does so with a greater minuteness of detail than
is usually found in his narrative. The incidents of St Paul's
preaching at Philippi especially, the first European town which
hears the truths of the Gospel from the lips of the Apostle, are
dwelt upon with singular fulness. Of these incidents the historian was himself an eyewitness. He had but lately joined
St Paul's company for the first time, and the scenes, in which
he now moved, would naturally dwell in his memory with all
the force of fresh and unwonted experiences. But beyond this
personal reason we can scarcely doubt that the fulness of detail
in this part of his narrative is due also to the conviction in his
mind that this visit heralded a new and important era in the
history of the Christian Church.

It was not only that the Apostle had surmounted the sea-barrier which separates two tracts of country bearing different names, and conventionally regarded as distinct continents[1]. The real significance of his journey lay in this, that it brought him in contact with new interests, new associations and ideas, or at least into closer contact with them than hitherto. He now occupied the ground which from its geographical position was the natural high road between the East and the West, and was mixing with that people whose mission it had been to fuse the whole civilised world, to bring the arts and intelligence of Greece and the political capacities of Rome into alliance with the nobler spiritual instincts and sublimer theological conceptions of Asia—above all, with the one specially revealed religion of Palestine—and thus to pioneer the way for the Gospel. The great Macedonian conqueror had appreciated the task which its natural position imposed upon his country. He can have been no mere selfish tyrant or vain profligate, who when advised by the wisest philosopher of the day to treat the Greeks as free subjects, the Orientals as slaves, repudiated the narrow counsels of his teacher, declaring that he had been 'sent by God to unite, pacify, and reconcile the whole world[2].' This generous sentiment of Alexander was an anticipation, however feeble, of the work of that great Reconciler, who broke down the partition walls between castes and nations[3], and may well recal the loftier utterance of St Paul, who proclaimed that there was now 'neither Greek nor Jew, Barbarian, Scythian, bond nor free,' but all were 'one in Christ[4].' And when again we read of the

---

[1] It is interesting to observe that 'Europe' is never once mentioned in the New Testament, and that 'Asia' denotes not the continent, but the Roman province. The words of the man in St Paul's vision are not 'Come over into Europe,' but 'Come over into Macedonia,' Acts xvi. 9.

[2] Plut. de Alex. Fort. 1. § 6. Op. Mor. p. 329 B Οὐ γὰρ, ὡς Ἀριστοτέλης συνεβούλευεν αὐτῷ, τοῖς μὲν Ἕλλησιν

ἡγεμονικῶς, τοῖς δὲ βαρβάροις δεσποτικῶς χρώμενον...ἀλλὰ κοινὸς ἥκειν θεόθεν ἁρμοστὴς καὶ διαλλακτὴς τῶν ὅλων νομίζων κ.τ.λ. The whole passage is worth reading.

[3] See Ephes. ii. 14, 15; and compare the expressions ἀποκαταλλάξαι τὰ πάντα Col. i. 20, and καταλλαγὴ κόσμου Rom. xi. 15.

[4] Col. iii. 11, Gal. iii. 28.

taunts levelled at the Macedonian king by narrower-minded Greeks, because he strove to conciliate the Oriental peoples whom he had vanquished, by conforming to their dress and habits as matters of indifference[1], we seem to trace the shadow of that large-hearted policy of the Apostle of the Gentiles, who in a like spirit, but with a nobler aim, braved the fierce hatred of his countrymen, consenting to be reviled as a subverter of the laws and institutions of his fathers, and, himself a Jew, became as a Greek to the Greeks that he might win them to Christ[2].

Alexander had not entertained this grand purpose in vain. Though he died young, he had accomplished a vast task, the importance of which to the future history of the world it is scarcely possible to overrate. If he had not realised his project, he had prepared the way for its realisation in a far higher sense than he himself could have imagined. He had diffused the literature and life, the habits and institutions, of Europe through the East. He had made the language of Greece a common instrument of communication throughout the civilised world. Now, at length, the completion of his great design, though very different, no doubt, from that which he himself had contemplated, was drawing near. And as his country had borne the chief part in preparing the way for this universal pacification of the world, so now in turn she was herself to receive the earliest and most striking earnest of its fulfilment. The tide, which had once flowed eastward through Macedonia bearing with it the civilisation of the West, was now rolled back through the same channel, laden with a nobler treasure, by which Asia more than discharged her debt of obligation to Europe.

Each successive station at which he halted might have reminded the Apostle of the great services rendered by Macedonia as the pioneer of the Gospel. The very names of the

---

[1] See Plutarch l. c. p. 329 C and p. 330 A Ἐκ τοῦ Μακεδονικοῦ καὶ Περσικοῦ τρόπου μεμιγμένην τινὰ στολὴν ἐφόρει καθάπερ Ἐρατοσθένης ἱστόρηκεν· ὡς μὲν φιλόσοφος τοῖς ἀδιαφόροις χρώμενος κ.τ.λ.

[2] 1 Cor. ix. 19 sq, Gal. ii. 14 sq.

places bore testimony to the part she had played in history. The seaport whence he embarked on leaving the Asiatic shore was surnamed, after the great conqueror of the East, Alexandria Troas.   In Philippi, the first European city which he visited, was perpetuated the memory of the monarch, who, by organizing the armies of Macedonia and establishing the supremacy of his country over Greece, prepared the way for the vast projects of Oriental conquest carried out by his greater son.   The name of the next town in which he planted the standard of the cross spoke of a later stage in the progress of events.   It recalled the partition of Alexander's empire, having been founded by one of his successors Cassander, in honour of his wife Thessalonica, the half-sister of the conqueror himself.   Whether St Paul, while visiting these scenes, recalled the past glories of Macedonia, whether he traced in this marvellous page of her history the hand of God moulding the selfish counsels of men to His own great purpose, it is vain to speculate; but we may at least be assured that he did in a measure forecast the future, and that he felt, when he entered Macedonia, that the Gospel was on the eve of some new and striking development.   The divine voice, which had first driven him coastward and then beckoned him across the seas, was a significant token.   The rapid and prosperous voyage to the European shores seemed the presage of a coming triumph[1].   The strange scenes, the new and varied types of character which he encountered there, the contact with purer forms of Western civilisation, the more direct influence of Greek and Roman institutions—all these fresh experiences crowding upon him spoke to him of more brilliant victories yet to be achieved, of wider and fairer provinces to be annexed to his Master's kingdom.   All the incidents of this epoch seem to assume vaster proportions, to be cast on a grander scale.   A success unparalleled in his previous career

---

[1] Acts xvi. 11, $\epsilon\dot{v}\theta\nu\delta\rho o\mu\dot{\eta}\sigma a\mu\epsilon\nu$. The distance which on this occasion seems to have been accomplished in two days' voyage, took *five* on a later occasion (Acts xx. 6).   See Conybeare and Howson *Life and Epistles of St Paul* p. 219 (*ed.* 1870).

both in extent and durability crowns his preaching in the first European city. A marvellous deliverance, a more signal interposition in his behalf than any elsewhere recorded, assures him of the protecting hand of God. The first visit to Macedonia stands out in the Apostle's history as an eventful epoch in a career singularly crowded with incidents and fertile in results.

I propose to call attention to a few points bearing on the history and character of the Macedonian Churches collectively. They are so closely linked together in the circumstances of their foundation, and present so many features in common, that it is especially instructive to consider them together.

1. The three stations in Macedonia, which St Paul selected for his missionary labours, are Philippi, Thessalonica and Berœa. A glance at any good map of this country will show at once the reasons which may have influenced this choice. The whole region of Macedonia Proper exclusive of the Chalcidic peninsula is divided by its natural barriers into three portions corresponding respectively to the water-courses of the Strymon, the Axius and the Haliacmon. Philippi stands on a tributary of the Strymon; Thessalonica, though planted on the banks of another less considerable river, occupies the most important position in the valley of the Axius; while Berœa, lying more inland, represents the third district watered by the Haliacmon near to which it is situated. In the first Roman partition of Macedonia—now long abandoned—these three towns had belonged to distinct provinces called respectively Prima, Secunda, and Tertia. Thus standing sufficiently wide apart from each other and commanding three separate districts, they recommended themselves to the Apostle by their geographical position, as good missionary centres.

2. But he was guided also by another consideration. It was necessary that there should be a sufficient Jewish population in those towns which were marked out as the mother Churches of their respective districts. Around the few believers of the

house of Israel, as a nucleus, the Gentile majority of the Church must gather. All three places satisfied this condition. At Philippi indeed there was no synagogue, but every Sabbath-day the faithful Jews met together for prayer by the riverside[1]. Their numbers appear to have been scanty, yet there was a sufficient body of them to render it necessary for the Apostle to warn his converts against 'the concision[2],' though in the admonition he may have been thinking more of Rome than of Philippi[3]. At Thessalonica, at all events, a synagogue existed[4], and the Jews play a prominent part in the narrative of the Acts[5]. This city appears to have been a favourite resort for Jews in the middle ages, and a recent writer, who gives the whole population as seventy thousand, sets down the Jewish element at fifty thousand souls[6]. At Berœa also was a synagogue[7], and the conduct of the Jews there is highly commended by the historian of the Acts[8].

---

[1] Acts xvi. 13, 16. The use of the word προσευχὴ here does not necessarily imply a building.

[2] Phil. iii. 2 βλέπετε τὴν κατατομήν.

[3] [See *Philippians*, p. 52.]

[4] Acts xvii. 1, ὅπου ἦν συναγωγὴ τῶν Ἰουδαίων. Textual criticism requires the suppression of the article before the word συναγωγή.

[5] See esp. Acts xvii. 5 sq., 13 sq.

[6] W. G. C. in *Macmillan's Magazine* for Feb. 1863 (vii. p. 313). This is the highest estimate I have seen, and I suspect some mistake in the numbers. Other estimates are given by Conybeare and Howson, p. 250.

[7] Acts xvii. 10 sq.

[8] If we are tempted to ask why St Paul chose Philippi and Berœa rather than Amphipolis or Pella for the scene of his preaching, the true answer may be somewhat of this kind. Philippi was the first town which he reached. He would naturally be anxious to commence his missionary work at once. An opportunity offered, and he availed himself of it. Though there was no regular synagogue here, there was, as we have seen, a nucleus of Jews, and in this respect Amphipolis would offer no greater facilities, for there certainly was no synagogue there. Besides, even if Philippi was not the chief town of the district, it was a place of great importance, and would command the Eastern districts better than Amphipolis.

Berœa was probably chosen in preference to Pella on account of the synagogue there. It is improbable that there should have been synagogues at both places. Besides this, Pella was on the decline; see Dion Chrysost. *Or.* xxxiii. (p. 460 *ed.* Emper.), νῦν εἴ τις διέρχοιτο Πέλλαν, οὐδὲ σημεῖον ὄψεται πόλεως οὐδὲν δίχα τοῦ πολὺν κέραμον εἶναι συντετριμμένον ἐν τῷ τόπῳ.

It seems a mistake to suppose that St Paul went to Berœa as an out-of-the-way town, a sort of hiding place,

Alexander himself had shown great favour to the Jews, and his successors in the Macedonian dynasties abroad seem to have inherited his policy in this respect.   The Syrian kings admitted them to equal privileges with the Macedonians and Greeks[1]. And the liberality of the Alexandrian princes[2] in this respect is witnessed by the LXX. translation of the Scriptures, by the building of the Temple at Leontopolis and by the large Jewish population at Alexandria.   There were occasional exceptions indeed to this wise liberality, but on the whole it seems to have remained the traditional policy of the successors of Alexander. Both in Egypt and Syria the Romans left the Jews in possession of the privileges which they enjoyed.   We may well suppose, though we have no direct evidence, that the like spirit prevailed at home, and that the Jews were at least protected, if they were not encouraged, by the rulers of Macedonia.   At all events, we may gather from the New Testament history that at the time of the Christian era they had settled there in considerable numbers,

as Alford seems to imply.   Cicero says of Piso, escaping from Thessalonica, where he was pestered with complaints, that he 'took refuge' in Berœa, 'in oppidum devium Beroeam profugisti' (*in Pison*. c. 36).   Piso's course would naturally have been along the Egnatian road, and therefore to him it was 'devium.'   But Berœa was a most important city (see Lucian *Asin.* § 34 ἐρχόμεθα εἰς πόλιν τῆς Μακεδονίας Βέροιαν μεγάλην καὶ πολυάνθρωπον), and would have been very ill-chosen as a lurking place, since there was a Jewish synagogue there, which doubtless kept up constant communication with that of Thessalonica, as the result seems to show.   It also lay near the road that he must ultimately take for Achaia.

It is not probable that St Paul on any subsequent occasion preached in other Macedonian towns.   In Romans xv. 19 it is true he speaks of having preached 'as far as Illyricum,' but if his visit to Berœa may not be con

sidered to justify the expression, the Gospel may well have been spread southward through the labours of his companions Silas, Timotheus and Luke between his first and second visits to Macedonia.   In the scanty fragments of his Apology which survive, Melito, addressing M. Antoninus, appeals to the fact that his father wrote letters to the people of Larissa, Thessalonica and Athens forbidding them to molest the Christians (ὁ δὲ πατήρ σου...ταῖς πόλεσι περὶ τοῦ μηδὲν νεωτερίζειν περὶ ἡμῶν ἔγραψεν· ἐν οἷς καὶ πρὸς Λαρισσαίους καὶ πρὸς Θεσσαλονικεῖς καὶ Ἀθηναίους καὶ πρὸς πάντας Ἕλληνας Melito in Eus. *H. E.* iv. 26, 10, see Routh *R. S.* I. p. 112).   The establishment of Christianity at Larissa is an interesting fact; see below, p. 267.

[1] See the curious illustration which Josephus gives (*Ant.* xii. 3, 1).

[2] See Winer's article on the Jewish Dispersion in his *Bibl. Realwörterbuch*, II. p. 727 sq. (1847).

and that the synagogue organisation was established in full force. The historical connexion of Macedonia with Syria and Palestine was of some centuries standing, and the Syrian cities of Edessa and Berrhœa, which had far outstripped their older namesakes, not to mention the Palestinian town of Pella, testify to the intimate relationship between the countries.

3. St Paul's communications with the Macedonian Churches were very close and frequent. This was partly due to their position on the high road between Asia on the one hand and Greece and Rome on the other, partly to other causes. These communications are of various kinds. *Firstly*, there are personal visits made by the Apostle. During his second missionary journey in the year 52 he founds the Macedonian Churches[1]. Five years or so later, on his third missionary journey he visits them twice, as he goes and again as he returns[2]. Another interval of five years elapses, and again he seems to have paid them another visit, immediately after his return from captivity, in fulfilment of his declared intention[3]. Lastly, once, probably more than once, we find him there again at the very close of his life[4]. *Secondly*, we read of constant communications made with the Macedonians through his disciples. When he departs after his first visit, he leaves Silas and Timotheus behind[5], and possibly after joining him at Athens they were despatched thither again[6]. But these are not the only companions delegated to watch over the infant Churches of Macedonia. It would appear that St Luke also remained at Philippi for a period of five or six years[7]. On his third missionary journey again the Apostle sends Timotheus and Erastus into Macedonia[8]. During the imprisonment at Rome, this intercourse is of the most intimate character. The narrative of the Epistle to the Philippians implies four journeys between Philippi and

[1] Acts xvi. 9–xvii. 15.
[2] Acts xix. 21, xx. 1, 3.
[3] Phil. ii. 24.
[4] 1 Tim. i. 3; cf. 2 Tim. iv. 13, 20.
[5] Acts xvii. 14, 15, xviii. 5.
[6] 1 Thess. iii. 1, 2, 6.

[7] This is inferred from the fact that the first person in the narrative is dropped after Acts xvi. 17 and resumed at ch. xx. 5.
[8] Acts xix. 22.

the place of St Paul's captivity, before the writing of the letter[1], and mention is made of the Apostle's intention of despatching Timotheus thither shortly[2]. And to this constant association, sustained, as far as we can trace it, throughout St Paul's life, must be added the frequent interchange of messages consequent upon the contributions made by the Macedonian Churches both towards the relief of the brethren in Judæa[3], and towards the Apostle's personal maintenance[4]. *Thirdly,* we find several Macedonian Christians in more or less constant attendance upon St Paul. These men are representative, and are taken from the three Churches of Macedonia. Thessalonica sends Aristarchus[5], a Jewish convert, to endanger his life with the Apostle at Ephesus and to share the captivity at Rome. Another Thessalonian, Secundus[6], is mentioned with Aristarchus as accompanying the Apostle during his voyage to the Capital. On the same occasion Berœa is represented by Sopater 'the son of Pyrrhus[7],' the patronymic being added perhaps to distinguish him from the Sosipater who sends his salutation to the Church of Rome[8]. From Philippi comes Epaphroditus, whose sickness at Rome aroused such a tender interest in the Church of which he formed a member[9]. Another Macedonian, Gaius, is mentioned as St Paul's companion in the tumult at Ephesus[10], unless indeed (as is possible, though hardly probable) he is to be identified with

[1] [Aristarchus however may have parted from the Apostle at Myra. See *Philippians* p. 37.]

[2] Phil. ii. 19.

[3] 2 Cor. viii. 1 sq., ix. 2 sq.

[4] Phil. iv. 15 sq.; 2 Cor. xi. 9.

[5] Acts xix. 29, xx. 4, xxvii. 2; Col. iv. 10; Philemon 24. His nationality appears from Col. iv. 11 where he is coupled with Mark and Jesus called Justus, as being 'of the circumcision.' He was a constant companion of St Paul who calls him ὁ συναιχμάλωτός μου (Col. iv. 10). The name occurs in the Bollandist *Acta Sanctorum* for Aug. 4.

[6] Acts xx. 4. Of Secundus we only hear in this passage, but the name is found in Macedonian inscriptions; thus in Boeckh *C. I. G.* II. no. 1957 (Pydna) Κάσιον Σεκοῦνδον. So in Thessalonian inscriptions L. Pontius Secundus is the name of one of the politarchs (Boeckh no. 1967), cf. no. 1969 Οὐάλης καὶ Σεκοῦνδος (where compare the name 'Valens' in Polycarp's Epistle to the Philippians § 11), no. 1988 [Σεκ]οῦνδος, no. 1988 *b*, 'Ιουλία Σεκούν[δα]...[Σ]εκουνδίων.

[7] Acts xx. 4 Σώπατρος Πύρρου Βεροιαῖος.

[8] Romans xvi. 21.

[9] Phil. ii. 25 sq.

[10] Acts xix. 29.

Epaphroditus[1]. Lastly, there is some reason for the supposition that Demas[2], whose desertion of the Apostle in his second imprisonment contrasts so painfully with his faithful companionship at an earlier period, hailed from Thessalonica[3].

But the most permanent result of St Paul's intercourse with the Macedonian Churches is embodied in the three letters which have come down to us addressed by the Apostle to his converts there. His two earliest Epistles—the two Epistles to the Thessalonians—were written to one Macedonian Church, a later Epistle—the Epistle to the Philippians—to another. Nor are we to suppose that these three extant letters exhaust the Apostle's literary activity in the case of congregations in which he took so special and so affectionate an interest. Even admitting that there is not sufficient evidence to warrant us in postulating a lost letter to the Philippians[4], yet his language in the Second Epistle to the Thessalonians becomes meaningless unless it presupposes more than one previous communication with the Church of Thessalonica[5].

The outward condition of the Macedonian Churches stands fully revealed in the Pauline Epistles which survive to us. They were baptized with the baptism of suffering, and this suffering was the result both of poverty and of persecution[6].

---

[1] The two names are borne together in an inscription of Thessalonica (Boeckh *C.I.G.* no. 1987 Γαΐῳ Κλωδίῳ Ἐπαφροδείτῳ [Κ]λωδία Φιλημάτιον τῷ [πά]τρωνι τὸ μνῆμα). Origen in Rom. xvi. 23 states a tradition that the Gaius there mentioned was a bishop of Thessalonica. The Gaius however in question was a Corinthian. There may however have been some confusion with the Gaius of Acts xix. 29. [On Epaphroditus see *Philippians* pp. 61, 62.]

[2] On the name Demas see the references in Meyer on Col. iv. 14, Lobeck *Pathol.* 505; cf. Boeckh *C.I.G.* III. no. 3817 (Δημᾶς καὶ Γάϊος). Demas is mentioned next to Aristarchus the Thessalonian in Philemon 24, and when he deserted St Paul he went to Thessalonica (2 Tim. iv. 10), probably home. The name Demetrius, of which Demas is a contract form, occurs twice among the list of politarchs of that city (Boeckh no. 1967).

[3] To complete the list of Macedonian Christians we must add Jason (Acts xvii. 6 sq.).

[4] [On the question of lost letters of St Paul see *Philippians* p. 138 sq.]

[5] 2 Thess. iii. 17 ὅ ἐστιν σημεῖον ἐν πάσῃ ἐπιστολῇ: cf. also 2 Thess. ii. 15.

[6] 2 Cor. viii. 2 ἐν πολλῇ δοκιμῇ θλίψεως...ἡ κατὰ βάθους πτωχεία of the Macedonian Churches. And yet there must have been sufficient wealth both at Philippi and at Thessalonica. Were

There is no warning against the temptations of wealth, no enforcement of the duties of the rich, in the Epistles to the Thessalonians or Philippians[1]. The former especially are addressed as those who have to work for their living[2]. On the other hand, the allusions to persecution undergone are prominent in all three Epistles[3]. And side by side with the external dangers which beset these infant communities we can discern the presence of a more subtle peril to which they were exposed from the tendencies of their national character. The old Macedonian spirit of independence showed itself in a factious self-assertion, a contempt for authority, to which the Apostle is constrained to draw attention with a significant and emphatic iteration[4].

But the better side also of the Macedonian character[5] made

the gold and silver mines at Philippi [see *Philippians* p. 47] still worked?

[1] The case is different in Polycarp's Epistle to the Philippians. Probably Christianity had by that time extended to the wealthier classes; see esp. §§ 4, 5, 6.

[2] 1 Thess. iv. 11; 2 Thess. iii. 7-12.

[3] Thessalonica (1 Thess. i. 6, ii. 14, iii. 2, 3, 4; 2 Thess. i. 4-7); Philippi (Phil. i. 28-30).

[4] Cf. 1 Thess. v. 12-14; 2 Thess. iii. 6, 7, 11, 14.

[5] The Macedonians were to Greece what the Piedmontese are to Italy, the rude highlanders speaking a mongrel dialect, regarded with a proud but impotent scorn by the pure bred Greeks, but in the highest moral qualities far their superiors, with a more genuine love of freedom and a stubborn perseverance. They were the one people which made the power of Greece felt throughout the world. On the Macedonian spirit of independence see especially Flatte *Gesch. Mac.* I. 45. Flatte's summary of the Macedonian character

is very striking and accurate. They appear to have had that peculiarly English virtue of not knowing when they were beaten. An excellent illustration of this sturdy perseverance and indomitable buoyancy of character which the Apostle commends (1 Thess. i. 6) is the passage of Mommsen (*History of Rome* Bk. III. ch. 8, Vol. ii. p. 229 Dickson's transl. 1868). 'In steadfast resistance to the public enemy under whatever name, in unshaken fidelity towards their native country and their hereditary government, and in persevering courage amidst the severest trials, no nation in ancient history bears so close a resemblance to the Roman people as the Macedonians; and the almost miraculous regeneration of the state after the Gallic invasion redounds to the imperishable honour of its leaders and of the people whom they led.'

A curious parallel to St Paul's language occurs in Dion Chrysost. *Or.* xxv. Ἀλέξανδρος [τοὺς Μακεδόνας] εἰς τὴν Ἀσίαν ἐξαγαγὼν ἅμα μὲν πλουσιωτάτους ἁπάντων ἀνθρώπων ἀπέδειξεν ἅμα

itself felt in the converts gained for Christianity from that region. The Macedonian Churches are honorably distinguished above all others by their fidelity to the Gospel and their affectionate regard for St Paul himself. While the Church of Corinth disgraced herself by gross moral delinquencies, while the Galatians bartered the liberty of the Gospel for a narrow formalism, while the believers of Ephesus drifted into the wildest speculative errors, no such stain attaches to the brethren of Philippi and Thessalonica. It is to the Macedonian congregations that the Apostle ever turns for solace in the midst of his severest trials and sufferings. Time seems not to have chilled these feelings of mutual affection. The Epistle to the Philippians was written about ten years after the Thessalonian letters. It is the more surprising therefore that they should resemble each other so strongly in tone. In both alike St Paul drops his official title at the outset, not wishing to assert his Apostolic authority where he could appeal to the higher motive of love. In both he opens his letter with a heartfelt thanksgiving expressed in terms of highest commendation. In both Epistles he speaks of his converts as his 'crown and joy[1]': in both he appeals freely to his personal example: and in both he adopts throughout the same tone of confidence and affection. In this interval of ten years we meet with one notice of the Macedonian Churches. It is conceived in terms of unmeasured praise. The Macedonians had been called upon to contribute to the wants of their poorer brethren in Judæa, who were suffering from famine. They had responded nobly to the call. Deep-sunk in poverty and sorely tried by persecution, they came forward with eager joy and poured out the riches of their liberality, straining their means to the utmost in order to relieve the sufferers. 'They exceeded our expectations,' says the Apostle; 'they gave themselves to the Lord, and to us by the will of

---

δὲ πενιχροτάτους, καὶ ἅμα μὲν ἰσχυροὺς ἅμα δὲ ἀσθενεῖς, φυγάδας τε καὶ βασιλέας τοὺς αὐτούς, comp. 2 Cor. vi. 10. Dion flourished at the close of the first

and the beginning of the second century A.D.

[1] 1 Thess. ii. 19; Phil. iv. 1.

God[1].' We may imagine that the people still retained something of those simpler habits and that sturdier character, which triumphed over Greeks and Orientals in the days of Philip and Alexander, and thus in the early warfare of the Christian Church the Macedonian phalanx offered a successful resistance to the assaults of an enemy, before which the lax and enervated ranks of Asia and Achaia had yielded ignominiously.

[1] 2 Cor. viii. 1–5.

[1863.]

VII.

THE CHURCH OF THESSALONICA.

Printed from Lecture-notes.

VII.

THE CHURCH OF THESSALONICA.

THE ancient name of Thessalonica [1] was Therme or Therma [2] 'the hot-spring,' and there are still warm springs in the neighbourhood, though not at Thessalonica itself [3]. At the time of the Persian invasion it was apparently only a small town [4], but it gradually grew in importance and appears occasionally in history. It was at all events sufficiently influential to give its name to the bay on which it stood [5].

On the site of Therma, the city of Thessalonica [6] was founded by Cassander. It was probably at the same time that he rebuilt the city of Potidæa [7]. If so, the date of the

---

[1] On the geography and antiquities of Thessalonica, see Cousinéry *Voyage dans la Macédoine* I. p. 23 sq. (1831); Leake *Northern Greece* III. p. 235 sq. (1835); Koch *Comm. üb. den ersten Brief an die Thessalonicher* (1855) *Einleit.* § 1, 2; Tafel *Historia Thessalonicae* (Tübing. 1835) and *de Thessalonica dissertatio geographica* (Berl. 1839); Pococke *Description of the East* II. (2) p. 148 sq. (1743); Belley *Observations sur l'histoire et sur les monuments de la ville Thessalonique*; Texier *Description de l'Asie Mineure* (1839–49); and for its ecclesiastical history Texier *Byzantine Church* p. 111 sq. (1864). I have not been able to investigate the work by Burgerhoudt *de coetus Christ. Thessalonicensis ortu* (1825), referred to by Koch, p. 8.

[2] Æschines (*de Fals. Legat.* §§ 31, 36) calls it Θέρμα, Herodotus (vii. 121, 123 etc.), Thucydides (i. 61, ii. 29) and Scylax (*Geog. Min.* p. 26 *ed.* Hudson) Θέρμη.

[3] See Tafel *H. Th.*, p. 3, and Pococke, p. 149, quoted by Koch, p. 2. For the name compare Crenides, 'Wells,' the ancient name of Philippi.

[4] So Tafel (p. 13), but Herodotus (vii. 127) speaks of it as a πόλις.

[5] Herod. vii. 121.

[6] The Greek form is Θεσσαλονίκη (Steph. Byzant. *s.v.*), or -κεία (Strabo vii. § 10).

The name Thessalonica first occurs in Polybius (xxiii. 4. 4, 11. 2, xxix. 3. 7).

[7] Diod. Sic. xix. 52.

foundation of the new city was apparently about the year B.C. 315[1]. Therma was named Thessalonica after Cassander's wife, the daughter of Philip and half-sister of Alexander: Potidæa he called Cassandreia[2] after his own name. Of the twin cities Thessalonica was destined far to outstrip her rival[3].

Its natural advantages were indeed great, both as regards the sea and as regards the land. It was situated, as Pliny describes it[4], in the middle of the bend of the Thermaic gulf. It had a good natural harbour, so excellent indeed that Xerxes, when on his march against Greece, had chosen it as his naval station[5]. Its dockyards are mentioned by Livy[6]. Nor did its excellence as a military and commercial centre fall short of the prominence which its situation as a seaport gave to it. It was the key to the whole of Macedonia. It commanded by a good land route the two levels—the level of the plain of the Strymon on the one hand, and on the other the level of the converging plains of the Axius, Haliacmon and Echedorus[7]. It was likewise conveniently situated with respect to that excrescence of Macedonia, the Chalcidic peninsula. For the purpose of inter-communication with more distant centres its situation was all that could be desired. The Via Egnatia[8], that great

---

[1] See Niebuhr *Ethnol.* I. 293.

[2] Cassandreia was probably his capital. Tafel (p. 8) quotes a coin ΚΑΣΑΝ-ΔΡΟΥ ΘΕΣΣΑΛΟΝΙΚΗΣ. Both however attained great prominence; thus Livy xlv. 30 says 'Secunda pars celeberrimas urbes Thessalonicam et Cassandream habet.'

[3] Another account of the city is that it was founded by Philip to commemorate a victory over the Thessalians. This does not deserve any credit. It appears first in Julian *Orat.* iii. about seven centuries after the event, and it is there given as a conjecture. In later writers it takes its place with the other account, e.g. Steph. Byzant. *s.v.* A third story combines the two former. It represents the city as founded by Philip in honour of his daughter Thes-

salonica. All three are given in a passage of Tzetzes quoted by Tafel (p. 5).

[4] Pliny *N. H.* iv. 10. 17 'medio litoris flexus [sinus Thermaici].'

[5] Herod. vii. 121.

[6] Livy xliv. 10. In a moment of despair Perseus had ordered them to be burnt. Five centuries later Constantine the Great, on the eve of his conflict with Licinius (A.D. 322), had the harbour enlarged for the reception of his fleet (Zosimus *Hist.* ii. 22).

[7] On the fertility of the Macedonian plain see Cousinéry II. p. 5, Perrot in the *Revue Archéologique* (1860) II. p. 49, and compare Appian *Bell. Civ.* iv. p. 105, Athen. xv. p. 682 B.

[8] On this great military road see a treatise of Tafel *De via militari Romanorum Egnatia* (Tübing. 1837).

highroad between Italy and the East which spanned the peninsula, passed through its walls—an advantage the full force of which is appreciated only when we recollect that, owing to the imperfect knowledge of navigation of the ancients, communication by sea was at all times precarious, and at some seasons of the year entirely closed. Such advantages fully justified Cicero's description of its inhabitants as 'lying in the lap' of the Roman Empire[1].

The city grew and flourished. In Strabo's time, a generation or two before St Paul, it was the most populous of the Macedonian cities[2]. A century later than the Apostle, Lucian speaks to the same effect[3]. And in spite of invasion, misrule and disaster, it has enjoyed from that time to this a continuous, if comparative, prosperity; fully bearing out Meletius' dictum upon it 'So long as nature does not change, Thessalonica will remain wealthy and fortunate[4].' It narrowly escaped being made the capital of the world[5]. At one time its population seems to have risen above two hundred thousand. At present it has fallen to about a third of that number. It still retains its ancient name, corrupted in Turkish into Selanik, in vulgar Greek into Σαλονίκη, but the educated continue to call it, as of old, Θεσσαλονίκη[6].

In illustration of the history of St Paul's labours in these parts, two points deserve to be considered (1) its political status, (2) its moral and religious condition.

1. The political importance of Thessalonica commences with the decline of Greece. It was the capital of the second of

[1] Cic. *de prov. consul.* 2 'Thessalonicenses positi in gremio imperii nostri.' Cicero resided at the place when in exile (*pro Planc.* 41).

[2] Strabo vii. 6. 4 ἣ νῦν μάλιστα τῶν ἄλλων εὐανδρεῖ.

[3] Lucian *Asinus* § 46 ii. p. 613 (*ed.* Hemsterhus.) πόλεως τῶν ἐν Μακεδονίᾳ τῆς μεγίστης Θεσσαλονικῆς.

[4] Cousinéry i. p. 24.

[5] Gibbon ch. xvii. (ii. p. 183, *ed.* Bohn) 'Before the foundation of Constantinople, Thessalonica is mentioned by Cedrenus (p. 283), and Sardica by Zonaras, as the intended capital.'

[6] Leake iii. p. 238. In the West it was called by the early German poets Salneck, *Salonicia* occurs in a twelfth century Italian chronicle (Muratori *Script. rer. Ital.* vii. 875), but Salonichi is the name by which it is now known in Western Europe: see Koch *Einl.* p. 3.

the four districts in the first quadripartite division of Macedonia[1]. At a later re-arrangement of the province it would seem to have been made the capital of Macedonia.

Its native poet Antipater about the time of the Christian era[2] says of it

$$\Sigma o\acute{\iota}\ \mu\epsilon,\ \Theta\rho\eta\ddot{\iota}\kappa\acute{\iota}\eta\varsigma\ \sigma\kappa\upsilon\lambda\acute{\eta}\phi o\rho\epsilon,\ \Theta\epsilon\sigma\sigma\alpha\lambda o\nu\acute{\iota}\kappa\eta,$$
$$\mu\acute{\eta}\tau\eta\rho\ \acute{\eta}\ \pi\acute{\alpha}\sigma\eta\varsigma\ \pi\acute{\epsilon}\mu\psi\epsilon\ M\alpha\kappa\eta\delta o\nu\acute{\iota}\eta\varsigma.$$

On coins (though of a much later date) it is styled the metropolis. In the civil wars it had the good fortune to take the winning side, espousing the cause of Octavius and Antony[3]. It would appear that it owed its privileges as a free city to the services thus rendered to the future master of the world[4].

Pliny speaks of it as *liberae conditionis*[5], and there are coins with the inscription ΘΕϹϹΑΛΟΝΙΚΕΩΝ ΕΛΕΥΘΕΡΙΑϹ (or -ριΑ)[6]. In the enjoyment of this constitution we find it at the time of the Acts.

Its chief magistrates are πολιτάρχαι[7], a word not known elsewhere in classical literature, but the account of St Luke is remarkably confirmed by an inscription still to be seen at Thessalonica on an arch at the western end of the town[8]. The Politarchs appear to have been seven in number[9]. There is

[1] Livy xlv. 18.

[2] Jacobs *Anthol. Gr.* ii. p. 98, no. xiv.

[3] Appian *Bell. Civ.* iv. p. 118, Plutarch *Brutus* 46. Brutus before Philippi appears to have held out to his soldiers the sacking of the city as an incentive to their valour in action.

[4] Tafel, p. 20.

[5] Pliny, *N. H.* iv. 10. 17.

[6] See Cousinéry I. p. 28 and the reff. in Tafel, p. 20.

[7] Acts xvii. 6.

[8] The inscription is given in Boeckh *C. I. G.* II. p. 53, no. 1967; Leake III. p. 236; Cousinéry I. p. 27; Conybeare and Howson (p. 258), and elsewhere. Quite recently a paper was read on it by Mr Vaux before the Royal Geographical Society, July 4, 1866, and a photograph of it produced.

[9] Not six, as stated by Tafel, p. 21, followed by Dean Howson in Smith's *Dictionary of Geography*. The latter is correct in his article 'Thessalonica' in Smith's *Dictionary of the Bible* and in his life of St Paul (p. 259). At least there must have been seven, if Boeckh's copy of the inscription is correct, but no two copies that I have seen agree.

This inscription illustrates St Paul and St Luke in other respects; first, in the prominence given to women, a fact noted elsewhere [see *Philippians*, p. 54 sq.]; secondly, in the names, Secundus, Gaius, Sosipater, see above, p. 246.

mention also in this inscription of a steward ($\tau a\mu ia\varsigma$) of the city, and a gymnasiarch ($\gamma \upsilon \mu \nu a\sigma \iota \acute{a}\rho \chi \eta \varsigma$)[1]. There was likewise a popular assembly ($\delta \hat{\eta} \mu o\varsigma$)[2]. The whole city then is essentially Greek, not Roman as Philippi was. As a free city it was spared the ignominy of a permanent Roman garrison within its walls[3].

2. The moral and religious condition of Thessalonica was probably not worse than that of any ordinary Greek town, perhaps better, for there was a more sterling moral basis in the Macedonian character than in the Greek[4]. Still it would be open to all the ordinary temptations of a Greek city and especially of a Greek seaport. Against such St Paul had to warn his converts both orally and by letter[5]. But no inference of especial immorality in Thessalonica can be drawn from the expressions which he employs. Scarcely a single Epistle of St Paul is without similar warnings.

There was however one element of immorality in Thessalonica which must not be passed over—of immorality which shielded itself under the protection of religion—the worship of the Cabiri, the mystic deities of Samothrace[6]. This worship

[1] The date of the inscription is uncertain. As read by Boeckh, it has the name P. Flavius Sabinus, which, as he truly remarks, points to a date not earlier than Vespasian. As read by others, only the Sabinus remains. Cousinéry (I. p. 28) on very insufficient grounds assigns the arch to the age of Augustus, supposing that it was erected to commemorate the battle of Philippi. Leake (III. p. 236) considers it to be later. The writer of the article in *Macmillan's Magazine* alluded to already (see above, p. 243) informs me that it was his impression that the inscription need not be part of the original arch.

[2] The word $\delta \hat{\eta} \mu o\varsigma$ likewise occurs in St Luke's narrative in reference to Thessalonica (Acts xvii. 5 $\acute{e}\zeta \acute{\eta} \tau o\upsilon \nu$ $a\grave{\upsilon} \tau o\grave{\upsilon} \varsigma$ $\pi \rho o\alpha \gamma a\gamma \epsilon \hat{\iota} \nu$ $\epsilon \grave{\iota} \varsigma$ $\tau \grave{o} \nu$ $\delta \hat{\eta} \mu o\nu$). He uses

it also twice in the analogous case of Ephesus (Acts xix. 30, 33).

[3] See Dirksen *Versuche zur Kritik* IV. p. 140 sq. (Lips. 1823).

[4] The story in Lucian (*Asinus* § 49 –56) has been put in evidence, as showing a very low state of morals in Thessalonica. This is unfair, as Tafel justly remarks (p. 25).

[5] 1 Thess. iv. 3—6.

[6] On the Cabiri see especially Lobeck *Aglaoph.* III. c. 5, p. 1202 sq. (and esp. p. 1256 sq., where he treats of their worship in Macedonia), Creuzer's *Symbolik und Mythologie* III. p. 17–36, p. 159 sq. (3rd ed.). The article in Pauly *Real-Encycl. der class. Alterthüm.* II. p. 2, by K. W. Müller, contains an abstract of the opinions of the principal writers on this subject.

had been patronised by Philip[1], and by Alexander[2]. It is especially identified with the Macedonians[3], and more particularly still with the Thessalonians[4]. About the time of St Paul a political sanction was given to the worship—or rather, a religious sanction to the political system as derived from the worship—by deifying the Emperor as a Κάβειρος[5].

To these Cabiric rites, in which gross immorality was promoted under the name of religion, we may suppose that St Paul alluded, when he deprecated any connexion between his gospel and uncleanness[6], a disclaimer which happily would sound strange from the lips of a minister of any religious denomination now, but which is quite intelligible in St Paul's day, when read in the light of the foul orgies of the Cabiric worship or of similar rites[7].

[1] Plut. *Vit. Alex.* c. 2.

[2] Philostr. ii. 43. 94.

[3] Lactant. *Div. Inst.* i. 15, Summa veneratione coluerunt...Macedones Cabirum.

[4] Firmicus *de Err. Prof. Rel.* c. 11, Hunc eundem Macedonum colit stulta persuasio. Hic est Cabirus, cui Thessalonicenses quondam cruento [ore] cruentis manibus supplicabant. Cabiric coins of Thessalonica are not infrequent (see Cousinéry i. p. 28, Pl. i.). On the Cabiric games see Tafel, p. 24.

Cousinéry supposes that this worship was not introduced into Thessalonica before the reign of Claudius, on the very insufficient ground that no Cabiric coins are found at an earlier date (i. p. 35 sq.). It is in the highest degree improbable that a worship which is especially connected with the Greek kings of Macedonia should not have found its way into the principal city of Macedonia earlier.

On less slender grounds still he finds a temple of the Cabiri in an ancient building still existing (*l. c.*).

[5] See the coins and esp. Cousinéry i. p. 38.

[6] 1 Thess. ii. 3.

[7] On the Jewish population of Thessalonica something has been said already; see above, p. 243. In the present day the Jews are probably the most numerous section of the inhabitants. They have a quarter of their own. Various estimates of their numbers are given (see Conybeare and Howson, p. 383), the largest being that of W. G. C. in *Macmillan's Magazine* Feb. 1863, see above, p. 243. The writer of the article informs me that he heard it on the spot, on authority that he cannot question. He adds moreover that the Jews have an interest in representing themselves as fewer than they are, owing to the polltax. Many of the Jews of modern Thessalonica settled there in the fifteenth century, having been driven out of Spain by the persecution in that country, but they must have been induced to settle there by the fact that there was already a large Jewish population. On the Rabbinical school at Thessalonica see Milman *History of the Jews* iii. p. 419 (*ed.* 1866), and on the whole question see Cousinéry i. pp. 19, 49; Leake iii. p. 249 sq.

Fresh from the insults and sufferings he had undergone at Philippi, but nothing daunted, he arrives at Thessalonica[1]. With the Jews he commences his labours[2]. On the Sabbath day he enters the synagogue. The details may be supplied from the similar scene recorded as having taken place at an earlier period in Antioch of Pisidia[3]. The law and the prophets read, he is invited, we may suppose, by the rulers of the synagogue to offer a word of exhortation. He avails himself of the opportunity, and preaches, arguing from the Scriptures. He sets himself to prove two things: (i) That it was ordained that Messias should suffer; (ii) that Jesus whom he preaches is the Messias. For three successive Sabbath-days ($\epsilon\pi i$ $\tau\rho ia$ $\sigma\acute{a}\beta\beta a\tau a$[4]) he preaches[5].

Of his missionary labours in the course of the week St Luke says nothing. We may supply the omission from his conduct at Athens (Acts xvii. 17). He would appear in the market place, engaging in conversation and trying to interest persons in his message. The account of St Luke however is silent as to his labours beyond the first three weeks of his stay. Had we merely the historian's narrative we might have supposed that he only stayed so long. It is plain however from the Epistles that the length of his sojourn was much greater[6]. At the close of these three weeks we may suppose that he devoted himself more exclusively to the heathen[7].

---

[1] 1 Thess. ii. 2.

[2] Acts xvii. 1 sq.

[3] Acts xiii. 15; and cf. Luke iv. 16 sq.

[4] It matters little whether we translate $\sigma\acute{a}\beta\beta a\tau a$ 'weeks' or 'sabbath-days.' The meaning is the same, viz. that for three weeks he repeated his preaching in the synagogue on the sabbath.

[5] We may imagine him doing so, as at the Pisidian Antioch, at the request of some of the congregation who, interested in his teaching, thronged about him as he left the synagogue (Acts xiii. 42), and requested him to resume his preaching; or he may even have

found favour with the ruler of the synagogue, as at Corinth. From whatever cause, however, he was allowed to repeat his message.

[6] We gather this (1) from the success of his labours among the Gentiles; (2) from the mention of the way in which he was engaged, especially his working 'day and night'; (3) from the notices given in Phil. iv. 16 of contributions sent to him more than once ($\ddot{a}\pi a\xi$ $\kappa a i$ $\delta i s$).

[7] The incidents at the Pisidian Antioch are here again a parallel (Acts xiii. 45, 46).

But meanwhile it was necessary that he should find means of support. He did not wish to hinder the Thessalonians. He did not wish to clog his message with the suspicion that would attach to it, if he sought any return for his labours. He would not appear to preach under 'a cloke of covetousness[1].' His wants were supplied in two ways, by the labours of his own hands[2], and by contributions received from Philippi[3].

Meanwhile he preached zealously. He alludes more than once to the subject of his preaching in the Epistles: and thus we are enabled to supplement the notice in the Acts, already alluded to, which refers mainly to his labours in the synagogue.

His preaching seems to have turned mainly upon one point —the approaching judgment, the coming of Christ. They had been invited at their conversion to await the Son of God from heaven[4]. They were warned that He would come, as a thief in the night[5]. At the same time they were told that many things must happen first, that Antichrist must gather strength, that 'the Restrainer' must be removed[6]. Around this one doctrine the Apostle's practical warnings and exhortations had clustered. He warned them that they must suffer tribulation[7], the tribulation which was to usher in the end of all things, the persecution from the power of Antichrist. He bade them abstain from impurity lest they should find vengeance in the day of the Lord's coming[8]. He had charged them to walk worthily of God who was calling them to His kingdom and glory[9].

But the flood of new experiences, poured in upon them, threatened to unsettle the foundations on which the social structure was built. In the immediate presence of the great

---

[1] 1 Thess. ii. 5, προφάσει πλεονεξίας.
[2] 1 Thess. ii. 5, 6, 9; 2 Thess. iii. 8. The notice in Acts xviii. 3 refers indeed to another town and to a few months later, but will show what the nature of these labours was.
[3] Phil. iv. 15–18. This however was not the main means of support, and is not inconsistent with the Apostle's language given above (see the preceding note); cf. τὸ ὑστέρημα 2 Cor. xi. 9.
[4] 1 Thess. i. 10.
[5] 1 Thess. v. 2, αὐτοὶ γὰρ ἀκριβῶς οἴδατε.
[6] 2 Thess. ii. 5 sq.
[7] 1 Thess. iii. 4.
[8] 1 Thess. iv. 6, 7.
[9] 1 Thess. ii. 12.

crisis which was to change all things, why should they attend to the petty details, the common avocations, of daily life? In the flush of fresh and glorious hopes, was it right, was it possible, to care for the things of this world? There were some, doubtless, who honestly drew this inference from the Apostle's teaching. There were many who, without examining their own motives, would greedily seize hold of so lofty a pretext for shirking the manifold responsibilities of their social position. This restless and feverish spirit had appeared while the Apostle was still at Thessalonica; and he had set himself to counteract it. He told them that their true ambition should be to keep quiet, to attend to their business, to labour with their own hands[1]. The bread of the Church was not for those who refused to work[2]. *Laborare est orare* is the true maxim of the Christian, be the Advent far or near.

In such spirit the Apostle preached. Of the results of his preaching we have ample evidence. 'His entrance in to them was not in vain[3].' They received the word in much affliction with joy of the Holy Ghost[4]. The fame of their conversion spread throughout Macedonia and Achaia, and 'in every place[5].' Among the Jews indeed his success appears not to have been great[6], yet among these two are mentioned by name, whose faithful adherence to the Apostle is placed on record. Jason, whose correct name was Jesus[7], but who had assumed the heathen name which most nearly resembled it, calls down the wrath of his countrymen upon himself by entertaining the Apostle while at Thessalonica. Aristarchus, another convert from the Circumcision[8], is his constant companion, suffering for him at Ephesus, and apparently sharing his imprisonment at

---

[1] 1 Thess. iv. 12.
[2] 2 Thess. iii. 10.
[3] 1 Thess. ii. 1.
[4] 1 Thess. i. 6.
[5] 1 Thess. i. 8. This is an indirect testimony to the central position of Thessalonica noticed above (p. 254).
[6] Acts xvii. 4, τινὲς ἐξ αὐτῶν, i.e. τῶν

Ἰουδαίων, ἐπείσθησαν.
[7] Cf. Joseph. *Ant.* xii. 5. 1, ὁ μὲν οὖν Ἰησοῦς Ἰάσωνα ἑαυτὸν μετωνόμασεν; cf. also Aristo of Pella in Routh *R. S.* i. pp. 97, 107; and see the article by B. F. W. in Smith's *Dict. of the Bible* s. v. Jason.
[8] Col. iv. 10, 11; see above, p. 246.

Rome. With the proselytes and with the heathen his success was greater[1]. It was from the last-mentioned however that the vast majority of the new disciples were drawn[2]. They turned from idols to serve the living and true God[3]. Among his converts were many ladies of the first rank[4].

These successes provoke the hatred of the Jews. They enlist on their side the profligate idlers of the city, of which in a seaport town there would be many, the lazzaroni of Thessalonica[5]. They besiege the house of Jason, where Paul and his companions were lodged, wanting to drag them before the people, probably in the theatre[6]. Not finding them there, they carry Jason and certain converts before the Politarchs. They accuse them of high treason. They are setting up a rival to the Roman Emperor, a king Jesus[7]. The main topic of the Apostle's preaching had given the handle to their accusation. He had, as we saw, laid great stress on the coming judgment, on the kingdom of Christ. Ignoring or misapprehending his true meaning, they represented him as setting up a temporal kingdom[8].

---

[1] Acts xvii. 4, τῶν τε σεβομένων [καὶ] Ἑλλήνων πλῆθος πολύ. The received text is τῶν τε σεβομένων Ἑλλήνων 'of devout Greeks' i.e. of Greek proselytes (so also ℵ). For this τῶν τε σεβομένων καὶ Ἑλλήνων is read by AD vulg. copt., but not by B, as Koch states. This brings the account into more direct agreement with the language of the Epistles; and in its favour may be urged (Koch Einl. p. 8) that σεβόμενοι elsewhere stands by itself (Acts xvii. 17) for proselytes. Koch refers to Burgerhoudt (p. 93); see also Paley Horæ Paul. p. 281.

[2] This appears from the evidence of the Epistles. For (i) he addresses his readers distinctly as having been converted from idol-worship, 1 Thess. i. 9, quoted below, cf. ii. 14, 16; (ii) he refrains from any direct allusion to the O. T., which would certainly have

occurred had he been addressing Jews chiefly or proselytes.

[3] 1 Thess. i. 9.

[4] Acts xvii. 4.

[5] Acts xvii. 5 'certain lewd fellows of the baser sort' (A.V.). This archaic use of the word 'lewd,' as equivalent to 'ignorant,' is not uncommon in early English literature: 'the leude man, the grete clerke Shall stonde upon his owne werke' Gower Conf. Am. i. 274; 'the lered and the lewed' Piers Ploughman's Vis. 2100, and other instances given by W. A. Wright Bible Word-book, s.v.

[6] As in the riot at Ephesus, Acts xix. 29, 30, 31.

[7] The exact parallel to John xix. 12, 15 is worth noticing.

[8] This is rightly regarded as an undesigned coincidence of a striking kind. The history supplies the ac-

The magistrates no less than the populace are alarmed at these representations. They take securities from Jason and the rest, as persons who had disturbed, or were suspected of disturbing, the public peace. The Apostle had hitherto lain concealed. Seeing that events had taken a turn so unfavourable to the continuance of his labours, he left Thessalonica in company with Silas under cover of night.

These events occurred on St Paul's second missionary journey —probably in the year 52. From Thessalonica he went to Berœa. Thence he was driven out at the instigation of some Jews from Thessalonica, who, hearing of his successes there, followed him. From Berœa he went to Athens, and from Athens to Corinth. As he does not seem to have remained long at either of these intermediate places, it was not many months—probably not many weeks—after he left Thessalonica that he entered Corinth.

But meanwhile his anxiety for his Thessalonian disciples was increasing daily[1]. He had made more than one unsuccessful attempt to revisit them[2]. The storm of persecution was gathering while he was yet at Thessalonica. He knew that he had left to his new converts a heritage of suffering. He had warned them of what awaited them. Would they yield to persecution and renounce their allegiance[3]? At length the suspense became too terrible. He could no longer contain himself[4]. He denied himself the services of Timothy, and despatched him—whether from Berœa or from Athens is uncertain —to visit Thessalonica and report to him of the condition of his new converts.

The Apostle is now at Corinth; Timothy returns. The report of the Thessalonian Church is most favourable. Their personal affection for the Apostle is as strong as ever; and undaunted by persecution they had remained steadfast in the

---

count of the charges brought against him. The Epistles supply the matter of his preaching (see esp. 1 Thess. ii. 12; 2 Thess. i. 5). The two coincide in a very remarkable way.

[1] 1 Thess. ii. 17.
[2] 1 Thess. ii. 18 ἅπαξ καὶ δίς.
[3] 1 Thess. i. 6; ii. 14, 15; iii. 3, 5, 7.
[4] 1 Thess. iii. 1, 2, 5.

faith and in deeds of love[1]. It was as new life to the Apostle
to hear these glad tidings[2]. In the first flush of joy and
gratitude he wrote to the Thessalonians to encourage them to
persevere and to advise them on certain matters, where they
seemed to need his advice. This is the *First Epistle to the Thessalonians.*

For notwithstanding that Timothy's report was so cheering,
there were some points on which they required correction or
instruction.

These points were as follows:—

(1) The error, of which he had discerned the beginnings
while he was still in Thessalonica, and which he had striven to
check, had gained ground meanwhile. The very intensity of
their Christian faith, dwelling too exclusively on the day of the
Lord's coming, had been attended with evil consequences. A
practical inconvenience of some moment had arisen. In their
feverish expectation of this great crisis, some had been led to
neglect their ordinary business[3]. There was a spirit of restlessness manifest in the Thessalonian Church. The Apostle rebukes this.

(2) In connexion with the doctrine of the Lord's advent
another difficulty had arisen—not a practical one, but a theo-
retical one—which had troubled the minds of many. Certain
members of the Church had died, and there was great anxiety
lest they should be excluded from any share in the glories of
the Lord's advent[4]. The Apostle sets himself to quiet this
anxiety.

(3) An unhealthy state of feeling with regard to spiritual
gifts was manifesting itself. Like the Corinthians at a later
day[5], they needed to be reminded of the superior value of
'prophesying,' compared with other gifts of the Spirit which
they exalted at its expense[6].

---

[1] 1 Thess. iii. 6; cf. i. 5 sq.; iv. 10.
[2] 1 Thess. iii. 8 νῦν ζῶμεν ἐὰν ὑμεῖς στήκετε.
[3] 1 Thess. iv. 11.
[4] 1 Thess. iv. 13–18.
[5] 1 Cor. xiv. 3, 4, 5, 22, 24.
[6] 1 Thess. v. 19, 20.

(4) There were symptoms of a tendency to despise lawfully constituted authorities, and generally a spirit of unruliness was showing itself—not unconnected, as I have already hinted, with that independence of temper which was characteristic of the Macedonians[1].

(5) There was the danger, which they shared in common with most Gentile Churches, of relapsing into their old heathen profligacy[2]. Against this the Apostle offers a word in season. We need not suppose, however, that Thessalonica was worse in this respect than other Greek cities.

The letter was written partly to correct these errors, but still more to express his satisfaction with his converts, and to cheer them under persecution[3].

Between the First and the Second Epistles no long interval seems to have elapsed. Some information as to the state of the Thessalonian Church has reached the Apostle meanwhile, by what source it is not known. Some of the vicious tendencies, which he had endeavoured to check, were still further developed. And some misunderstanding as to his teaching had arisen.

To meet these he wrote the *Second Epistle*. The two prominent points in the Epistle are as follows:—

(i) Misapprehension had spread as to the nearness of the Advent. It was maintained that the Apostle had declared it to be imminent[4].

(ii) The restless and unruly spirit, which he had before rebuked, was gaining ground[5].

At the same time, and not unconnected with these errors, St Paul's personal relations with the Thessalonians had become less satisfactory. His authority had been tampered with, and an unauthorised use was made of his name. It is difficult to ascertain the exact circumstances of the case from casual and indirect allusions, and indeed we may perhaps infer from the

[1] 1 Thess. v. 12–14; see above, p. 248.
[2] 1 Thess. iv. 3–8.
[3] 1 Thess. ii. 14; iii. 2, 4.
[4] 2 Thess. ii. 1 sq.
[5] 2 Thess. iii. 6–12.

vagueness of the Apostle's own language that he himself was
not in possession of definite information; but at all events his
suspicions were aroused. Designing men might misrepresent
his teaching in two ways, either by suppressing what he actually
had written or said, or by forging letters and in other ways
representing him as teaching what he had not taught. St
Paul's language hints in different places at both of these modes
of false dealing. He seems to have entertained suspicions of
this dishonesty even when he wrote the First Epistle. At the
close of that Epistle he binds the Thessalonians by a solemn
oath, 'in the name of the Lord,' to see that the Epistle is read
'to all the holy brethren'[1]—a charge unintelligible in itself,
and only to be explained by supposing some misgivings in the
Apostle's mind. Before the Second Epistle is written, his
suspicions seem to have been confirmed, for there are two
passages which allude to these misrepresentations of his teaching. (1) In the first of these he tells them in vague language,
which may refer equally well to a false interpretation put upon
his own words in the First Epistle, or to a supplemental letter
forged in his name, 'not to be troubled either by spirit or by
word or by letter, as coming from us, as if the day of the Lord
were at hand.' They are not to be deceived, he adds, by any
one, whatever means he employs (κατὰ μηδένα τρόπον, ii. 2, 3).
(2) In the second passage at the close of the Epistle he says,
'The salutation of Paul with mine own hand, which is a token
in every Epistle: so I write' (iii. 17), evidently a precaution
against forgery[2].

And not only so. If there were unscrupulous persons, who
tampered with his authority, there were also unruly ones who
denied it, or were disposed to deny it. St Paul asserts his office

---

[1] 1 Thess. v. 27.

[2] That such precautions were not
unnecessary is proved by the complaint
of Dionysius of Corinth (in Eus. *H. E.*
iv. 23, see Routh *R. S.* I. p. 181), ἐπισ-
τολὰς γὰρ ἀδελφῶν ἀξιωσάντων με
γράψαι ἔγραψα. καὶ ταύτας οἱ τοῦ δια-
βόλου ἀπόστολοι ζιζανίων γεγέμικαν· ἃ
μὲν ἐξαιροῦντες, ἃ δὲ προστίθεντες· οἷς τὸ
οὐαὶ κεῖται. οὐ θαυμαστὸν ἄρα εἰ καὶ τῶν
κυριακῶν ῥαδιουργῆσαί τινες ἐπιβέβληνται
γραφῶν, ὁπότε καὶ ταῖς οὐ τοιαύταις ἐπι-
βεβουλεύκασι.

much more strongly in this Epistle than in the former[1].   Yet
still these were but slight blemishes on a Church with which
generally the Apostle was thoroughly satisfied.   The errors were
confined to a few, and had not assumed a virulent form.   The
Apostle is bound to thank God for the exceeding growth of
their faith and the abundance of their love[2].

The Thessalonian Church is now but a very few months old
—a little more than a year at most.   From this time forward it
disappears from the Apostolic history.   As regards the Churches
of Macedonia generally we have the Apostle's testimony to their
satisfactory condition, and we can well believe that the Thessalonians were included in his commendation.   But of Thessalonica
especially we know absolutely nothing.   Even the name occurs
but twice in the New Testament at a later date[3].   One of these
passages refers to incidents within the period of its infancy
which I have already considered : in the other it occurs quite
incidently.   Neither throws any light on its condition.

And this is true of its subsequent ecclesiastical history.
The Church of Thessalonica passes through a period of thick
darkness, from which it emerges at length in the fourth century.
So far as I know, there are but two notices of it during two
centuries and a half or more, and these are of the briefest and
most meagre character[4].   From Melito's Apology it appears that
the Emperor Antoninus Pius had written to the people of Thessalonica, among other places, telling them to take no new steps
against the Christians[5].   This would seem to show an important
and a struggling Church at Thessalonica in the middle of the
second century.   At the beginning of the next century,
Tertullian[6] couples it with Philippi as a Church where the

---

[1] 2 Thess. iii. 14, 15; cf. ii. 15, iii. 4.

[2] 2 Thess. i. 3.

[3] Phil. iv. 16, 2 Tim. iv. 10.

[4] On the other hand Conybeare and
Howson (p. 250) speak of Thessalonica
'boasting of a series of Christian annals
unbroken since the day of St Paul's
arrival.'

[5] Melito *Apology*, μηδὲν νεωτερίζειν
περὶ ἡμῶν (i.e. τῶν Χριστιανῶν).   The
passage is given above, p. 244, from
Eus. *H. E.* iv. 26 : it has escaped the
diligence of Tafel, pp. 9, 30.

[6] Tertull. *de praescr.* 36, 'apud quas
ipsae authenticae literae eorum reci-
tantur.'

letters of the Apostles are read in the original. Of its early
bishops two are mentioned, Aristarchus in Bede's martyrology[1],
and Gaius by Origen[2], if this latter be not a confusion with
Gaius of Macedonia[3]. It could boast of a martyr in the Dio-
cletian persecution[4], and the church raised in his honour, the
church of St Demetrius, now a mosque, is the most splendid in
Thessalonica[5]. Nor does Demetrius appear to stand alone, if
an epithet ($\phi\iota\lambda o\mu\acute{a}\rho\tau\upsilon\rho\epsilon\varsigma$) applied to the congregation at large
be something more than a complimentary title[6]. More than
once the names of its bishops appear on the records of ecclesiastical councils, and at the Council of Sardica (A.D. 343) its
bishop Aetius claimed for the metropolis of the people of Thessalonica the consideration due to its importance and its population[7].
While the glories of Antioch and Alexandria gradually pale,
Thessalonica rises into splendour. In the fourth century Theodoret in a striking passage[8] points to the city as the greatest
and most populous in the district. Its resistance to the successive attacks of the barbarian hordes—whether Goths or

[1] On Aug. 4; see Le Quien *Or. Chr.*
II. p. 27.

[2] Origen on Rom. xvi. 23; see above,
p. 247.

[3] Acts xix. 29.

[4] The year of the martyrdom of
Demetrius must be fixed at A.D. 303
or 306, according as the Maximianus
mentioned in the acts of his martyrdom (Anastatius Bibliothecarius p. 88;
Photius *Biblioth.* 255) is considered
to be Herculius or Galerius. Simeon
the Metaphrast (for Oct. 8, pp. 90,
96) and an anonymous biographer of
the sixth century call him Maximianus
Herculius, but on the other hand he
is represented as having conquered
the Sarmatians, which was done, not
by Herculius, but by Galerius (Oros.
Hist. vii. 25; see Cornelius Byeus
Acta Sanctorum Octobris iv. Brussels
1780). Demetrius' festival is kept by
the Western Church on Oct. 8 (*Martyrol.*

Roman. Vet.), by the Eastern Church
on Oct. 26. His cult sprang rapidly
into prominence in the fifth century.
He received the title of $\mu\upsilon\rho o\beta\lambda\acute{\upsilon}\tau\eta\varsigma$
from the streams of holy oil, which
were said to issue from his relics and
to cure diseases.

[5] Cousinéry I. p. 41, Leake III. p.
242.

[6] It occurs in an anonymous writer
quoted by John of Thessalonica (*Act.
Sanct.* IV. 48, p. 121). A little lower
down, one saint, a virgin called Ma-
trona, is mentioned by name.

[7] Canon. xvi. Ἀέτιος ἐπίσκοπος εἶπεν·
Οὐκ ἀγνοεῖτε ὁποία καὶ πηλίκη τυγχάνει
ἡ τῶν Θεσσαλονικέων μητρόπολις κ.τ.λ.
(Mansi *Concil.* III. p. 17; cf. Hefele
Conciliengesch. I. p. 577).

[8] Theodoret *H. E.* v. 17, Θεσσαλονίκη πόλις ἐστὶ μεγίστη καὶ πολυάνθρω-
πος. The whole passage is important.

Sclavonians—and the noble share which it took in the conversion to Christianity of each successive tribe of invaders won for it the proud title of ' the orthodox city[1].'

At present its population represents more fully the creed of the adversaries of St Paul than the creed of St Paul himself— the Jewish than the Christian faith. Only a minority of the inhabitants are Christians[2]. But the memory of the great Apostle lives and is honoured by those who deny the truths which he first taught within its walls. Two pretended relics of St Paul the city possesses in two rival pulpits which stand in two of the principal mosques, and contend for the honour of having been the place from which the Gospel was first preached by the Great Apostle of the Gentiles[3].

---

[1] This title was given to it by Cameniata in the tenth century (τὸ ὀρθόδοξον αὐτὴν καὶ εἶναι καὶ ὀνομάζεσθαι § 3). Tafel, who has studied the medieval history of the city with great care, couples it with Constantinople as the twin bulwark of Eastern Christendom. Though frequently besieged, the city was only captured three times, by the Saracens (A.D. 904), the Normans (A.D. 1185), and finally the Turks (A.D. 1430).

[2] For a most interesting account of Jewish life in those parts, and on the general relation of Judaism and Christianity, see Renan Les Apôtres p. 284 sq. (ed. 1866). On the present ecclesiastical organization of the district see Leake III. p. 250.

[3] Macmillan's Magazine Feb. 1863 pp. 314, 5.

[1867.]

VIII.

THE MISSION OF TITUS TO THE CORINTHIANS.

Reprinted from the 'Journal of Classical and Sacred Philology,'
Vol. II. p. 194 sq. (1855).

VIII.

THE MISSION OF TITUS TO THE CORINTHIANS.

THE mission of Titus, which occupies so prominent a place in the Second Epistle to the Corinthians, has been the subject of much discussion with regard to its object and relation to other communications of St Paul with the same Church, especially the similar and almost contemporaneous mission of Timotheus. The explanation here offered has not, as far as I have seen, been anticipated: it is certainly not the view maintained by the most recent critics, English or German. At the same time it seems so far to recommend itself by its simplicity, and to offer so adequate a solution of all the difficulties which the problem presents, that it can scarcely have failed to suggest itself to the minds of others besides myself[1].

But perhaps it may not be superfluous to say a few words on the previous communications of St Paul with the Church of Corinth, not only by way of introduction to my immediate subject, but also because they offer considerable difficulties in themselves.

[1] This paper had been partly written and the substance of the whole collected, before Mr Stanley's book appeared. It was no slight satisfaction to me to find that with regard to one main point, the identification of the mission of Titus with that of the brethren mentioned in the First Epistle, the distinguished editor supports the view here maintained. Though so far anticipated, I have ventured to send this paper to the press, because the results were obtained independently, and, where they agree with those of Mr Stanley, are worked out more fully than his plan admitted.

I have alluded several times to Mr Stanley's book in my notes, chiefly where I have had occasion to differ from him; but I would not be thought to disparage so valuable a contribution to the history of the apostolic times. I would wish the same remark to apply to my mention of other distinguished names.

It must have been some time during St Paul's three years' residence at Ephesus (from A.D. 54 to 57), that he received information of the critical state of the Corinthian Church, which he had himself founded a few years earlier. His presence seemed to be required, and he accordingly crossed the Ægæan, and paid a short visit to the capital of Achaia, returning to Ephesus to complete his missionary work there. This seems to be the most probable account of St Paul's second visit to Corinth, of which little more than the fact is recorded. For though the circumstance is not noticed by St Luke, yet his silence is easily accounted for, supposing it intentional, when we reflect that his object was not to write a complete biography of St Paul, but a history of the Christian Church, and that he has accordingly selected out of his materials such facts only as throw light upon Christianity in all ages—*representative* facts, as we might call them; while on the other hand, if it be supposed that he was unacquainted with the circumstance, this supposition again is easily explained from the short duration of St Paul's stay at Corinth, and the facility of intercourse between the two coasts of the Ægæan. At all events, there are passages in the epistles (e. g. 2 Cor. xii. 14; xiii. 1, 2) which seem inexplicable under any other hypothesis, except that of a second visit—the difficulty consisting not so much in the words themselves, as in their relation to their context[1]. It appears necessary therefore to

---

[1] I cannot think, for instance, that Mr Stanley's explanation of the context of 2 Cor. xii. 14, τρίτον τοῦτο ἑτοίμως ἔχω ἐλθεῖν πρὸς ὑμᾶς, on the ground of the *designed* visit, is at all satisfactory. And yet he calls attention to the opposition between the tenses κατενάρκησα and καταναρκήσω, which leads to the true solution, 'I have not been burdensome to you...I am on the eve of paying you a third visit, and I will not be burdensome,' *i.e.* I will observe the same practice as on the two former occasions. But the appeal to his projected visit as a proof of his affection (for this is Mr Stanley's explanation) is quite out of place in this connexion, to say nothing of the ambiguity of expression. His interpretation of 2 Cor. xiii. 1 in relation to its context is scarcely less objectionable.

At all events, admitting Mr Stanley's explanations as possible, it must seem strange that the Apostle should *twice* have veiled his mention of his designed visit under language which applies at least as well (in 2 Cor. xiii. 1 τρίτον τοῦτο ἔρχομαι, far better) to an actual visit, and in both cases have introduced it in a manner which so rudely interrupts the obvious train of thought.

On the other hand, 1 Cor. xvi. 7

abandon the opposite view, chiefly known to the English student through the advocacy of Paley, who seeks to explain these passages on the ground of a visit designed, but never actually paid.

The Apostle's visit seems not to have been effectual in checking the evils which called for his interference. It would appear that the shameless profligacy, for which the city was proverbial, had already found its way into the Christian community. He therefore wrote to the Corinthians, warning them to shun the company of offenders in this kind. This letter, which was probably brief and of no permanent interest to the Christian Church, has not been preserved, and we only know that it was written, from a passing allusion to it in a subsequent epistle[1]—the First to the Corinthians in our Canon. It was probably in this lost letter that he informed them of the design,

has been unjustifiably pressed into the service. The words οὐ θέλω γὰρ ὑμᾶς ἄρτι ἐν παρόδῳ ἰδεῖν have been interpreted 'I will not *now* pay you a passing visit;' implying that he had done so before, and, as St Paul on his first visit to Achaia stayed eighteen months (Acts xviii. 11), necessarily alluding to a second and shorter visit. Against this Meyer alleges the order of the words, and de Wette repeats this argument. So far as I can see, the order would admit this interpretation well enough, and Wieseler (*Chron.* p. 240) has a right to make use of the passage in spite of this protest. The real objection seems to be that the natural, if not the necessary, antithesis to ἄρτι 'just now' (when used of present time) is the future, and not the past. On this ground I should object to Mr Stanley's explanation, 'now according to my present, as distinguished from my late intention.'

[1] 1 Cor. v. 9 Ἔγραψα ὑμῖν ἐν τῇ ἐπιστολῇ μὴ συναναμίγνυσθαι πόρνοις: but as undue weight has been assigned to these words, as showing that a previous letter had been written, it will be

as well to see how far they favour such a view. (1) No such conclusion can be drawn from the aorist ἔγραψα. That this word is frequently used in reference to the letter in which it occurs, any concordance will show; I must also confess myself unable to discern the latent 'philosophical' objections to its being so employed, even at the commencement of a letter (Davidson, *Introd.* ii. p. 140, *ed.* 1); the grammar, at all events, seems unexceptionable. Cf. *Martyr. Polyc.* c. 1: ἐγράψαμεν ὑμῖν, ἀδελφοί, τὰ κατὰ τοὺς μαρτυρήσαντας, where the words occur immediately after the salutation. (2) It is unnecessary to accumulate instances to show that ἡ ἐπιστολή may refer to the letter itself. (3) It has been found difficult to explain the allusion by anything which has preceded. This difficulty must be allowed: verses 2, 6, 8, do not supply what is wanted: but is it necessary to seek any reference beyond the passage itself? Would it not be quite in accordance with this epistolary usage of the aorist to look for the explanation in the same sentence, so that the corresponding English

which he at this time entertained but was afterwards obliged to abandon, of paying them a double visit, on his way to and return from Macedonia (1 Cor. xvi. 5; 2 Cor. i. 15).

How long an interval elapsed before St Paul again communicated with the Corinthian Christians, we cannot ascertain; but it was towards the close of his stay at Ephesus, that he despatched Timotheus through Macedonia on his way to Corinth, though apparently with some apprehensions that he might not reach that city, and not long after addressed a second letter to them—the First Epistle of our Canon. This he placed in the hands of certain brethren, whom he expected to arrive at Corinth a little before or at any rate not later than Timotheus (1 Cor. xvi. 10–12), so that they might return together, and rejoin the Apostle in company. Have we any means of discovering who these brethren were?

It seems more than probable in the first place, that Timotheus never reached Corinth, but was detained in Macedonia so long, that he had not advanced beyond this point, when he was overtaken by St Paul on his way from Ephesus to Achaia. At all events he must have been in St Paul's company when the Second Epistle was written, as his name appears in the salutation, and there are sufficient grounds for concluding that this Epistle was sent from Macedonia. But there are numerous reasons for

to the words ἔγραψα ὑμῖν μὴ συναναμίγνυσθαι would be, 'I *write* to you not to keep company'?

The only substantial argument in favour of a previous letter seems to be contained in the words ἐν τῇ ἐπιστολῇ, which are quite superfluous in reference to the First Epistle itself, and the comparison with 2 Cor. vii. 8 makes the allusion to a previous letter even more evident. This argument appears to be insuperable.

I suppose that the Chev. Bunsen's 'Restoration' of the 'Former Epistle of Peter' will carry conviction to few German and still fewer English minds (*Hippol.* i. p. 24, *ed.* 2, in *Anal. Anten.* i.

p. 35 sq.), but it is perhaps worth while observing how completely his argument founded on 1 Pet. v. 12 δι' ὀλίγων ἔγραψα, which he finds it necessary to refer to a former and shorter letter, is met by such passages as Hebr. xiii. 22 διὰ βραχέων ἐπέστειλα ὑμῖν, Ignatius *ad Polyc.* c. vii. (shorter Greek) δι' ὀλίγων ὑμᾶς γραμμάτων παρεκάλεσα. For not only is the aorist used in both these passages in a way which M. Bunsen seems to think inadmissible, but the writers have also ventured to characterize their epistles as brief, though they considerably exceed in length that to which he considers such a term inappropriate.

supposing that this was the limit of Timotheus' journey. In the *first* place: St Paul himself in announcing this projected visit of Timotheus to Corinth, has evidently some misgivings as to its fulfilment, and consequently speaks of it as uncertain, ἐὰν δὲ ἔλθῃ Τιμόθεος (1 Cor. xvi. 10). Probably he foresaw circumstances which would detain his missionary on the way. *Secondly*, Timotheus is represented in the Acts (xix. 22) as being sent with Erastus into Macedonia, as if the sacred historian were not aware of his journey being continued to Corinth. *Thirdly*: if Timotheus had actually visited Corinth, he must have brought back some information as to the state of the Church there; and, if he arrived, as was expected, subsequently to the receipt of the First Epistle, he must also have been able to report on a subject which lay nearest to the Apostle's heart—the manner in which his letter was received by the Corinthian Christians. But we do not find this to have been the case. For while in the Second Epistle to the Corinthians St Paul dwells at great length on information derived from another source—the epistle in fact arising entirely out of this—there is not the slightest inkling of any knowledge obtained through Timotheus on any subject whatever. And *fourthly*, in one passage where St Paul is enumerating visits recently paid to the Corinthians by the Apostle himself or by his accredited messengers, the name of Timotheus does not occur, though it could scarcely have been passed over in such a connexion (2 Cor. xii. 17, 18).

For these reasons we may infer with extreme probability, that Timotheus, finding it advisable to prolong his stay in Macedonia, was prevented from carrying out his original intention of visiting Achaia, before he joined St Paul. For, though each of these arguments separately is far from conclusive, they seem when combined to form such a body of circumstantial evidence, as fully to justify this verdict. Again, if this conclusion be admitted, it simplifies the problem, and the subsequent communications of the Apostle with the Church of Corinth become easily explicable. This consideration is of course not without weight.

On the other hand attempts have been made to impugn some of these arguments. It will be as well to dispose of these before proceeding.

In answer to the *second* argument, it has been maintained that the journey of Timotheus to Macedonia (Acts xix. 22) was different from, and subsequent to, his mission to Corinth. If such a method of reconciling the accounts can in any way be avoided, it should not be resorted to. The philosopher's rule with entities should be the historian's with facts. They should not be unnecessarily multiplied. Here so far is there from being any necessity, that it is not easy to account for these repeated journeys, which moreover in some degree perplex the chronology, there being a difficulty in compressing all the events within the given time.

In the statement on which my *third* argument is based, I am at issue with Wieseler (*Chron.* p. 58) in a matter of fact. I can therefore only state the case and leave it for the judgment of others. He argues thus. The language with which the Epistle opens (i. 12—ii. 11) was evidently prompted by St Paul's distress at the opposition which his former letter had occasioned. Now this language describes his state of mind before the arrival of Titus. Therefore some other messenger must have reached him meanwhile from Corinth. Who can this messenger have been but Timotheus? With Wieseler's hypothesis as to the composition of the Second Epistle, built upon the argument here given, I have no concern. The argument itself too is unexceptionable, if the premise be once allowed. But does not his statement arise from an entire misconception? I believe ordinary readers will discern no such traces of tidings received before the arrival of Titus. They will read in the opening of the Second Epistle nothing more than the vague apprehensions and misgivings, which would naturally arise in the Apostle's mind as to the manner in which a condemnatory letter, expressed in such fearless and uncompromising language—written moreover in much affliction and anguish of spirit (2 Cor. ii. 4)—would be received in a community where the most flagrant irregularities prevailed, and where his own apostolic authority was denied by a considerable number, and perverted to factious purposes by others. Surely the language would have been far different; his fears would have been far more clearly defined, if he had actually received tidings; especially if these tidings had been brought by a messenger as trustworthy as Timotheus.

The *fourth* argument has been answered on the supposition that St Paul in 2 Cor. xii. 17, 18 is only speaking of those who took part in the collection of alms, and that, as the mission of Timotheus was quite independent of any such object, his name is properly omitted. But where does it appear that the list of names is so restricted? The word ἐπλεονέκτησεν, judging from the context, seems to refer rather to the abuse of the Corinthians' hospitality, than to the gathering of the contributions. Meyer again accounts for the omission of Timotheus' name on the ground that only the most recent visits to Corinth are here alluded to. Yet granting that his view is true, as probably it is, still the visit of Timotheus must have preceded that of Titus by a few weeks at most, and could not have been omitted on this account. The same able critic even considers that any mention at all of Timotheus in the third person would be quite out of place, when his name is found in the superscription of the letter (on 2 Cor. xii. 18, cf. *Einl.* § 1); and Mr Alford urges the same argument, though less strongly (Vol. II. Prol. p. 56). It is a sufficient reply to Meyer to observe that, whether out of place or not, it is what St Paul has done elsewhere (e.g. 1 Thess. iii. 3, 6), and what therefore he might be supposed to do here.

On the other hand, the direct arguments which have been employed by those who consider it improbable that Timotheus should have abandoned his design, do not seem to have much force. Mr Alford for instance considers the purpose of his mission as stated in 1 Cor. iv. 17, to be 'too plain and precise to be lightly given up.' That the mission should have been entirely abandoned is certainly unlikely. That it should have been transferred to other hands, when it was found incompatible

with the discharge of Timotheus' duties in Macedonia, so far
from being an improbable supposition, seems to commend itself
by its very probability. Again it is suggested by Meyer, and
here too Mr Alford endorses the suggestion, that the abandonment of the intended journey of Timotheus would have furnished
another handle for the charge of fickleness against St Paul, and
that we should have found the charge rebutted in the Second
Epistle. This reason will probably not be considered of sufficient weight to counterbalance the amount of evidence on
the other side. For if we take into account that the charge
would lie primarily at the door of Timotheus, and not of the
Apostle himself—that St Paul in announcing the design had
expressed some doubts as to the possibility of its fulfilment—that
the objects of the mission were not abandoned when it was
found impossible for Timotheus to carry them out—and lastly,
that the messengers sent by St Paul in his stead had a satisfactory explanation to offer to the Corinthians of this change of
purpose—we can hardly suppose that the most captious of
St Paul's enemies would have thought it worth their while to
employ such a lame expedient to injure his credit. In short,
this case is no parallel at all to the circumstance of which his
opponents did avail themselves to bring him into disrepute
(2 Cor. i. 17).

On the whole then, so far from finding anything conflicting
in the evidence with regard to this mission of Timotheus, it
seems that, combining the hint of the possible abandonment of
the design in the First Epistle, the account of the journey to
Macedonia in the Acts, and the silence maintained with regard
to any visit to Corinth or any definite information received
thence through Timotheus in the Second Epistle, we discover an
'undesigned coincidence' of a striking kind ; and that it is
therefore a fair and reasonable conclusion that the visit was
never paid.

By whom then was this mission fulfilled? At the close of the
First Epistle (xvi. 11, 12) certain 'brethren' are mentioned, who
appear to have been the bearers of the letter, and whom St Paul

expected to rejoin him in company with Timotheus. The Apostle
had urged Apollos to accompany this mission to Corinth (v. 12),
but he for reasons easily intelligible had declined, considering
that his visit would be unseasonable. Now there is no mention
of the names of these brethren in the First Epistle, but we find
St Paul subsequently after his departure from Ephesus at Troas
awaiting the return of Titus from Corinth with tidings of the
reception of his letter there (2 Cor. ii. 12), and falling in with
him at length in Macedonia (2 Cor. vii. 6). From this we might
have supposed that Titus was alone. But from another allusion
to this mission in the Second Epistle we find he was accompanied
by a 'brother,' whose name is not given (2 Cor. xii. 18)[1]. What
more probable than that Titus and 'the brother' accompanying
him of the Second Epistle, are 'the brethren' of the First?

But why is Titus not mentioned by name? Might we not
rather ask, why he should be so mentioned? His name never
occurs in the Acts. His influence on the interests of the Church
at large was probably not so great as that of Tychicus or
Trophimus, certainly not as that of Apollos or Timotheus. He
is brought into prominent notice in reference to the Churches of
Corinth and Crete in particular; but we should doubtless be
wrong in judging of his position in the Christian Church by the
special importance with which he is invested in regard to individual communities. The fact that an Epistle of St Paul bears
his name leads us almost unconsciously to assign a rank to him
which he probably did not hold in the estimation of his con-
temporaries. Titus then does not appear to have had a church-
wide reputation at this time, and there is no reason to suppose
that he was known specially to the Christians at Corinth. If so,
the omission of his name presents no difficulty, and it is in

---

[1] I am at a loss to discover why Mr
Stanley says, 'This mission was composed of Titus and *two* other brethren'
(on 1 Cor. xvi. 12). The Syriac version indeed in 2 Cor. xii. 18 reads the
plural 'the brethren' (I assume this
to be the case on Mr Stanley's authority, though I have not found any
confirmation), but this has evidently
arisen from a confusion with the subsequent mission, mentioned 2 Cor. viii.
16. Mr Stanley does not give his
reasons elsewhere (2 Cor. viii. 16; xii.
18).

accordance with St Paul's manner to speak thus of his fellow-labourers (2 Cor. viii. 18, 22). No doubt Titus' strength of character was well known to the Apostle when he despatched him upon this difficult mission, but it only approved itself to the Corinthians during his stay among them; and his earnestness and devotion, while there, raised him so far above his colleague, that St Paul in writing to the Corinthians subsequently speaks in such a manner as to show that 'the brother' who accompanied him had sunk by his side into comparative insignificance.

Titus then, we may suppose, had been selected by St Paul as one of the bearers of the letter, that in the event of Timotheus being unable to prosecute his mission to Corinth, it might be fulfilled by one who would act in the same loving and devoted spirit. But there is one link yet to be supplied. How did Titus communicate with Timotheus? How was it known that Timotheus would be detained in Macedonia? Here we are left to mere conjecture; but it seems not improbable that Titus and his companion took the less direct route to Achaia by way of Macedonia. They certainly returned that way, and there was, as far as we can see, no more reason for haste in the one case than in the other. And if it was the apprehension of danger which deterred them from crossing the open sea at that early season of the year, they would have much more cause to entertain such fears on their journey thither than on their return, when the season was farther advanced. Probably the greater security of the indirect route was thought to compensate for the advantage, in point of time, gained by sailing straight across the Ægæan[1]; while the opportunity of communicating with Timotheus would be an additional motive in influencing their choice.

If the view here taken be correct, it will overthrow all Wieseler's chronological results with regard to the interval

[1] The movements of St Paul in the following spring throw some light on this point. He had intended to sail *direct* from Corinth to Syria. His departure however was hastened by the discovery of a conspiracy against him, and he went by way of Macedonia, apparently on account of the early season of the year. He left Philippi μετὰ τὰς ἡμέρας τῶν ἀζύμων (Acts xx. 6). Cf. Conybeare and Howson, II. p. 206.

between the writing of the First and Second Epistles. The facts are few and lead to no satisfactory conclusion; but as far as they go, they do not conflict with anything I have advanced.

The data for determining the relative chronology of this period are these; (1) St Paul stayed at Ephesus 'for a season' after sending Timotheus into Macedonia (ἐπέσχεν χρόνον, Acts xix. 22). (2) Timotheus had left before the First Epistle was written (1 Cor. iv. 17; xvi. 10). (3) There is an allusion which makes it not improbable that the First Epistle was written shortly before Easter (1 Cor. v. 7, 8). (4) St Paul here declares his intention of setting out to visit Corinth quickly (iv. 19). (5) We also learn from the same source that he expected to stay at Ephesus till Pentecost (xvi. 8): and lastly (6) there is reason to suppose that he was subsequently led to hasten his departure. It is not evident indeed that his life was endangered by the tumult at Ephesus[1], but such an outbreak must have interfered with his preaching, and rendered his further stay there useless. At all events the language of St Luke places his departure in immediate connexion with this disturbance, in such a manner as scarcely to leave a doubt that it was determined by this circumstance (Acts xix. 41; xx. 1). It is probable, therefore, that he left before he had intended; and this explains another incident. We find St Paul, after his hurried departure from Ephesus, expecting to meet Titus at Troas, and when he was disappointed of this hope, advancing into Macedonia, where he was ultimately joined by him. Wieseler (*Chron.* p. 59) uses

---

[1] Wieseler considers it necessary to bring Timotheus back from Macedonia to Ephesus, because the plural in 2 Cor. i. 8 seems to show that he shared the danger with St Paul on the occasion of the outbreak. The question of the use of the plural is beset with difficulties; but, waiving this, the language of St Paul (θλίψεως, ἐβαρήθημεν, ἐξαπορηθῆναι) must refer to something more than the mere momentary danger arising from the uproar. St Paul seems to have been subjected to a continuous persecution at Ephesus, which must have begun before the departure of Timotheus, and may have been shared by him. St Paul speaks in the First Epistle of his many adversaries (xvi. 9), and compares his struggles at Ephesus to a contest with wild beasts in the arena (xv. 32). It is strange that ἐθηριομάχησα should ever have been understood literally, when the same image is used 1 Cor. iv. 9 ὡς ἐπιθανατίους, ὅτι θέατρον ἐγενήθημεν.

this as an argument, that St Paul's departure cannot have
taken place much earlier than he had originally intended; for
otherwise he could not have expected to find Titus so soon at the
place of meeting determined upon. This seems to be a mistake.
There is no reason for supposing that they had agreed to meet
at Troas. The true state of the case appears to be this.
St Paul had intended to await the return of Titus and his
colleague at Ephesus. Subsequently being obliged to hasten
his departure, he calculated they would have advanced as far as
Troas before they met. In this calculation he proved to be
wrong.

If this view be correct, the hurried departure from Ephesus
will obviously not affect the chronological question, which thus
assumes a very simple form. We have the period from the
writing of the First Epistle, shortly before Easter (if we may
lay so much stress on a doubtful allusion), till after the feast
of Pentecost, when St Paul expected to leave Ephesus, for the
double journey of Titus, to Corinth and back. I have supposed
that he went and returned by way of Macedonia. Even assuming
that he travelled from Macedonia to Achaia by land, the interval
is sufficiently great. Hug (*Introd.* II. p. 381) calculates the
single journey from Corinth to Ephesus at thirty-one days, but
then he allows a wide margin which is quite superfluous. But,
if it be thought that in this case more time would be required,
we may suppose that Titus took ship at some port of Macedonia
(Thessalonica for instance), as St Paul seems to have done on
one occasion on leaving Berœa (Acts xvii. 14; Wieseler's *Chron.*
pp. 42, 43), and returned the same way. This would be a
considerable saving of time, and the perils of the open sea
would in great measure be avoided.

[1855.]

IX.

THE STRUCTURE AND DESTINATION OF THE EPISTLE TO THE ROMANS.

A.

M. RENAN'S THEORY OF THE EPISTLE TO THE ROMANS.

Reprinted from the 'Journal of Philology,' Vol. II. p. 264 sq. (1869).

B

ON THE END OF THE EPISTLE TO THE ROMANS.
BY DR HORT.

Reprinted from the 'Journal of Philology,' Vol. III. p. 51 sq. (1871).

C.

THE EPISTLE TO THE ROMANS.

Reprinted from the 'Journal of Philology,' Vol. III. p. 193 sq. (1871).

IX.

THE STRUCTURE AND DESTINATION OF THE EPISTLE TO THE ROMANS.

A.

IN the introduction to his recent volume on St Paul, M. Renan has offered a novel theory to account for certain phenomena connected with the Epistle to the Romans. If, for reasons which I shall give hereafter, this theory seems to me to be unsatisfactory, it is yet sufficiently ingenious and striking to claim a fair discussion; and, as the subject itself possesses great critical interest independently of M. Renan's views, I gladly avail myself of the opportunity to investigate it in detail.

The documentary facts which demand explanation, and which have served as the foundation for several theories more or less allied to that of M. Renan, are the following:

(1) In Rom. i. 7 one MS. (G) for τοῖς οὖσιν ἐν Ῥώμῃ ἀγαπητοῖς Θεοῦ reads τοῖς οὖσιν ἐν ἀγάπῃ Θεοῦ; while in i. 15 it omits the words τοῖς ἐν Ῥώμῃ. Again the cursive 47 contains the following marginal note on i. 7, τὸ ἐν Ῥώμῃ, οὔτε ἐν τῇ ἐξηγήσει οὔτε ἐν τῷ ῥητῷ μνημονεύει, where however it is not clear to what authority the scribe refers, though apparently he is speaking of some commentator. Moreover I seem to see other traces of the omission (at least in i. 7), which hitherto have not been recognised. Though Origen elsewhere quotes the common reading (II. p. 301, IV. p. 287), and though it is given as the text in Rufinus' translation of his commentary on this very passage, yet the comment itself, even as disguised by its Latin dress, still appears to me to indicate that Origen here had before him a text in which the words ἐν Ῥώμῃ were omitted; 'Benedictio haec pacis et gratiae quam dat dilectis Dei ad

quos scribit apostolus Paulus' (IV. p. 467).   The same inference
also, if I mistake not, is suggested by the language of the Ambrosian Hilary; 'Quamvis Romanis scribat, illis tamen scribere
se significat qui in caritate Dei sunt'; though here again the
text has 'qui sunt Romae dilectis Dei,' but with the important
various reading (in one MS.) of 'in caritate Dei' for 'dilectis
Dei.'   These, it will be remembered, are the two oldest extant
commentaries on the Epistle to the Romans.   Still further; I
am disposed to think that the reading ἐν ἀγάπῃ Θεοῦ (for
ἀγαπητοῖς Θεοῦ), which is found in several other authorities,
has arisen out of a combination of the two readings τοῖς οὖσιν
ἐν ᾽Ρώμῃ ἀγαπητοῖς Θεοῦ and τοῖς οὖσιν ἐν ἀγάπῃ Θεοῦ, and
thus bears indirect testimony to a still wider diffusion of a
recension omitting the words ἐν ᾽Ρώμῃ.   This reading occurs
in the Latin of D (the Greek is wanting), and in the two
oldest MSS. of the Vulgate.

(2)   The ascription of praise, with which according to the
received text (xvi. 25–27) the epistle closes, occupies different
places in different copies.   In ℵ, B, C, D, f, Vulg., Pesh., Memph.,
Æth., and in the commentaries of Origen, Hilary, and Pelagius,
it occurs at the end of the xvith chapter, as in the received
text; in L, 37, 47, and by far the greater number of cursives,
in the Harclean Syriac, in the commentaries of Chrysostom,
Theodoret, and others, and in Cyril of Alexandria, its place is
at the close of the xivth chapter: in A, P, 17, Arm. (MSS. and
Zohr.), it is found in both places; while in F, G, it is omitted
in both (a blank space however being left in G between the
xivth and xvth chapters).   This variation of position moreover
is at least as early as Origen, who commenting on xvi. 25–27
writes; 'Caput hoc Marcion, a quo scripturae evangelicae atque
apostolicae interpolatae sunt, de hac epistola penitus abstulit ; et
non solum hoc, sed et ab eo loco ubi scriptum est, *Omne autem
quod non est ex fide, peccatum est* (xiv. 23), usque ad finem
cuncta dissecuit.   In aliis vero exemplaribus, id est in his quae
non sunt a Marcione temerata, hoc ipsum caput (i.e. xvi. 25–27)
diverse positum invenimus.   In nonnullis etenim codicibus post

eum locum quem supra diximus, hoc est *Omne autem quod non est ex fide peccatum est*, statim cohaerens habetur *Ei autem qui potens est vos confirmare*. Alii vero codices in fine id, ut nunc positum est, continent.' From this language we may perhaps assume that the authorities for either position seemed to Origen to be nearly evenly balanced. Whether in 'ut nunc positum est' he refers to the position which he himself adopts in this commentary, or to the position which was most common in his day, does not distinctly appear. He makes no mention of any MSS. as having it in both places, or (except Marcion's copies) of any as omitting it in both. St Jerome however (on Ephes. iii. 5) speaks of this passage as occurring 'in plerisque codicibus,' thus implying that it is omitted in some; but he may have been deceived by not finding it in the place where he expected to find it.

(3) As appears from the statement of Origen just quoted, Marcion's recension of the epistle closed with the end of the xivth chapter. Moreover Tertullian (*adv. Marc.* v. 14) refers to *tribunal Christi* (xiv. 10) as occurring *in clausula* of the epistle; but, as he is refuting Marcion, we might reasonably suppose that he here takes Marcion's own copy and argues from it. On the other hand, it does not appear that he himself elsewhere quotes from the xvth or xvith chapters of the epistle, though the omission may be accidental. Neither is there, so far as I know, any reference to these last two chapters in Irenæus, but here also no stress can be laid on the omission, as there was no special reason for his quoting them. Again, Wetstein says, '*Codex Latinus* habet capitula epistolae ad Romanos 51, desinit autem in cap. xiv.', but later critics have not been able to identify the MS. and thus to verify the statement.

To explain these documentary facts, as also to account for certain phenomena in the closing chapters of the epistle itself, various theories have from time to time been suggested, which I shall here attempt to classify.

(i) BAUR, with characteristic boldness, *denied the genuineness of the last two chapters*, or, in other words, accepted the recension of Marcion as preserving the original proportions of the epistle (*Paulus* p. 398 sq.). This solution does not take into account all the facts stated. Thus, for instance, it passes over in silence the omission of the words ἐν ῾Ρώμῃ in one or more copies. For this reason it must be rejected on the ground of external criticism alone. But again, when we come to examine the xvth and xvith chapters themselves, whatever may be our conclusion as regards their *destination*, we are forced to recognise their *genuineness*. M. Renan expresses his surprise ' qu'un critique aussi habile que Baur se soit contenté d'une solution aussi grossière. Pourquoi un faussaire aurait-il inventé de si insignifiants détails ? Pourquoi aurait-il ajouté à l'ouvrage sacré un liste de noms propres ?' (p. lxxi. sq.) If the argument is just, the surprise is hardly reasonable ; for in spite of his acknowledged ability, Baur's prompt method elsewhere is entirely consistent with the rejection of these chapters. But indeed we need not rely on this negative argument derived from the inadequacy of the motive for such a forgery. The style and the substance of the chapters afford conclusive testimony, that we have here not only the thoughts, but the words, of the Apostle himself. To this it must be added that the incidental notices, of which Paley has made use to establish the time and place of writing, hang together in a manner which would suppose not only the most consummate skill, but also the most minute knowledge, on the part of a forger.

From this solution which maintains the spuriousness of the last two chapters, we pass to others which, accepting them as genuine, assume their *displacement* to a greater or less degree. And here we may subdivide, according as these chapters are supposed to have been addressed wholly to the Romans or partly (at least) to some other Church.

(ii) Among those who accept the Roman destination of the whole, but assume some displacement, is HEUMANN[1]. He

---

[1] The views of Heumann, Paulus, Griesbach, and Semler, are here given at second hand from Reiche *Erklärung des Briefes an die Römer* 1833, as I have had no opportunity of verifying the references.

supposes that the original epistle comprised the first eleven chapters, to which were added two postscripts, xvi. 1–24, and xvi. 25–27. The intermediate matter (cc. xii–xv.) formed a separate letter to the Romans written on account of some intelligence received meanwhile from Rome. The two letters were afterwards combined (but not by the Apostle himself), in such a manner as to throw the postscript to the end.

In like manner PAULUS (*de Orig. Ep. ad Rom.*, Jena 1801) offered another solution on the same basis. The xvth chapter was a sort of supplementary letter, addressed to the enlightened. The xvith chapter, written on a separate parchment, contained recommendations of Phœbe the bearer of the letter to the principal members of the Church, and instructions to her to salute certain persons. Finding that there was space remaining on this leaf, the Apostle availed himself of it to add some directions to the presbyters. The doxology at the end belonged originally to the general letter, but was afterwards displaced when the several documents were put together.

Another hypothesis, which like the two last mentioned supposes the epistle to consist of a number of Sibylline leaves stitched together almost at random, is that of GRIESBACH (*Curæ in Hist. Test. Gr. Epp. Paul.* p. 45). He believes that the original letter ended with xiv. 23, the parchment being exhausted. The final doxology, xvi. 25–27, was attached on a separate leaf. Another parchment contained the salutations from certain friends of St Paul, with a benediction, xvi. 21–24. St Paul then found leisure to continue the subject, where he had broken off, in a postscript (xv.), to which he added another benediction. A fourth parchment contained the names of the Roman Christians who were saluted, together with a warning against intriguers; and here again a benediction was appended. At a later date, when these various leaves were attached together, different places were assigned to the doxology, and in some copies it was entirely omitted.

The three solutions last mentioned, while disintegrating the epistle, assume that all the component parts were addressed to

19—2

the Roman Church. This is not the case with those which follow.

(iii) SEMLER (*Paraphr.* 1769) supposes that the letter to the Romans closed with the xivth chapter; that the bearers of the letter were charged to distribute copies to the leading members of certain churches which they would visit on the route; and that an authoritative list of these persons (xvi.) was given to them at the same time. To these persons, not to the Roman Church, the xvth chapter was addressed. The bearers would visit Cenchreæ, the residence of Phœbe, and Ephesus, where Aquila was staying. The places where the others dwelt are not mentioned by name, because they were well known to the bearers.

Not very different is EICHHORN's hypothesis (*Einl.* Th. iii.). The parchment destined for the original letter, he supposes, ended with the xivth chapter. A separate leaf contained on one side the final doxology, on the other the salutations and benediction. This formed the whole of the letter as originally conceived. But some time intervening before it was sent, the Apostle added on a separate leaf (which was interposed) certain warnings and personal explanations (xv.). The remainder of the present epistle (xvi. 1–20) was not addressed to the Romans, but was a letter of introduction for Phœbe, perhaps intended for Corinth. Phœbe forgot to deliver it, and took it with her to Rome.

From these complex theories, which hardly deserve credit for ingenuity, it is a relief to turn to simpler solutions. Allowing the xvth chapter to stand as part of the Epistle to the Romans, several critics have separated the xvith chapter from the rest, and assigned it to some other letter. Thus SCHULZ (*Stud. u. Krit.* 1829, p. 609) supposed it to be a portion of an epistle written from Rome to Ephesus: and this view has been recently adopted by EWALD (*Sendschr. des Apostels Paulus* p. 428 sq.), who however restricts the intrusive fragment to xvi. 3–20. On the other hand SCHOTT (*Isagoge* p. 250 sq.) regards the xvith chapter as a congeries of fragments written by the

Apostle from Corinth to some Christian community in Asia Minor.

It will be seen at once that in this last class of solutions the documentary facts are entirely neglected, the theories being built on certain phenomena in the chapter itself. But indeed the same charge lies, though in a less degree, against all the solutions enumerated under the heads (ii) and (iii). No regard at all is paid to the remarkable omission of the mention of Rome in the opening verses; and, as attempts to explain the textual phenomena of the last two chapters, they are in most cases at once superfluous and defective. At the same time they are condemned by their highly artificial character.

I hope to show that M. Renan's theory also must be rejected, both as involving strong improbabilities in itself, and as being more complex than the phenomena demand. But, in so far as it grapples fairly with the documentary facts, it has a higher claim to attention than the others.

M. Renan then supposes that the so-called Epistle to the Romans was a circular letter, of which several copies with distinct and appropriate endings were sent to different churches, the body of the letter being the same for all. One of these was despatched to Rome, a second to Ephesus, a third to Thessalonica, and a fourth to some unknown Church. Our epistle is the work of a later editor, who had these four copies in his hands, and combined all the endings so that nothing might be lost. The following table will show what parts of our epistle (according to M. Renan's view) belonged to each of these:

Romans.	Ephesians.	Thessalonians.	Unknown Church.
i–xi.	i–xi.	i–xi.	i–xi.
	xii, xiii, xiv.	xii, xiii, xiv.	xii, xiii, xiv.
xv.			
	xvi. 1–20.		
		xvi. 21–24.	
			xvi. 25–27.

In the last three some modification would be made also in the first chapter. The mention of Rome (vv. 7, 15) at all events must have been expunged.

M. Renan founds this theory of a quadripartite epistle on the assumed fact that in the existing recension we meet with four successive endings, xv. 33, xvi. 20, xvi. 24, xvi. 25–27. His reasons for assigning the several portions to letters addressed to the several churches above mentioned will appear in the sequel.

The most convenient method of dealing with M. Renan's opinions will be first to consider the difficulties which he feels in the received view that the whole epistle was written to the Romans and which oblige him to substitute another hypothesis, and then to state the objections which lie against his own theory.

The difficulties then, which M. Renan proposes to remove by his theory, are the following:

1. Certain phenomena in the body of the letter are perplexing, if it was written to the Romans. He selects as instances, the passages ii. 16, xi. 13, xvi. 25. Of these he says that they are 'only moderately adapted to the faithful of Rome, and would amount to indiscretion if addressed to these last alone' (p. lxxiv.). This objection rests on the assumption that the Roman Church consisted wholly of Jewish Christians; an assumption which I shall consider hereafter. At present I would only remark that, inasmuch as the letter (on M. Renan's hypothesis) was specialized by attaching an appropriate ending and thus became to all intents and purposes an Epistle to the Romans, it is difficult to see how the 'indiscretion' would be affected by the fact that other copies with other endings were despatched to other churches.

Again, M. Renan, building on the assumption already mentioned that the Roman Church must have been Judæo-Christian, claims for his theory the merit of explaining 'the hesitation of the best critics on the question whether the letter was addressed to converted heathens or to Jewish Christians'; for on his hypothesis 'the principal parts of the epistle would have been com-

posed to serve for several churches at once' (p. lxxiv.). The
answer to this argument is the same as to the former; and
to the same extent I must reserve what I have to say in
reply.

2. Moreover M. Renan thinks it surprising that St Paul
should have composed 'un morceau si capital,' 'having regard
solely to a church which he did not know and over which he
had not incontestable rights' (p. lxxiv.). Considering the general
and comprehensive character of the epistle, it seems to me
that the church of the metropolis would naturally be chosen
for such a purpose, and that the Apostle saw a distinct advantage in addressing such a letter to a community with which he
had no special relations, so that he would run no risk of
being diverted from his aim by any personal interests.
But to this subject again I shall have occasion to return
hereafter.

3. When he reaches the xiith, xiiith, and xivth chapters,
M. Renan sees many difficulties in supposing that St Paul can
have addressed such language to the Romans. He regards it
as a departure from the Apostle's principle 'Each on his own
ground' (p. lxiii.). He cannot understand that one who is so
unsparing towards those who 'build on other men's foundations'
should himself give such bold counsel to a church which he
had not founded. He discovers a difference in tone between
these chapters and the xvth, which he supposes to be really
addressed to the Romans, and which seems to him to hold
gentler language. I am not sure that others would find out
this difference; but if any such exists, the Apostle's own
words supply the explanation. In xv. 15 he himself apologizes
for speaking to the Romans 'with over-boldness' ($\tau o\lambda\mu\eta\rho\acute{o}$-
$\tau\epsilon\rho o\nu$). But indeed, if this interference with the Roman
Christians be truly a violation of the Apostle's rule not to
build on another man's foundation, he has already violated
it in addressing to them a letter of instruction of which the
doctrinal portion is at least as peremptory as these special precepts, and he has expressed his intention of still further violating

it by paying them a visit and by communicating to them some spiritual gift (i. 11). This argument proves nothing, because it proves too much.

4. The opening verses of the xvth chapter also occasion some surprise to M. Renan on the common supposition as to the integrity and destination of the letter. They seem to him merely to repeat and to enfeeble what has gone before. 'It is hardly supposable,' he says, 'that they occurred in the same letter' with the foregoing chapters (pp. lxiv., 461). Moreover ' the verses 1–13 appear to be addressed to Judæo-Christians. St Paul there makes concessions to Jewish ideas' (pp. lxiv., 462). These remarks seem to me to show a strange misapprehension of the Apostle's drift. At the close of the preceding chapter he has taught that in the matter of meats there must be mutual concession and forbearance; that the man who can conscientiously eat may do so, but that in so doing he must take care not to scandalize his weaker brother. At the opening of the xvth chapter he turns round and addresses, not Jewish Christians who were too scrupulous about such matters, but ultra-Pauline Christians who were only too ready to go their own way and to ignore the effects of their conduct on others; 'But it is the duty of *us*—the strong—to support the infirmities of the weak and not to please ourselves.' A comparison with 1 Cor. viii. 1, Gal. vi. 1, Phil. iii. 15, where there is the same touch of irony in St Paul's language, will show the force of $\dot{o}\phi\epsilon\acute{\iota}\lambda o\mu\epsilon\nu$ $\delta\grave{\epsilon}$ $\dot{\eta}\mu\epsilon\hat{\iota}\varsigma$ $o\acute{\iota}$ $\delta\nu\nu\alpha\tau o\acute{\iota}$, as addressed to the extravagant disciples of liberty. I am somewhat confident therefore that most persons who will read the xivth and xvth chapters continuously, bearing this in mind, will not only not agree with M. Renan, but will find it difficult to believe that the two did *not* occur in the same letter[1].

Another argument, of which M. Renan makes use against the Roman destination of these chapters, admits a still more direct refutation: 'Il s'y sert du verbe $\pi\alpha\rho\alpha\kappa\alpha\lambda\hat{\omega}$, verbe d'une nuance très-mitigée sans doute, mais qui est toujours le mot

---

[1] 'Es ist unleugbar,' says de Wette, 'dass Cap. xv. 1–13 zu Cap. xiv. gehört.'

qu'il emploie quand il parle à ses disciples.' If this argument is to have any force, it must mean that παρακαλῶ is never used by St Paul except to his disciples. If so, he has forgotten that it occurs in xv. 30, παρακαλῶ δὲ ὑμᾶς κ.τ.λ., a passage which on M. Renan's own showing was addressed to the Roman Church.

It should be added that throughout his remarks on this xvth chapter M. Renan is hampered by the hypothesis that the Roman Church was Judæo-Christian. In one passage indeed he seems ready to make a concession, for he speaks of the *majority* as Judæo-Christian (p. lxiv.); but this has no practical influence on his argument. Yet surely the expression προσλαμβάνεσθε ἀλλήλους (xv. 7), not less than the whole tenour of the epistle, points to a mixed community of Jews and Gentiles, in which it was the Apostle's aim to conciliate the discordant elements. If the expression *Christ a minister of the Circumcision* (xv. 8) points (as M. Renan justly infers) to Jewish prepossessions among St Paul's readers, yet on the other hand the Apostle's language a few verses below, xv. 15, 16, 'Reminding you by the grace which was given to me by God that I might be a minister of Christ Jesus *unto the Gentiles*,' shows still more clearly that he looked upon the Roman Church as in some sense Gentile, and therefore under his own jurisdiction.

5. The objections which M. Renan brings against the Roman destination of the xvith chapter are partly his own and partly adopted from others.

The Apostle, he urges, concludes the xvth chapter with a benediction and a final *Amen*. This therefore must be the end of a letter, since St Paul never adds salutations after such a close (p. lxv.). As he mentions the final Amen twice, it must be supposed that he lays great stress on the occurrence of the word here. We are therefore the more surprised that he has not consulted the critical editions of the text. In this case he would have found that ἀμὴν is omitted by Griesbach, and placed in brackets by Lachmann and Tregelles. As the bias of scribes is always in favour of inserting rather than omitting an

Amen in such cases, and as in this place it is wanting in some good copies (though present in the majority), these editors have justly regarded it with suspicion. Deprived of the Amen, the passage has a very close parallel in Phil. iv. 9, καὶ ὁ Θεὸς τῆς εἰρήνης ἔσται μεθ᾽ ὑμῶν (comp. 2 Cor. xiii. 11, Gal. vi. 16), which occurs in the body of the letter. But indeed doxologies and benedictions, with or without the accompanying Amen, are very frequent in St Paul, in other places than at the close of an epistle, as e.g. Rom. xi. 36, Gal. i. 5, Ephes. iii. 20, 21, Phil. iv. 19, 20, 1 Thess. iii. 11–13, v. 23, 2 Thess. ii. 16, 17, iii. 5, 1 Tim. i. 17, vi. 16, 2 Tim. iv. 18; comp. Heb. xiii. 20, 21. In some cases these occur immediately before the salutations, as in the present passage.

6. In the salutations themselves M. Renan finds the same difficulties which have been a stumbling-block in the way of others before him. He and they are surprised that St Paul should salute so many persons in a church which he had not visited, when he is so sparing of individual salutations in writing to churches with which his relations are most close and intimate. Let us ask in reply, What is the common experience in such matters? Will not a man studiously refrain from mentioning individual names where he is addressing a large circle of friends, feeling that it is invidious to single out some for special mention, where an exhaustive list is impossible? On the other hand, where only a limited number are known to him, he can name all, and no offence is given. This in fact is exactly what we find in St Paul. So far as the data are sufficient to establish any rule, it may be said that the number of names mentioned is in the inverse proportion to his familiarity with the church to which he is writing. In the Epistles to the Corinthians and Thessalonians no individuals are saluted. In the Epistle to the Philippians again there are no salutations properly so called, though a special warning is addressed to two persons by name and a commission given to another. On the other hand, in the Epistle to the Colossians, whom the Apostle had never visited, certain persons are saluted by name.

This preliminary difficulty therefore is no difficulty at all. But—M. Renan proceeds—there is great improbability in supposing that St Paul knew so many members of a church which he had never visited, that he should have had such intimate relations with several of them, and that he should be so well acquainted with their circumstances. In the case of almost any other church such a supposition would indeed be improbable. But Rome with its vast and ever-growing population of immigrants from the East, and especially from Syria and Palestine, could not but contain a large number of residents known directly or indirectly to one who had travelled so long and so wide as St Paul. On this point let M. Renan himself be witness; 'By the side of the Apostles who attained celebrity,' he writes, ' there was also another obscure apostolate, whose agents were not dogmatists by profession, but which was only the more efficacious on that account. The Jews of that time were *extremely nomadic*. Tradesmen, domestic servants, small craftsmen, they overran all the great towns on the coast (p. 96). Rome was the rendezvous of all the Oriental religions, the port of the Mediterranean with which the Syrians had the closest relations. They arrived there *in enormous bands*... With them disembarked troops of Greeks, of Asiatics, of Egyptians' (p. 97).

But again, when he examines the names in detail, M. Renan is more than ever convinced that these salutations were not addressed to the Church of Rome. On the one hand he cannot find in the list any names known to have belonged to the Church of Rome at this time, and to substantiate this assertion he refers to 2 Tim. iv. 24, which, with some little ingenuity, he describes as a 'passage which has its historical value, *though the letter is apocryphal*.' I too allow the historical value of the passage (though, if I thought the letter apocryphal, I should hardly venture to build an argument on it); but I cannot see that the mention of four other names and only four in an epistle written from Rome after an interval of several years throws any discredit on this earlier list, as a catalogue of Roman Christians. On the other hand M. Renan finds in the list

'several persons who assuredly never formed part' of the Roman
Church.   Of these he singles out Aquila and Priscilla, remarking that as 'every one knows,' 'only some months' (quelques
mois) elapsed between the writing of the First Epistle to the
Corinthians and the Epistle to the Romans, and that, when the
former was written, they were still at Ephesus (1 Cor. xvi. 19).
Now it is just in a case like this that words should be carefully
chosen.   Yet on M. Renan's own showing (and the fact can
hardly be disputed) the Epistle to the Romans was not despatched till the early part of the year 58 (see pp. 459, 498);
whereas the First Epistle to the Corinthians was written about
the same time or a little later in the preceding year ('probable-
ment à l'époque même de Paques,' are M. Renan's own words,
p. 383); so that by the 'some months' we must understand
'at least ten months.'   Elsewhere indeed (p. 6) he places even
the Second Epistle to the Corinthians in the year 56, thus
making a longer interval; but I presume that this is a slip
of the pen.   Is there then any real difficulty in supposing that
they returned to Rome in this interval of a year more or less,
and that St Paul should have been made acquainted with their
return, seeing that his own travels meanwhile had lain mainly
on the route between Ephesus and Rome ?   Aquila and Priscilla appear first at Rome, then at Corinth, then at Ephesus
(Acts xviii. 2, 18, 19, 26, 1 Cor. xvi. 19).   All this M. Renan
admits.   But he will not allow their return to Rome.   This
would be 'leur prêter une vie par trop nomade.'   Why, does not
M. Renan himself afterwards in a passage already quoted (p. 275)
describe the life of these itinerant Jewish artisans and traders
exactly in this way ?   Does not the narrative of the Acts distinctly assign to this couple a 'nomadic' life, which indeed was
the direct consequence of the peculiar trade which they plied ?
But 'to bring them back to Rome, without their sentence of
banishment being rescinded, on the very morrow of the day
(juste le lendemain du jour) when Paul had bidden them farewell at Ephesus,' this in M. Renan's opinion is to 'accumulate
mprobabilities.'   But how does he know that a special sentence

of banishment was pronounced against them individually or that, if pronounced, it was not revoked? On this point however I will appeal to a witness, whose testimony ought to be conclusive, so far as M. Renan is concerned, and who (I confess) seems to me to put the matter in the right light; 'These expulsions' (the writer is speaking of the edict of Claudius) 'were never more than temporary and conditional. The flood, arrested for a moment, always returned. The measure of Claudius had in any case very little result; for Josephus does not mention it, and in the year 58 Rome had already a new Christian Church' (*Saint Paul* p. 111). But again, M. Renan, though he holds the 2nd Epistle to Timothy to be spurious, yet cannot refrain from using it to increase the supposed difficulty, because in that epistle Aquila and Priscilla appear again at Ephesus (2 Tim. iv. 19). Is it at all improbable that after an interval of nearly ten years they should again revisit this important city? They were wanderers not only by the exigencies of their trade, but also by the obligations of their missionary work. Why should we deny them a rapidity of movement, which we are obliged to concede to Timotheus, to Tychicus, to St Luke, to St Paul himself?

But 'this is not all. In ver. 5 St Paul salutes Epænetus, the first-born of Asia in Christ.' 'What!' exclaims M. Renan, 'had all the Church of Ephesus assembled at Rome?' Let us dissect this sentence. This 'all' in plain language consists of three persons. Of one, Epænetus, we do not know that he belonged to Ephesus, but only that he was a native of the province. The other two belonged no more to Ephesus than to Pontus, to Corinth, to Rome, though about a year before this they happened to be residing in Ephesus. But once again, is there any improbability in imagining two or three Asiatic Christians resident or sojourning in Rome? Does not M. Renan himself speak of the 'troops of Asiatics' that flocked thither? And history teaches that this language is not an exaggeration.

'But,' M. Renan continues, 'the list of names which follows is in like manner better suited to Ephesus than to Rome.' He allows indeed that 'the earliest Church of Rome for the most part spoke Greek': but he argues that in examining the Jewish inscriptions in Rome 'Garrucci has found that the number of Latin proper names was double the number of Greek names,' whereas in this list 'of twenty-four names, sixteen are Greek, seven Latin, one Hebrew, so that the number of the Greek names is more than double that of the Latin.' To this objection it would be a sufficient answer that St Paul's acquaintances must necessarily have lain, not among the native Latin population, but among the Greek and Oriental immigrants whom he had crossed in his travels. But a little examination will show that the argument is fallacious, even as applied to the Church of Rome generally. A better test of its composition, than these Jewish inscriptions, is the list of the Roman bishops in the first two centuries. Analysing this list, we find that in a catalogue of fifteen names (from Linus A.D. 67 ? to Callistus A.D. 219), twelve are Greek, while three only (Clemens, Pius, Victor) are Latin. After Callistus the proportions are about reversed; the Roman Church was becoming gradually Latinized and there is a corresponding preponderance of Latin names. This fact illustrates the fallacy of M. Renan's comparison. Garrucci's Jewish inscriptions (I am repeating M. Renan's own statement elsewhere, p. 106, note 3) for the most part belong to a much later date than St Paul's age. We should therefore expect to find in these, as we find in the Christian lists at the same time, an increase of the Latin names at the expense of the Greek.

But among these numerous Greek names, which thus create a difficulty to M. Renan, he especially remarks on the fact that 'the names of the masters of houses, Aristobulus and Narcissus, are Greek also.' This remark seems to me peculiarly unfortunate. It so happens that we know of two great 'chefs de maison' at Rome about this time, bearing these very names. The former was a Jew, a member of the Herodian family, and therefore among his slaves and dependents the Apostle was most likely to have formed friendships; nor is it an unimportant coincidence, as I have remarked elsewhere[1], that after the mention of the household of Aristobulus the next person specified is one Herodion, whom St Paul calls his kinsman and who therefore was a Jew by birth, while at the same time his name seems to indicate a dependent position in the family of this Jewish prince. Again in a foot-note M. Renan for some reason or other (probably thinking of his name-sake, the writer on prodigies, who was a native of Tralles) singles out *Phlegon*, as a name more suited to Ephesus than to Rome. Even the Trallian Phlegon however, who was a freed man of Hadrian, resided at Rome: and in fact the inscriptions show that this name was by no means of rare occurrence in the metropolis[2].

On this point therefore I cannot but think that M. Renan is entirely wrong, though he can quote the authority of some important critics on his side. How far I have succeeded, I am not competent to say; but I seem to myself to have shown elsewhere[3] that the names in this list are quite appropriate on the hypothesis that the salutations were addressed to the Romans, and that on this supposition alone they present several coincidences which go far to establish its truth. I am glad also to be able to quote on my side the opinion of a writer whose bias would certainly have led him to take a different view, if he had shared M. Renan's difficulty. Baur, who goes so far as to deny the genuineness of the last two chapters of the epistle, explains the salutations by supposing that the forger inserted 'a catalogue of those who were known at the time as the notabilities of the oldest Roman Church' (*Paulus* p. 414).

'So,' M. Renan concludes decisively, 'the verses Rom. xvi. 3–16 (containing the salutations) were not addressed to the Church of Rome; they were addressed to the Church of Ephesus.' 'No more,' he continues, 'can the verses 17–20 have been addressed to the Romans.' The strength of his affirmations seems at this point to be in the inverse proportion to the

---

[1] See *Philippians* p. 173, where I have interpreted the expressions οἱ ἐκ τῶν Ἀριστοβούλου, οἱ ἐκ τῶν Ναρκίσσου to mean *Aristobuliani*, *Narcissiani*.

[2] The index to Gruter gives only three inscriptions, where this name occurs, DCLXXI. 6, DCCLIX. 12, DCCCLVIII. 3, and all three are Roman.

[3] *Philippians*, p. 169 sq.

strength of his evidence. He appeals here again to the use of
the word παρακαλῶ (ver. 17)—an argument demonstrably erroneous, even on his own showing, as I have already pointed out
(p. 296). He quotes the expression ἐφ' ὑμῖν χαίρω, which he
explains as 'the language of a master to his scholars,' not
remembering that St Paul uses a similar expression in writing
to the Colossians (ii. 5) whom he had never visited, and apparently not entertaining any objection to the allied phrase εὐχα-
ριστῶ περὶ πάντων ὑμῶν (i. 8) as addressed to the Romans.
He remarks that St Paul knows the condition of the church he
addresses, and glories (se fait gloire) in its good reputation; but
why should he not do all this in the case of Rome? And thus
he infers 'il est là en famille.' Then by a rough and ready
method he argues that the verses could only be addressed to
the Corinthians or to the Ephesians; and, as the epistle at the
close of which they occur was written at Corinth, they must
have been addressed to Ephesus. I seem to myself to have
shown that the reasons for questioning their Roman destination
are wholly insufficient to counteract the weight of external
evidence. But, I would ask, are there no difficulties in the
counter hypothesis that they were written to the Ephesians?
Why in this case have the personal allusions no points of coincidence either with the narrative of St Paul's long residence at
Ephesus which terminated not a year before, or with his address
to the Ephesian elders which was held only a few months
afterwards? Why again is there no mention of Tychicus or of
Trophimus, who were with St Paul at this time? Of the
benediction, which closes the 20th verse and which M. Renan
takes to be the conclusion of the Ephesian letter, I shall have
something to say presently.

7. The next few verses also (vi. 21-24), containing salutations from divers persons in St Paul's company, 'cannot any
more than the preceding have formed part of an Epistle to the
Romans.' 'Why,' he exclaims, 'should all these people who
had never been at Rome, who were not known to the faithful
at Rome, salute these last? What meaning could these names

of unknown persons have to the Church of Rome ?'   As much
meaning, I would reply, as the names of the persons saluting
the Colossians could have to the Church of Colossæ (Col. iv. 10
sq.).   They might or they might not be known to the Roman
Church by name; personal acquaintance was not necessary to create
Christian sympathy; and, being about the Apostle at the time,
they might well pour out their hearts in this expression of good
wishes.   What more natural for instance than that Gaius in
whose house St Paul was staying, and Tertius who acted as the
Apostle's amanuensis, should join in the salutation ?

But M. Renan goes on to remark, as an important fact, that
the names mentioned in these verses 'are *all* names of Macedonians or of persons who might have known the Churches of
Macedonia.'   Will this statement bear examination ?   Eight
names are mentioned in all.   Of *Tertius* the amanuensis and
Quartus 'the brother' we know nothing.   Of *Lucius* also we
are equally ignorant, unless he be the Lucius of Cyrene mentioned Acts xiii. 1, in which case he is as likely to have had
relations with Rome as with Thessalonica.   *Timotheus*, it is
true, was well known in Macedonia; but as the constant companion of the Apostle, his fame must have reached Rome also.
Erastus too, himself a Corinthian, had accompanied the Apostle
on a missionary visit to Macedonia (Acts xix. 22); but the descriptive addition, 'the steward of the city,' is much more appropriate, if addressed to those to whom his name was unknown or
scarcely known, than to those with whom he was personally
acquainted.   *Gaius* of Corinth (1 Cor. i. 14) again (for he must
not be confused with Gaius of Macedonia, Acts xix. 29) had—so
far as we are aware—no personal relations with Macedonia.
Thus as regards six out of the eight persons sending salutations,
M. Renan's remark has no force.   The remaining two, *Jason*
and *Sosipater*, were seemingly Macedonians.   The former may
be identified with St Paul's host at Thessalonica, Acts xvii. 5
sq. (though the name, as a Grecized form of Jesus or Joshua, is
common among Hellenist Jews at this date); and the latter is
most probably 'Sopater the son of Pyrrhus the Berœan,' who

accompanied St Paul when he left Corinth on this occasion[1] and was probably with him now. Both these however, as faithful friends and constant attendants of the Apostle, might very well append their salutations to his letter. On the other hand there is no mention of Aristarchus and Secundus the Thessalonians, who were with St Paul at this time (Acts xx. 4)[2], as might have been expected in a letter written to Thessalonica.

At this point again M. Renan calls attention to the benediction in xvi. 24 and adds, 'verse 24 is the conclusion of a letter. The verses xvi. 21–24 may therefore be an end of a letter addressed to the Thessalonians.' He has failed to observe that this benediction is wanting in the best critical editions, but to this matter I shall have to revert presently.

8.   Thus we have arrived at the close of M. Renan's third epistle. His fourth is suggested by the documentary evidence. As the final doxology, xvi. 25–27, is found in many copies at the close of the xivth chapter, he concludes that it must have occurred in this place in one of the four copies of the circular letters which were welded together to form our recension. His fourth epistle in fact coincides in limits with Baur's Epistle to the Romans, though M. Renan himself supposes it to have been addressed to some unknown church. How much nearer to probability this part of his theory approaches than the rest, I hope to show hereafter.

I have thus examined in detail M. Renan's objections to the integrity of the letter, considered as addressed to the Romans; and, if I mistake not, have reduced them to very small dimensions. Every complex historical fact involves some improbabilities, prior to evidence; and in this case such improbabilities as remain are not greater than we might reasonably expect. On the other hand the direct documentary evidence is

---

[1] Acts xx. 4, Σώπατρος Πύρρου Βεροιαῖος, the correct reading. The very fact however that St Luke takes such pains to identify him, seems to show that he was not the only person of the name about St Paul at this time.

[2] M. Renan himself makes them accompany him to Corinth (p. 458).

exceptionally strong here, as this epistle seems to have been more widely known from the very earliest ages than any of St Paul's letters, and therefore the probability of such a manipulation as he supposes having occurred without leaving any traces in the MSS. is correspondingly diminished.

This examination has also brought out incidentally the positive grounds on which M. Renan constructs his own theory, and they have been severally considered. One point however has been reserved. The *quadripartite* character of the closing chapters of this epistle is a remarkable fact, if true, and indeed may be regarded as the foundation of his theory. If it fails, the theory must crumble and fall. I propose therefore to ask whether the epistle has or has not these *four distinct endings*.

Inasmuch as the establishment of this fact is all important to his theory, it is strange that M. Renan should not have glanced beyond the received text, except to suggest (with what bearing, it does not appear) a possible fifth ending; 'Nous arrivons donc à ce singulier resultat que l'épître finit quatre fois, et dans le *Codex Alexandrinus* cinq fois' (p. lxxi.; comp. p. 461).

These four endings then (in the received text) are:

(1) xv. 33 ὁ δὲ Θεὸς τῆς εἰρήνης μετὰ πάντων ὑμῶν. ἀμήν.

(2) xvi. 20 ἡ χάρις τοῦ Κυρίου ἡμῶν Ἰησοῦ Χριστοῦ μεθ' ὑμῶν.

(3) xvi 24 ἡ χάρις τοῦ Κυρίου ἡμῶν Ἰησοῦ Χριστοῦ μετὰ πάντων ὑμῶν. ἀμήν.

(4) xvi. 25–27 τῷ δὲ δυναμένῳ...μόνῳ σοφῷ Θεῷ διὰ Ἰησοῦ Χριστοῦ, ᾧ ἡ δόξα εἰς τοὺς αἰῶνας. ἀμήν.

Now the *first* of these has not the character of St Paul's final benedictions at all. The ἀμήν (this is a matter of little moment) is, as I have pointed out already, open to grave suspicion (see p. 297). The form of the prayer has many parallels in the body of the Apostle's letters, as I have also shown. But the final benedictions *in every other instance* are framed on the type of (2) or (3) ἡ χάρις κ.τ.λ., consisting of more or fewer words, but preserving this characteristic feature. Any one who reads in succession the concluding benedictions of all St Paul's epistles will, I think, feel the force of this argument.

The *second* and *third* do exhibit the character of final benedictions. But here M. Renan has made an important oversight[1]. The two editors, to whom we are indebted for the best texts, Lachmann and Tregelles, omit the third. In fact a comparison of the oldest uncials will show, that these two benedictions are in reality the same, which occupies one or other place in the better authorities, but which in later copies is sometimes inserted in both. Thus we have to make a choice between xvi. 20 and xvi. 24, but we cannot retain both. In this respect the phenomena of this benediction present an exact parallel to those which attend the position of the long doxology (xvi. 25–27), as given above, p. 288.

The following is a conspectus of the facts relating to this benediction.

xvi. 20 ἡ χάρις τοῦ Κυρίου ἡμῶν Ἰησοῦ [Χριστοῦ] μεθ' ὑμῶν.

ins. ℵ, A, B, C, rel., Orig.

om. D, F, G.

xvi. 24 ἡ χάρις τοῦ Κυρίου ἡμῶν Ἰησοῦ Χριστοῦ μετὰ πάντων ὑμῶν. ἀμήν.

om. ℵ, A, B, C, Am., Fuld., Harl., Memph., Æth., Orig.

ins. D, F, G, (17), 37, 47, L, (P), Demid., Tol., (Syr. Pesh.), Syr. Harcl., (Arm.), [*om.* ἡμῶν, 37; *om.* Ἰησοῦ Χριστοῦ, F, G].

---

[1] Perhaps 'oversight' is hardly the correct term, for he adds in a note, 'Sur l'incertitude des manuscrits à propos de la place du verset 24, voir Griesbach, *Nov. Test.* II. p. 222.' But here his curiosity ends. As his theory mainly depends on the position of these benedictions, it is only the more strange that he should have accepted the received text without examination, knowing that it was open to question.

As F, G, 37, L, Goth., omit xvi. 25–27, it becomes the end
of the epistle in these.

In 17, P, Syr. Pesh., Arm., it occurs after xvi. 25–27 [*om.*
ἡμῶν P].

It will thus be seen that Lachmann and Tregelles are right
in placing this benediction at xvi. 20; and that it has been
transplanted thence into the later positions, whether at xvi. 24
or after xvi. 27, by editorial revision, with a view to restoring it
to what seemed to be its proper place. To this subject also I
shall have to revert again.

M. Renan's *fourth* ending is different in character from the
others, being a doxology and not a benediction. I shall reserve
my explanation of it.

Thus then it will appear that the basis of M. Renan's theory,
the quadripartite character of the epistle, has fallen away. But
before dismissing this theory, I must point out some objections
to which, even if it rested on more solid ground, it would be
exposed, and which might in themselves prove fatal to it.

(1) In our existing Epistle to the Romans the topics in
the last two chapters occur in the following order. (*a*) xv.
Special injunctions and explanations concerning the Apostle's
movements. (*b*) xvi. 1–20. A recommendation of the bearer
of the letter and several salutations to divers persons, with a
warning against divisions appended. (*c*) xvi. 21–24. Salutations from divers persons in St Paul's company. (*d*) A
doxology (xvi. 25–27). This sequence is natural. In fact the
topics follow each other in the same order in the Epistle to the
Colossians, which, as regards the concluding matter, is the most
complete of all the Apostle's letters. On the other hand all
M. Renan's four epistles are incomplete, and incomplete in a
remarkable way. The first—to the Romans—contains personal
explanations without salutations to or from any one. The second
—to the Ephesians—contains no personal explanations but only
salutations to several brethren. The third—to the Thessalonians
—has neither the one nor the other, but only salutations from
several friends of the Apostle. Lastly, the fourth—to some

unknown Church—has none of the three but only a bare
doxology. We are required therefore to suppose that these
four copies were defective in such a way that, when they were
combined at some distance of time by a chance editor, they
fitted together exactly, each supplying what was lacking in the
rest, and all together forming a complete whole.

(2) But again; M. Renan's theory, though contrasting in
this respect favourably with many of its predecessors, nevertheless fails to account for all the phenomena of the MSS. Thus,
whereas the reading preserved in G τοῖς οὖσιν ἐν ἀγάπῃ Θεοῦ
obliterates the mention of any individual church, M. Renan's
theory supposes that in the several copies appropriate modifications were introduced to adapt them to particular churches.
In this case we should rather have expected traces of such a
reading as τοῖς οὖσιν ἐν Ἐφέσῳ (or ἐν Θεσσαλονίκῃ) ἀγαπητοῖς
Θεοῦ, or at all events (as in the somewhat parallel case of the
canonical Epistle to the Ephesians) τοῖς οὖσιν ἀγαπητοῖς Θεοῦ,
the space which was originally left for the name having disap-
peared in the course of transcription and the words closed in
upon the blank. On the other hand the substitution of ἐν ἀγάπῃ
for ἀγαπητοῖς seems to have been made with a view to *obviating
the necessity of mentioning any name.* This suggests a solution
somewhat different from M. Renan's.

Again; as regards the concluding chapters of the epistle, it
will be seen that the documentary facts point only to the *fourth*
of M. Renan's four copies, and give no indication whatever of
the other three. This fourth copy, as I hope to show, does
represent a truth, though the destination was not what
M. Renan supposes.

(3) M. Renan speaks with some vagueness about the body
of the letter. In one passage in his introduction (p. lxxiii.) he
seems to imply that the copy sent to the Romans consisted of
chapters i–xi., xv., exactly as we have them; for he mentions
'modifications in the first half of the first chapter,' as introduced into the three remaining copies. This I suppose to be his
meaning. But, if so, what becomes of half his objections to the

received view? These are based on the assumption that the
Roman Church was Judæo-Christian. Of the truth or false-
hood of this assumption I shall have something to say presently.
I would simply ask now, how it is reconcilable with the Epistle
to the Romans, as he leaves it. This is M. Renan's own statement of the case; 'Les passages de l'Épître aux Romains qui
supposeraient (why not 'supposent'?) l'Église de Rome composée pour la plus grande partie de païens et de prosélytes,
Rom. i. 6, 11, 13, vi. 14, 17 et suiv., vii. 1–6, xi. 13, 25, 28, 30,
xiv. 1 et suiv., xv. 7 et suiv., viennent de ce que les Romains
n'étaient pas les uniques destinataires de l'Épître en question.
Ces formules sont, du reste, si vagues que de bons critiques en
ont pu conclure, les uns que l'Épître aux Romains a été écrite à
des païens convertis les autres qu'elle a été écrite à des Judéo-
Chrétiens' (p. 483).   Yet M. Renan lets all these passages
remain in the copy sent to the Roman Church. It may be
inferred however from his language here that these passages
made a deeper impression upon him when he came to analyse
the epistle towards the close of his volume, than when he wrote
the introduction. For though he argues in the introduction on
the hypothesis of a strictly Judæo-Christian Church, and even
in this later passage speaks of it as 'en général composée
d'Ebionites et de Judéo-Chrétiens,' he yet adds here 'Elle
renfermait aussi cependant des prosélytes et des païens convertis'; and altogether his language seems to betray a vague
misgiving that his theory is not very consistent with the
hypothesis on which it is built.

It was not my intention, when I commenced this paper, to
take up a merely negative position. As M. Renan has endeavoured fairly to grapple with the documentary facts, it is
only due to him, while rejecting his theory, to attempt to
suggest some other solution which shall account for them as
well or better, and shall not be open to the same objections.
The view that the Epistle to the Romans was early circulated in a longer and a shorter form, i.e. both with and without

the xivth and xvth chapters, is in some shape or other not new.
Bertholdt and others, for instance, explained the phenomena of
the different positions of the doxology by supposing that these
two chapters were omitted in the public lessons[1]. More recently
Mr Westcott (Vaughan's *Romans*, p. xvi.) says, ' Whether it may
be possible that the epistle proceeded in two forms from the
Apostle's hands, the one closing with chap. xiv. and the doxology,
the other extended by the addition of the two last chapters after
the omission of the doxology, or whether any other more satisfactory explanation can be offered of the phenomena of omission,
repetition, transposition, authenticity, must be left for further
investigation.' In an article on the epistle in Smith's *Dictionary
of the Bible* I myself adopted the theory of a twofold edition, and
further examination has confirmed me in this view. But the
subject has never, so far as I am aware, received that ' further
investigation' which Mr Westcott desires, and in the hope that
I may be able to throw a little light on it, I venture now to
examine the question more closely.

But by way of preface it is necessary to say something about
the composition of the Church of Rome at this time, for (as we
have seen already) much depends on the view adopted in this respect. M. Renan, in the passage quoted above (p. 311), offered
his own explanation of the fact that the ablest critics were
divided on the question whether the epistle was addressed to
Jewish or to Gentile Christians. Would not the more natural
explanation be that St Paul is here addressing a mixed church,
composed of both in equal or nearly equal parts, and that he
turns now to one, now to the other, as the tenour of his argument
demands ? Certainly the Gentile element is very strong ; and I
think few will agree with M. Renan, that such passages as i. 5,
6 ἐν πᾶσιν τοῖς ἔθνεσιν...ἐν οἷς ἐστε καὶ ὑμεῖς, or i. 13 ἐν ὑμῖν
καθὼς καὶ ἐν τοῖς λοιποῖς ἔθνεσιν, or xi. 13 ὑμῖν λέγω τοῖς ἔθνεσιν
(with its whole context), or xv. 16 ἐπαναμιμνήσκων ὑμᾶς διὰ τὴν
χάριν τὴν δοθεῖσάν μοι ὑπὸ τοῦ Θεοῦ εἰς τὸ εἶναί με λειτουργὸν

---

[1] This however is shown not to have been the case. See Reiche, *Comm.
Crit.* p. 118.

Χριστοῦ Ἰησοῦ εἰς τὰ ἔθνη, are explained on the assumption that the Roman Church was strictly Judæo-Christian, together with (what M. Renan very reluctantly concedes) a sprinkling of Gentile Christians among them. St Paul, if I mistake not, starts from the fact that the Roman Church stood on Gentile ground, and that very large and perhaps preponderating numbers of its members were Gentiles. This is his justification for writing to them, as the Apostle of the Gentiles. It never once occurs to him, that he is intruding on the province of others. Yet at the same time it is equally clear that a considerable part of the argument is directed against Judaizing tendencies, and occasionally he appeals directly to Jewish readers (ii. 17, iii. 9, vii. 4 sq.). The inference from these two classes of facts seems to be plain.

Nor is there any prior improbability in such a mixed church. M. Renan insists that the Roman brotherhood must have been founded and built up by emissaries from Palestine. But why should the Christianity of Rome be due to Jerusalem solely, and not also to Antioch and Corinth and Ephesus, with which cities communication must have been even more frequent ? Why at Rome alone should the Judaic element be all powerful, and the Pauline insignificant ?

And, while the hypothesis of such a mixed church is probable in itself, it also harmonizes with the notices elsewhere. St Paul's language to the Philippians implies that, when he arrived at Rome, he found two parties of Christians there, the one friendly to him, the other hostile, but both alike stimulated to activity by his presence (Phil. i. 14–18). It may be truly said also that this view is quite consistent with all the notices of the Roman Church during the first two centuries of its existence, and that some of these seem to require it.

To this obvious inference from the Apostle's own language, M. Renan can only oppose the testimony of one or two much later writers. He refers especially to the commentator Hilary (p. 483), whom he commends as ' fort au courant des traditions de l'Église romaine' (p. 115). It may be granted that this

writer has preserved more than one true tradition, but the mere
fact that he wrote quite three centuries after St Paul deprives
his statements of any value when they conflict with the natural
interpretation of the Apostle's language. And after all, is not
M. Renan mistaken in supposing that this writer here professes
to give a tradition? His words are, 'Constat itaque temporibus
apostolorum Judaeos, propterea quod sub regno Romano age-
rent, Romae habitasse; ex quibus hi qui crediderant, tradiderunt
Romanis ut Christum profitentes legem servarent; Romani
autem audita fama virtutum Christi faciles ad credendum fue-
runt, utpote prudentes: nec immerito prudentes, qui male in-
ducti statim correcti sunt et permanserunt in eo. Hi ergo ex
Judaeis, *ut datur intelligi*, credentes Christum non accipiebant
Deum esse de Deo, putantes uni Deo adversum; quamobrem
negat illos spiritualem Dei gratiam consecutos ac per hoc
confirmationem eis deesse' (Ambros. *Op.* ii. app. 25). He appears to state as matter of history ('constat') only that there was
a large Jewish population in Rome. Beyond this his language
is apparently based on the interpretation of the epistle itself
('datur intelligi'; comp. p. 30). He sees that a considerable
portion of the epistle is directed against Judaizing views, and
he therefore infers that the Judaizers were a very strong party
in the Roman Church. M. Renan again appeals to the Clementine Homilies, which he asserts confidently were written at
Rome, and which exhibit Ebionite views. The Roman origin
of this work seems to me more than doubtful; but even if
granted, it does not prove his point, for the cautious disguise,
which the writer wears throughout, shows that he must have
belonged to a comparatively small minority. That there was
such a compact and active Judaizing minority in Rome in
the early ages, few probably would deny. On the other hand,
M. Renan omits to mention the one genuine document of
subapostolic times, which was issued in the name of the Roman
Church, and which may therefore reasonably be supposed to
represent the views of that church. The Epistle of Clement
exhibits no leaning to Judaism.

To the Church of Rome then, as a mixed body of Jewish and Gentile converts, the epistle was addressed. The destination of the letter was in harmony with its subject. Indeed it may very reasonably be conjectured, that the subject in the Apostle's mind was prior to the destination. To the Corinthians he had written rebuking the errors of Gentile licence. To the Galatians he had denounced the deadening effects of Judaic bondage. The letters to these churches had been called forth by special emergencies, and this fact gave a special direction to them. Thus the Apostle's mind for a year or more had been led to dwell especially on the relation of these two extremes separately to the doctrine of grace and liberty. It would not unnaturally occur to him to treat them together in a comprehensive manner, and to show where Judaic and Gentile feeling might find their true meeting point. This is exactly what he does in the Epistle to the Romans. Its aim from beginning to end is *conciliation*—conciliation of claims, conciliation of doctrine, conciliation of practice. The manner in which the question of forbidden meats is treated in the xivth chapter is only a special example of the motive which pervades the whole work. The Apostle, it is true, had a personal reason for writing to the Romans, as he contemplated visiting them soon and wished to prepare them for his visit: but above all this, there was singular propriety in addressing such an exposition to the Church of the metropolis, composed, as we have seen, in almost equal parts of the same two discordant elements which he strove to combine. Thus the epistle, though not a circular epistle itself, yet manifested the general and comprehensive character which might be expected in such. It is more of a treatise than a letter.

This was our Epistle to the Romans. The shorter recension, in which the two last chapters were omitted, was, I suppose, an after-thought, being an attempt to divest it of all personal matter, and to make it available as a circular letter or general treatise. So far, it was a carrying out of the spirit of the original work. When and how this was done I shall en-

deavour to make out; but by way of introduction I will set
side by side what I consider to have been the contents of these
two recensions respectively.

Epistle to the Romans.	*Abridged Recension.*
i–xiv.	i–xiv.
	[Substituting τοῖς οὖσιν ἐν ἀγά-
	πῃ Θεοῦ for τοῖς οὖσιν ἐν 'Ρώ-
	μῃ ἀγαπητοῖς Θεοῦ in i. 5, and
	omitting ἐν 'Ρώμῃ in i. 17].
xv.	
xvi. 1–23	
[omitting the benediction (xvi. 24), and the doxology (xvi. 25–27)].	xvi. 25–27.

Of the abridged recension we have distinct traces in
Marcion's copy (though he omitted the doxology), in FG,
and less decidedly in other authorities; and some such hypothesis alone will explain the varying positions of the doxology
in different MSS.

The MS. F is unfortunately defective in the first chapter,
but doubtless preserved here the same phenomena which we
find in G. These two MSS. are very closely allied, and must
have been copied mediately or immediately from the same
prototype. They themselves may probably be referred to the
ixth century, having belonged to two neighbouring Swiss monas-
teries, the one to Reichenau, the other to St Gall. Either their
common prototype, or a still earlier MS. from which it was
copied, must have preserved the abridged recension. The
space of about five lines, which is left blank between chapters
xiv. and xv. in G, would be about sufficient for the doxology
(xvi. 25–27), which however is omitted in both places. These
features in the MS. suggest that the copyist of an earlier MS.,
from which it has descended, transcribed a MS. of the abridged

recension till the end of chapter xiv., and then took up a MS. of the original Epistle to the Romans to supply the lacking matter, omitting however the doxology as inappropriate to what had thus become the middle of the letter, and perhaps intending to give it a place afterwards, but abandoning his purpose. It is an instructive fact that in the allied MS. F no space is left after ch. xiv., but the text is written continuously.

My reasons for supposing that the doxology (xvi. 25–27 of the received text) belonged to the abridged recension and not to the original epistle are the following:

(1) It has nothing in common with the usual endings of St Paul's Epistles, which close with a benediction of the type mentioned above (p. 307).

(2) On the other hand, such an abridged recension as I have supposed, whether issued by the Apostle or by some later editor, would hardly have been left to terminate abruptly with $\pi\hat{\alpha}\nu$ $\delta\hat{\epsilon}$ $\hat{o}$ $o\hat{\upsilon}\kappa$ $\hat{\epsilon}\kappa$ $\pi\hat{\iota}\sigma\tau\epsilon\omega\varsigma$, $\hat{\alpha}\mu\alpha\rho\tau\hat{\iota}\alpha$ $\hat{\epsilon}\sigma\tau\hat{\iota}\nu$. The addition of a doxology, or of some equivalent, would seem necessary.

(3) If it had occurred at the end of the xivth chapter in the original epistle, it would have been a violent interruption of the sense, for the xvth chapter continues the thread of the xivth, and there is nothing to call for such a thanksgiving. On the other hand, if its position was at the end of the epistle, the displacement to the close of the xivth is somewhat difficult to explain.

(4) The difference of style between this doxology and the rest of the epistle has often been noticed, and has led some critics to question or deny its genuineness. The real fact is, that though it does differ somewhat in thought and diction from the epistles of this date, it has very strong affinities to the later letters of the Apostle, as the following table will show:

τῷ δὲ δυναμένῳ...
κατὰ τὸ εὐαγγέλιόν μου...

τὸ κήρυγμα Ἰησοῦ Χριστοῦ κατὰ ἀποκάλυψιν μυστηρίου χρόνοις αἰωνίοις σεσιγημένου φανερωθέντος δὲ νῦν διά τε γραφῶν
προφητικῶν, κατ' ἐπιταγὴν τοῦ
αἰωνίου Θεοῦ εἰς ὑπακοὴν πίστεως εἰς πάντα τὰ ἔθνη γνωρισθέντος.

τῷ δὲ δυναμένῳ, Eph. iii. 20.
κατὰ τὸ εὐαγγέλιόν μου (2 Tim.
ii. 8, but also Rom. ii. 16).
κατὰ ἀποκάλυψιν ἐγνωρίσθη
μοι τὸ μυστήριον...ὃ ἑτέραις
γενεαῖς οὐκ ἐγνωρίσθη...ὡς νῦν
ἀπεκαλύφθη τοῖς ἁγίοις ἀπο-
στόλοις αὐτοῦ καὶ προφήταις
ἐν πνεύματι, εἶναι τὰ ἔθνη κ.τ.λ.
Eph. iii. 3, 5, 6.
τοῦ μυστηρίου τοῦ ἀποκεκρυμ-
μένου ἀπὸ τῶν αἰώνων...ἵνα
γνωρισθῇ νῦν, Eph. iii. 9, 10.
ἣν ἐπηγγείλατο...πρὸ χρόνων
αἰωνίων ἐφανέρωσεν δὲ καιροῖς
ἰδίοις τὸν λόγον αὐτοῦ ἐν κη-
ρύγματι ὃ ἐπιστεύθην ἐγὼ κατ'
ἐπιταγὴν τοῦ σωτῆρος ἡμῶν
Θεοῦ (comp. 1 Tim. i. 1), Tit.
i. 2, 3.
τὴν δοθεῖσαν...πρὸ χρόνων αἰωνίων, φανερωθεῖσαν δὲ νῦν διὰ
τῆς ἐπιφανείας κ.τ.λ., 2 Tim. i.
9, 10.

τοῦ αἰωνίου Θεοῦ...μόνῳ σοφῷ
Θεῷ διὰ Ἰησοῦ Χριστοῦ ᾧ ἡ
δόξα εἰς τοὺς αἰῶνας [τῶν αἰώ-
νων]. ἀμήν.

τῷ δὲ βασιλεῖ τῶν αἰώνων...
μόνῳ [σοφῷ] Θεῷ τιμὴ καὶ δόξα
εἰς τοὺς αἰῶνας τῶν αἰώνων.
ἀμήν. 1 Tim. i. 17.

These facts seem to show that though written by the Apostle
it was not written at the same time with the letter itself[1].

In order to account for all these data, I suggest the follow-

---

[1] Dean Alford (*G. T.* III. Prol. p. 80)
points out the resemblance of this doxology to the Pastoral Epistles, though
not to the Epistle to the Ephesians,
and suggests that it was appended to
the epistle 'in later times by the
Apostle himself, as a thankful effusion
of his fervent mind.' This view seems
not to supply an adequate occasion for
the addition.

ing hypothesis. At some later period of his life, not improbably during one of his sojourns in Rome, it occurred to the
Apostle to give to this letter a wider circulation. To this end
he made two changes in it; he obliterated all mention of Rome
in the opening paragraphs by slight alterations; and he cut off
the two last chapters containing personal matters, adding at
the same time a doxology as a termination to the whole. By
this ready method it was made available for general circulation,
and perhaps was circulated to prepare the way for a personal
visit in countries into which he had not yet penetrated (i. 11
sq.). The idea of a circular letter was not new to him; for he
had already addressed one to the Churches of Asia. M. Renan
pertinently remarks that the First Epistle of St Peter makes
use chiefly of the Epistle to the Romans and the Epistle to the
Ephesians, 'c'est-à-dire des deux épîtres qui sont des traités
généraux, des catéchèses' (p. lxxii.).

Thus I believe that the last, and the last alone, of
M. Renan's four epistles represents a historical fact. It was
not however a special copy, as he supposes, addressed to some
individual church now unknown, but an adaptation of the
original epistle for general circulation. A copy of this fell into
the hands of Marcion, but (unless Rufinus in his translation has
misrepresented Origen's meaning) he removed the doxology,
as he well might have done with a doctrinal aim. Another
was the prototype of FG. All the phenomena relating to the
doxology arose from the combination of copies of this abridged
recension with copies of the original epistle in different ways.
The notice of Origen shows that such combinations took place
at a very early date.

One point still remains to be settled—relating however not
to the abridged recension, but to the original epistle. Where
are we to place the benediction which occurs (1) at xvi. 20,
(2) after xvi. 23, whether before or after the doxology, or (3)
in both places, in different copies, as explained above (p. 308)?
To this question the great preponderance of authority allows
but one answer. It must stand at xvi. 20, and must be

omitted from the later place. If so, ver. 20 is the true close of the epistle, and the salutations from the amanuensis and other companions of St Paul were added irregularly as a sort of postscript, as was very likely to have been done, considering the circumstances under which St Paul's epistles were written. The desire of later transcribers to get a proper close to the letter would lead them to transplant to the end of these salutations the benediction of xvi. 20, with or without modification, or to supply the defect with the doxology from the abridged recension. Either expedient appears in different MSS., and in some both are combined.

B.

By Dr Hort.

DR LIGHTFOOT in this Journal (II. 264 ff.) has demolished M. Renan's ingenious theory about the composition of the Epistle to the Romans, and along with it some others of inferior merit. He proposes instead a simpler view, which one could wish to believe true, so admirably does it harmonize the most salient phenomena of the text, and so free is it from broad historical improbability. A close examination however reveals difficulties which I am constrained to think fatal.

Dr Lightfoot supposes that the letter originally addressed to the Romans was our present epistle as it stands in the Received Text and Authorized Version, wanting only the last four verses, i.e. the second Benediction (xvi. 24) and the Doxology (25–27); but that at a later time St Paul himself 'made it available as a circular letter or general treatise' by cutting off the last two chapters, substituting the Doxology, and omitting the name of Rome in i. 7, 15. The direct evidence lies in three chapters, i. xiv. xvi., which I will consider separately and in inverse order.

I. The apparently triple ending of xvi. in the Received Text, when taken as a whole, rests on absurdly small and worthless evidence, three or four obscure cursives and the inferior MSS. of the Latin Vulgate: it is a mere jumble of the Latin and the late Greek traditions, which owes its place in the printed text to Erasmus[1]. If the Doxology be put out of

---

[1] His account of his own proceeding is intelligible, while his carelessness grossly misrepresents the evidence; indeed his statement is further from the truth as it could be known at that date than it would be now. 'Hanc partem usque ad *Debemus autem* quidam codices omnino non habent, qui-

sight, we are met by a still worse confusion of incongruous traditions; that is, the doubling of the Benediction (20 and 24). The great mass of early authorities of various groups concur in placing the Benediction at 20 only: so ℵABC 5 137 lat.vg (best MSS.) memph aeth Orig.ruf. The pure 'Western' group D*FG (with Sedulius and perhaps the Gothic version) places it only at 24[1], evidently from the feeling that it must be the close of the epistle. Minor shiftings and other like freedoms taken by the same group of authorities occur in almost every chapter of St Paul: two whole verses 1 Cor. xiv. 34 f. are pushed 5 verses forward by DFG 93 and some Latin Fathers: compare 1 Cor. xv. 26. The scribes of the fourth century, bringing together MSS. from different regions, here as in countless other instances heaped up without omission whatever they found, and so the Benediction was set down in both places. The compound reading appears first in the Greek commentators of the fifth century from the Syrian school, then in the Harclean Syriac (A.D. 508–616): in extant MSS. it is found only in L (= J) of the ninth century and the great mass of cursives. There is however a similar combination in a few respectable authorities who retain the Doxology and place the second Benediction after it (P 17, the vulgar Syriac and the Armenian versions, and the Ambrosian Hilary): and this implies the previous existence of MSS. which simply transposed the Benediction to *their* end of the epistle, as (D*)FG transposed it to *theirs*[2]. Thus

dam in fine adjiciunt epistolae. Nos, quoniam id non videbatur ad hunc locum pertinere, semovimus in finem hujus epistolae' (note on xiv. 23 in ed. princeps of 1516). 'Haec est pars quae in plerisque Graecorum codicibus non additur, in nonnullis alió additur loco, sicut indicavimus, in quibusdam adjicitur in fine. Id quod et nos fecimus, praesertim assentientibus Latinis exemplaribus' (note on xvi. 25 ff.).

[1] D* and Sedulius add the Doxology after the Benediction. The nature of both authorities, as evinced by their readings generally, explains this singular collocation. D is not so purely Western as FG: Sedulius combines the Old with the Hieronymic Latin. In each case the Doxology must be a later accretion. The Gothic has the Benediction at 24 and (in xvi.) no Doxology: the extant fragments fail to shew whether the Benediction was at 20 likewise.

[2] If, as is probable, the shifting of the Benediction and the dropping of the Doxology were simultaneous in the common source of D*FG Sed., P 17 etc.

the historical relations of the authorities clearly shew that, be the claims of the double Benediction as a 'harder reading' what they may, it is as a matter of fact the last term in a series of changes.

Thus far there is no reason to suppose that Dr Lightfoot would dissent. He places the Benediction at 20 and there alone, and gives what is doubtless the right explanation of the order in saying that 'v. 20 is the true close of the epistle, and the salutations from the amanuensis and other companions of St Paul were added irregularly as a sort of postscript, as was very likely to have been done, considering the circumstances under which St Paul's epistles were written' (p. 319). Whoever will read the chapter through as far as 24 according to this arrangement, will find everything straightforward and intelligible; while the nature of the postscript is such as might easily mislead a mechanical transcriber. The difficulty begins when we go on to 25–27. Supposing however that we had no evidence about these three verses except as to their presence or absence *in this place*[1], I do not see why we need hesitate to take them as an ending to the postscript, just as 20 is the ending to the epistle proper[2]. Having once made that fresh start to introduce the salutations sent by present companions, St Paul might gladly seize the opportunity to close the whole by a solemn giving of glory to God, as his first ending had carried grace to men. Compare xi. 36 in connexion with xi. 32 and the adjoining verses; also v. 2; xv. 5, 6. Similar pauses of adoration occur elsewhere in the epistle; i. 25; (viii. 39;) ix. 5; xi. 36; xv. (13,) 33, where I believe Ἀμήν to be genuine:

---

[1] Their total omission will be considered further on.

[2] The postscript is evidently St Paul's own, notwithstanding the first person used for the moment in 22 by Tertius the amanuensis in sending his own greeting. Otherwise ὁ συνεργός [μου], οἱ συγγενεῖς μου *before* the mention of Tertius would not be intelligible. The subsequent ὁ ξένος μου καὶ τῆς ἐκκλησίας is also the language of an apostle.

differ merely in taking one step instead of two: the writer of their common original was willing to transpose but not to omit. The two transpositions were however apparently independent of each other.

and it is to be observed that, when St Paul's own salutations to
Christians at Rome were ended, he was not able to refrain (xvi.
17–20) from breaking out afresh into renewed exhortations to
mutual peace through willing obedience to the common Lord.
As he had gone back to the perils and hopes of the Church
after the one set of individual greetings, so we can imagine him
joyfully returning to the yet higher sphere of God's universal
purposes after the other set of individual greetings[1]. Nay the
parallelism between 17–20 and 25–27 is one of contrast as
well as likeness. The first passage gives vent to somewhat of
the anxious dread which lurks behind many a phrase of xv.
14–33, especially 30, 31. If these were St Paul's last words
to the Romans except the two sets of greetings and the Benediction of 20 b, the epistle might have appeared to end in a
note of discord: at all events its exulting comprehensiveness
would have died back into the rebuke and controversy proper
for the Galatians. The sudden upward flight of the Doxology
seems therefore to be almost demanded, to swallow up not only
trivial individualities of salutation but also the temporary strifes
of the Church.

But it is said that the Doxology differs too much in style
from the rest of the epistle to form part of it. I used to
suspect that it might be the ending to one of the forms of the
encyclical epistle to the Ephesians, which was preserved from
being lost to the Canon by being appended to St Paul's longest
epistle. Dr Lightfoot (after Dean Alford) points out its resemblance to the Pastoral Epistles as well, and accordingly treats
it as marked by the Apostle's later style generally. Before
scrutinizing words and phrases, let us look at the subject. The
starting-point is doubly personal; an anxiety about the stability
of the converts addressed, such as tinges the hopefulness of the
first and last words spoken to and about the Romans (i. 11;

---

[1] Dr Lightfoot says (p. 317) that the
Doxology 'has nothing in common
with the usual endings of St Paul's
Epistles, which close with a benediction of the type' ἡ χάρις κ.τ.λ. But
none of his other epistles have a postscript, following a benediction in that
form already given.

xvi. 17–20); and a bold lifting up of what friend and foe knew as the distinctive 'Gospel' of St Paul, (and that in its distinctive form of 'preaching,' and with its distinctive appeal to 'faith,') such as marks the time of the conflict with Judaism within the Church (i. 1, 5, 9, 16; xv. 16; x. 8, 14, 15). Here the pronouns 'you' and 'my' face each other with an emphasis which in such a context is hard to explain till we remember the presaging instinct with which St Paul saw in the meeting of himself and the Roman Christians, if indeed it was to be vouchsafed, the pledge and turning-point of victory (i. 10 ff.; xv. 29–32; cf. Acts xix. 21; xxviii. 31). Then comes the idea in which the Doxology culminates, the counsel of the far-seeing God, the Ruler of ages or periods, by which the mystery kept secret from ancient times is laid open in the Gospel for the knowledge and faith of all nations. This idea no doubt pervades the Epistle to the Ephesians, though with considerable enrichments. But is it foreign to St Paul's earlier thought? The second chapter of 1 Corinthians at once shews that it was not and explains why the fact is not obvious. St Paul is dealing there with converts who were in danger from pride of eloquence and wisdom (from i. 5 onward). For fear of this danger, he says (ii. 1 ff.), he himself kept back all excellency of speech or of wisdom when he came among them, and confined himself to the bare preaching of the Cross as alone fitted to their imperfect state. But for all that he desired them to know that he too had in reserve a wisdom which he spoke among the perfect. Its nature he briefly hints in words that closely resemble our Doxology ('We speak a wisdom of God in a mystery, that hidden wisdom which God fore-ordained before the ages unto the glory of us' etc. ii. 7), and then hastens to explain that, even after being laid open, it demands a spiritual power to discern it. The Churches to which he wrote about this time, at Corinth, in Galatia, at Rome, were not in a state to profit by an extended exposition of a belief which yet was strong in the Apostle's own mind, and so the traces of it in the early period are few. Later it filled a larger space in his thoughts, it acquired new extensions and associations, and he had occasion to write to Churches which by that time were capable of receiving it. But it is not really absent even from the Epistle to the Romans. Kindred thoughts find broken and obscure utterance in viii. 18–30. The belief itself is the hidden foundation of the three chapters (ix–xi.) in which God's dealings with Jew and Gentile are expounded, and comes perceptibly to light in their conclusion (xi. 33–36). Now it is precisely in these chapters, as F. C. Baur (*Paulus* 341 ff.) saw long ago, that the main drift of the epistle is most distinctly disclosed: all its various antitheses are so many subordinate aspects of the relation of Jew and Gentile which in this seeming episode is contemplated in its utmost generality as reaching from the one end of history to the other. The whole epistle could hardly have a fitter close than a Doxology embodying the faith from which its central chapters proceed. Here at last that faith might well be articulately expressed, though a wise economy compelled it to be latent as long as the Apostle was simply instructing the Romans. This Doxology is in fact a connecting link between the epistle at large and the earlier concentrated doxology of xi. 36. In both alike human sin and hindrance are triumphantly put out of sight[1]: but here the eternal operation of Him 'from Whom, through Whom, and unto Whom are all things' is translated into the language of history.

An examination of single phrases is attempted in the following table, which includes some less obvious coincidences of thought[2].

---

[1] They could not be left out in the latter part of the Epistle, when St Paul's own position and the dangers of the Romans had to be spoken of (xv. 14–33; xvi. 17–20). But for this very reason it was the more necessary that the ground conquered at the end of xi. should be maintained at the final close of the Epistle. See p. 324.

[2] References to the later epistles are in []: the chief passages are set out at length by Dr Lightfoot, p. 318.

Τῷ δὲ δυναμένῳ ὑμᾶς στηρίξαι

Rom. xiv. 4...στήκει ἢ πίπτει· σταθήσεται δὲ, δυνατεῖ γὰρ ὁ κύριος στῆσαι αὐτόν. Δύναμαι, δυνατός, δυνατέω with an infinitive are used of God Rom. iv. 21; xi. 23; 2 Cor. ix. 8; (xiii. 3;) Gal. iii. 21; [2 Tim. i. 12: τῷ...δυναμένῳ...Eph. iii. 20.] Στηρίζω in St Paul is found elsewhere only Rom. i. 11 (ἐπιποθῶ γὰρ ἰδεῖν ὑμᾶς...εἰς τὸ στηριχθῆναι ὑμᾶς) and 4 times in 1, 2 Thess. 'Standing fast' is a common phrase in 1, 2 Thess., 1, 2 Cor., Gal., Rom.; though also found later: 'falling' is confined to 1 Cor., Rom.

κατὰ τὸ εὐαγγέλιόν μου

So Rom. ii. 16; [2 Tim. ii. 8.] So also κατὰ τὸ εὐαγγέλιον Rom. xi. 28, for here as there the inclusion of the Gentiles must be chiefly meant. (The 'stablishment' of the Romans would presuppose the harmony of Jew and Gentile among them.) In this light μου is illustrated by i. 1–6, 9, 16; xv. 16.

καὶ τὸ κήρυγμα Ἰησοῦ Χριστοῦ

Compare Rom. ii. 16; x. 8–12; xv. 5 f.; 1 Cor. i. 21; xii. 12 f.; 2 Cor. i. 19 f.; Gal. iii. 26–29; [2 Tim. iv. 17; Tit. i. 3: also 1 Tim. ii. 7; 2 Tim. i. 11.] The double name appears to have special force in this connexion.

κατὰ ἀποκάλυψιν μυστηρίου χρόνοις αἰωνίοις σεσιγημένου φανερωθέντος δὲ νῦν

Rom. i. 16 f....εἰς σωτηρίαν παντὶ τῷ πιστεύοντι, Ἰουδαίῳ τε [πρῶτον] καὶ Ἕλληνι· δικαιοσύνη γὰρ θεοῦ ἐν αὐτῷ [sc. τῷ εὐαγγελίῳ] ἀποκαλύπτεται ἐκ πίστεως εἰς πίστιν·: here the historical δικαιοσύνη is a part of the μυστήριον: and so iii. 21 νυνὶ δὲ χωρὶς νόμου δικαιοσύνη θεοῦ πεφανέρωται, μαρτυρουμένη ὑπὸ τοῦ νόμου καὶ τῶν προφητῶν, δικαιοσύνη δὲ θεοῦ διὰ πίστεως [Ἰησοῦ] Χριστοῦ εἰς πάντας τοὺς πιστεύοντας: cf. Gal. iii. 22 f. Rom. xi. 25...τὸ μυστήριον τοῦτο...ὅτι πώρωσις ἀπὸ μέρους τῷ Ἰσραὴλ γέγονεν ἄχρι οὗ τὸ πλήρωμα τῶν ἐθνῶν εἰσέλθῃ, καὶ οὕτως πᾶς Ἰσραὴλ σωθήσεται. 1 Cor. ii. 6, 7, 10 σοφίαν δὲ λαλοῦμεν ἐν τοῖς τελείοις...θεοῦ σοφίαν ἐν μυστηρίῳ τὴν ἀποκεκρυμμένην, ἣν προώρισεν ὁ θεὸς πρὸ τῶν αἰώνων...· ἡμῖν γὰρ ἀπεκάλυψεν ὁ θεὸς διὰ τοῦ πνεύματος. [Eph. iii. 3–11. Πρὸ χρόνων αἰωνίων 2 Tim. i. 9; Tit. i. 2.]

διά τε γραφῶν προφητικῶν

Rom. i. 2...εὐαγγέλιον θεοῦ ὃ προεπηγγείλατο διὰ τῶν προφητῶν αὐτοῦ ἐν γραφαῖς ἁγίαις; iii. 21 (above); and ix–xi. passim.

κατ' ἐπιταγὴν

[1 Tim. i. 1; Tit. i. 3.] But the meaning is given by Rom. i. 1, 5 δι' οὗ [sc. Ἰ. Χ.] ἐλάβομεν...ἀποστολὴν εἰς ὑπακοὴν πίστεως ἐν πᾶσιν τοῖς ἔθνεσιν; x. 15; and the mere formula κατ' ἐπιταγήν 1 Cor. vii. 6; 2 Cor. viii. 8.

τοῦ αἰωνίου θεοῦ

1 Cor. ii. 7 (above); x. 11; cf. Rom. xi. 33–36. [1 Tim. i. 17 τῷ βασιλεῖ τῶν αἰώνων: also Eph. iii. 9, 11; Col. i. 26; 2 Tim. i. 9; Tit. i. 2.]

εἰς ὑπακοὴν πίστεως

Verbatim in this connexion Rom. i. 5 (above). This enlarged sense of ὑπακοή, ὑπακούω, is confined to the early epistles (Rom. vi. 17; x. 16; xv. 18 εἰς ὑπακοὴν ἐθνῶν; ? xvi. 19; 2 Thess. i. 8; 2 Cor. vii. 15; ? x. 5 f.).

εἰς πάντα τὰ ἔθνη   Rom. i. 5 above; xi. *passim;* xv. *passim;* xvi. 3 f. Γνω-
γνωρισθέντος,   ρίζω is *similarly* used Rom. ix. 22 f. ; 1 Cor. xv. 1; ? Gal.
    i. 11; as well as (often) in the later period.

μόνῳ σοφῷ θεῷ   Rom. iii. 29, 30 ἢ Ἰουδαίων ὁ θεὸς μόνων; οὐχὶ καὶ ἐθνῶν;
    ναὶ καὶ ἐθνῶν, εἴπερ εἷς ὁ θεὸς ὅς κ.τ.λ. [Μόνῳ θεῷ 1 Tim. i.
    17 a kindred passage, which early caused τῶν αἰώνων to be
    inserted here after τοὺς αἰῶνας, and in its turn received
    σοφῷ hence in the fourth century: cf. 1 Tim. vi. 15; but
    also Jud. 4, 25; John v. 44 etc.] Σοφία is predicated of
    God by St Paul with reference to the working out of a
    distant purpose by unexpected means: so Rom. xi. 33;
    1 Cor. i. 21, ? 30; ii. 7; [Eph. i. 8; iii. 10; Col. ii. 3.]

διὰ Ἰησοῦ Χριστοῦ   Rom. v. 1 f.; xv. 6 f.; Gal. i. 4 f.; [Eph. i. 5 f., 11–14;
[ᾧ][1] ἡ δόξα εἰς τοὺς   iii. 21; Col. i. 27; 1 Tim. i. 11, 17.]
αἰῶνας· ἀμήν.

A minute examination of the passages briefly indicated in
this table will shew that the dominant thoughts of the Epistle,
—the thoughts which inspired its beginning (i. 1–17), its
primary close (xv. 6–33), and its three characteristic chapters
in which the old faith and revelation are invoked on behalf
of the new,—are precisely those expressed in the final Doxology; and that the separate words and phrases of the Doxology
are for the most part what have already occurred in the
Epistle, while there are hardly any not to be found in epistles
of the same or an earlier period[2]. If this be so, the obvious
resemblances to parts of the later epistles lose all force as
evidence of date. The Doxology and 1 Cor. ii. 6–10, a passage
absolutely inseparable from its context, support each other
in shewing that St Paul's late teaching was his early belief;
while in each case there was an adequate motive for his exceptional transgression of the limits imposed on him by the
present imperfection of his converts. The condensed and
cumulative style, which he used more freely afterwards, arises
naturally from the compression of varied thoughts and facts
into a single idea in a single sentence under the impulse of

---

[1] ᾧ is probably an intrusion, notwithstanding the presumption in favour
of an irregular construction.

[2] The only clear exception is χρόνοι
αἰώνιοι (2 Tim. i. 9; Tit. i. 2), the idea
of which is preserved in 1 Cor. ii. 7;
x. 11. On the other hand ὑπακοὴ (πίστεως), both phrase and sense, is peculiar to the early epistles.

eager feeling. Rom. i. 1–7; iii. 21–26; 2 Thess. i. 3–10 offer a true analogy: what distinguishes them is their articulation, which was hardly possible in a doxology. But we may go further. As is the Epistle to the Romans itself in relation to the monuments of St Paul's early teaching, gathering up, harmonizing, concluding, such is the Doxology in relation to the Epistle. It looks at once backwards and forwards. Springing from the keen sense of a present crisis, it gives old watchwords of action a place in the dawning vision of thought which the epistles from Rome were to expound, and anticipates in its style as in its ideas the habitual mood of the time when the crisis was victoriously ended, and the unity of the Church secured.

II. The course thus far has been smooth, because the chief textual difficulties have been out of sight. The end of the fourteenth chapter is a point at which various phenomena present themselves which nothing in the context would have led us to expect. Some of them (*a*) on the surface mark only an interruption of the Epistle. The Doxology is inserted either (1) here alone or (2) both here and in xvi. In (3) a single MS. G, one of the twin MSS. which alone omit the Doxology altogether, an empty space is left here, occupying half a line at the bottom of an otherwise full page and 5 lines of the next page. Secondly (*β*) the whole of the two following chapters are supposed to have been omitted (1) by Marcion (on the authority of Origen), (2) perhaps by Tertullian and even Irenæus, and (3) in the capitulation of an unknown Latin MS. mentioned by Wetstein. The variety of this evidence, if it stands proof, is a strong argument in favour of any theory which will account for all the particulars.

The testimony of Origen requires consideration first. We have it only in the greatly abridged version of Rufinus, a careless and licentious translator. This is not a passage with which he is likely to have consciously tampered; but there is no certainty that the language is Origen's own. Characteristic

terms of expression as well as ideas may be recognized through
Rufinus's Latin in almost every page; but none such are conspicuous here: rather the sentences are short and simple for
Origen. The comment on the Doxology (after xvi. 23) begins
thus. "Caput hoc Marcion, a quo Scripturae Evangelicae
atque Apostolicae interpolatae sunt de hac epistola penitus
abstulit: et non solum *hoc,* sed et *ab* eo loco ubi scriptum est
'Omne autem quod non ex fide peccatum est' [xiv. 23] usque
ad finem cuncta dissecuit. In aliis vero exemplaribus, id est
in his quae non sunt a Marcione temerata, hoc ipsum caput
diverse positum invenimus. In nonnullis etenim codicibus post
eum locum quem supra diximus, statim cohaerens habetur 'Ei
autem qui potens est vos confirmare.' Alii vero codices in fine
id ut hunc[1] est positum continent. Sed jam veniamus ad capi-
tuli ipsius explanationem." As the text stands, it asserts plainly
that Marcion removed from the Epistle both the Doxology and
xv. xvi.; and that of the MSS. unaffected by Marcion's proceeding some had the Doxology after xiv., some after xvi.

So the passage has been universally understood. On the
other hand for many years I have had a strong impression
that the Benedictine text is wrong in three letters, and that
on the removal of this tiny corruption the whole interpretation
collapses. De la Rue's notes on this book often mention the
readings of a certain Paris MS. (Reg. 1639). Wherever I have
examined them, they have appeared usually to give the truest
text against all other known authorities, and very seldom to
be evidently wrong. In this place Reg. 1639 has *in* instead
of *ab.* If the preceding *hoc* is likewise altered to *hic,* and so
small a variation may easily have escaped notice, we get an
entirely new and, I venture to think, more probable statement.
Origen begins by saying merely that 'Marcion, the falsifier[2]
of the Gospels and [St Paul's] Epistles, removed this paragraph

---

[1] ['hunc' is a misprint for 'nunc.']

[2] *Interpolo* in ancient Latin, it will
be remembered, does not mean to interpolate, but properly to give a spurious look of newness to old things, and
so generally to falsify.

completely from the Epistle.' Then it appears to strike him
that some reader might know the Epistle in a copy which
had the Doxology at the end of xiv. (if not there alone), and
acquit Marcion as having at most only removed a superfluous
repetition[1]. He adds therefore explicitly 'And not only here
but also' at xiv. 23 'he cut away[2] everything quite to the
end.' Then, for fear the remark might not be understood
by those who knew the Doxology only in xvi., he explains
'But in other copies, that is in those which have not been
corrupted by Marcion, we have found this very paragraph
differently placed' etc.

Of these three statements the end of the second might be
thought a mere repetition of the first, according to the corrected
reading. But I think Origen wished to make it perfectly clear
that Marcion's offence, as he understood it, was no mere erasure
of an obnoxious phrase but utter excision of the entire paragraph. Nor is it unlikely that the Greek original contained
intermediate digressive sentences which gave a resumptive
force to the repetition. No one, I presume, would seriously
find a difficulty in the words 'to the end' as inappropriate to
the removal of the Doxology alone, in the case of MSS. in which
it had stood at xiv. 23: their correctness in reference to its
normal position would make them sufficiently descriptive for

---

[1] Reasons will be given further on
for suspecting that the MSS. here noticed by Origen had the Doxology in
both places. At this point the difference is without importance.

[2] This is not, it must be confessed,
the natural meaning of the single word
dissecuit: but will the context on any
view tolerate another? As regards the
Doxology, *abstulit* is decisive. Is it
conceivable that Marcion only '*separated*' xv. xvi. from the rest of the Epistle,
while still acknowledging their authority, whether he joined them to another
epistle or not? or that such an operation would be unrecorded? The difficulty surely lies in the translation.

Dissecuit would not be an unnatural
rendering of περιέκοψεν or possibly πε-
ριέτεμεν, either of which would mean
simply 'cut away.' Compare Epiph.
Haer. 309 D οὐ μόνον δὲ τὴν ἀρχὴν ἀπέ-
τεμεν [of St Luke's Gospel]..., ἀλλὰ καὶ
τοῦ τέλους καὶ τῶν μέσων πολλὰ περιέ-
κοψε τῶν τῆς ἀληθείας λόγων κ.τ.λ.: and
again ἀλλά τινα αὐτῶν περιτέμνων, τινὰ
δὲ ἀλλοιώσας κεφάλαια. In the first sentence, so closely resembling Rufinus's
in form, ἀποτέμνω and περικόπτω must
be practically synonymous, for the
preceding sentence describes the Gospel as περικεκομμένον ἀπὸ τῆς ἀρχῆς by
Marcion.

Origen's purpose. *Hoc ipsum caput* is perhaps a slightly stronger phrase than we might have expected: how far it represents the Greek, and, if supposed exact, how far a knowledge of the unabridged context would explain it, we need not try to conjecture: even as it stands, it has a certain force in binding together the first and second statements.

On the other hand the internal evidence for the truth of the corrected reading is substantial. The order of the sentences, which Rufinus is not likely to have changed, runs naturally upon this view. By the common reading Origen keeps till last the only fact specially concerning the passage on which he is commenting: his first two sentences might have been written with equal force and appropriateness on any group of verses in the two chapters. He begins with saying that Marcion removed this paragraph, three verses, and then condemns, as an aggravation of the main offence, his removal of 59 verses, of which these three are nothing more than the end. Why should he choose this particular place for the remark, if Marcion's operation was really on that extensive scale? Why not mention it at the proper place, xiv. 23? It may be urged that possibly he was forgetful there, as he is certainly silent about the Doxology, but gladly repaired his omission when the Doxology brought to mind by association the earlier critical point in the Epistle. Certainly it might be so. But in that case we should expect him to begin with the transposition of his immediate text, and having so been carried to xiv. 23 to append by way of digression an account of Marcion's proceeding. The reverse order, which we actually find, has no logical justification on the common interpretation, unless Origen himself saw in Marcion's supposed omission of xv. xvi. and in the transposition of the Doxology two facts connected by community of origin. That however is a step in criticism which there is not the slightest evidence that he took. He regarded Marcion's omission, whatever its extent, as an original and unprecedented act; and he gives no hint that the transposition or repetition in certain MSS. was a consequence of Marcion's mutilation: in

other words the two facts were in his eyes two independent
phenomena. How then came the one to suggest the other? If
Marcion omitted two chapters, the sole point of contact is xiv.
23; and thus the transposition, which alone forms a bridge
from xvi. 24 to xiv. 23, must have preceded the omission in
Origen's account. If on the other hand Marcion cut out only
what the scribes transposed, then no bridge is needed. The
first and the last sentences refer alike to the same subject, the
paragraph on which Origen is avowedly about to comment.
The second sentence refers partly to this place, partly to the
other; and likewise serves to anticipate an erroneous criticism
of the first statement, which might occur to Origen's readers.

The commentary of Jerome on Eph. iii. 5 explains diffusely
how St Paul could say that 'the mystery of Christ in other
generations was not made known to the sons of men' notwithstanding the language of the prophets. At the outset he
repudiates the doctrine *juxta Montanum* that the prophets
spoke in ecstasy, not knowing what they said. Three columns
further on he repeats ' Those who will have it that the prophets
understood not what they said, and spoke as it were in ecstasy,
bring to confirm their doctrine not only the present text, but
also that which is found [in the epistle] to the Romans in most
MSS., reading *Now to Him, etc.*' The inference is obvious, that
the writer had seen or heard of MSS. which did *not* contain the
Doxology. But who is the writer? Jerome in his preface
tells us that he had partly followed the three books of Origen
on this Epistle. Comparison of the Greek fragments proves
how freely he drew on his great predecessor's ample stores;
and any one familiar with Origen's style will recognize it in
many places where the Greek is entirely lost. Throughout this
long disquisition Origen's hand cannot be mistaken, though
Jerome may have added or altered this or that sentence. The
controversy with Montanistic doctrine belongs moreover to the
third, not the fourth century[1]. The character of the MSS.

---

[1] The dislike of the early Alexandrians to the Montanist theory of 'prophecy' or inspiration is well known.

hinted at as wanting the Doxology is sufficiently indicated
in the two sentences which follow the refutation of the Montanists. 'And in like manner it is to be observed that the
mystery of our faith cannot be revealed except through the
Prophetic Scriptures and the coming of Christ. Let those
therefore know who understand not the Prophets, and desire
not to know, protesting that they are content with the Gospel
alone' etc. This evident allusion to the Marcionists, the other
great sect which threatened the Church in Origen's days, suggests the strong probability that the passages from his two
commentaries relate to the same subject. What he calls
'most MSS.' here are identical with 'those copies which have
not been corrupted by Marcion.' In the former case the
Doxology is said to have been omitted[1]: may we not infer, in
the absence of evidence to the contrary, that this and this alone
constituted Marcion's offence? Whatever the argument might
be worth taken independently, it appears to me a striking
corroboration of the result obtained thus far.

Tertullian's language is ambiguous. After confuting Marcion out of Galatians and 1, 2 Corinthians, he proceeds to
Romans (*adv. Marc.* v. 13). Henceforth, he says, he will touch
but briefly on what has come before him already, and pass over
altogether what has come before him frequently. He is tired
of arguing about the Law, and about God as a Judge, and so
an Avenger, and so a Creator. Yet he must point out the
plain references to justice and judgement which meet him at the
beginning of the Epistle (i. 16 ff.; ii. 2). It will be enough for
him, he declares, to prove his point from Marcion's negligences
and blindnesses, from the sayings which he left undisturbed[2].

---

[1] The words are 'Qui volunt Pro-
phetas etc., cum praesenti testimonio
illud quoque quod ad Romanos in plerisque codicibus invenitur ad confirmationem sui dogmatis trahunt, legentes
Ei autem' etc. They do not formally
negative the omission of the two whole
chapters; but other language would
surely have been chosen had the Doxo-

logy been the mere conclusion of a
large section omitted.

[2] He notices but one omission by
Marcion in this epistle, that of c. ix.
The limits are not given, but there is
little room for doubt. Eight other
(short) omissions are recorded by Epiphanius, who professes to furnish only
a selection (*Haer.* 317 f.). It is singu-

He then runs over the Epistle in 5 pages, just half what he had bestowed on the little epistle to the Galatians, passing over in silence some long spaces of text containing appropriate matter, as iii. 1–20 and x. 5–xi. 32. The ethical paragraph xii. 9–xiii. 10 tempts him to give examples of the anticipation of its teaching in the Old Testament, and he concludes with insisting on the harmony of Law and Gospel in inculcating love of neighbours. There apparently he intended to stop, the doctrinal part of the Epistle being ended, but his eye was caught by the words 'judgement-seat of Christ' at xiv. 10. He therefore adds (14 s. f.) rather awkwardly, with evident reference to what he had said on the beginning of the Epistle[1], 'Bene autem quod *et in clausula* tribunal Christi[2] comminatur, utique *judicis et ultoris*, utique *creatoris*, illum certe constituens promerendum quem intentat timendum, etiamsi alium praedicaret.' And then he proceeds to another epistle. The absence of allusions to anything in xv. xvi. requires no explanation: it is hard to see what could have been cited except xv. 4, 8, 18, which are slight and contain nothing new in relation to Marcion, and the Doxology, which all agree to have been omitted by him. But *in clausula* certainly means 'in the close of the Epistle,' and it is a natural inference that such a phrase would not have been used if xv. xvi. had stood in Tertullian's MS., whether that was his own or one of Marcion's recension. Natural but not conclusive. The verse quoted is not in the actual close on any view; thirteen verses follow of xiv. But the force of the word must be estimated by the context.

lar that Epiphanius should pass over the loss of three consecutive verses: but his silence would be far more astounding if two whole chapters were missing. Nothing could be safely inferred in any case from his employment of the word ἀκρωτηριάζω as applied to St Paul's epistles (καὶ αὐτῶν δὲ ἠκρωτηριασμένων συνήθως τῇ αὐτοῦ ῥᾳδιουργίᾳ 317 D): his wide use of it is manifest when he says (311 D) that the Gospel, as ἠκρωτηρίασται μήτε ἀρχὴν ἔχον μήτε μέσα μήτε τέλος, ἱματίου βεβρωμένου ὑπὸ πολλῶν σητῶν ἐπέχει τὸν τρόπον.

[1] So not long before he had said, not it is true of a book but of a passage (1 Cor. ix. 10–x. 11), 'Denique et in clausula praefationi [apostolus] respondet' (c. 7).

[2] The true reading is τοῦ θεοῦ, but confusion with 2 Cor. v. 10 was easy.

Antithesis to the beginning of the Epistle, not by any means the very beginning but i. 16 ff., ii. 2, is the motive of the remark. If xiv. 10 is included in a section of the Epistle, however large, which can fairly be called in any sense its close, the point of the remark is saved. Now Tertullian had to all appearance virtually ended his comments at xiii. 10. What follows to the end, with the partial exception of xv. 3 f., 8–12, is either hortatory or personal. The business of the Epistle, so to speak, is over : to the eye of a rhetorician, accustomed to study the members of a speech, the remainder would all constitute the close. Tertullian uses the word more loosely still on another occasion, again for the sake of an antithesis. To reinforce his position that Christ's command to flee from city to city under persecution became obsolete when the apostles went forth to convert the Gentiles, he urges that St Paul, who at an early time had consented to escape in a basket, in the close of his ministry (*in clausula officii*) rebuked those who urged him not to go up to Jerusalem lest he should suffer there (*de Fuga in Pers.* 6). Yet this incident (Acts xxi. 13) preceded the events at Jerusalem, the two years' imprisonment at Cæsarea, the voyage and shipwreck, and the two years at Rome; to say nothing of later occurrences not told in the Acts.

It remains true that Tertullian does not cite any words out of xv. xvi. in other parts of his writings[1] : nor does Irenæus or perhaps Cyprian[2]. Negative facts of this kind are by no means to be contemned, but their value depends on the attendant circumstances. Seventeen verses only of the two chapters (xv. 1–13; xvi. 17–20) were likely to be quoted. Of these Origen once quotes one (setting aside the commentary), Clement three; while of others it so happens that Origen quotes five, Clement three, besides the Doxology.

---

[1] Semler and Oehler indicate 5 references to xv. 4, 14; xvi. 18 : but they are imaginary.

[2] Fell's index gives only xvi. 18 'ventri serviunt: E[pist.] 233.' Doubtless he means p. 283 (*Ep.* 65 § 3) 'nec ante se religioni sed *ventri* potius et quaestui profana cupiditate *servisse*'; a very doubtful reference.

Lastly Wetstein has a note at the end of xiv.: 'Codex Latinus habet capitula epistolae ad Romanos 51, desinit autem in caput xiv.; ex quo conficitur ista capitula ad editionem Marcionis fuisse accommodata.' 'Later critics,' says Dr Lightfoot [p. 289], 'have not been able to identify the MS. and thus to verify the statement.' Their failure however matters little. The phenomenon here obscurely described is not peculiar to a single MS.: it belongs to what was probably a widely current Latin capitulation, found e.g. in the earliest (540–550) MSS. of the Vulgate, the Amiatinus and the Fuldensis. The sections or *breves* of Romans are 51, § 50 beginning at xiv. 15, and § 51 at xv. 4. In the table of contents before the Epistle § 50 is headed 'De periculo contristante [sic] fratrem suum esca sua, et quod non sit regnum Dei esca et potus sed justitia et pax et gaudium in Spiritu Sancto,' a fair description of the section; and § 51 'De mysterio Domini ante passionem in silentio habito post passionem vero ipsius revelato,' which in strictness applies only to the Doxology[1]. If the marginal figures were lost, it would be a natural inference that § 50 ended with xiv., that § 51 consisted of the Doxology, and that xv. xvi. were absent from the MS. on which the capitulation was originally formed. But as on this view the table and the marginal figures contradict each other, it seems hopeless to attempt to clear up the confusion while the origin of the capitulation remains unknown[2]. There is no Latin authority whatever for associating the Doxology with xiv. 23; so that it would be rash to assume the table of headings to be alone authentic, and the marginal figures to have been inserted at xv. 4 by a misunderstanding. Yet that is certainly a possible solution. Only it must be

---

[1] Either Wetstein examined only the table of headings, or he overlooked the inconspicuous figures li. at xv. 4, a place where he would scarcely expect them. This is the sole point of difference.

[2] Internal evidence proves that the sections cannot, in their present form,

answer to ecclesiastical lessons. Otherwise one might have thought that the Doxology was appended to xv. 13 or 33 for public reading, and the rest of xv. xvi. neglected. Some sections are described only by their end, as others only by their beginning.

remembered that the table of headings, with all its obscurities, would stand as the sole direct piece of evidence for the omission of xv. xvi. by any authority.

One indirect testimony Dr Lightfoot finds in the space left after xiv. 23 in the single MS. G, as noticed above (p. 329). His inference [p. 316] is that 'the copyist of an earlier MS., from which it has descended, transcribed a MS. of the abridged recension [i.e wanting xv. xvi.] till the end of chapter xiv., and then took up a MS. of the original Epistle to the Romans to supply the lacking matter, omitting however the doxology as inappropriate to what had thus become the middle of the letter, and perhaps intending to give it a place afterwards, but abandoning his purpose. It is an instructive fact that in the allied MS. F no space is left after ch. xiv., but the text is written continuously.' 'Either their common prototype[1], or a still earlier MS. from

---

[1] The above was written on the assumption that F and G were independently copied from the archetype, as all considerable writers on the subject except Wetstein had laid down on apparently sufficient grounds. A query by Dr Westcott has recently induced me to examine the matter anew, and so led me to the conclusion that the scribe of G alone used the archetype, and that F is a copy of G. The few verbal (not orthographical) variations of F that might have seemed to preserve the readings of the archetype crumble away on examination. F often interchanges ὑμεῖς with ἡμεῖς, not seldom against all sense, and 6 times alters ὑπό to ἀπό: it omits the article 23 times, and perhaps once inserts it: it omits other words 16 times, and inserts them at most thrice (Rom. vii. 19 μεισῶ as in 15; ix. 31, with a special mark, δικαιοσύνης as in the line above; Gal. fin. ἀμήν; all from the Vulgate): and the remaining changes, I believe fourteen, of which most are favoured by the Vulgate, are all trivial and natural. On the other hand FG agree in count-less blunders, evidently such and not traditional variants, which cannot all, to say the least, be set down to the archetype. Again the confusion of spellings has its uniformities. To take only the more frequent cases, F incessantly interchanges ε η, ο ω, ι υ, δ θ (τ); in almost every line FG *together* interchange ι ει, ε αι, very rarely either MS. separately; and I have failed to detect any permutations approximately peculiar to G. Misspellings of the promiscuous sort swarm in FG together and in F separately; in G separately they are rare and always so simple as to be within the capacity of the scribe of F to correct. Precisely the same may be said of the divisions of words; F is free from no outrageous portent found in G, but has to answer for many of its own. No one can believe that two scribes independently arrived at e.g. Ποτυπουσιν εχαι ὑγεισεμνον των λογων (both FG have ω over -νον: F further divides ὑγεισ. εμνον) for ὑποτύπωσιν ἔχε ὑγιαινόντων λόγων: and the absence of division of words in the archetype is proved by the numerous

which it was copied, must have preserved the abridged recension.' In other words (1) the scribe of G copied i.–xiv. from one MS. and xv. xvi. from another; and (2) the scribe of F copied in like manner from the same *two MSS.*, though he left no mark of the transition from the one to the other. If the first of these hypothetical facts were true, we ought surely to find some evidence of it in the respective texts; whereas the closest study fails to detect a shadow of difference in the character of the readings before and after the blank space. The partial adherence of D excepted, this character is unique among existing Greek MSS.: that it should prevail equally in two MSS. accessible to the scribe of G is possible certainly, but not likely; and the hypothesis involves this further anomaly that

self-corrections of the scribe of G, where he has added to the end of one word the first letters of the next, seen his error, and begun the second word afresh with a space between. In these cases he sometimes has forgotten to put in the cancelling dots or line, and then the writer of F confidingly transcribes the whole. But usually he is careful to follow only corrected readings. In 1 Cor. xi. 31 f. ἀπό translated by *a* happens to be under the end of ἑαυτούς in G; and the stroke or accent which, as usual in G, caps *a* looks like a cancelling line to the final ς: hence F reads ἑαυτόν though the verb is διεκρίνομεν. Other instances might be given of the dependence of F on accidents in G. The relations of the Latin accompaniments (fg) are complicated, but tend to the same result. The body, so to speak, of g must have at least a double origin, from a pure Old Latin text and from one or more altered texts, either the true Vulgate or one of the intermediate revised texts or both. Where none of his materials represented the Greek literally enough, the scribe evidently devised new renderings of words and still oftener changed their order. This is shown not only negatively by comparison with the mixed and fragmentary yet frequently copious evidence of all sorts as to variations in Latin MSS. and Fathers, but also positively by mistakes arising from the wrongly divided Greek words and the like. Sometimes g offers two or more alternative renderings, either all traditional or part traditional part original. The body of f is tolerably pure Vulgate, unequally but always imperfectly assimilated to the Greek with, I believe, the aid of no document except g, all the elements of which may be recognized. In 1 Cor. x., singled out by Mr Scrivener for its frequent departure from the Vulgate, out of the 46 variants 23 agree with d and 42 with g, while the remaining 4 consist of 2 blunders, one correction of an obvious blunder, and one interpretative change of tense. The concordance of evidence so various seems decisive against any claim of F to represent the archetype where it differs from G. Nothing however in the text of this article is substantially affected by the result except the sentences in brackets.

the two originals, so singularly alike in the main, must have differed on the capital point, the omission of xv. xvi. [When F is taken into account, fresh embarrassments arise. Either the scribe of F copied one MS. throughout or he did not. If he did not, an exact repetition of the circumstances attending the writing of G is demanded, without such evidence as the blank is said to afford. If he did, what becomes of the primary original of G?] The blank may, I believe, be easily explained by a simple process. The Greek text of F and G alike was copied from a single archetype wanting only the Doxology. [The scribe of F wrote down exactly what lay before him.] The scribe of G on arriving at xiv. 23 remembered the Doxology as occurring there in some other MS. that he had read (all extant MSS. but 9 have it there, 4 older, 5 younger), held faithfully to his archetype, but satisfied his conscience by leaving a space which might be filled up hereafter if needful. He did in fact only what the scribe of B had done four centuries before, when he left a blank column for the supplement to St Mark's Gospel (xvi. 9–20). It follows that FG attest the omission of the Doxology alone, while the blank in G vouches merely for the vulgar Greek text as it prevailed from the fourth century onwards.

That reading of the vulgar text however remains to be explained if possible, and remarkable without doubt it is. The intrusion of the Doxology after xiv. 23 appears in two forms: conjointly with its retention at the end in AP 5 17[1], and some Armenian MSS.: in this place alone in L (= J) and all Greek cursives but 8 (or 10), some MSS. known to Origen (above, p. 330), the Harclean Syriac and the Gothic[2] (with, it is said,

---

[1] There is a doubt about 2 or 3 others, and more will probably be found in due time: see also p. 341, note 1. The introduction at xiv. 23 by the second hand of the Latin text in the trilingual 109 is doubtless due to an imperfect assimilation to the Greek.

[2] The fragments of this version do not comprise xiv. 20–xv. 3. But the presence of the Doxology after xiv. would make the gap exactly equal in length to the adjoining leaves of the Codex Carolinus, which alone has preserved the verses before and after. The 4 existing leaves of this MS. shew that xi. 33–xv. 13 was written on 8 leaves; and all the measures give the same length to a leaf within a line.

two other late and obscure versions), Chrysostom[1] and the Greek commentators who follow him, and perhaps Cyril and John of Damascus. Perplexities abound here. The first small group is select[2] though not trustworthy: by the analogy of other passages it indicates a reading of high antiquity, probably current at Alexandria, but a correction. Origen's MSS. being waived, the certain portion of the second group is practically rubbish: that is, it contains no authority of the slightest value hereabouts except as a rare adjunct to some primary authority left nearly in solitude. That some MSS. known to Origen should have attested a reading of the first group is exactly what might have been expected: their association with the second is passing strange. It suggests a doubt (more is not permissible) whether Origen after all did not speak of those MSS. which had the Doxology at xiv. 23 as having it also at the end. Rufinus's clumsy scissors may easily have shorn off the additional fact, especially as the antithesis became clearer in consequence: on this view the words about Marcion's doings 'not only here but also in that place etc.' would have increased force, though it must be allowed they do not require it. But another difficulty remains. We might have supposed the double position of the Doxology to be owing to the combination of texts from two sets of MSS., each of which had it in a different place and there alone; yet the character of the authorities inverts this order. In cases like this it is ultimately found safer to trust to the historical relations of the evidence than to any speculations about probability. But indeed here the only tolerable explanation that offers itself of the introduction of the Doxology at xiv. 23 in *either* group would point to the first group as exhibiting the earlier form of corruption. Changes in the Greek text of the New Testament, chiefly by

---

[1] One Vatican MS. of Chrysostom according to Mr Field (p. 547) has both text and commentary in both places, and so might be added to the first group. But internal evidence proves that Chrysostom himself used only the vulgar Greek text.

[2] Though inferior to 17, 5 is a cursive of the first rank.

interpolation, arising from the modifications required for Church lessons are common in MSS., though they have rarely found their way into printed texts. The salutations in xvi. might easily be thought to disqualify the bulk of the chapter for public reading[1], especially at a time when but a few select lessons were taken from the whole Epistle[2]: and yet some church, for

---

[1] The Greek 'Euthalian' capitulation found in divers MSS. (printed by Mill *N. T.* 418 and elsewhere) has for the heading of its § 18 περὶ [τῆς] μιμήσεως τῆς Χριστοῦ ἀνεξικακίας, of §19 περὶ τῆς λειτουργίας αὐτοῦ τῆς ἐν ἀνατολῇ καὶ δύσει, and nothing after. These must correspond to xv. 1–13, 14–33. It follows that xvi. (but not xv.) is omitted, evidently because not publicly read in *some* church. The latest sectional number (24) in P stands at xv. 14, doubtless for a similar reason. By a singular coincidence § 18 of the Vatican capitulation begins with xv. 1 as in the 'Euthalian' capitulation: but they do not coincide in the earlier chapters, and the Vatican sections proceed to the end, commencing § 19 at xv. 25, § 20 at xv. 30, and § 21 at xvi. 17. Fritzsche (*Rom.* i. p. xlvii.) pleads that on the same grounds we might argue the exclusion of 1 Cor. xvi. from public reading, since no trace of its contents appears in the 'Euthalian' capitulation for that epistle. Why not? The last sectional numeral (20) in the margin of P in 1 Cor. is at xv. 51. Thus again both independent capitulations equally agree with what the nature of the chapter renders intrinsically likely. The Capuan Lectionary in the Fulda MS. of the Latin Vulgate takes no lesson from Rom. xv. xvi. except xv. 8–14 (for the Circumcision), and none from 1 Cor. xii.–xvi.

[2] Dr Lightfoot (p. 312) refers to Reiche as having shewn that xv. xvi. were not omitted in public reading. Reiche depends on Fritzsche and after him

Meyer, who argue (1) that the profound reverence of the early Christians must have saved every letter of the N. T. from being unheard in the churches; (2) that the lectionaries prove the whole epistle to have been actually read. But this continuous reading noted in the lectionaries belongs only to the Daily Lessons, which E. Ranke (Herzog *R. E.* xi. 376 ff.) shews to be of late date, perhaps not earlier than the 12th century. The ancient lessons for Sundays and Saturdays are all more or less selected, continuous only in certain definite cases. The existing Synaxaria, *valeant quantum*, give Rom. xiv. 19–23 *plus* the Doxology as the lesson (an appropriate one) for Saturday before 'Tyrophagus' Sunday (Quinquagesima): see the tables in Scrivener *Introd.* 72; Scholz *N.T.* ii. 459; Matthæi *Rom.* xxiv. They have but two other lessons from this part of Romans, xv. 1–7 for the 7th S. and xv. 30–33 for the Saturday before the 10th S. after Pentecost (Scrivener 69 f.; Scholz 458; Matthæi *ib.*). All these arrangements however are probably Constantinopolitan, and originally derived from the 'use' of Antioch. An Alexandrine Table of Lessons is preserved in a Vatican MS. (46 Paul. of Wetstein), and has been edited by Zacagni *Coll. Mon.* 712–722; but the first leaf, containing from Easter to the 3rd S. after Pentecost, is missing. In the part of the year where Romans is chiefly read, xiii. 1–8, xv. 1–6, 13–19, 30–33 occur consecutively; but no other lesson from this Epistle after xiv. 11 appears

instance that of Alexandria, may have been glad to rescue the striking Doxology at the end for congregational use by adding it to some neighbouring lesson[1]. It could not well be used by itself, even if it were longer: it craved to follow some passage which in like manner craved a close. Many would find in the benedictions at xv. 13, 33 a reason against appending the Doxology in either place[2], while it would make an impressive termination to a lesson formed out of the latter verses of xiv. which when alone have both a harsh[3] and an unfinished sound.

anywhere. A few scattered lessons agree with those in the common Synaxaria, but the coincidences are such as might easily be accidental: the systems are independent throughout, though partly analogous. Saturday lessons are wanting, according to the custom of the early Alexandrine and Roman Churches (Socrat. v. 22), except in Lent. But as it is the long eight-week Lent of *late* Alexandrine usage, comparison as to 'Tyrophagus' Saturday is out of the question. All the Lenten Saturdays have in place of a definite lesson the single obscure formula Ἐκ τοῦ ἀποστόλου εἰς ἁγίους: the 4 lessons εἰς μνείας ἁγίων, Rom. v. 1–5; viii. 28–34; Heb. x. 32–38; xi. 33–xii. 2, can hardly be meant, as Zacagni seems to suppose; but the reference may be to a Menologium, or Table of Lessons for Holy-Days, not preserved in the MS.: the common Synaxaria have lessons from Hebrews on the Saturdays of their Lent. 'Tyrophagus' *Sunday* is one of the days of coincidence, the lesson being Rom. xiii. 11–xiv. 4. In short nothing can be clearly made out, except the prevalence of variety of usage and the utmost freedom in the selection of lessons; that is, Fritzsche's and Meyer's arguments are found to have no support from facts.

[1] The late Alexandrine lesson for St Stephen's Day begins Acts vi. 8 and ends vii. 60. As the other lessons are all short, this must have been made up of two passages, the speech being omitted. A similar Old Latin lesson for St Stephen's Day has been printed by Ceriani (*Mon. S. et P.* i. ii. 127 f.), combining vi. 8–vii. 2 with vii. 51–viii. 4. Ranke in Herzog *R. E.* x. 81 notices two Mozarabic lessons from Jeremiah, one of which omits 13 verses in the midst, and the other is a cento of 5 fragments.

[2] Gabler in Griesbach *Opusc.* ii. p. xxvi.

[3] This is the ground taken by J. A. Bengel (*App. Crit.* 340 Burk), to whom we owe the first suggestion about Church Lessons. He says 'Videntur Graeci, ne lectio publica in severam sententiam *Quicquid non est ex fide peccatum est* desineret, hanc ei clausulam attexuisse. Conf. var. Matth. iii. 11.' His note on the omission of καὶ πυρί in this last place is worth quoting. 'Citra haec verba finierunt Graeci, v. gr. in *Aug.* 4 [the Lectionary numbered 24], lectionem ecclesiasticam, ne tristis esset clausula. Simili euphemismo et Judaei post ultimum eumque severum Iesaiae, Malachiae, Threnorum, et Koheleth versum rescribere penultimum solent: et Graeci nonnulli post ultimum Malachiae versum ponunt antepenultimum. Etiam in *Byz.* [86] τέλος primum post haec verba, deinde his erasis ante, notatum est."

Scribes accustomed to hear it in that connexion in the public lessons would half mechanically introduce it into the text of St Paul, just as they seem to have introduced a liturgical doxology after the Lord's Prayer into the text of St Matthew (vi. 13). Then in the course of time it would be seen that St Paul was not likely to have written the Doxology twice over in the same epistle, and it would be struck out in one place or the other; while familiar use would override any effort of critical judgement[1], and so the Doxology would vanish from the end of xvi., nothing in the context seeming to demand its retention. Such I conceive is the history of the position which the Doxology holds in the vulgar Greek text, a position which it would probably retain in the Received Text and in the popular versions of Europe but for the confused impulse which led Erasmus in this instance to adhere to the Latin tradition.

III. In the two places of the first chapter (7, 15), where the name of Rome is mentioned, it disappears in the single MS. G. Some leaves are wanting at the beginning of F; doubtless if extant they would shew the same omission. At the first passage there is a note in the margin of 47 to the effect that 'he [or 'it': no nominative] mentions the phrase ἐν 'Ρώμῃ neither in the commentary nor in the text.' The subject may be some unknown commentator, but is more likely to be an 'ancient copy' of St Paul's Epistles which is expressly cited in a similar marginal note on vi. 24[2], and which like 47 itself may have been provided with a marginal catena or 'commentary'[3]. Dr Lightfoot thinks he sees a trace of the

---

[1] Yet ancient criticism, *finding* the Doxology between xiv. and xv., would probably see nothing to object to; while it would readily stumble at the apparent violation of epistolary correctness in xvi. 25 ff. The influence of MSS. like FG may also have helped to expel the final Doxology, while it would be powerless to displace the same words where imbedded firmly in the text.

[2] The reading there quoted from τὸ παλαιὸν ἀντίγραφον is both rare and excellent: the other marginal readings of 47 are of no interest, nor is there I believe any other reference to another authority. Cf. Griesbach *Symb. Crit.* i. 155 ff.

[3] An uncial MS. with a catena, like Ξ of St Luke, might be called 'the ancient copy' in the 11th or 12th century.

same omission in Origen's criticism as rendered by Rufinus, notwithstanding the presence of *Romae* in the text. But the context gives another turn to the language used. 'Benedictio autem pacis et gratiae, quam dat *dilectis Dei* ad quos scribit apostolus Paulus, puto quod non sit minor ea quae fuit bene-dictio in Sem et in Japheth, quoniam per Spiritum impleta est erga eos qui fuerant benedicti etc.' 'Ad quos scribit' is substituted for 'qui erant Romae' because the point is that St Paul's benedictions had not less dignity and effect than the sacred benedictions of the Old Testament; as Origen proceeds 'Non ego his omnibus inferiorem duco hanc Apostoli bene-dictionem, qua benedixit ecclesias Christi,' while any inference from the generality of 'ecclesias' is precluded by the further remark that 'haec Apostoli consuetudo scribendi non erga omnes ab eo servatur ecclesias,' and by the classification which follows. Still less can I recognize any sign of the omission in the Ambrosian Hilary's words 'Quamvis Romanis scribat, illis tamen scribere se significat, qui *in caritate Dei* sunt.' For he goes on 'Qui sunt hi nisi qui de Dei filio recte sentiunt? Isti *sancti* sunt et *vocati* dicuntur: sub lege enim agentes[1] male intelligunt Christum' etc. Every word becomes clear on com-parison with a passage in the Prologue (25 AB) in which he contrasts the 'Romani' with the Judaizers who were equally at Rome (ἐν Ῥώμῃ): the meaning is that St Paul writes not to all 'at Rome' indiscriminately, but to those at Rome who were in caritate Dei.' The true text in full is πᾶσιν τοῖς οὖσιν ἐν Ῥώμῃ ἀγαπητοῖς θεοῦ κλητοῖς ἁγίοις. A Western correction (D* lat. [the Greek lost] G, the 2 best MSS. of the Vulgate, apparently the Ambrosian Hilary, and perhaps Hilary of Poitiers) substitutes ἐν ἀγάπῃ θεοῦ for ἀγαπητοῖς θεοῦ, doubt-less on account of the κλητοῖς following ('who…through the love of God are called to be saints'). The result is that ENPΩMH and ENAΓAΠHΘY were left contiguous, each beginning with ἐν. The loss of one or other out of a pair of such groups of letters

---

[1] Not 'they *agentes*' but 'they who *agunt*.'

is common in MSS. of any form, and would be peculiarly liable to occur in one written in columns of short lines, such as was assuredly the archetype of FG[1]. These two MSS. have further a trick of omitting words that do not appear necessary to the sense, as might easily be the case with ἐν ʻΡώμῃ here when the following words were changed: so εἰς σωτηρίαν i. 16; ἡ ἐκ

---

[1] Hug pointed out (*Einl. in N. T.* i. 252 ff.) the evidence afforded by the frequent capitals in G that it was copied from a 'stichometrical' MS. resembling D, and perhaps older. In F many of the capitals are wanting, and probably even the scribe of G neglected a large proportion. It has not however been noticed, I believe, that the three equal chasms in the Greek text common to F and G measure for us the contents of each leaf of the archetype, about 20 lines of the 'Oxford Lloyd,' a convenient standard for reference. Now in these three places (1 Cor. iii. 8–16; vi. 7–14; Col. ii. 1–8) a leaf of D contains on the average 24 lines of Lloyd, Greek alone. If then the archetype of FG had like D a Latin column, we might form a fair impression of the general appearance by cutting off 2 lines from each page of D. If there was no Latin, each leaf of the archetype must have contained rather less than those of any extant Biblical MS.: the nearest approach would be to the purple and silver N (21 Lloyd lines) and the peculiar Z (23), apparently once a MS. of the same class. E of the Acts has indeed but 12 Greek Lloyd lines; but there is the Latin in addition. One exception might have been found in the lost archetype of a part of C. A fortunate displacement of text in the midst of a page of the Apocalypse (x. 9, 10; vii. 17–viii. 4; xi. 3–12) proves, on accurate measurement and calculation, notwithstanding the loss of the preceding leaf, that the arche-type hereabouts was made up of quires of 8 sheets, with 12 Lloyd lines to a leaf, while a leaf of C itself has 100 Lloyd lines. The outer sheet but one of a quire must have been somehow turned inside out before stitching, and so the scribe of C, copying on without thought, interchanged vii. 17–viii. 4 and x. 10–xi. 3. But it is possible, though unlikely, that the archetype of C was bilingual: the Græco-thebaic fragments of T have 21 Greek Lloyd lines to a leaf, nearly double. The great primary Eastern MSS. of the 4th and 5th centuries, ℵABC (with 160, 148, 131, 100 Lloyd lines to a leaf respectively), owe I believe their state-ly appearance to the new impulse to exhibit together the settled and completed Canon of Scripture. Before Constantine the parchment copies were in all likelihood small and portable. Our two earliest MSS, ℵ and B, seem to represent the older period in the narrowness of their columns, not in the ample structure of their pages, which may or may not have been suggested by a partly opened papyrus roll. During the time when most variations arose, narrow columns were assuredly general, to say the least. The date when 'stichometry' proper began is still unknown: the evidence which refers it to the middle of the 5th century is most precarious. And the example of E of the Acts shews on how different scales stichometrical arrangements might be made.

φύσεως ἀκροβυστία ii. 27; (οὐ πάντως iii. 9;) Ἰησοῦ iii. 26;
μόνον iv. 16; ὁ θάνατος v. 12; (ταῖς ἐπιθυμίαις αὐτοῦ vi. 12;)
ὅτι ἐμοὶ τὸ κακὸν παράκειται vii. 21; εἰ δὲ Χριστὸς ἐν ὑμῖν
viii. 10; υἱοθεσίαν viii. 23; &c. The omission in i. 7 might therefore be neglected without further thought but for the parallel
omission of τοῖς ἐν Ῥώμῃ in i. 15, the name of Rome being
confined to these two passages in the Epistle. The coincidence
would certainly be noteworthy if it were sustained by other
documentary evidence, or if there were independent reasons for
believing a recension of the Epistle to have existed in which
the marks of a special destination were purposely obliterated.
There is no such reason apart from the supposed removal of
xv. xvi. : the hypothesis is suggested by the reading of G at
i. 7, 15. We may therefore be content to suspect that in these
two verses like causes produced like results.

All the phenomena of text alleged to prove a double
recension have now been examined. The enigmatical Latin
capitulation excepted, they have been found, if I mistake not,
to be more naturally explicable by other causes. This result
becomes clearer still when the hypothesis is examined as a
whole. The second recension, it will be remembered, was said
to consist of chapters i. to xiv., with the Doxology, and without
the two namings of Rome. How is it then that every authority, which supports, or may be thought to support, some part
of this combination, contradicts some other part ? For the
omission of xv. xvi. the one direct testimony, if such it be, is
that of Marcion: and yet the one incontrovertible fact about
him is that he omitted the Doxology. If G is to be added on
the strength of the blank space after xiv., yet again it leaves
out the Doxology. Once more there is no lack of authorities
of a sort for subjoining the Doxology to xiv. We may waive
the fact that they all retain xv. xvi. We cannot forget (1) that
they all make mention of Rome at i. 7, 15; and (2) that they
have no sort of genealogical affinity with the MS. that ignores
Rome, or with Marcion. In few words, the authorities, which

as a matter of fact contain the rude outlines of the first
recension, supply the main data for constructing the second.
Meanwhile neither recension is represented in the great mass
of good authorities, Greek, Latin, Syriac, Egyptian, or other,
on which the text of St Paul stands in ordinary cases. *Both
recensions, as wholes, are purely conjectural.* If Rome and the
transposed Benediction are set aside, the first recension is
vouched for by FG (standing for a single archetype) alone of
extant documents and by some traditional evidence. The
second recension can be reached only through a hypothetical
text which Marcion altered, and a hypothetical duplicate
original of G.

Such being the relations of the textual evidence, little requires to be said on the intrinsic probability of the hypothesis.
There is nothing in it that we need hesitate to accept if only
the evidence were stronger. But it surely has not that kind of
verisimilitude which would raise the feeling that it cannot but
be true. The only analogous instance known to us is the
encyclical epistle addressed to the Ephesians and other neighbouring churches. But that letter appears (1) to have been
sent simultaneously to its different recipients; and (2) to have
been general in form in the first instance, not a special appeal
trimmed for general use. Analogy apart, it is difficult to
imagine St Paul deliberately cutting out in after years the
words that spoke of personal bonds to definite churches and
believers, and the passionate hopes and fears which they had
once called forth. If for any purpose he needed an impersonal
treatise on the old subjects, he would surely have written it
anew. Indeed the fitness of our Epistle, however altered, may
well be doubted. Its catholicity springs from the marvellous
balance that it holds between Jew and Gentile, which in its
turn rises historically out of the equal or almost equal combination of the two bodies in the metropolitan Church, as Dr
Lightfoot has justly insisted (p. 312 ff.). Is it probable that the
same characteristics would recur in the unlike 'countries into
which he had not yet penetrated' (p. 319)? Even that single

point of connexion disappears when we recall the pregnant paradox of his relation to the Romans, that, though he had not seen them, he knew them so well.

The inverse theory of several critics, that the original letter to the Romans ended with xiv. and, some add, with the Doxology, and that St Paul afterwards appended xv. xvi., escapes these difficulties to plunge into worse. Paley proves convincingly that xv. can belong only to the time when the body of the Epistle was written and can have been addressed only to the Romans : and there is cogent evidence which he has overlooked. Dr Lightfoot has shewn how much can fairly be elicited from xvi. to the same effect. The slight break more-over after xiv. is onesided, and on the wrong side. The opening words of xv. furnish a tolerable beginning : the last words of xiv. make a very bad end, even when the Doxology is allowed to follow.

When all is said, two facts have to be explained, the inser-tion of the Doxology after xiv., and its omission. The former has occupied us enough already : the latter now claims a few words. If the view taken in this paper be right, the omitting authorities are FG, Marcion, and certain MSS. twice noticed by Origen, once distinctly and both times implicitly, as having been corrupted by Marcion. The readings of D* and Sedulius, mixed authorities substantially akin to FG, likewise imply omission as antecedent. Origen accuses Marcion of wilful omission : is the charge just ? There is analogy favourable to either answer. It is now equally certain that Marcion some-times mutilated the text of his favourite apostle, and that some variations or omissions imputed to his pen were in fact simply the readings which he found already in his MS. The reference to ' prophetic Scriptures' in v. 26 might conceivably annoy him, though, as far as we know, he tolerated much of the same kind that was less likely to please him. But the removal of four words, an operation more in his manner, would have served every purpose. Though copies of his Apostolicon were seemingly current here and there in the Church, no extant document can

be shewn to have been affected by any of his wilful alterations.
Indeed 'copies corrupted by Marcion' need mean to us no more
than 'copies agreeing in a certain reading with Marcion's copy':
and Marcion's copy, prior to his own manipulations, appears by
various signs to have had much in common with the authorities
associated with him in the omission of the Doxology. On the
whole it is reasonably certain that the omission is his only as
having been transmitted by him, in other words that it is a
genuine ancient reading.

Genuine: but right or wrong? The question cannot be
answered off-hand. Not right merely because shewn to be as
old as the first quarter of the second century: not wrong merely
because the outward evidence for omission is small and at the
same time virtually responsible for many impossible readings.
Experience shews that authorities, rarely or never in the right
when they alter or add, are often in the right when they omit.
Such is preeminently the case with the Western group of which
DFG form an important section. Yet the omissions of DFG
without the accession of B, when examined together, are for the
most part suspicious. Thus on the whole authority is in favour
of the Doxology. Internal evidence is likewise not all on one
side. So considerable an omission might be expected to proceed
only from a strong and evident motive, such as cannot be
decisively recognized here. On the other hand the singular
and yet unobtrusive correspondence with those parts of the
letter which best reveal its purpose is an argument hardly
to be gainsayed without strong documentary testimony. Pure
accident is not to be rejected from the imaginable causes of the
loss. The last or outer column of a papyrus roll, the outer leaf
of a parchment book, would be subject to peculiar risks, as
every keeper of MSS. can avouch; and it is probable that an
epistle as long as that to the Romans would often form a book
to itself in early times[1]. Nor again dare we assume that the

---

[1] On the scale of the archetype of C
this epistle would occupy 90 leaves.
They would necessarily be small, and
usually of coarse thick parchment, the
delicate thin vellum of our great MSS.
being a recognized mark of luxury;

rash hands which shifted the Benediction would hesitate to let go the Doxology, in their zeal to give the Epistle a correct ending. Having once lost the vantage ground of possession from whatever cause, the Doxology would not easily recover it. Henceforth conservatism and criticism would be on the same side. Presently, when the Doxology had found a home after the fourteenth chapter, every motive for replacing it at the end of the Epistle was gone. We cannot wonder that the evidence for retaining it there, and leaving inviolate the continuity of the fourteenth and fifteenth chapters, is exclusively ancient and good[1].

F. J. A. HORT.

and would thus form a sufficient volume. The variety of order in the Pauline epistles in early times, of which there is good evidence, would be promoted by their separate use. On this view the language used by Constantine and Eusebius (*V. Const.* iv. 36 f.) about the new Imperial Bibles, 'sumptuously prepared,' with their quires of 3 or 4 sheets, has more force: Constantine's word σωμάτιον (=*corpus*), the technical term for a combination of single works, doubtless expresses the change from books and groups of books to the full Canon.

[1] Since this article has been in type, Dr Lightfoot has kindly pointed out to me an oversight in pp. 337 f., 347. In the Codex Fuldensis the table of headings to Romans agrees with that in the Codex Amiatinus etc. only in the latter part, as Ranke himself observes, p. xxiii. The first 23 headings belong to a totally different capitulation, and exhaust the Epistle down to xiv. 13. Then follows No. 24 of the other table, describing ix. 1–5; and so on. The previous or peculiar headings have no marks or divisions answering to them in the text itself. The scribe evidently saw that his tale of 51 sections could not be made up without borrowing elsewhere, and he ventured to save appearances at the cost of sense. Whether he had actually reached the end of the first table or only saw it near at hand, is less clear. The headings are not so exactly descriptive as to forbid the inclusion of xiv. 14–23 in § 23; and thus it is certainly possible that we have two complete and independent Latin capitulations in which xv. xvi. are omitted. More cannot be said till ancient capitulations generally have been properly investigated, and this demands a wide examination of MSS. Meanwhile it should be observed that (1) the Fulda headings have no trace of the Doxology; and (2) they are loaded with Augustinian or Anti-Pelagian phraseology, and cannot therefore be dated much before 400 at earliest.

The sectional numerals in P, I now likewise see, may possibly once have been continued after Rom. xv. 14; 1 Cor. xv. 51: some numerals have faded out of sight in almost every epistle, and in Rom. i.–x. all have vanished; cf. Tischendorf *M.S.I.* v. p. xiv. But as the § 1 of each epistle (10) except 1 Cor. begins after the salutation, analogy favours the view taken above (p. 342, n. 1).

C.

IN the last number of this Journal (III. p. 51 sq.) Mr Hort
criticised and condemned a theory which I had suggested
in the preceding number (II. p. 264 sq.) to account for certain
facts connected with the text of the Epistle to the Romans.
The *facts*, it will be remembered, were mainly these; (1) One
or more ancient writers used a copy of the Epistle containing
only the first fourteen chapters, with or without the doxology
which in the common text stands at the close of the whole (xvi.
25–27). (2) In the existing copies this doxology appears sometimes at the end of the xivth chapter, sometimes at the end of
the xvith, sometimes in both places, while in some few instances it is omitted altogether. (3) At least one text omits
ἐν Ῥώμῃ in i. 7, 15. The *theory*, by which I sought to combine and explain these facts, was this; that St Paul at a later
period of his life reissued the Epistle in a shorter form with a
view to general circulation, omitting the last two chapters,
obliterating the mention of Rome in the first chapter, and
adding the doxology, which was no part of the original Epistle.
Mr Hort impugns some of these assumed facts and explains
away others. Having done this, he attacks the theory itself,
and endeavours to show that it is untenable.

No one, who is really anxious to ascertain the truth, would
object to such a criticism as Mr Hort's, even though it should
lead to the rejection of a darling theory. I am especially
obliged to him for the thoroughness with which he has applied
the test of textual criticism to my hypothesis. And, if I venture, notwithstanding his arguments, to maintain that the facts
themselves are stubborn and in some respects even stronger
than I had supposed, and to uphold my theory as the most

probable explanation of the facts, until a better is suggested, I trust that I am not blinded by partiality. At all events I will give my reasons as briefly as possible, taking the facts first and then proceeding to the theory.

I. The first and most important of the facts is the existence, in early times, of copies containing only fourteen chapters. Of this the indications are various, and (as it seems to me) conclusive.

(i) The statement of Origen respecting Marcion has been 'universally understood,' as Mr Hort himself allows (p. 330), to mean that this heretic struck out not only the paragraph containing the doxology, but the two last chapters also; 'Caput hoc [*i.e.* the paragraph containing the doxology] Marcion, a quo Scripturae evangelicae atque apostolicae interpolatae sunt, de hac epistola penitus abstulit; et non solum hoc, sed et ab eo loco ubi scriptum est *Omne autem quod non ex fide peccatum est* (xiv. 23) ad finem cuncta dissecuit. In aliis vero exemplaribus, id est, in his quae non sunt a Marcione temerata, hoc ipsum caput diverse positum invenimus.' An universal understanding may be wrong, but most frequently it is correct; and I cannot doubt that this is the case here. Mr Hort however adopts a reading of a Paris MS. (Reg. 1639) which has '*in* eo loco' for '*ab* eo loco,' and himself alters '*hoc*' into '*hic*.' Thus he makes Origen say that Marcion cut out the doxology, not only at the end of the xivth chapter, but also at the end of the Epistle. Now my reply to this is threefold; (1) Though we may allow the general value of the readings in this MS., whose date however is not earlier than about the 12th century, yet its text is far from faultless, so that only a slight presumption is raised in favour of a reading from the fact of its being found there. In the present instance however the reading '*in* eo loco' has no meaning, unless with Mr Hort we likewise change *hoc* into *hic*—an alteration for which there is no MS. authority. (2) Mr Hort's reading and interpretation destroy the force of individual expressions in the context.

'*Usque ad finem cuncta dissecuit*' is natural enough when applied to two whole chapters, but not to the doxology alone; and again in 'hoc *ipsum* caput' the *ipsum* becomes meaningless, unless it is contrasted with some other portion. If the words be taken as they stand and interpreted in the ordinary way, the sequence commends itself; 'Caput *hoc*...non solum *hoc* sed...*usque ad finem cuncta*...*hoc ipsum* caput'; but it is entirely broken up if they are read and explained as Mr Hort wishes. (3) One who reads continuously not only the passage quoted above, but the whole paragraph of Origen as given by Mr Hort (see p. 330) or by myself (p. 288), will hardly fail, I think, to see how Mr Hort's interpretation involves and confuses the natural order of the topics.

When again Mr Hort supposes the statement of Jerome (on Ephes. iii. 5), that the doxology was found *in plerisque codicibus*, to have been derived from Origen's commentary on the same Epistle, I allow that this supposition is probable. But I do not see that Mr Hort's view gains strength thereby. Commenting on Ephes. iii. 5, Origen would be concerned only with the doxology in which 'the mystery' is mentioned, and he would be going out of his way, if he said anything about the omission of the xvth and xvith chapters, with which he was not in any way concerned. Moreover it must be observed that, when there is a question of a various reading, Jerome sometimes manipulates Origen's statements in such a manner as entirely to disfigure their meaning. Such is the case for instance with the opening verse of this very Epistle to the Ephesians, where Origen, having before him a text which omitted ἐν Ἐφέσῳ, interprets τοῖς οὖσιν in an entirely lucid though highly artificial way, but Jerome, repeating his great predecessor's comment, holds language which can hardly be called intelligible.

As regards the statement of Tertullian, when arguing against Marcion (v. 14), that the threat of the *tribunal Christi* (Rom. xiv. 10) occurs *in clausula* of the Epistle, I agree with Mr Hort that the inference which supposes Tertullian to refer to a copy of the Epistle wanting the xvth and xvith chapters, though 'natural,' is not 'conclusive.' Let the fact that the inference is natural have no more than its proper weight. I should not have laid much stress on the expression, if it had stood alone; but in connexion with Origen's account of Marcion it cannot be overlooked.

(ii) For the negative argument that the last two chapters are nowhere quoted by certain early writers I claim a *supplemental* value. More than this it does not deserve. The fact however remains that neither Irenæus nor Tertullian nor Cyprian (except in a very doubtful allusion) refers to them. I will only add that this omission occurs in Western writers[1], whereas they are more than once quoted by Clement and Origen. The importance of this fact will appear hereafter.

(iii) I owe it to Mr Hort's candour that my attention was directed to the capitulations of the Latin Bibles, and the evidence derived thence seems to me to strengthen my case enormously. In my former article I had referred to Wetstein's note: 'Codex Latinus habet capitula Epistolae ad Romanos 51, desinit autem in caput xiv.; ex quo conficitur ista capitula ad editionem Marcionis fuisse accommodata'; and, misled with others by his careless expression *desinit* (where *desinunt* would have been clearer), I had naturally supposed that the MS. itself, to which he refers, ended with the xivth chapter, and accordingly remarked that 'later critics had not been able to identify the MS. and thus verify the statement.' I have no doubt however that Mr Hort is right, and that Wetstein refers to such a phenomenon as the Codex Amiatinus exhibits, where (though the Epistle itself is complete) the capitulations end with the end of the xivth chapter, there or thereabouts. I have since

---

[1] The first distinct quotation by any Western writer, so far as I can discover, occurs in Victorinus c. *Arium* iii. p. 280 c, a treatise written about A.D. 365—where xvi. 20 is quoted. Even Hilary of Poitiers (if the index may be trusted) cites nothing from these two chapters but the doxology. The 'very doubtful reference' in Cyprian is given by Mr Hort, p. 336, note 2.

been investigating the subject[1]; and the results of this investigation seem to be sufficiently important to justify my taking up a few pages in recording them.

In fact, there is evidence of two distinct capitulations—both ending with the xivth chapter—the first very widely spread, the second only preserved in a single though very early MS.

Of the *first* of these, the Codex Amiatinus affords the oldest and best example. In this MS. the table of contents prefixed to the Epistle gives 51 sections, the 50th section being described ' De periculo contristante fratrem suum esca sua, et quod non sit regnum Dei esca et potus sed justitia et pax et gaudium in Spiritu Sancto,' and the 51st and last ' De mysterio domini ante passionem in silentio habito, post passionem vero ipsius revelato.' Corresponding to these, the sections are marked in the text, and agree with the descriptions in the table of contents as far as the 50th. The 50th is marked as beginning at xiv. 15, and here again the description is accurate; but the 51st commences with xv. 4, and has no connexion with the description. The description of the 51st in fact corresponds to the doxology (xvi. 25-27), and to nothing else in the remainder of the Epistle. The natural inference therefore is, that the capitulation was made for a copy of the Epistle, containing only fourteen chapters and the doxology; and that the scribe who first adapted it to a full copy with the sixteen chapters, not finding anything corresponding to the 51st section in the immediate context, extended the 50th section as far as the subject allowed him and made the 51st section include all the remainder of the Epistle. This solution, which Mr Hort allows to be certainly possible, seems to me to commend itself as in the highest degree probable.

This capitulation appears to have prevailed very widely. It is found in not less than seven MSS. enumerated by Card.

[1] After I saw Mr Hort's article in type, I began to look into the matter; and, before it was finally struck off, I mentioned the remarkable phenomenon of the capitulations in the Codex Fuldensis. To this conversation he refers in a note appended to his article (p. 351).

Tommasi (Thomasii *Op.* I. p. 388 sq. ed. Vezzosi), and dating from the age of Charles the Great downwards. It occurs again in the British Museum MS. *Add.* 10,546, an Alcuinian copy, generally called 'Charlemagne's Bible,' but really written in one of the succeeding reigns; in the important MS. *Harl.* 1772 belonging to the 8th century; in the Oxford Bodleian MS. *Laud. Lat.* 108 (E. 67) of the 9th century (in which however the number is expanded from 51 to 67 by a subdivision of one or more of the earlier sections); in the MS. B. 5. 2 of Trin. Coll., Cambridge, belonging to the 11th or 12th century[1]; and in the Cambridge University MS. Ee. 1. 9 written apparently late in the 13th century[2]. In *Add.* 10,546 the sections correspond in number and position with those of the Amiatinus, but the words are occasionally varied, e.g. *de non contristando fratre* for *de periculo contristante fratrem suum.* In *Harl.* 1772 the number of sections in the table of contents is reduced to 49 by combining §§ 43, 44, 45 in one section, while (except unimportant various readings) the words of the Amiatinus are strictly followed. In the text however the whole 51 sections are marked; of these the first 49 correspond to those of the Amiatinus, but the 50th commences not with the beginning of xiv. 15 *Si enim propter,* but with the middle *Noli cibo* (while on the margin in a later hand stands xlviiij. opposite *Si enim propter*), and the 51st not with xv. 4 *Quaecumque enim,* but with the middle of xiv. 22 *Beatus qui* (the Q of *Quaecumque* being however illuminated). And again in Cambr. Univ. Ee. 1. 9, where the number of sections is similarly reduced to 50, the beginning of the 50th and last section 'de mysterio etc.' stands at xv. 1 *Debemus autem nos,* i.e. at the precise point where it would have stood, if the MS. had con-

---

[1] In the older Trin. Coll. MS. of St Paul's Epistles B. 10. 5, of the 9th century, the Epistle to the Romans and part of the First to the Corinthians are wanting. The Amiatinian capitulations are given for the other Epistles.

[2] In the Cambr. Univ. MS. Ff. 4. 40, which came from the Library of Christ Church, Canterbury, and was written probably early in the 13th century, though the Amiatinian capitulations are not given, I find this note 'Haec epistola capitula li. dicitur habuisse.'

tained only the doxology after the xivth chapter. These variations show the difficulty which was felt in adapting the end of the imperfect capitulation to the complete Epistle: and they answer any objection founded on the fact that in the Amiatinus itself the last section does not commence at the exact place in the text which the hypothesis seems to require.

In more than one MS. however, which I have examined, this capitulation is completed. The British Museum MS. *Add.* 28,107 formerly belonged to the monastery of S. Remacle at Stavelot, and was written in the year 1097, 'ipso eodem anno quo versus hierusalem facta fuerat gentium plurimarum profectio,' as is stated at the end. The capitulation to the Epistle to the Romans gives 63 sections. Of these §§ 1–41 correspond with those of the *Amiatinus;* §§ 42, 43, 44, 45, are formed out of § 42 of the latter subdivided; and §§ 46–53 correspond to §§ 43–50 of the latter. Thus the heading of § 53 is 'Periculum contristantis fratrem suum esca sua etc.' There is nothing corresponding to § 51 of Amiatinus, which comprises the doxology, but § 54 (xiv. 19) is 'Quae pacis sunt sectanda et fratres propter escam minime judicandi,' and § 55 (xv. 4) 'De doctrina et consolatione scripturarum et quod unanimiter sit honorificandus deus et pater domini nostri jesu christi'; while the last section of all (§ 63), beginning at xvi. 21, runs 'Salutatio timothei et caeterorum etiam et ipsius pauli qui epistolam in domino se scripsisse dicit.' The compiler was vigilant enough to see that the section ' de mysterio etc.' of the capitulation before him did not correspond to anything which followed, and therefore ejected it, and supplied (though not very intelligently) the remaining sections which were required to complete the Epistle.

Another complete capitulation, founded on the Amiatinian, occurs in the British Museum MS., *Reg.* 1. E. viii., which belonged to Christ Church, Canterbury, and may have been written about the middle of the tenth century. This capitulation, which is very brief and very slovenly, comprises 29 sections. The last of these are as follows:

xxiiii. de redditione unicuique omnium debitore (*sic*).
xxv. de periculo contristante fratrem esca sua.
xxvi. de mysterio domini ante passionem in silentio habitat (*sic*).
xxvii. post passionem domini ipsius mysterio revelatus.
xxviii. obsecratio pauli ad dominum ut liberetur ab infidelibus.
xxix. salutatio pauli ad fratres.

The retention and subdivision of the section comprising the doxology, where it has no meaning, is a curious pheno- menon.

A third instance of completed capitulation is found in the MS. B. 5. 1 of Trin. Coll., Cambridge, belonging to the 12th century. Here the scribe has retained all the Amiatinian sec- tions, including the doxology; but by combining two in the earlier part, he reduces them to 50 in number. Thus the 49th is 'de non contristando fratrem, etc.', and the 50th 'de mysterio domini, etc.' To these he adds two new sections, which are the same as those described in the last MS.:

li. obsecratio pauli ad dominum, etc.
lii. salutatio pauli ad fratres.

In the text the 49th section begins at xiv. 50, the 50th at xv. 4, the 51st at xv. 30, and the 52nd at xvi. 1. The inequality of scale in these superadded sections shows that they did not pro- ceed from the same hand as the rest[1].

These facts have been elicited by an examination of such MSS. as came conveniently within my reach[2]. Doubtless a wider investigation would produce more striking results. But I have seen enough to convince me that the Amiatinian capitu-

[1] The relation between the two MSS. last described is curious. For, while other indications would suggest that the capitulations of Brit. Mus. *Reg.* 1. E. viii. were derived from those of Trin. B. 5. 1, the former presents the older form of the Amiatinian 50th sec- tion 'de periculo contristante fratrem,' while the latter substitutes the amend- ed form 'de non contristando fratrem,' which perhaps appears first in the Al- cuinian copies.

[2] My examination has not extended beyond the British Museum MSS. to the 11th century (inclusive), and the MSS. in the Cambridge University and Trinity College Libraries. The infor- mation respecting Bodl. *Laud. Lat.* 108 I owe to Mr Coxe, the Librarian.

lation, though originally framed, as will be seen hereafter, for a
short copy of the Old Latin, yet maintained its ground as a
common mode of dividing the Epistle, until it was at length
superseded by the present division into 16 chapters in the latter
half of the 13th century.

The *second* capitulation, of which I spoke, is found in the
Codex Fuldensis which, like the Amiatinus, was written about
the middle of the 6th century. The sections in the text correspond exactly with the Amiatinian. Not so in the table of
contents. Of the latter Ranke remarks (*Codex Fuldensis*, p.
xxiii, 1868): 'Quae epistolae ad Romanos praemissa sunt capitula
duabus in partibus constant, quarum altera (i.–xxiii.), *totius
fere epistolae argumentum* in se continens, per se ipsa stare
videtur, altera (xxiii.–li.) iis respondet quae iisdem sub numeris
in cod. Amiatino proferuntur.' The words which I have itali-
cised are not very exact. These 23 sections, which belong to
a different capitulation from the remainder, reach to about the
end of the fourteenth chapter, the last (§ xxiii.) being 'Quod
fideles dei non debeant invicem judicare cum unusquisq. secundum regulas mandatorum ipse se debeat divino judicio praepa-
rare ut ante tribunal dei sine confusione possit operum suorum
praestare rationem.' The 24th Amiatinian section, which follows next, begins with ix. 1, so that six chapters (ix.–xiv.) are
included twice. The natural inference is that the scribe, remembering that the text contained 51 sections and seeing that
the table of contents gave less than half that number, applied
himself to another source, and completed the headings of the
remaining sections from the Amiatinian capitulation. Whether
the capitulation from which §§ i.–xxiii. are taken contained the
doxology or not, must remain doubtful. The analogy of the
Amiatinian sections would suggest that it did. The 23 sum-
maries peculiar to the Fuldensis are very broad and general;
thus § xxii. 'de mundanis potestatibus honorandis quia oportet
oboediri his quib. ad mundanum regumen dominus tribuit
potestate,' though including the whole of our 13th chapter, omits
to take account of the last half, vv. 8–14; and in like manner

in § xxiii. the doxology may not have been thought worthy of any special attention in this heading[1].

Mr Hort indeed impugns the value of this Fuldensian capitulation on the ground that the headings 'are loaded with Augustinian or Anti-Pelagian phraseology, and cannot therefore be dated much before 400 at earliest' (p. 351, note). I have no wish to deny that there is force in this argument; which nevertheless does not seem to me conclusive. The strongest expressions in this direction are 'pro fide romanorum...deo apostolus gratias agit *ut probetur fidem in deum muneris est divini*,' and 'in Christo Jesu qui solus sic humana [humanam] naturam recepit ut eum *contagia veteris originis* non tenerent.' The African fathers were more or less Augustinian before Augustine's time, and (so far as I can see) might have held such language[2].

On any showing however the Latin Bibles bear strong testimony to the existence of the shorter form of this Epistle at an early date. The alternative hypothesis, that these sections were determined by the lessons read in Churches, is devoid alike of evidence and of probability. With this single exception, the Amiatinian capitulation in the New Testament includes, I believe, the entire book in every case. It does not bear the slightest trace of being intended for lectionary purposes. Nor indeed is there any reason why the 15th chapter should be excluded from the lessons; for it is much more fit for public

---

[1] Besides the capitulations mentioned in the text, I have noticed one other which is unconnected with either. It contains 18 sections and includes the whole epistle. This capitulation is found in:

(1) Brit. Mus. *Add.* 11,852, a MS. which belonged to the monastery of St Gall, and was written in the 9th century.

(2) Brit. Mus. *Add.* 24,142 'Monasterii S. Huberti in Ardvenna,' supposed to have been written about A.D. 900.

In this last MS., though the table of contents gives 18 chapters, the Epistle itself is divided by marginal numbers into smaller sections, 125 in number.

[2] e.g. Cyprian *Ep.* 64, says 'Secundum Adam carnaliter natus, *contagium mortis antiquae* prima nativitate contraxit.' Compare also Tertull. *de Anim.* 40, 41; and see Neander *Hist. of Christian Dogmas*, I. p. 185 sq. (Eng. Trans.). Augustine's own dogmatic views on these points were enunciated before Pelagius took up the subject: ib. p. 347 sq.

reading than many sections elsewhere, which are retained. Even the 16th chapter would be treated with exceptional rigour on this showing, for in other epistles the paragraphs containing the salutations are religiously recorded in the capitulation. Moreover, the oldest evidence which we possess on the subject exhibits lessons for Sundays and Festivals taken from the 15th chapter; and if so, *a fortiori* it would not be neglected in the daily lessons, supposing (which seems improbable) that daily lessons had been instituted at the time when this capitulation was made.

When my attention was first directed to the Amiatinian capitulation, I naturally inferred that it had belonged originally to the Old Latin and was later adapted to the Vulgate. A further examination has shown this inference to be correct. The capitulation preserves at least one crucial reading of the Old Latin. In § xlii. the words 'de tempore serviendo' show that its author for τῷ κυρίῳ δουλεύοντες read τῷ καιρῷ δουλεύοντες in xii. 11, a reading which Jerome especially quotes as condemning the Old Latin and justifying his own revision (*Epist.* 28, *Op.* I. 133, ed. Vallarsi).

Thus, taking into account all the evidence, the statement of Origen respecting Marcion (confirmed by the incidental expression of Tertullian), the absence of quotations in several early fathers, and the capitulation (or capitulations) of the Latin Bibles, we have testimony various, cumulative, and (as it seems to me) irresistible, to the existence of shorter copies of the Epistle containing only fourteen chapters with or without the doxology in early times. Even though it be granted that Mr Hort has given a possible explanation (I cannot allow that his explanations are probable) of each of these facts singly on a different hypothesis, still the convergence of so many independent testimonies direct or indirect towards this one point must be regarded, if I mistake not, as conclusive.

II. However the evidence does not end here. The fact that in existing MSS. the doxology occurs in different places (see p. 352) is very intimately connected with the fact or class of facts considered under the first head.   And here again I cannot help remarking that my position has this great advantage over Mr Hort's, that whereas I postulate only one unknown fact to explain all or most of the phenomena, he is obliged to postulate a distinct one to account for each several phenomenon in turn.

As regards the varying position of this doxology, Mr Hort's explanation supposes the following stages. (1) The original place was at the end of the Epistle. (2) It was afterwards attached to xiv. 23 for reading in Church. (3) 'Scribes accustomed to hear it in that connection in the public lessons would half mechanically introduce it into the text of St Paul' at this place. (4) It would then be struck off from the end of the Epistle, that the same doxology might not occur twice. Thus we arrive at the vulgar Greek text, which has it at the end of the xivth chapter only.

Now, waiving for the present the consideration of its original position, I wish to point out two great improbabilities involved in the other assumptions in this sequence. *First.* There is no such obvious connexion between the paragraph at the end of chapter xiv. and the doxology, as should lead to their being connected together[1], if separated in their original position by two whole chapters, while on the other hand these intervening chapters present material for more than one excellent lesson. Bengel indeed suggests, as Mr Hort points out, that the *severa sententia* ἁμαρτία ἐστίν, with which chapter xiv. closes, would be deemed unfit for the end of a lesson and that this inauspicious termination was got rid of by tacking on the doxology. But how much more easily would the difficulty have been overcome by continuing the lesson a little further

---

[1] In a note (p. 342) Mr Hort remarks that 'the Synaxaria, *valeant quantum*, give Rom. xiv. 19–23, *plus* the doxology as the lesson' for the Saturday before Quinquagesima. But since the doxology occurs here in the vulgar Greek text which prevailed at Antioch and Constantinople and from which the Synaxaria are taken, they would naturally read it here. I would add that the Synaxaria (see Scrivener's *Introduction*, p. 68 sq.) present no parallel to the omission of two whole chapters.

and closing with the 2nd or 4th or 6th verse of the next chapter. The instance which Mr Hort quotes (p. 343, note 1), Acts vi. 8–vii. 2 combined with vii. 51–viii. 4, as a lesson for St Stephen's day, will hardly bear out his hypothesis, for there the combination is naturally suggested by the subject. *Secondly.* This solution requires us to believe that all the three steps numbered (2), (3), (4), had taken place before Origen's time, so that he can speak of some MSS. as having the doxology in the one place and some in the other, without suspecting how the variation had come to pass. This supposes such an early development of the lectionary as (I believe) there is no ground for assuming.

III.   Lastly there are the phenomena in the first chapter to be considered.   Here the important fact is, that in one extant MS. (G) certainly, and in another (F) probably, the mention of Rome has been obliterated in *two distinct* passages. In i. 7 Mr Hort explains the omission by the fact that 'a Western correction substitutes ἐν ἀγάπῃ Θεοῦ for ἀγαπητοῖς Θεοῦ,' so that the words would run ενρωμηεναγαπη, where the repetition of ἐν might occasion the omission of one of the two clauses, especially as the archetype of this MS. appears to have been written stichometrically and each ἐν might commence a new line. Thus the omission would be *accidental.* But apparently dissatisfied with this solution he offers a second suggestion, that the omission was *intentional;* for he adds, 'These two MSS. (F and G) have further a trick of omitting words that do not appear necessary to the sense,' and gives instances. The accidental omission I could understand, but the intentional (thus explained) seems hardly credible, for the words ἐν 'Ρώμῃ are essential to an Epistle to the Romans. Of the omission in i. 15 he gives no direct explanation, except so far as it may be involved in the words ' we may be content to suspect that in these two verses like causes produced like results' (p. 347). I do not understand this, unless by like causes is meant the desire in both cases to *obliterate a superfluous clause.* I too maintain that ' like causes produced like results,' but I cannot allow that the historical fact involved in the mention of Rome could be regarded as a super-fluity in an Epistle to the Romans; and, if the omission was intentional in both cases, it must have been (so far as I can see) from the desire of obliterating the proper name, because the proper name was no longer applicable. The hypothesis, that a coincidence so remarkable as the omission of the same name in two distinct passages could have been purely accidental, seems to me to be the most improbable of all.

That the twin MSS. F, G, did not stand alone in this omission, appears from the marginal note in 47, on which Mr Hort has some remarks, p. 344. Whether to these authorities we should add the commentaries of Origen and the Ambrosian Hilary, must remain uncertain. I certainly should not have discovered the omission in them, if it had not occurred independently, and I am not prepared to say that Mr Hort's explanation (p. 345) of their language is not right. At the same time to my own mind the 'Benedictio quam dat *dilectis Dei* ad quos scribit' of Origen, and the '*Quamvis* Romanis scribat, illis tamen scribere se significat *qui in caritate Dei sunt*' of Hilary, still leave the same impression; but probably they will strike others differently.

It will thus be seen that Mr Hort denies some of my facts, and impugns the significance of others. As the facts give him no trouble, it follows that the hypothesis, which has no other *raison d'être* but to explain them, should not find favour with him. But, if (as I think I have shown) the facts are even more cogent than they appeared at first, being reinforced by the Latin capitulations, an explanation is still demanded. I cannot indeed say that my hypothesis is free from objections. But *a priori* improbabilities could be detected by the keen eye of criticism in the most certain events of history; and a theory, which is based on circumstantial evidence, cannot hope to escape objection on this ground. But, if no other hypothesis has been offered which does not involve more or greater improbabilities, and if some hypothesis is needed to account for the facts, I must still venture to claim a hearing for my own.

In Mr Hort's criticism of the theory itself, as distinct from the facts which evoked it, there are three points especially which call for a reply.

(i) I had assigned the doxology (xvi. 25–27) to the shorter recension of the Epistle, which I supposed to have been issued by St Paul himself at a later date, and had produced parallels to show that its style very closely resembles that of the Apostle's later Epistles. Mr Hort himself considers it to have been the termination of the original Epistle. His argument is threefold: (*a*) that it is appropriate; (*b*) that St Paul at the time entertained the ideas contained in it; (*c*) that it presents numberless close parallels of expression to the earlier Epistles.

(*a*) As regards its appropriateness, I entirely agree with him. I cannot indeed assent to Baur's opinion which he adopts, that the main drift of the Epistle is revealed in chapters ix.–xi. The central idea, as I conceive it, is the *comprehensive offer of righteousness* to Jews and Gentiles impartially, following on the *comprehensive failure* of both alike before Christ's coming. After this idea has been developed, the objection arises that, however comprehensive may be the *offer*, the *acceptance* at all events is partial and one-sided; that while the Gentiles seem gladly to accept it, the Jews stand aloof; and that thus the promises of the Old Testament appear to be nullified, and indeed reversed. It is to meet the objection which thus starts up, that St Paul pierces the veil of the future and discerns the gathering of the Jews into the same fold whither the Gentiles have preceded them. Thus the *result* will be comprehensive, as the *offer* has been comprehensive. But however fit a consummation of the Apostle's teaching this prophetic announcement may be, it does not in itself contain the nucleus of that teaching.

To the whole body of the Epistle however, in which the comprehensive failure, the comprehensive grace, the comprehensive acceptance, have been set forth in succession, the doxology forms an eminently appropriate close. An outburst of thanksgiving for the revelation of this 'mystery' of the impartial Fatherhood of God in Christ is the proper sequel to the contents of the Epistle. This adaptation would not indeed be easily reconcileable with any other authorship than St Paul's; but if written by him, whether written early or late, we should expect it to be appropriate.

(b) And again I grant that its main idea—the impartiality and universality of God's grace as a truth revealed in Christ—was not foreign to St Paul's thoughts at this time, though it assumed a much greater prominence afterwards. Indeed it may be said that this idea necessarily flowed from his commission as the Apostle of the Gentiles.

(c) But, as regards the expression of the idea, I join issue with him. The general style seems to me to be cast essentially in the mould of the later Epistles. The diffusive syntax of the paragraph is exactly what we find, for instance, in the Epistle to the Ephesians. And, when we come to individual phrases, there is (if I mistake not) a very wide difference in point of closeness between Mr Hort's parallels with the earlier Epistles and mine with the later. Compare for example his parallel of Rom. xiv. 4 with mine of Eph. iii. 20 for τῷ δυναμένῳ, or of Rom. iii. 29, 30 with mine of 1 Tim. i. 17 for μόνῳ σοφῷ Θεῷ. The only exceptions in favour of the earlier Epistles occur exactly where on my hypothesis we should expect to find them. The expression ὑπακοὴ πίστεως is repeated in this final doxology from the opening paragraph of the Epistle (i. 5), and the reference to the prophetic Scriptures also has a parallel in the same paragraph (i. 2). On my hypothesis the opening portion was read over and altered, when some years later the Epistle was issued by the Apostle in this second and shorter form; and it was therefore natural that the thanksgiving which was then appended, should embody not only thoughts but also expressions taken from the commencement, thus binding together the beginning and the end of the Epistle.

(ii) The character and condition of the text of the twin MSS., F and G, is one of the points on which Mr Hort lays most stress; and certainly, if his account of my theory were

correct, I should find it difficult to answer him. Expressing
my hypothesis in his own words, he represents me as holding
(1) that 'the scribe of G copied i.–xiv. from one MS. and xv.
xvi., from another,' and (2) that 'the scribe of F copied in like
manner from the same *two MSS.*, though he left no mark of the
transition from the one to the other' (p. 339). He then remarks
that 'If the first of these hypotheses were true we ought surely
to find some evidence of it in the respective texts; whereas
the closest study fails to detect a shadow of difference in the
character of the readings before and after the blank space';
and that 'when F is taken into account, fresh embarrassments
arise.'   But I did not for a moment contemplate the scribes of
F and G each of them copying *directly* from these two MSS.,
containing respectively the shorter and the longer recension of
the Epistle.   I was well aware that the phenomena of these
MSS. would not admit of such a supposition.   And I venture
also to think that my language, which Mr Hort himself quotes
just before (p. 338), cannot be taken in this sense: 'The
copyist of an *earlier* MS., from which it [G] *has descended,*
transcribed a MS. of the abridged recension till the end of
chapter xiv., and then took up a MS. of the original Epistle to
the Romans'; 'Either their common *prototype* [i. e. of F and G]
or *a still earlier* MS. from which it was copied, must have preserved the abridged recension.'   This language was expressly
intended by me to leave open the question, as to the length of
the pedigree which connected F and G with the scribe who first
combined the two recensions; and the idea of *direct parentage,*
which Mr Hort has imposed upon me, never once entered my
mind.   Thus I left ample room for the development of the
peculiarities of F and G.   Only I assumed that the retention of
the vacant space at the end of chapter xiv., which I took to
indicate the end of the Epistle in one of the two original MSS.,
had survived this development.   But though I still think that
(taking it in connexion with all the other textual phenomena
on which I dwelt) my account of this blank space is the most
probable, yet this is only a subsidiary support to my view, and

I could abandon it without any material injury to the main hypothesis.

But let us enquire what Mr Hort's statement, that 'the closest study fails to detect a shadow of difference in the character of the readings before and after the blank' (p. 339), really amounts to, when considered in its bearing on my hypothesis.

The characteristics of F and G, which differentiate them from what we may call the standard text of St Paul's Epistles, as based on the coincidence of the best authorities, are twofold: (1). Those which they exhibit in common with the Western authorities, and more especially that type of Western authorities which appears in the Old Latin Version; and (2) Those which are peculiar to these two MSS.

To the *first* class, comprising those readings which must be referred to the Western type, belong the most important, as well as the most numerous, variations from the standard text, whether in the first fourteen or in the last two chapters of the Epistle. If the two MSS. (containing respectively the long and the short form), from which on my hypothesis the text of FG was *ultimately* derived, were both of them Western, as on all accounts we might probably conclude that they were, then we should expect to find these readings pervading the xvth and xvith chapters, as well as the earlier part of the Epistle. It is difficult to explain the origin and prevalence of the Western type of text at all; but this difficulty was not introduced by my hypothesis, nor do I see that it is increased thereby.

Speaking of the peculiar features of F and G, Mr Hort says, 'The partial adherence of D excepted, this character is unique among existing Greek MSS.' On this statement I should wish to make two remarks. (1) The expression *partial* seems to me inadequately to express the degree of coincidence between D on the one hand, and FG on the other. Certainly in the two last chapters of this Epistle, with which we are mainly concerned, by far the greater number of the important deviations from the standard text are shared by D in common with FG. (2) These three are the *only*[1] *three Greek uncial MSS.* which, whether on external or internal grounds, can be assigned to the Western family. Whatever distinctive features therefore they possess in common, it is reasonable to set down to the Western type of MSS. generally. The Old Latin Version (with the exception of a few fragments) is only known to us through these same MSS., which are bilingual; for other independent copies, which contain a more or less pure Old Latin text, have not been collated: and its phenomena entirely accord with this supposition. The remaining source of evidence—the *early* patristic quotations— does not offer any obstacle to this conclusion; and indeed in the last two chapters of the Epistle, this evidence, as has been mentioned, is entirely wanting. On the whole then, I think it may be said that the coincidence of D with F and G represents very fairly the Western text.

The *second* class of readings, those peculiar to F and G, are in the xvth and xvith chapters comparatively unimportant. The divergences of these twin MSS. from D may be taken as *approximately* representing their peculiarities, though in the course of the analysis it will be seen that in many cases these divergences are supported by other, and especially by Western, authorities[2].

These are as follows:

xv. 1 αρεσκον [αρεσκειν]; 3 ουκ [ουχ]; 7 ὑμας [D* ἡμας, but D** ὑμας with most authorities, including Western]; 11 επαινεσατε [D επαινεσα-τωσαν, but the Latin of D has *Magnificate* with many other authorities, and the variation is easily explained in a quotation from the LXX.]; 13 πληροφορησαι...παση χαρα και ειρηνη [D πληρωσαι...πασης χαρας και

---

[1] I pass over E, which is now acknowledged (at least so far as regards the Greek) to be a direct copy of D, and therefore to have no independent value.

[2] I have not recorded either the accidental errors of G when these have been corrected at the time when the MS. was written, or the divergences of F from G. Mr Hort's view, that F was copied directly from G, deserves consideration, and may prove true, though his arguments do not seem quite conclusive. So far as it has any bearing on my hypothesis, it is rather favourable than otherwise. The converse proposition, that G is copied from F, could not be maintained for a moment.

ειρηνης, but B agrees with FG, inserting however εν before παση. The Old
Latin has *repleat...omni gaudio et pace*]. 16 Ιησου Χριστου [D Χριστου
Ιησου, but the Latin of D has *Jesu Christi* which also has the vast
preponderance of authority in its favour]. 18 ὁ Χριστος [om. ὁ]. 21
αναγγελη [ανηγγελη]. 24 ελπιζω [D adds γαρ with the preponderance of
authorities, but the Latin of D omits it, and so do the Latin fathers].
25 νυν [νυνι]. 26 Μακαιδονες [Μακεδονες]. 27 οφειλεται γαρ [om. γαρ, but
the Latin of D and Ambrosiaster have it] ; αυτων εισιν [εισιν αυτων]. 28
ουν αρα [om. αρα. The Latin of G is *Hoc ergo igitur ergo*]. ὑμας [ὑμων].
29 γινωσκω γαρ [D οιδα δε, but the Latin of D has *scio enim*, and other
authorities, especially Latin Fathers, have the same conjunction]. 30 προσ-
ευχαις [add ὑπερ εμου, but several Latin authorities, including the Latin of
D, omit the words]. 31 προσδεκτος [ευπροσδεκτος. The Latin of D is
acceptalis (sic)]. 32 αναψυχω [αναψυξω]. 33 υμων [add. αμην, but A and
others omit it].

    xvi. 1 ὑμων [ἡμων, but the Latin of D has *vestram*, and AP also have
ὑμων]. 2 παραστατεις [προστατις]. 3 ασπασθαι [ασπασασθε. This blunder
recurs]. 8 Αμπλιατον [Αμπλιαν, but the longer form occurs in the Latin
of D]. 10 Αριστοβολου [Αριστοβουλου, but the Latin of D has *Aristoboli*
and this form is found in B and elsewhere]. 11 συγγενη [D συγγενην, but
corrected by a later hand]. 14 ασπασασθε...εν κυριω om. with A. 15 Ιουνιαν
[D Ιουλιαν, which is correct, but C* has Ιουνιαν]. Ολυμπειδα [D Ολυμπιαν,
but Latin authorities, including the Latin of D itself, have *Olympiada* or
Olympiadem]. 17 παρακαλω [D* ερωτω, but corrected. The rest have
παρακαλω]. παρα [D* περι, but corrected]. 18 κυριω [τω κυριω], δουλευ-
σουσιν [δουλευουσιν]. 23 ὁλαι αἱ εκκλησιαι [ὁλης της εκκλησιας. The Latin
of DFG alike is *universæ ecclesiæ*, which would cover both readings.
Another reading is ὁλη ἡ εκκλησια. The Æth. is said to have ὁλαι αἱ
εκκλησιαι with FG]. 24 om. Ιησου Χριστου.

    This analysis of the readings in the last two chapters shows
two things: (1) That in almost every point even of minor importance, in which the text of FG diverges from the correct
standard, it agrees with the Western text as exhibited by D or
by some other authority; and (2) that the exceptions, which
thus form the peculiarities of FG, are in almost every instance
trivial and are easily explained by carelessness or caprice in
copying. Hence it follows: *first*, that the scribe, who (on my
hypothesis) wrote the archetype of F and G, taking up an
average copy of the Western text to supply the xvth and xvith
chapters, would find a text substantially such as we actually
have here; and *secondly*, that no long pedigree need have been

interposed between this archetype and FG, in order to develope
the phenomena which they exhibit in these chapters; but that
the intervention of a single scribe, or two at most, would explain everything. If so, the argument from the character of the
text cannot be considered a substantial objection to my view.

(iii) Mr Hort advances another argument against my hypothesis based on the assumption that the textual phenomena
on which my theory is built are gathered together from *incongruous* sources; and he even goes so far as to ask, ' How is it
that every authority, which supports, or may be thought to
support, some part of this combination [i. e. the Short Recension, involving (*a*) the omission of the word Rome in the first
chapter, (*b*) the omission of the xvth and xvith chapters, (*c*) the
presence of the doxology], contradicts some other part ? ' (p. 347).

To this statement I demur. I allow indeed that all these
phenomena do not coexist in any extant authority. If this had
been the case, I should not have had to frame a hypothesis,
for the existence of this Shorter Recension would have been
an absolute fact. But that there is any contradiction in my
authorities, which prejudices the hypothesis, I cannot allow.

This attack has led me to marshal my troops to better
effect. I wish especially to call attention to the fact, that
the authorities, on which I chiefly rely, have for the most
part a close affinity to one another and that they belong to
the Western type. The Latin capitulations derived, as I have
shown, from the Old Version are essentially such. The copy
or copies, to which they refer, presented two (*b*, *c*) out of the
three phenomena, and (for anything we know) may have presented the third (*a*) also. The remarkable absence of quotations from the last two chapters in the earlier Latin Fathers
points in the same direction. The MSS. FG, which are the
only indisputable vouchers for (*a*), are essentially Western.
Their relation to (*b*), (*c*), is a matter of dispute between Mr
Hort and myself; but the fact that there is a great break in G
at the end of the xivth chapter (however explained) cannot
but be held to favour my hypothesis to a greater or less

degree. The exception to the Western origin of the evidence is Marcion, who, being an Eastern, used a copy of this Epistle in which the two last chapters including the doxology were wanting. But even Marcion is known to have resided for many years in Rome; and if, during his sojourn in the West, he fell in with a copy of the Short Recension, he might have welcomed it gladly, as sparing him the superfluous use of his scissors, which would be required to eliminate such passages as xv. 8, 27.

Hitherto there is no incongruity in the sources from which my data are taken. But the position of the doxology in the several authorities still remains to be considered; and it is evidently here that Mr Hort considers the main 'contradiction' to lie. Though 'there is no lack of authorities of a sort for subjoining the doxology to xiv.,' he writes, yet 'they have no sort of genealogical affinity with the MS. that ignores Rome, or with Marcion.' Now to this I would reply that the capitulations of the Latin Bibles certainly have this affinity, and that (for all we know) the MSS. mentioned by Origen as placing the doxology in this position may have had it also. On the other hand his statement, so far as regards the extant MSS. and the patristic authorities generally, which exhibit it at the end of the xivth chapter, is indisputably true. They belong to the great Antiochene or Constantinopolitan family, which though by far the most numerous, is of inferior authority. On the contrary the place of the doxology in the extant Western authorities is at the end of the xvith chapter. But, allowing the fact, I cannot accept the inference. For suppose that a scribe had before him copies of the two recensions (according to my hypothesis), the one comprising the 14 chapters together with the doxology, the other including all the 16 chapters but omitting the doxology and ending with xvi. 23 Κούαρτος ὁ ἀδελφός. If he set himself to combine the two so as to omit nothing, is it not at least as likely that, when he arrived at the end of the xivth chapter, he would reserve the doxology for the end of the whole Epistle where it seemed to be required to finish

off an abrupt conclusion, as that he would leave it at the end
of the xivth chapter? The same motive which led others
to transpose the benediction (ἡ χάρις κ.τ.λ.), which properly
stands at xvi. 20, to xvi. 24, might even more easily induce
him to treat the doxology in a similar way, inasmuch as he
would still leave it at the *end* of the Epistle as he found it,
though the Epistle had been lengthened out by the two additional chapters. Thus the fact that the Western authorities
place the doxology after ch. xvi. seems to me to prove nothing
as to the want of *affinity* between the several authorities for
my hypothesis.

But this investigation leads me to observe (and I think
the observation is pertinent) how entirely this Western character of the authorities coincides with my hypothesis. I suggested that 'at some later period of his life, not improbably
during one of his sojourns in Rome, it occurred to the Apostle
to give to this letter a wider circulation'; and that for this purpose he made the alterations which resulted in the shorter
edition, so that it was rendered 'available for general circulation,
and perhaps was circulated to prepare the way for a personal
visit in countries into which he had not yet penetrated' (p. 319).
This hypothetical change is made in the West and for the
West; and it cannot be considered a matter of indifference
that to this same region we owe the authorities which suggested the hypothesis, though at the time when I propounded
it I did not see the full significance of this fact.

With these remarks I will leave the theory. For a reply
so thorough and so suggestive as Mr Hort's I can only feel
grateful. It has led me to consolidate the different elements
of my hypothesis, and, unless I am mistaken, to present a
stronger front to attack. From criticisms of inferior merit I
might have found less to dissent, but I certainly should have
found less to learn.

[1871.]

X.

THE DESTINATION OF THE EPISTLE TO THE EPHESIANS.

Printed from Lecture-notes.

X.

THE DESTINATION OF THE EPISTLE TO THE EPHESIANS.

IS the common designation of this Epistle correct or not? We are accustomed to style it an 'Epistle to the Ephesians.' But was it really addressed to the Christians of Ephesus, either solely or primarily? This is not merely a curious question of criticism, devoid of any ulterior interest. It has a very direct bearing on the genuineness of the letter, and it is intimately connected also with the scope and purpose of the writer.

Many facts converge from various quarters, which suggest an answer unfavourable to the commonly received title of this Epistle.

1. In the first place it is quite clear that in the early ages of the Church a very large number of copies were in circulation, in which the words 'in Ephesus' were omitted from the opening verse.

(i) ORIGEN [† A.D. 253], whose commentary on this Epistle must have been written during the second quarter of the third century, speaks in such a way as to show not only that they were absent from the text which he himself used, but that he was unaware of their existence in any copies of the Epistle within his reach. His words are as follows:

"In the case of the Ephesians alone have I found the expression '*to the saints that are*,' and I am led to ask,

unless the clause '*that are*' is superfluous, what can be
meant by it?   May it not be then, that as in Exodus He
who speaks to Moses declares His name to be '*He that is*'
(or '*the Absolute Being*'), so also they who partake of the
Absolute Being, themselves become existent, when they are
called as it were from not being into being: for, says the
same Paul, '*God chose out the things that are not, that they
might bring to nought the things that are*,' *etc.*[1]"

The inference from this passage is inevitable.   In the first
place, the interpretation itself tells its own tale.   No one, seeing
the words ἐν Ἐφέσῳ immediately following, would have thought
of separating them from the preceding τοῖς οὖσιν, thus abandoning the obvious construction of the passage and having recourse
to a highly strained and unnatural explanation.   In the second
place, Origen could not possibly have said that this statement is
made of the Ephesians alone, if he had read the words as they
stand in the common texts.   In this case he would have found
several parallels in the Epistles of St Paul.   He would have
found the Apostle, for instance, addressing 'all that are in Rome,'
'the Church of God that is in Corinth,' 'all the saints that are
in the whole of Achaia,' 'all the saints in Christ Jesus that are
in Philippi[2].'   But indeed the fact that the words 'in Ephesus'

---

[1] Origen, Ἐπὶ μόνων Ἐφεσίων εὕρομεν
κείμενον τὸ τοῖς ἁγίοις τοῖς οὖσι· καὶ
ζητοῦμεν, εἰ μὴ παρέλκει προσκείμενον τὸ
τοῖς ἁγίοις τοῖς οὖσι, τί δύναται σημαίνειν.
ὅρα οὖν εἰ μὴ ὥσπερ ἐν τῇ Ἐξόδῳ ὄνομα
φησὶν ἑαυτῷ ὁ χρηματίζων Μωσεῖ τὸ ὤν,
οὕτως οἱ μετέχοντες τοῦ ὄντος γίνονται
ὄντες, καλούμενοι οἱονεὶ ἐκ τοῦ μὴ εἶναι
εἰς τὸ εἶναι· ἐξελέξατο γὰρ ὁ Θεὸς τὰ μὴ
ὄντα, φησὶν ὁ αὐτὸς Παῦλος, ἵνα τὰ ὄντα
καταργήσῃ κ.τ.λ.   Should the position
of τὸ be altered, προσκείμενον τοῖς ἁγίοις
τὸ τοῖς οὖσι?   At all events Origen's
meaning seems to be 'unless τοῖς οὖσι
attached to τοῖς ἁγίοις is redundant or
superfluous.'   For this sense of παρέλκει, which is common in late writers,

comp. Clem. Alex. *Strom.* vi. 16, p.
807 Potter, ὅτι μὲν ἱερὰ ἡ δεκάς, παρέλκει λέγειν τὰ νῦν.   There is an allusion
to these words of Origen in the scholia
of Matthæi, Ὠριγένης ὡς ἐπὶ Ἐφεσίων
κείμενον παρέλκον οἴεται, where the writer
perhaps misunderstands and certainly
obscures Origen's meaning.   The reference is given in Resche *Comm. Crit.*
p. 104 note.

[2] Rom. i. 7 πᾶσιν τοῖς οὖσιν ἐν Ῥώμῃ,
1 Cor. i. 2 τῇ ἐκκλησίᾳ τοῦ Θεοῦ τῇ
οὔσῃ ἐν Κορίνθῳ, 2 Cor. i. 1 τοῖς ἁγίοις
πᾶσιν τοῖς οὖσιν ἐν ὅλῃ τῇ Ἀχαίᾳ, Phil.
i. 1 πᾶσιν τοῖς ἁγίοις ἐν Χριστῷ Ἰησοῦ
τοῖς οὖσιν ἐν Φιλίπποις.

are wanting in some very early copies leaves no doubt upon this point.

The importance of this notice will be felt when it is remembered that Origen was the most learned and enquiring of the fathers in all matters relating to the text of the Scriptures. To him it was a subject of special study.

(ii) From the third century we pass to the fourth, from Origen to BASIL [✝ A.D. 379]. The testimony of this father runs thus:

> "Moreover, when writing to the Ephesians, as men truly united with the Absolute Being through perfect knowledge, he uses a peculiar expression and styles them ' being,' saying ' to the saints that are and faithful in Christ Jesus.' For so we learn from the statements of previous writers ; and we ourselves have found (this reading) in those copies which are ancient[1]."

Here it will be observed that Basil repeats the interpretation of Origen, of whom he was a diligent student and to whom doubtless he was indebted in this instance. When therefore he appeals to ' the statements of previous writers,' he cannot be considered to add anything to the testimony of the Alexandrian father. But the information, which he adds respecting the copies extant in his own day, is highly important. He does not say that the words were wanting in some old copies, or in many old copies; but his statement is absolute. He is not even content with saying ' in the old copies ' (ἐν τοῖς παλαιοῖς ἀντιγράφοις); but he expresses himself still more strongly ' in those copies which are old ' (ἐν τοῖς παλαιοῖς τῶν ἀντιγράφων). Thus it appears that, while in the first half of the third century Origen (if we may draw the inference from his silence) was not acquainted with any manuscript which

---

[1] Basil contr. Eun. ii. 19 (ed. Garn. I. p. 254) ἀλλὰ καὶ τοῖς Ἐφεσίοις ἐπιστέλλων ὡς γνησίως ἡνωμένοις τῷ ὄντι δι' ἐπιγνώσεως, ὄντας αὐτοὺς ἰδιαζόντως ὠνόμασεν, εἰπών· τοῖς ἁγίοις τοῖς οὖσι καὶ πιστοῖς ἐν Χριστῷ Ἰησοῦ. οὕτω γὰρ καὶ οἱ πρὸ ἡμῶν παραδεδώκασι, καὶ ἡμεῖς ἐν τοῖς παλαιοῖς τῶν ἀντιγράφων εὑρήκαμεν.

contained the words, Basil, writing more than a century later, found them in some copies, but these were all recent.

(iii) The statements of these two fathers are in strict accordance with the phenomena exhibited by extant documents. Two Greek MSS. and two only, which contain this Epistle, have any claim to be dated as far back as the fourth century (they may not improbably be assigned to the earlier decades, at least to the first half of this century); and in both these the words 'in Ephesus' are wanting. In the *Codex Sinaiticus* (א) they were absent originally, but are supplied by the third hand. In the *Codex Vaticanus* (B) they have no place in the text, but are supplied in the margin by a later corrector. The testimony of these—the two most ancient uncials—is further supported by another authority of weight. The second corrector of the cursive 67 has marked the words ἐν Ἐφέσῳ as spurious. The corrections by this hand have the highest value, having been evidently made from some very early text. It may be safely said that a reading in St Paul's Epistles which is supported by such a combination as א B 67** can never be neglected, and almost always represents the original text.

(iv) To these facts it must be added that Marcion in his Canon called this letter an Epistle to the Laodiceans[1]. The obvious inference is, that at all events he did not read 'in Ephesus' in his text. Whether he found other words substituted for these, I shall enquire hereafter[2]. The Canon of Marcion, it will be remembered, must have been drawn up before the middle of the second century[3].

With these facts before us, it seems plain, that in the Greek MSS. which were in circulation during the second and third

---

[1] This fact about Marcion is derived from the passages in Tertullian given below (see p. 381 sq.).

[2] See below, p. 392.

[3] As the question is purely critical and has no bearing on the doctrinal views of Marcion, his testimony is free from suspicion; and due weight must be attached to the evidence of one who lived in a neighbouring province of Asia Minor in the first half of the second century. Tertullian's assertion, that he falsified the title (see below, p. 382), is unworthy of credit, though no doubt uttered in good faith.

centuries, the omission of the words ἐν Ἐφέσῳ was not the exception, but the rule. The silence of Origen is confirmed by the direct statement of Basil; and their joint testimony, sufficiently strong in itself, is further strengthened by the phenomena of the extant MSS. and by the belief of Marcion. On the other hand, we have no direct evidence that a single Greek manuscript during this period contained the words in question. The recent manuscripts, to which Basil refers in the latter half of the fourth century, are the earliest of which this can be distinctly affirmed. On the other hand, the fact, to which I shall advert presently, that the letter was commonly and persistently styled the 'Epistle to the Ephesians' from the latter half of the second century at least, suggests that the words occurred in some manuscripts from a very early date, perhaps from the Apostle's own age. But this is a critical inference, of which there is no positive proof.

From the Greek manuscripts I turn to the Latin. The original form of the Old Latin Version in the Pauline Epistles can only be ascertained very imperfectly from the existing copies. The three chief extant manuscripts of this Version of St Paul's Epistles are bilingual. The Latin stands in close proximity to the Greek, being written either in a parallel column as in DE, or over the words as in G. Under such circumstances the Latin text would almost inevitably be made to conform to the Greek in a case like the present, where the omission would appear obvious. Moreover of these three manuscripts only one was written as early as the sixth century, and the remaining two are as late as the ninth. For the original form of the text therefore we must have recourse to the notices and commentaries of the Latin Fathers.

(i) Of these the testimony of Tertullian, as the oldest, is the most important. He refers twice to the title which this Epistle bore in the Marcionite Canon. In the first passage he writes:

> "I say nothing here about another Epistle which we (Catholics) have with the heading '*to the Ephesians*,' but the heretics '*to the Laodiceans*.'"

In the second passage he is more explicit:

'According to the true belief of the Church,' he writes, 'we hold this Epistle to have been despatched to the Ephesians, not to the Laodiceans; but Marcion had to falsify its title, wishing to make himself out a very diligent investigator. The question of titles however is of no consequence; seeing that the Apostle wrote to all, when he wrote to some[1].'

It seems probable from the expressions here used, that the words 'in Ephesus' were wanting in the copies used by the Latin father. He speaks of Marcion's falsifying[2] the *title*; he appeals to the received *heading* of the letter. He neither directly states, nor indirectly hints, that anything in the letter itself contradicts this hypothesis. His argument in fact seems to be this: "It must be confessed that the letter itself does not say to whom it was written; but the Catholic Church has always regarded it as addressed '*To the Ephesians*.' It was therefore a wanton and arbitrary proceeding of Marcion to give it another title '*To the Laodiceans*,' for the sake of gaining credit, as an enquiring critic."

Thus strictly interpreted, the language of Tertullian refers only to the title. This interpretation however is rendered uncertain by the fact that Tertullian elsewhere uses the expressions *titulus* and *praescribere*, not of the actual title or heading, but of the opening words of an Epistle[3]. Still, as he appeals

---

[1] Tertullian *adv. Marc.* v. 11, 'Praetereo hic et de alia epistula, quam nos ad Ephesios praescriptam habemus, haeretici vero (i.e. the Marcionites) ad Laodicenos;' *ib.* v. 17, 'Ecclesiae quidem veritate epistulam istam ad Ephesios habemus emissam, non ad Laodicenos, sed Marcion ei titulum aliquando interpolare gestiit, quasi et in isto diligentissimus explorator. Nihil autem de titulis interest, cum ad omnes apostolus scripserit, dum ad quosdam.' This treatise was written A.D. 207.

[2] 'Interpolare' is used loosely by Tertullian in the sense 'to corrupt or falsify' whether by omission, insertion, or alteration, e.g. *adv. Marc.* v. 21, 'Affectavit, opinor, etiam numerum epistularum interpolare.' Marcion only accepted ten epistles of St Paul as genuine. See also *adv. Marc.* iv. 1, 'evangelium...quod interpolando suum fecit.' Cf. Anger *Ueber den Laodicenerbrief* (Leipzig 1843), p. 41.

[3] e.g. *adv. Marc.* v. 5, 'Praestructio superioris epistulae ita duxit, ut de

not to the ancient copies, but to the authority of the Church, the inference is that he could not refute Marcion out of the manuscripts of the Epistle which were in his hands[1].

titulo ejus non retractaverim, certus et alibi retractari eum posse, communem scilicet et eundem in epistulis omnibus, quod non utique salutem *praescribit* eis quibus scribit, sed gratiam et pacem.' Generally however 'titulus' is the heading, the title, e.g. *adv. Marc.* iv. 2, 3, *de Pudic.* 20; see Anger *Laodic.* p. 97.

[1] Tertullian's testimony to the identity of the Laodicean Epistle of Marcion with the Ephesian Epistle of the Catholic Church is positive and explicit; and, if it had stood alone, would have excited no suspicion. Two other witnesses however appear, whose testimony is scarcely reconcileable with his statement. (1) About a generation before Tertullian's time, an anonymous writer of the Muratorian Canon of Scripture, after enumerating the Epistles of St Paul adds, 'Fertur etiam ad Laudicenses alia ad Alexandrinos Pauli nomine finctae ad haeresem Marcionis et alia plura quae in catholicam ecclesiam recipi non potest' (*Fragm. Murator.* Credner *Gesch. des N.T. Kanons,* p. 148). If 'finctae' refers to the Laodicean and Alexandrian Epistles mentioned just before, we must suppose the writer to be in error. He knew of an Epistle to the Laodiceans in the Marcionite Canon, but not being aware of its identity with this Epistle to the Ephesians assumed that it was an apocryphal writing. But in this case no account can be given of 'alia ad Alexandrinos,' for no such Epistle is elsewhere mentioned as belonging to the Marcionite Canon. Not without reason therefore, considering that the fragment is a blundering translation from a Greek original, much mutilated in the course of transcription, Credner (p. 160) sepa-

rates 'finctae' from the preceding words. The words will then mean: 'Besides the Canonical Epistles, there is an Epistle to the Laodiceans in circulation, another to the Alexandrians, both bearing the name of Paul; others again adapted to the heresy of Marcion, etc.' The phrase 'finctae ad haeresem Marcionis' well describes the process of mutilation and alteration, by which Marcion shaped St Paul's Epistles to his own views. In this case the Epistle to the Laodiceans was probably some apocryphal writing which has not survived. The allusion in Col. iv. 16 must have tempted more than one heretical writer to forge an Epistle in St Paul's name, as a means of gaining Apostolic sanction for his own opinions. (2) At the close of the fourth century, Epiphanius (*Haeres.* xlii.) speaks of the Marcionite Canon in a way which is very perplexing. He says that Marcion recognised ten Epistles of St Paul (the Pastoral Epistles being of course excluded), and mentions the Epistle to the Ephesians in his enumeration of these, p. 310, *ed. Petav.* He then adds that he recognises also 'portions of the so-called Epistle to the Laodiceans' (ἔχει δὲ καὶ τῆς πρὸς Λαοδικέας λεγομένης μέρη, p. 310; cf. p. 321, p. 374). Later on, he gives several extracts from the Epistle to the Ephesians (p. 371) identical with our text, except that in one instance Marcion omitted a few words (πρὸς τὴν γυναῖκα αὐτοῦ Ephes. v. 31), and one passage as from the Epistle to the Laodiceans (p. 374), which also is found in our Epistle to the Ephesians (Ephes. iv. 5). Epiphanius is aware of this, for, speaking of this last passage, he says that Marcion did not adduce this testimony from the Epistle to the

(ii)   And this inference is supported by the interpretations of the earlier Latin commentators, whose language seems to show that the word *Ephesi* was wanting, or that its position fluctuated in some Latin copies and thus betrayed its later introduction.   Thus Victorinus Afer [c. A.D. 360] writes: 'But when he says these words "To the saints who are the faithful of Ephesus," what does he add?   "In Christ Jesus."'[1]   The importance of this fact is not seriously diminished by the circumstance that immediately below he quotes the words as they stand in the existing manuscripts[2]: because we meet with numberless examples in which the commentator explains one reading and the scribe gives another.   The natural tendency of the transcriber was to conform to the commonly received text. In all such cases therefore a deviation has far higher value, as evidence, than a coincidence.

(iii)   I believe also that traces of a variation from the common reading may be discerned in the next Latin commentator in point of time, the Ambrosian Hilary.   Here too the text conforms to the common type; but the commentary ignores the word *Ephesi* altogether.   It runs as follows: 'He writes not only to the faithful, but also to the saints, to prove that men are then truly faithful, if they are saints in Christ Jesus[3].'

Ephesians, but from that to the Laodiceans, which is not contained in the Apostle's writings (οὐ γὰρ ἔδοξε τῷ ἐλεεινοτάτῳ Μαρκίωνι ἀπὸ τῆς πρὸς Ἐφεσίους ταύτην τὴν μαρτυρίαν λέγειν, ἀλλὰ τῆς πρὸς Λαοδικέας, τῆς μὴ οὔσης ἐν τῷ ἀποστόλῳ, p. 375).   The explanation of Epiphanius' language seems to be this. Some of the later Marcionites abandoned the title of the Epistle adopted by their founder, and designated it according to Catholic usage the Epistle to the *Ephesians*.   In the copy of the Marcionite ἀποστολικὸν used by Epiphanius it was so designated (Anger *Laodic.* p. 41 sq.).   At the same time he found in some writings of Marcion, or of his followers, quotations from

St Paul's 'Epistle to the Laodiceans'; and in ignorance assumed that the Epistle thus quoted was another, not contained in the Catholic Canon.

[1] Victorinus quoted in Mai *Script. Vet. Nov. Coll.* III. p. 87 (1828), 'Sed haec cum dicit *Sanctis qui sunt fidelibus Ephesi*, quid adjungitur?   *In Christo Jesu.*' [On this commentator see *Galatians* p. 231.]

[2] Victor. *op. c.* p. 88, '*Sanctis qui sunt Ephesi et fidelibus in Christo Jesu.*'

[3] Ambrosiaster *Com.* in Eph. i. 1 (Migne *P. L.* XVII. p. 373), 'Non solum fidelibus scribit, sed et sanctis: ut tunc vere fideles sint, si fuerint sancti in Christo Jesu.'

It would almost seem as though this commentator (or some earlier writer whose note he adopts) had in his mind the reading τοῖς ἁγίοις τοῖς οὖσιν καὶ πιστοῖς, and that, like several modern interpreters, he translated them 'the saints who are also faithful.' If so, he can hardly have read *sanctis qui sunt Ephesi et fidelibus* in his Latin copy; since this would have saved him from the misinterpretation. His language however is not so clear as to leave this inference free from doubt.

(iv) The only later Latin father whose language tends in the same direction is Sedulius Scotus, who in the eighth or ninth century compiled a commentary on St Paul's Epistles. He writes:

> '*To the saints.* Not to all the Ephesians, but to those who believe in Christ. *And faithful.* All the saints are faithful, but not all the faithful are saints etc. *Who are in Christ Jesus.* There are many faithful who are not faithful in Christ, etc[1].'

No stress can be laid on the omission of *Ephesi* here, because the inserted fragments of the text are more often discontinuous than not in this writer; and indeed he omits the corresponding names of places in other Epistles. But the position of *qui sunt* is striking. It would seem as though some transcriber, finding the reading *sanctis qui sunt et fidelibus in Christo Jesu* in his copy and stumbling at the order, had transposed the words so as to read *sanctis et fidelibus qui sunt in Christo Jesu.* This altered reading may have been before Sedulius, or some earlier writer whom he copies.

(v) On the other hand the note of St Jerome on the passage suggests that some centuries before Sedulius *Ephesi* was commonly read in the Latin copies. He writes:

> 'Some persons, with more ingenuity than is needed, think that, according as it is said to Moses *These things*

---

[1] Sedul. Scot. *Com.* in Eph. i. 1 (Migne *P. L.* CIII. p. 195), '*Sanctis.* Non omnibus Ephesiis, sed his qui credunt in Christo. *Et fidelibus.* Omnes sancti fideles sunt, non omnes fideles sancti etc. *Qui sunt in Christo Jesu.* Plures fideles sunt, sed non in Christo, etc.'

shalt thou say to the children of Israel, He that is hath sent me, so also *those who are at Ephesus saints and faithful* are addressed under the title of (absolute) existence; that is to say, just as (they are called) holy after the Holy One, righteous after the Righteous One, and wise after the Wise One, so also they are designated *Those that are* after *Him that is.* Others however take it simply, and think that it is written not to *those that are,* but to *those that at Ephesus are saints and faithful* [1].'

This father has expressed himself in a hasty and obscure manner. When he speaks of 'some persons,' he doubtless alludes to Origen, to whose work he was largely indebted in his own commentary on this Epistle. But it does not appear clearly what view he took of Origen's explanation. In the former part of this note he speaks only of a difference of interpretation, not of reading; and hence we might infer not only that he had the words 'in Ephesus' in his own text, but that he was unaware of their omission in any copies, and therefore did not see the difficulty with which Origen had to contend. On the other hand the word *scriptum* in the closing sentence seems to point to a difference of reading also. But he may have used the word loosely and without any such intention. On the whole it seems probable that he overlooked the omission. Yet even then his language suggests that his Latin copy may have had the words *qui sunt Ephesi* in some other than the ordinary position.

(vi) The extant copies of all the other Versions, early as well as late, contain the words in the text. The unanimity however does not carry any great weight in the present instance. Our existing manuscripts of these Versions are all far too late

---

[1] Hieron. *Com.* in Eph. i. 1 (vii. p. 545, *ed.* Vallarsi), 'Quidam curiosius quam necesse est putant ex eo quod Moysi dictum sit *Haec dices filiis Israel, Qui est, misit me* (Exod. iii. 14), etiam eos qui Ephesi sunt sancti et fideles essentiae vocabulo nuncu- patos: ut quomodo a Sancto sancti, a Justo justi, a Sapiente sapientes, ita ab Eo qui est hi qui sunt appellentur... Alii vero simpliciter, non ad eos qui sint (*al.* sunt), sed qui Ephesi sancti et fideles sint scriptum arbitrantur.'

to assure us of their original reading in a case where the insertion would be irresistible to scribes. The contest between the testimony of the earlier and that of the later Greek MSS., as already stated, shows how little dependence can be placed on any but the most ancient authorities under such circumstances. The earliest extant manuscript of any of these Versions containing this opening verse of the Ephesian letter, is at least two centuries later than ℵ B, to say nothing of the manuscripts consulted by Origen and Basil.

2. But if the diplomatic evidence throws considerable doubt on the common designation of this Epistle, our suspicions are deepened when we examine the general character and tone of the Epistle itself.

St Paul had spent a great part of three years at Ephesus. He had 'gone about among them preaching the kingdom of God[1].' He had testified 'both to Jews and to Greeks[2].' 'He had ceased not to warn every one day and night with tears[3].' On his last journey to Jerusalem he summoned the elders of the city to meet him at Miletus. He poured forth his whole heart to them in affectionate remembrances and earnest warnings. Parting from him at length, 'they fell on his neck and kissed him, sorrowing most of all for the words which he spake, that they should see his face no more[4].'

The interview at Miletus is a striking picture of St Paul's intimate relations with the brethren of Ephesus. There was no Church on which he spent more time and labour, none in which he felt a warmer personal interest, none with which fonder or more sacred memories were bound up. Might it not be expected then that a letter written to the Church of Ephesus would be full of personal reminiscences, that there would be a marked individuality of character in it, that the Apostle would pour out his heart to his converts, as a friend speaking to friends?

[1] Acts xx. 25.
[2] Acts xx. 21.
[3] Acts xx. 31.
[4] Acts xx. 37, 38.

The Epistle to the Ephesians does not answer these conditions. Much stress indeed has been laid on the absence of
salutations to individual members of a Church so familiar to
him. To this argument there is a ready answer. In writing
to brotherhoods with whom he was most intimate, to the
Corinthians and Philippians, for instance, he sends no special
salutations: in writing to the Roman Church, which he had
never visited, he greets by name a large number of individual
members. The reason for this is obvious. In a community of
strangers it is easy to single out and enumerate friends. Where
all alike are known to us, it becomes irksome, if not invidious,
to select any for special salutations.

The absence of such salutations therefore is natural enough
in an Epistle to Ephesus. But the general character of the
Epistle admits of no explanation on this hypothesis. Of all
St Paul's letters it is the most general, the least personal. In
this respect it more nearly resembles the Epistle to the Romans
than any other [1]. Both alike partake of the character rather
of a formal treatise than of a familiar letter. Yet even the
Epistle to the Romans betrays deeper personal feeling, and
exhibits more distinct traces of individual relations and local
colouring. In writing to the Ephesians of their faith and
progress in the Gospel, he might be expected at all events to
allude to his own labours among them, their attachment to
him, the memories and experiences which they shared in
common [2]. Far different is his language. 'Having *heard* of
your faith in the Lord Jesus and your love towards all the
saints, I cease not to give thanks for you [3].' 'For this cause I
Paul, the prisoner of Christ Jesus for you Gentiles, if indeed

---

[1] Theodore of Mopsuestia, with his
usual penetration, discerns the likeness
of these two Epistles 'Scribit Ephesiis
hanc epistolam beatus Paulus, eo modo
quo et Romanis dudum scripserat quos
necdum ante viderat' (*Argum. ad
Ephes.* I. p. 112 *ed.* Swete).

[2] Theod. Mops. *l. c.* is driven to
assert that the letter was written

before St Paul visited Ephesus, and so
does Severianus (see Cramer's *Catena*);
but not Theodoret, as De Wette asserts.
Recent writers adduce it as an argument against the genuineness of the
Epistle. Mr Burgon does not attempt
an explanation of the facts.

[3] Eph. i. 15.

ye were instructed in the dispensation of the grace of God which was given me to you-ward[1].' 'But ye did not so learn Christ, if so be ye heard of him and were taught in him, as the truth is in Jesus[2].' All this is general and comprehensive, not necessarily excluding personal intercourse with those he addresses, but still scarcely natural if addressed to his own converts solely. It is strangely at variance with the language in which he generally writes to his own children in the faith, the Corinthians and Philippians, for instance. It even presents a very striking contrast to the contemporaneous letter to the Colossians, for whom he shows an intense personal interest, and to whose special dangers and temptations he is fully alive, though they had not seen his face in the flesh[3].

3.   Yet, though this Epistle so little fulfils our expectations of what St Paul would have written to his converts, it is beyond a question that the Early Church universally regarded it as an Epistle to the Ephesians. It is distinctly referred to as such by the writer of the Muratorian Canon, by Irenæus, by Tertullian, by Clement of Alexandria, even by Origen himself, in whose text, as we have seen, there was no direct mention of Ephesus[4]. Thus the tradition is carried back to the earlier decades of the last half of the second century, and at the close of that century, at least, the title seems to have been received without question by the Catholic Church, so much so that, as we have seen, Tertullian accused Marcion of forgery because he denied it. Earlier than this we cannot trace the opinion, unless the existing text of the Old Latin and the Syriac Versions, which have the words 'in Ephesus', may be put in evidence[5].

---

[1] Eph. iii. 2.
[2] Eph. iv. 20, 21.
[3] Col. ii. 1.
[4] The references are as follows: *Murat. Canon*, p. 148 *ed.* Credner; Iren. *Haer.* i. 3. 1, 4, pp. 14, 16, i. 8. 4, p. 40, v. 2. 36, p. 294 *ed.* Stieren; Tert. *adv. Marc.* v. 17 (see above, p. 382),

de praescr. 36, *de monogam.* 5 ; Clem. Alex. *Strom.* iv. 65, p. 592, *Paed.* i. 18, p. 108 *ed.* Potter; Origen *contr. Cels.* iii. 20 (XVIII. p. 273 *ed.* Lomm.).
[5] Ignatius, writing in the first decade of the second century to the members of the Ephesian Church, alludes to St Paul as 'making mention

4. Only one exception to this general belief during the earliest ages is on record. But this exception is most important. I have mentioned before that Marcion considered it to be addressed to the Laodiceans. Now (1) Marcion lived nearer to the times of the Apostles than any of the Catholic writers above mentioned. (2) He was moreover a native of Pontus, a neighbouring province of Asia Minor, and therefore not unfavourably situated for forming an opinion. And, (3), as the question has no theological bearing whatever, his opinion is free from all suspicion of bias, and must be received with the respect due to so ancient a writer. Did Marcion then maintain this opinion, as a tradition received from others, or as a result arrived at by his own independent criticism? We have not sufficient information to form any judgment on this point. If the former idea be correct, this tradition is of the highest value: if the latter, as Tertullian assumes, he may be supposed to have built an inference on the mention of a Laodicean letter in Col. iv. 16. Anyhow it is still clear that the destination of the Epistle was open to question, for it is most unlikely that Marcion would have changed the received title merely because he found an allusion elsewhere to a Laodicean letter, if this title were hitherto undisputed, and if the Epistle itself stated that it was addressed to the Church of Ephesus. The former view is more probable in the infancy of criticism. Criticism would only step in where history was silent or confused.

5. But whether Marcion's opinion was founded independently of the mention of a Laodicean Epistle in the letter to the Colossians or not, this mention has undoubtedly a very important bearing on the question. The Ephesian and Colossian letters

of them in every epistle' (*Eph.* § 12 ὃς ἐν πάσῃ ἐπιστολῇ μνημονεύει ὑμῶν). Attempts have been made to translate ἐν πάσῃ ἐπιστολῇ as though it were ἐν πάσῃ τῇ ἐπιστολῇ 'throughout his epistle,' and thus to claim this personal disciple of the Apostles as a further witness to this tradition; but grammar forbids the interpretation. [See the note on the passage in *Apostolic Fathers* Pt. II. Vol. II. p. 65 *ed.* 2.]

were written and despatched about the same time. Tychicus
seems to have been the bearer of both letters[1]. At all events
he is expected to visit the persons to whom they were addressed
about the time when they were delivered. Simultaneously
with these also a private letter was sent to Philemon, an
individual member of the Church of Laodicea or of Colossæ.
Thus three letters were despatched at the same time. But in
the Epistle to the Colossians they are directed to exchange
letters with the Laodiceans. Are we then to add to the three
letters already mentioned a fourth letter no longer extant? Or
is the Laodicean Epistle to be identified with one of these? If
the latter alternative be adopted, it can only be our Epistle to
the Ephesians, for the letter to Philemon is addressed to an
individual Christian on a matter of strictly private interest, and
does not therefore answer to the designation.

Let us now combine the evidence gathered from these
various sources, and what is the result? We must frame some
hypothesis which recognises our Epistle both as an Epistle to the
Laodiceans and an Epistle to the Ephesians, and yet neither
the one nor the other. It must moreover be sufficiently elastic
to adapt itself to the general tone in which the letter is
couched.

The required hypothesis is not far to seek. It was an
encyclical letter addressed to the Churches lying within a
certain area, which we may perhaps venture to define roughly
as coextensive with Proconsular Asia. On this supposition all
the varying forms of the opening salutation are fully explained.
The facts before us are these :—

(1) The words $\epsilon \nu$ 'Εφέσῳ were omitted in the old MSS.
(see above, p. 377 sq.).

(2) The general character of the Epistle is quite incapable of explanation, if it were written solely or
specially to the Ephesians (see above, p. 387 sq.).

[1] Eph. vi. 21; Col. iv. 7.

(3) At the same time the Epistle was regarded from very ancient times as an 'Epistle to the Ephesians,' and so it was entitled (see above, p. 389).

(4) Marcion, however, the earliest writer whose opinion is known (except doubtfully and inferentially), believed that it was written to the Laodiceans (see above, p. 390).

(5) It is certain that St Paul despatched an Epistle to Laodicea, at or about the same time that the Epistle (so called) to the Ephesians reached its destination (see above, p. 390 sq.).

We have to seek a theory which will account for and combine all these facts, and that of Archbishop Ussher alone satisfies these requirements.

(i) In the original letter a vacant space would be left after the words 'To the saints that are.' In the copies made for distribution the blank would be filled in with the names of the individual Churches for which they were intended, 'in Ephesus,' 'in Smyrna,' 'in Laodicea,' 'in Thyatira' and so forth. In the Church at large some copies would be circulated with the vacant space. When these were again transcribed, the blank would be disregarded, and the text closing in upon it would run 'To the saints that are and faithful brethren.' This explains the reading of the texts of Origen and Basil, and of our two best extant MSS. Not a few again would be circulated from the metropolitan Church of Ephesus. Hence the received text and the recognised title. Lastly a MS. would here and there be found transcribed from the copy sent to some other Church. A transcription from the Laodicean copy fell into Marcion's hands and led to his designation. (ii) And in this way a satisfactory account may be given of the notice in the Colossian Epistle. The letter would be sent only to the mother Church in each district, with the injunction to circulate it among the lesser communities scattered throughout that district. Laodicea would be selected, as she is selected in the Apocalypse, as of superior importance to either Hierapolis or Colossæ, which lay in her immediate neighbourhood[1].

Moreover the hypothesis adopted fits in with the exact terms of that notice. Two points are to be observed: (1) The Epistle in question is called not the 'Epistle *to the Laodiceans*', but the 'Epistle *from Laodicea.*' The former designation would not be very well suited to our Epistle: the latter exactly describes it, for the Colossians got it from Laodicea. (2) If St Paul had written directly and solely to the Laodiceans, he would naturally have given his salutations to the Church of Laodicea and to individual members of it in the letter addressed to them. On the contrary we find him sending his salutations *through the Colossians*, not only to the Church of Laodicea generally, but to Nymphas, who was certainly, and Archippus, who was perhaps, a member of that Church (Col. iv. 15, 17). (iii) Again, the entire absence of special allusions, with the sole exception of the mention of Tychicus, has created much perplexity and suspicion. On the supposition adopted, both the rule and the exception are satisfactorily explained. On the one hand the encyclical character of the letter required that all personal matters should be excluded. But at the same time, with some of the Churches thus addressed St Paul was on terms of affectionate intimacy. To such he must needs address some words of special import. These were entrusted to the bearer of the letter: 'But that ye *also* may know my affairs, how I do, Tychicus, the beloved brother and faithful minister in the Lord, shall make known to you all things: whom I have sent unto you for this very purpose, that ye may know our affairs, and that he may comfort your hearts[2]'. The very expression 'ye *also*' points to the encyclical character of the letter. Private instructions, salutations to individuals, strictly personal matters of all kinds would be reserved for him to deliver.

I have suggested Proconsular Asia as the probable limit of the district through which the Epistle was intended to be

---

[1] See *Colossians*, pp. 7, 8.   [2] Eph. vi. 21, 22.

circulated. The seven Churches of the Apocalypse at once occur to us, and St Paul's letter was probably destined for a circle of readers not much wider nor much narrower than St John's Revelation. The Apocalypse was written probably not many years later, and by that time these Churches had passed through many vicissitudes, had been proved by many trials, had grown old and in some instances lukewarm in the faith. It is most probable therefore that they were in existence when St Paul wrote. During his residence of three years in Ephesus, the knowledge of the Gospel through his influence, direct or indirect, had spread throughout the neighbourhood. It had certainly reached Laodicea, with her attendant satellites Hierapolis and Colossæ, lying at the extreme verge of this Pleiad of the Christian heavens, and the more central points of the constellation would not have been passed over. There was little, if any, exaggeration in the language of Demetrius when he said 'not only at Ephesus, but almost throughout all Asia, this Paul hath persuaded and turned away much people[1].' During great part of the second century the Asiatic Churches are without question the most energetic and lively members of Christ, whether we regard their missionary zeal or their literary activity.

What motive then may be supposed to have prompted St Paul to write this letter? A beloved disciple, Epaphras, had brought tidings of the errors which threatened the safety of the Christian brotherhood in his own native place, Colossæ, in itself a comparatively small and unimportant Church. At Colossæ the symptoms were so clear, that there was no mistaking the form which the disease might assume. For these strongly marked errors the Apostle prescribed. The true medicine was found in the doctrine of the Person of Christ. In writing to the Colossians therefore he applied this as a special remedy, with a view to a special complaint[2]. But in the course of writing, it would occur to him to set forth these grand truths in a broader form and in their more general relations. This he

---

[1] Acts xix. 26; cf. v. 10.　　　[2] See *Colossians*, p. 41 sq.

could do, if, while writing, he were free from any of the disturbing forces which special local interests must exert upon him.

The Churches of Asia would offer themselves as fit recipients for such an exposition. He was known personally to some of these; his influence had been felt by all. A trusty messenger was at hand in Tychicus, a member of the Church of Ephesus, the most important in the district, and himself a tried companion and fellow-labourer of the Apostle. To these therefore St Paul wrote a circular letter, for while speaking to all collectively, he was not obliged to speak to any individually. He thus felt himself free and unfettered. At the same time, the area chosen was not too large to prevent his adapting his teaching to the wants of his hearers. A certain tone of feeling pervaded all the Churches of Asia, a certain class of errors would find a welcome among them. If false opinion did not take exactly the same form at Ephesus or Thyatira or Smyrna, for instance, as at Colossæ, it would take a similar form. Thus St Paul still dwells in this Epistle on the same class of truths as in the Epistle to the Colossians. Only whereas in the Colossians he combats error directly[1], he here combats it indirectly: whereas there he is special, distinct, personal, here he speaks broadly and generally[2].

Thus the Epistle to the Ephesians stands to the Epistle to the Colossians in very much the same relation as the Romans to the Galatians. The one is the general and systematic exposition of the same truths which appear in a special bearing

[1] On the character of the heresy which assailed the Colossian Church, see *Colossians*, p. 72 sq.

[2] Besides this, St Paul has given to his teaching a new centre. In this Epistle it revolves about the doctrine of the Church. The same truths which in the Epistle to the Colossians are advanced to combat a peculiar phase of false doctrine have here a place as leading up to the doctrine of the Church, e.g. compare the treatment

of the subject of Christ the Logos in Col. i. 15, ii. 9 with Eph. i. 22, or of the law of ordinances in Col. ii. 14 with Eph. ii. 14, 15, or again the practical lessons of the relations of husbands and wives in Col. iii. 18, 19 with Eph. v. 25 sq., 32. The propriety of this new centre of teaching is obvious when we remember that it is addressed, not in a special letter to an individual Church, but in an encyclical to several Churches.

in the other. For though the Roman is not strictly a circular letter[1], yet, being addressed to a very large and varied community, it was enabled to maintain this general character.

Thus the resemblances between the language of the Epistles to the Ephesians and Colossians are explained. Analogous resemblances between expressions used to the Galatians and Romans are not quite so close, but there the interval between the two letters is longer[2].

[1] See above, p. 315.

[2] This hypothesis best explains the relation between this letter and 1 Peter, which, like it, is addressed to the Churches of Asia Minor and obviously makes use of the Epistle to the Ephesians. Compare the following pairs of passages :

1 Pet. i. 3.	Eph. i. 3.
ii. 5.	ii. 21, 22.
ii. 18 sq.	vi. 5.
iii. 1 sq.	v. 22.
iii. 7 sq.	v. 25.
iii. 22.	i. 20, 21.
iv. 3.	ii, 2, iv. 17.
etc.	etc.

[1873.]

XI.

THE DATE OF THE PASTORAL EPISTLES.

Printed from Lecture-notes.

XI.

THE DATE OF THE PASTORAL EPISTLES.

THE date of the Pastoral Epistles has been more canvassed than perhaps any other point in the chronology of St Paul[1]. While it has been generally acknowledged that the Second Epistle to Timothy was the Apostle's dying strain, though even this opinion has not been allowed to pass unchallenged[2], the First Epistle to Timothy, and the Epistle to Titus have occupied almost every conceivable position in the systems of different critics. This circumstance is in itself a sufficient proof of the difficulties which beset the question, and might perhaps lead us to despair of a solution. A little more careful examination, however, tends to a more hopeful view. Taking into account all the conditions of the problem—the internal character of the Epistles themselves as regards style and teaching, no less than the historical notices which they contain, whether relating to the Church at large, or to personal matters—we arrive at this simple result, that they cannot be placed within the compass of the history contained in the Acts, and that they must have been written after the other letters of the Apostle, towards the close of his life. The later criticism, based on a deeper appreciation of the style of the Pastoral Epistles, is obviously tending to

---

[1] Various opinions respecting this question will be found collected and classified in C. W. Otto *Die Geschichtlichen Verhältnisse der Pastoralbriefe* etc. Leipz. 1860. The writer however, like most of his countrymen, is igno-rant of all recent English Theological works.

[2] For a list of these exceptions see Davidson *Intr.* iii. p. 52 *ed.* 1, and Otto, p. 16.

this result, though there are still some important exceptions[1], and it may be safely predicted that the alternative of placing them at the close of the Apostle's life, or of abandoning the Pauline authorship, will be accepted by both impugners and defenders alike, as common ground.

The two points, which we have to consider, are (1) The style and intrinsic character of the Epistles themselves; (2) The historical matter which they contain.

I. THE STYLE AND INTRINSIC CHARACTER OF THE PASTORAL EPISTLES.

Those who have examined St Paul's Epistles with reference to their time of writing, will have observed a strong resemblance in style and character between the letters belonging to the same chronological group, while at the same time a letter of one group, placed by the side of a letter of another, though betraying the strongest indications of the same mind, shows marked and unmistakable differences. So strong does this impression become on closer study, that the evidence of date derived from style takes the first place in our minds, and when, as in the case of the Galatian Epistle, the historical notices are few and vague, we still feel an absolute certainty in a result derived solely or chiefly from this source. This phenomenon of a difference in a resemblance is much more clearly exhibited in the Pastoral Epistles than in any other of St Paul's letters[2]. With the resemblance I have no concern here. At present I shall dwell simply on the differences, as a proof, first, that they belong to the same period one with another, and secondly, that they cannot have been contemporaneous with the other Epistles of St Paul.

These differences may be gathered up under the following

---

[1] Such as Wieseler, Davidson and Schaff. The most recent writer, Otto, is also an exception. I regard his criticism as retrograde.

[2] Coleridge calls them Παυλοειδεῖς (*Table talk* p. 253).

heads, (1) vocabulary, (2) syntax, (3) modes of thought and teaching.

1. *The Vocabulary.* Words used in these Epistles alone, or with far greater frequency in them. The following classification is more or less artificial, but will assist in apprehending the character of these differences. For convenience of reference the First and Second Epistles to Timothy and the Epistle to Titus are designated by the letters a, b, c, respectively, the number of occurrences, where more than one, being placed immediately above each letter.

(*a*) A new set of terms to describe moral and religious states.

βέβηλος 'profane' a³b. Not used elsewhere by St Paul, occurs in Heb. xii. 16.

εὐσέβεια 'godliness' a⁸bc εὐσεβῶς bc εὐσεβεῖν a, thirteen times in all, and not once elsewhere in St Paul's Epistles.

καθαρός 'pure' a²b²c² (in four out of the six cases used of the conscience); only once elsewhere (Rom. xiv. 20) in St Paul.

καλός 'good' 'beautiful' a¹⁶b³c⁵, twenty-four times in the Pastoral Epistles, and only sixteen times elsewhere in St Paul.

σεμνότης 'gravity' a²c σεμνός a²c. σεμνός occurs Phil. iv. 8, and nowhere else in the New Testament.

(*b*) A new set of terms relating to doctrine, many of them bringing out the contrast between true and false doctrine.

διδασκαλία 'teaching' a⁸b³c⁴, used most frequently objectively 'doctrine.' The word only occurs elsewhere in St Paul four times, and then with its ordinary sense of the 'art of teaching.'

ἐκζητήσεις, ζητήσεις 'questionings' a²bc, not elsewhere in St Paul.

λογομαχία, -εῖν of 'combats of words' ab, not elsewhere in the New Testament.

παραθήκη 'the deposit of the faith' ab², not elsewhere in the New Testament.

ὑγιής, ὑγιαίνειν 'sound' 'healthy' as applied to doctrine a²b²c⁵, not elsewhere in St Paul, or in this sense in the New Testament. Also the opposite νοσεῖν a, here only in the New Testament.

(*c*) Certain formulæ and maxims.

διαμαρτύρεσθαι ἐνώπιον ab². The word διαμαρτύρεσθαι only occurs once elsewhere at all in St Paul.

χάρις, ἔλεος, εἰρήνη ab and perhaps c, contrasted with the earlier salutation χάρις καὶ εἰρήνη.

πιστὸς ὁ λόγος a³bc. Peculiar to this group.

(*d*) Modes of speaking of God the Father, and Christ.

μακάριος θεὸς a².

σωτήρ applied to God a³c³.

ἐπιφάνεια in the sense of παρουσία ab³c.
None of these are found elsewhere in St Paul.   In 2 Thess. ii. 8
however there is ἡ ἐπιφάνεια τῆς παρουσίας.

(e)   Other expressions not falling under any of these classes.
ἀρνεῖσθαι ab³c².
διάβολος, 'false-accuser' abc.
δεσπότης 'master' a²bc, elsewhere in St Paul κύριος.
διαβεβαιοῦσθαι περί τινος ac.
παραιτεῖσθαι a²bc.
All these are peculiar to this group of Pauline Epistles.

2.   *The Syntax.*

(a)   It is stiffer and more regular than in the earlier Epistles, more
jointed and less flowing.   The clauses are marshalled together,
and there is a tendency to parallelism.
e.g. 1 Tim. i. 9, ii. 1, 2, iii. 16, iv. 12, 13, 15, v. 10, vi. 9, 11, 12,
13, 15, 18; 2 Tim. ii. 11, 12, iii. 1–8, 10–13, 16, iv. 2, 4, 5,
7; Tit. i. 7, 8, 9, ii. 7, 12, iii. 1–3.

(b)   There is a greater sententiousness, an abruptness and positive-
ness of form.   Imperative clauses are frequent.
e.g. 1 Tim. iv. 11, 15, 16, v. 7, 8, 22–25, vi. 2, 6, 11, 20; 2 Tim.
i. 13, 14, ii. 1, 3, 7, 8, 14, 19, 22, 23; iii. 1, 5, 12, 16.

3.   *The tone of thought* manifest in these Epistles has a character of
its own.

(a)   There is an increased tendency to the directly moral side of
duty.   The Apostle's former preaching of faith and grace is
not lost sight of, but it occupies a much smaller space and
a less prominent position.   Stress is laid upon good works
(1 Tim. ii. 10, v. 10, 25, vi. 18; 2 Tim. ii. 21; Tit. i. 16, iii. 7,
14).   In describing the Christian state the principles of
εὐσέβεια and σωφροσύνη stand forward.   Long and frequent
lists of virtues are given, often descending into minute
details of practical life.   (b) On the other hand, apparently
in contradiction to the characteristic just mentioned but not
really so, the Apostle dwells more on orthodoxy of belief in
comparison with his previous Epistles.   There is more of the
doctrine of Christianity as a creed, and less as a life.   Altogether we may say that the teaching of the Pastoral Epistles
is more definite and positive, than that of the earlier letters.
There is more of detail in it, and less of principles.

These distinguishing features, it must be observed, are
found in all these three Epistles alike.   It is an obvious and

almost irresistible conclusion (i) that they must all three have been written at or near the same time, (ii) that some considerable period must be interposed between them and the remaining Epistles of St Paul. Now, no hypothesis framed on the supposition that St Paul was not released, and that therefore the Pastoral Epistles fall within the limits of time comprised in the Acts, satisfies these conditions. Indeed it is impossible that such an hypothesis could satisfy them; for the Second Epistle to Timothy is generally allowed to have been written from Rome at the very close of his life, while the First Epistle to Timothy and the Epistle to Titus were written when he was at liberty, and supposing his first captivity to have terminated fatally, this consideration alone interposes a period of four years at least between them[1].

Thus judging from the style and character of these Epistles alone we are led to this very definite conclusion.

II. The historical notices.

These are of two kinds: those relating to (1) actual incidents, affecting himself and his friends; (2) the general condition of the Church.

i. *Historical incidents.*

From the opening verses of the First Epistle to Timothy

---

[1] Wieseler's hypothesis (*Chron.* p. 286), the most plausible of those constructed on this supposition, arranges the Epistles in the order—Galatians, 1 Timothy, 1 Corinthians, Titus, 2 Corinthians. Thus we get a series of Epistles in which St Paul's styles alternate—for Galatians, 1 Corinthians, 2 Corinthians are closely allied to each other, and widely different from 1 Timothy and Titus. According to this hypothesis, 2 Timothy follows Titus after an interval of five or six years, and with six Epistles of an entirely different style intervening. The difficulty is not at all met by saying that as private letters written to intimate friends, the Pastoral Epistles might be supposed to have a character of their own. The peculiarities of style are for the most part not of a kind to be accounted for in this way, though some of them might be so explained. And we have an instance of St Paul's familiar style at this earlier date in the Epistle to Philemon, which has none of the characteristic features of the Pastoral Epistles. Otto (p. 9) has quite failed to grasp the conditions of the problem when he dismisses these considerations so summarily.

we learn that St Paul, when departing for Macedonia, had charged Timothy to remain at Ephesus to superintend the Church there[1]. There are only two visits to Ephesus recorded in the Acts[2]. On the first of these, which was very brief, St Paul scarcely did more than prepare the way for the foundation of a Church, and it is excluded by the fact that he was then travelling not to Macedonia but in a direction the very opposite, viz. to Jerusalem[3]. On the second, he remained at Ephesus for three years, and on departing did go into Macedonia[4]: but the following reasons are decisive against this being the visit in question. (i) He did not leave Timothy in Ephesus, but sent him on to Macedonia[5], intending that he should also go to Corinth[6]. That Timothy did actually reach Corinth is improbable, but that he did not return to Ephesus before St Paul left is clear: for St Paul joins him in Macedonia[7] and is accompanied by him to Corinth[8]. (ii) St Paul had no such intention of revisiting Ephesus soon, as he declares in this letter[9]. On the contrary, he was bound for Greece, intending to sail thence direct to Jerusalem to pay his farewell to the Holy city before visiting Rome and the West[10].

This difficulty may indeed be got over by supposing that St Paul may have paid a visit from Ephesus to Macedonia during his three years' stay there—a visit unrecorded in the Acts, as he is known from 2 Corinthians to have paid a visit to Corinth likewise unrecorded[11]. But this is an arbitrary assumption, and two unsurmountable difficulties still remain: (i) to account for the growth of the heresies in so short a time during St Paul's actual presence at Ephesus; and (ii) to reconcile the appearance of these heretics at Ephesus, as stated in this Epistle, with the prediction to the Elders at Miletus[12]

---

[1] 1 Tim. i. 3.
[2] Acts xviii. 19, and xix. 1.
[3] Acts xviii. 21.
[4] Acts xix. 21.
[5] Acts xix. 22.
[6] 1 Cor. iv. 17, xvi. 10, 11.
[7] 2 Cor. i. 1.

[8] Rom. xvi. 21.
[9] 1 Tim. iii. 14.
[10] Acts xix. 21.
[11] This hypothesis is put in the best form by Wieseler, *l. c.*
[12] Acts xx. 29 μετὰ τὴν ἄφιξίν μου.

that they would appear hereafter, the fact being on this hypothesis earlier than the prediction[1].

The notices in the Epistle to Titus enhance the difficulty on any such hypothesis. St Paul leaves Titus in Crete to organize the Churches there[2]. There is no record in the Acts of any such visit to Crete. We have also mention of a winter to be spent in Nicopolis[3]—which Nicopolis is meant, I need not stay to enquire at present. This also is passed over in silence in the Acts. But not only are these incidents unrecorded; there is no place in the narrative of St Luke where we can interpolate them[4]. It has been suggested indeed that they must be taken out of the long residence at Ephesus, extending over from two to three years. That St Paul paid a brief visit to Corinth during this period, unrecorded by St Luke, we are forced to conclude by some incidental allusions in the Epistles to the Corinthians. But if we add to this a visit to Macedonia, as required by the First Epistle to Timothy, and then a residence more or less prolonged in Crete, and a winter passed at Nicopolis, as inferred from the Epistle to Titus, and make allowance for the journeys to and fro, we have to assume a prolonged absence from Ephesus which could not have been unknown to St Luke, or, if known, passed over in silence, and which would render St Paul's language to the Ephesian Elders at Miletus[5] quite incorrect and inappropriate. It may be added also that the projected mission of Artemas or Tychicus to Crete[6], or the expected visit of Zenas and Apollos and of Titus himself[7], have no points of correspondence with the incidents of St Luke's narrative—a remarkable circumstance if they fell within the same range of time.

The notices in the Second Epistle to Timothy are still more unaccountable. This Epistle, as is generally supposed, was

---

[1] Futile attempts are made to meet this difficulty in Hemsen, Paulus, and Davidson III. p. 25.

[2] Tit. i. 5.

[3] Tit. iii. 12.

[4] For various shifts see Davidson

III. p. 79 sq., Wieseler, p. 286 sq., Otto, p. 357 sq.

[5] Acts xx. 31 τριετίαν νύκτα καὶ ἡμέραν οὐκ ἐπαυσάμην νουθετῶν.

[6] Tit. iii. 12.

[7] Tit. iii. 13.

written while St Paul was a prisoner at Rome, and when his
captivity was soon to terminate in death. According to the
hypothesis which I am now considering, this was the same
captivity with which the history of the Acts closes. Thus he
had been a prisoner for more than four years, first at Cæsarea,
then at Rome. The incidents therefore which occurred when
St Paul was in the East—the sojourn of Erastus at Corinth[1],
and his leaving Trophimus ill at Miletus—must have happened
previously to this. Even if we suppose with some that it was
written at the beginning of his stay at Rome, there is still a
period of two or three years, yet he feels it necessary to inform
him by letter of these occurrences after so long a lapse of time.
Nay more, Timothy had been staying with the Apostle meanwhile at Rome[2]; he was in fact with him during this very tour
in Greece and Asia Minor when, on the supposed hypothesis,
these incidents must have occurred. Why then should the
Apostle offer this information so superfluous and uncalled for?
But indeed the incidents themselves militate against the hypothesis. Erastus indeed might have remained at Corinth on
that occasion, for about him St Luke is silent. But Trophimus
was certainly not left at Miletus sick, for we find him with the
Apostle immediately afterwards at Jerusalem[3]. It is unnecessary to dwell on minor difficulties, such as his leaving the
cloak and books at Troas[4] so many years[5].

This accumulation of historical contradictions is quite unsurmountable on the supposition of the earlier date of these Epistles. De Wette's phrase of the 'historical unaccountableness' of
the Pastoral Epistles then becomes most appropriate. And if no
alternative remained, there would be an overwhelming difficulty
in accepting these writings as genuine. This historical difficulty
disappears, if we prolong St Paul's life beyond the period comprised in the Acts, and place the Pastorals at a later date.

[1] 2 Tim. iv. 20.
[2] Phil. i. 1; Col. i. 1; Philem. i. 1.
[3] Acts xxi. 29.
[4] 2 Tim. iv. 13.

[5] To escape this difficulty Hug and
Hemsen take ἀπέλειπον to mean 'they
left' (see Davidson III. p. 53). Who
'they' are, is not clear.

ii.   *The condition of the Church.*

Very exaggerated and unwarrantable views have been taken
of the notices in the Pastoral Epistles relating to the condition
of the Church, as indicating a later date, and this circumstance
may perhaps prejudice the consideration of them.   But on the
other hand these Epistles leave on the mind the impression of
a definite and various organization, which must have taken
some time in forming, and of a progress and development of
opinion and action for good or evil, inconsistent with a very
early stage of the Church.   This consideration becomes of
importance when we apply it to the particular case of the
Church of Ephesus.   According to the hypothesis we have
been combating, the First Epistle to Timothy was written not
later than A.D. 57, before the close of St Paul's protracted stay
in that city.   Now that stay was practically the foundation
of the Church there, for on his previous brief visit St Paul did
but break ground.   Thus on this theory in the course of two or
three years the Church has attained this advanced development,
and what is more improbable still, false and heretical opinions
have grown up and spread before the Apostle's own eyes.

The three points which deserve considering in the condition
of the Church are (*a*) the ministry and in general the offices
connected with Church government, (*b*) the heresies, (*c*) the
traces of a Church literature.

(*a*) I do not lay any stress on the existence of the two
orders of *presbyters* and *deacons*, as a recognised institution.
Evidence is not wanting to show that these existed in some
Churches at least at a very early date[1]; but the directions
given (1 Tim. iii. 1 sq., v. 17–21; Tit. i. 7) imply that these
offices had assumed a very definite form, that serious irregularities had crept into the ministry of the Church and that altogether there had been long experience of the working of the
system.   I would point particularly to the direction that the
presbyter must not be 'a novice, lest he be lifted up with pride[2],'

---

[1] Acts xi. 30, xiv. 23; Phil. i. 1.   [2] 1 Tim. iii. 6.

as savouring of a later date. Again the term πρεσβυτέριον[1] implies that the office was consolidated. Provision is also made for the maintenance of church officers[2]. Altogether the tone of these injunctions is inconsistent with the very first stage of the Church before carelessness and insincerity had grown with the growth of its numbers.

Again, the systematic employment of *women* in offices connected with the ministry is another proof of a later date. We read of a deaconess of the Church of Cenchreæ[3], about the time when on the hypothesis of the earlier date the First Epistle to Timothy was written, but with this single exception there is no distinct trace in the other Epistles of St Paul of a special ministry of women. Here on the contrary the deaconesses are a recognised class of officials[4]. The diaconate of women however would not create any serious difficulty. It is more important to observe that 'the widows[5]' also are spoken of as a separate class, specially appointed (καταλεγέσθω) with functions of their own, and spoken of in such a way as to show that the institution had been working for some time.

(*b*) The picture drawn by St Paul of the state of opinion in theological matters tends to the same result—'the endless fables and genealogies,' 'the questionings and battles of words,' 'the profane and vain babblings[6].' The 'oppositions of science so called[7]' must have come to the surface after a long seething of speculation, and betoken the conflict of various elements of philosophical opinion with the Gospel, so that a considerable time is required for their development. Again, if we compare these notices in the Pastoral Epistles with those elsewhere, we arrive at the same conclusion. In the Apostle's farewell address to the Ephesian Elders at Miletus, these irregularities in the Church

[1] 1 Tim. iv. 14.
[2] 1 Tim. v. 17. On the other hand promotion from one office to another is not implied in 1 Tim. iii. 13, as some have supposed (e.g. Blunt, Wordsworth).
[3] Rom. xvi. 1.
[4] 1 Tim. iii. 11.
[5] 1 Tim. v. 3 sq.
[6] 1 Tim. i. 4, iv. 1, vi. 20; 2 Tim. ii. 16; cf. also 2 Tim. ii. 23, iii. 13; Tit. i. 10, iii. 9 sq.
[7] 1 Tim. vi. 20.

of Ephesus are an anticipation, a prophecy; here they are a painful fact. Thirdly, comparing them with the phase of heresy prevalent in these same regions of Asia Minor, as presented in the Epistles to the Colossians and Ephesians, we find that though they have much in common, the latter are an advance upon the former[1]. Whereas in the former no charge of immorality is brought against the false teachers, but on the other hand they are reproved for their strict asceticism, in the Pastorals the heretical spirit is one of profligate, reckless self-seeking. Without pressing the *prophetical* passages[2], this tendency is apparent enough[3]. Now this sequence is natural. Loose and idle speculation, freedom from restraint in matters of opinion, ultimately begets immorality of conduct, for it throws off the sanctions of authority which kept it in check. But all this requires time. Lastly, it should be observed that the heretics of the Pastoral Epistles made a traffic of their false doctrines. They found advantage in vending their wares to foolish purchasers who in turn were interested in being deceived[4]. Now all this militates against a very early date. There is little chance of deceiving and nothing to be gained by it, where all are poor and all honest alike. It is only later that the theological adventurer has any chance and that, having first deceived himself, he finds it worth his while to deceive others[5].

(*c*) We find here and there in the Pastoral Epistles traces of a liturgical form, snatches of hymns, and fragments of creeds or formularies. It will be sufficient to point out one or two of these. They are to be distinguished by their balanced, rhythmical form, as if framed to assist the memory and perhaps to be sung. They are besides introduced in many cases by

---

[1] On the relation of these two heresies see the additional note at the end of this Essay (p. 411 sq.).

[2] 1 Tim. iv. 1 sq.; 2 Tim. iii. 1 sq., iv. 3 sq.

[3] See below, p. 415.

[4] 1 Tim. vi. 5 νομιζόντων πορισμὸν εἶναι τὴν εὐσέβειαν: 2 Tim. iii. 6 αἰχμαλωτίζοντες γυναικάρια σεσωρευμένα ἁμαρτίαις, ἀγόμενα ἐπιθυμίαις ποικίλαις.

[5] 2 Tim. iii. 13.

the formula 'faithful is the saying.' Such are especially 2 Tim. ii. 11 εἰ γὰρ συναπεθάνομεν, καὶ συνζήσομεν κ.τ.λ. and 1 Tim. iii. 16 ὃς ἐφανερώθη ἐν σαρκὶ κ.τ.λ. Now we should perhaps expect to trace the origin of a devotional and ecclesiastical literature back to the close of the Apostolic age, but not much earlier. At first the oral teaching, the communion of soul with soul, 'the spirit and not the letter,' was the paramount, as it always will be the most effectual, mode of instruction; but as the Apostles foresaw their speedy removal from the scene of their labours, it is not unnatural that they should have countenanced efforts of this kind, for the guidance and instruction of the Churches after their death. It is worth observing here, that outside the Pastoral Epistles there is no distinct trace of a liturgical or devotional form of words in St Paul's writings but one. Both the rule and the exception are instructive. The rule shows the practice of the earlier Apostolic age. The exception occurs in the Epistle to the Ephesians[1], probably the latest of St Paul's Epistles antecedent to the Pastorals. It is therefore the first trace of the transition to the fixed form and prepares the way naturally for the phenomena of his latest group of letters.

[1862.]

---

[1] Ephes. v. 14, διὸ λέγει· Ἔγειρε ὁ καθεύδων‖καὶ ἀνάστα ἐκ τῶν νεκρῶν‖ καὶ ἐπιφαύσει σοι ὁ Χριστός. With the expression διὸ λέγει compare the later formula πιστὸς ὁ λόγος.

ADDITIONAL NOTE ON THE HERESY COMBATED
IN THE PASTORAL EPISTLES.

The form of heresy presented to us in the Pastoral Epistles has been much canvassed. Some have recognised in it a Judaism of the extreme Pharisaic type. To others, it has appeared in the directly opposed form of strictly Gentile Gnosis. Some again have traced one form of error in this group of Epistles, while others have discovered as many as four distinct heresies.

It will be necessary to start from a careful examination of the passages in which the false doctrine is alluded to. From the results thus obtained, with the light thrown by the false teaching combated in the Epistle to the Colossians and by the form of heresy known to have prevailed in the age which followed upon the Apostles, we are enabled to draw a tolerably vivid and consistent portrait of this branch of false doctrine.

From the Pastoral Epistles themselves these five characteristics of the heresy are elicited :—

(1)   It was Jewish in its origin, promulgated chiefly by converts from Judaism and maintaining the observance of the law as a fundamental tenet.

Cf. 1 Tim. i. 7, 8 θέλοντες εἶναι νομοδιδάσκαλοι κ.τ.λ., Tit. i. 10 εἰσὶν γὰρ πολλοὶ ἀνυπότακτοι, ματαιολόγοι καὶ φρεναπάται, μάλιστα οἱ ἐκ τῆς περιτομῆς, 14 μὴ προσέχοντες Ἰουδαϊκοῖς μύθοις καὶ ἐντολαῖς ἀνθρώπων, iii. 9 μωρὰς δὲ ζητήσεις καὶ γενεαλογίας καὶ ἔριν καὶ μάχας νομικὰς περιίστασο.

(2)   It vaunted a superior knowledge (γνῶσις) and busied itself in idle speculations. Under this head the three points, on which we may fix attention, are (a) its foolish and profane disputations and combats of words, (b) fables, (c) genealogies.

Cf. 1 Tim. i. 4 προσέχειν μύθοις καὶ γενεαλογίαις ἀπεράντοις αἵτινες ἐκζητήσεις παρέχουσι μᾶλλον ἢ οἰκονομίαν θεοῦ τὴν ἐν πίστει, 6 ἐξετράπησαν εἰς ματαιολογίαν, iv. 7 τοὺς βεβήλους καὶ γραώδεις μύθους, vi. 4 νοσῶν περὶ ζητήσεις καὶ λογομαχίας, 20, 21 ἐκτρεπόμενος τὰς βεβήλους κενοφωνίας καὶ ἀντιθέσεις τῆς ψευδωνύμου γνώσεως κ.τ.λ., 2 Tim. ii. 14 μὴ λογομαχεῖν ἐπ' οὐδὲν χρήσιμον, 16 τὰς βεβήλους κενοφωνίας, 23 μωρὰς καὶ ἀπαιδεύτους ζητήσεις, iv. 4 ἀπὸ μὲν τῆς ἀληθείας τὴν ἀκοὴν ἀποστρέψουσιν ἐπὶ δὲ τοὺς μύθους ἐκτραπήσονται, and Tit. iii. 9 already quoted.   It would seem that in some cases at least this speculation assumed the form of denying the resurrection of the dead (2 Tim. ii. 18).

(3)   Its adherents practised mysterious or magical rites. They are spoken of as wizards.

Cf. 2 Tim. iii. 13 πονηροὶ ἄνθρωποι καὶ γόητες, to which perhaps we may refer 1 Tim. iv. 1 προσέχοντες πνεύμασι πλάνοις καὶ διδασκαλίαις δαιμονίων.

(4)   There was a strongly ascetic tendency in their teaching. Marriage was forbidden, and they distinguished between meats clean and unclean.

Cf. 1 Tim. iv. 3 κωλυόντων γαμεῖν, ἀπέχεσθαι βρωμάτων, 8 ἡ σωματικὴ γυμνασία πρὸς ὀλίγον ἐστὶν ὠφέλιμος, Tit. i. 15 πάντα καθαρὰ τοῖς καθαροῖς κ.τ.λ.

(5)   In character they were corrupt, deceitful and selfseeking.

Cf. 1 Tim. iv. 2 κεκαυστηριασμένων τὴν ἰδίαν συνείδησιν, vi. 5 διαπαρατριβαὶ διεφθαρμένων ἀνθρώπων τὸν νοῦν καὶ ἀπεστερημένων τῆς ἀληθείας, νομιζόντων πορισμὸν εἶναι τὴν εὐσέβειαν, 2 Tim. iii. 6, 8 ἐνδύνοντες εἰς τὰς οἰκίας...ἀνθίστανται τῇ ἀληθείᾳ ἄνθρωποι κατεφθαρμένοι τὸν νοῦν, ἀδόκιμοι περὶ τὴν πίστιν, iv. 3 κατὰ τὰς ἰδίας ἐπιθυμίας ἑαυτοῖς ἐπισωρεύσουσιν διδασκάλους κνηθόμενοι τὴν ἀκοήν, Tit. i. 16 θεὸν ὁμολογοῦσιν εἰδέναι, τοῖς δὲ ἔργοις ἀρνοῦνται, βδελυκτοὶ ὄντες καὶ ἀπειθεῖς καὶ πρὸς πᾶν ἔργον ἀγαθὸν ἀδόκιμοι.

In this enumeration I have made two assumptions. *First*, that all the passages refer to one and the same heresy. Now there is nothing in the Epistles themselves from which to infer that distinct forms were contemplated. The characteristic elements, which I have elicited, do not refuse to combine, and, strange as the resulting compound may appear to modern habits of thought, it was in one guise or another a common phenomenon when Oriental mysticism and Greek thought came in contact for the first time with the ordinances of the law and the spiritual truths of the Gospel. On the other hand, it would be anticipating history to regard the heresy as having assumed a definite creed or a distinct organisation. Floating speculation, vague theories, coalescing gradually to a greater consistency and tending more or less in one direction—this, and not more than this, we are at liberty to assume at the date of the Pastoral Epistles.   Indeed the phenomena do not justify more.

Secondly, I have drawn my deductions not less from the prophetical warnings than from the historical statements. Whoever will read these predictions in connexion with their context will see that they are but a declaration of the inevitable consequences to which the spiritual insight of the Apostle foresaw the irregularities of the present would lead, that in fact these irregularities were in themselves the beginning of the end.

Now, combining these features together, we obtain a portrait of an early phase of *Jewish Gnosticism*, very similar in character to, but more advanced and definite than, that which appears in the Epistles to the Colossians and Ephesians. The later date appears in the directions for dealing with the heretics, pointing to them as recognisable enemies to be treated as such (e.g. Tit. iii. 10 αἱρετικὸν ἄνθρωπον...παραιτοῦ).

On a previous occasion[1] I devoted some time to the study of the origin and character of Gnosticism; it will therefore suffice to recapitulate as briefly as possible some of the most important points arrived at, as serving to explain the allusions in the Pastoral Epistles. The three notes of Gnosticism were found to be (1) its intellectual exclusiveness; (2) certain speculative tenets chiefly relating to the creation of the world and the existence of evil, creation being accounted for by the doctrine of emanations, the existence of evil by postulating matter as an antagonistic principle independent of God; (3) as a practical consequence of these speculations, a twofold and divergent result upon the ethical systems of their advocates, either rigid asceticism, or unrestrained licence. I proceeded to point out distinct traces of all these three characteristics of Gnosticism in the heresy portrayed in the Epistle to the Colossians. St Paul is there confronting false opinion itself; he argues against it directly, and opposes to it the truths of the Gospel. Consequently from that Epistle we get a fuller conception of its general principles and bearing. Here the case is different. St Paul is writing to a friend, and instructing him to deal practically with the question. No lengthy exposition is necessary, nor would such be in place. It is from a single word here and there—a descriptive epithet or attribute—that we gather the character of the heresy in the Pastoral Epistles. But these notes are significant enough when we get the key to their interpretation; and with the light of the Colossian Epistle thrown on the previous era and the light of the heresiologists on the succeeding, we are at no loss to elucidate the intermediate stage in the progress of the error. The heresy in both cases has its root on the same ground, in Asia Minor, the fittest meeting-point of Oriental mysticism, of Greek thought, of Judaism,

[1] See *Colossians*, p. 73 sq., esp. pp. 76—80.

and of Christianity. It is evidently the same in most of its features, though, as was natural, in the earlier Epistle the picture given us is fuller, the canvas broader, but on the other hand, the individual features of the landscape are less clearly marked.

1. With respect to the esoteric spirit, the intellectualism of Gnosticism.

The phase of heresy in the Pastoral Epistles is an advance on that exhibited in the Colossians. 'Knowledge' is in the Colossian Epistle a favourite word with the false teachers, a word constantly on their lips; but it has not yet become the watchword of the sect. In these later Epistles, we find it as a distinct title, adopted by them and vaunted as peculiarly their own (1 Tim. vi. 20 τῆς ψευδω-νύμου γνώσεως). We may compare also the antithesis between knowledge and faith implied in 1 Tim. i. 4 αἵτινες ἐκζητήσεις παρέ-χουσι μᾶλλον ἢ οἰκονομίαν θεοῦ τὴν ἐν πίστει. Perhaps the emphatic declaration of the universality of the Gospel (1 Tim. ii. 4–6) is a protest against this intellectual aristocracy in religion. From this intellectualism arose those questionings, vain-talkings and combats of words, which the Apostle so frequently and so severely rebukes.

2. Again, in the speculative theories which characterize the Gnostic system—especially as regards the doctrine of emanations—we have an advance upon the γνῶσις of the Colossian Epistle. There the emanation of angels, the mediation of superior essences, appears in a vague, shadowy form (Col. ii. 18 θρησκείᾳ τῶν ἀγγέλων). Here it has assumed a definite shape. The 'genealogies' are mentioned twice over (1 Tim. i. 4, Tit. iii. 9), in the former passage with the epithet 'endless' (ἀπέραντοι). The term certainly does not explain itself, but by the light of the later Gnostic systems it becomes clear enough. It refers to the successive generations of æons, or emanations from the *pleroma*, which occupy so important a place in the speculations, for instance, of the Ophites and Valentinians. To the Apostle they are but tiresome pedigrees. To the same feature in Gnosticism may be referred the expression 'fables' or 'myths.' No term would better express the manner in which the Gnostics embodied these speculations, representing them in the concrete form of stories, as nobler teachers, like Plato, had done before them. There may be a reference to these false mediators in the emphatic declaration of the one, only mediator in 1 Tim. ii. 5, and perhaps also to the dualistic tendencies of the heresy in the doxology of 1 Tim. i. 17 (μόνῳ θεῷ).

These theories respecting the invisible world, proceeding from, or at least fostered by, a love of the marvellous, found a practical expression in mystic or magical rites, the common refuge of oriental superstition. Hence the Apostle says that these heretics were misled by 'doctrines of devils' (1 Tim. iv. 1), and calls them 'wizards,' 'enchanters' (2 Tim. iii. 13).

3.   We saw that in the case of the Colossian heretics the doctrine that matter was the source of evil led to the nobler of the two extremes, a rigid asceticism. In this earlier stage there is no trace of immorality. In the Pastoral Epistles, however, we find that we are on the confines of a new development of Gnostic ethics. It is true the ascetic theory still prevails. This asceticism, as in the case of the Colossians, is partly based on the Mosaic law, partly independent of, and contrary to, the spirit of Judaism. Of the former class is the abstaining from meats (1 Tim. iv. 3), though doubtless it went beyond the Mosaic distinction of meats clean and unclean ; of the latter the prohibition of marriage (*ib.*), a tenet of many of the Gnostic sects. Having debarred themselves from the lawful use of God's creatures under the idea of keeping themselves clean from the contamination of matter, they fell into vices of another kind. Avarice, selfishness and deceit are their prevailing sins (see esp. 1 Tim. vi. 5).

But there are besides this traces, more or less distinct, of the opposite extreme, deduced from the Gnostic principle—a reckless sensuality, an indulgence in profligate habits themselves and a pandering to the vices of others (Tit. i. 16, 2 Tim. iii. 6). The wild and unbridled profligacy of some of the later Gnostic sects is a constant theme of reproach with the writers of the Church. In the Pastoral Epistles we discern only the first beginnings of this tendency, which is spoken of as future rather than present, having hitherto, it seems, manifested itself only in a few.

All the later Gnostic sects were essentially anti-Judaic ; but this is not the case with the earlier forms of Gnosis. Arising as it did from an oriental mysticism, it took up its sojourn first in Judaism and Judaic Christendom, with which it came in contact first. But it was only by violent wresting and distortion that the teaching of the Old Testament could be brought into any sort of fellowship with the Gnosis. The fundamental principle of the Old Testament, the immediate and direct control of the supreme Lord over the material world and over the affairs of men, was diametrically opposed to the fundamental principle of Gnosticism, which was dualism in some form or other. The whole spirit of the Mosaic legislation, the high honour in which marriage was held, especially, was a protest equally against the asceticism and the unbridled profligacy of the two extremes of Gnostic practice.   Thus Gnosticism soon found that it was unequally yoked with Judaic Christianity, and betook itself to a more congenial, or at least a less impracticable, companionship in Gentile Christendom.   Here at all events it was not fettered by any allegiance to the Mosaic dispensation.   So it severed its connexion with the Old Covenant, and assumed a position of direct antagonism to Judaism.

But the earlier forms of Gnosticism are all, or nearly all, Judaic.   The uses which it made of Judaism were twofold—both of them abuses.

(1) The narrative of the Old Testament, its antiquity and its supernatural element, yielded a rich harvest for mystic application. The real significance of this narrative, as the history of the progressive dealings of God with man, was entirely lost sight of.

(2) The ordinances, especially with reference to clean and unclean things, were made a starting-point for asceticism.   It is needless to say that in this their spirit was entirely misapprehended. They were intended to serve as a disciplinary training.   They were perverted into a condemnation of God's creatures.

Speaking then of the heresy of the later Epistles with reference to its position in the Gnostic systems, we may call it *Judaic Gnosticism*.   Speaking of it with reference to its position as a phase of Jewish thought, we may call it *Essene Judaism*.

Having thus drawn the portrait of this heresy, the infancy of which we trace in the Epistles of the First Roman Captivity, and the early childhood in the Pastoral letters, we are led to enquire whether it corresponds to any form of error of which we have a historical record.

The discovery of the treatise of Hippolytus on heresies has thrown great light on this, as on many other points in early Church History.   First in the series of his heresies, before Simon Magus, before Cerinthus, he places the *Ophites* or *Naasenes*, so called from the fact that the serpent (ὄφις נָחָשׁ) was the symbol of their worship (Hippol. *Refut.* v. 6, p. 132 *ed*. Duncker et Schneid. οἱ οὖν ἱερεῖς καὶ προστάται τοῦ δόγματος γεγένηνται πρῶτοι οἱ ἐπικληθέντες Ναασσηνοί, τῇ Ἑβραΐδι φωνῇ οὕτως ὠνομασμένοι· νάας δὲ ὁ ὄφις καλεῖται).   His order is generally chronological, interrupted now and then to keep the same knot of heresies together.   We may therefore assume that the origin of the Ophites was contemporaneous with the Apostles. On the other hand, in the documents of the sect, which he quotes largely, we find citations from the Gospel of St John, and perhaps traces of the influence of Gnostic speculations of the second century. We must not therefore suppose that he presents the original form of the heresy. It is evident that later accretions have gathered about it.

Now as to this heresy we have the following facts from Hippolytus.

(1) It took its rise, or flourished chiefly, in Phrygia. It delighted especially in the Phrygian rites of Cybele (p. 170 παρεδρεύουσι τοῖς λεγομένοις Μητρὸς μεγάλης μυστηρίοις), and Phrygian legends are referred to frequently in the books of the sect (e.g. p. 154 τοῦτον Θρᾷκες Κορύβαντα καλοῦσι καὶ Θραξὶν οἱ Φρύγες παραπλησίως, p. 156 τοῦτον Φρύγες καὶ Πάπαν καλοῦσι, p. 160 οὗτος ὑπὸ τῶν Φρυγῶν καὶ ἄκαρπος καλεῖται, p. 162 λέγουσι δὲ αὐτὸν Φρύγες καὶ χλοερὸν στάχυν τεθερισμένον, etc.).

(2) It was Jewish. The name 'Naasene' indicates this. The Ophites professed to derive their Gnosis from James the Lord's brother (p. 134 ταῦτα ἐστί...τὰ κεφάλαια ἃ φησὶ παραδεδωκέναι Μαριάμνῃ τὸν Ἰάκωβον τοῦ Κυρίου τὸν ἀδελφόν). Some of their mystical formulæ were derived from the Hebrew of the Old Testament (p. 150 καυλακαῦ σαυλασαῦ ζεησάρ : cf. Is. xxviii. 10).

(3) They called themselves 'Gnostics.' Indeed Hippolytus seems to imply that they were the first to assume that name (see esp. p. 132 μετὰ δὲ ταῦτα ἐπεκάλεσαν ἑαυτοὺς γνωστικοὺς φάσκοντες μόνοι τὰ βάθη γινώσκειν : cf. p. 160 οἱ γνωστικοὶ τέλειοι, p. 176 τὰ κεκρυμμένα τῆς ἁγίας ὁδοῦ γνῶσιν καλέσας).

(4) They dealt largely in mystic rites. The mysteries of Osiris (p. 142 l. 11), of the Assyrians (p. 140 l. 90), of Samothrace (p. 152 l. 80), of Eleusis (p. 146 l. 80, p. 162 l. 58), but especially, as remarked before, of the Phrygian Cybele, all contributed their quota to the Ophite system. We may believe that many of these were incorporated at a later date into their system, to give a comprehensiveness and universality to it; and that originally it dealt with the Old Testament chiefly or solely, putting a mystical sense upon it. Thus the Apostle might well refer to them the term γόητες.

(5) As the whole of Hippolytus' account shows, they taught by myths (e.g. p. 134 ὅθεν αὐτοῖς οὗτος ὁ μῦθος).

(6) They forbad marriage (p. 170 παραγγέλλουσιν ἀπέχεσθαι ὡς ἀποκεκομμένοι τῆς πρὸς γυναῖκα ὁμιλίας).

(7) They maintained that the resurrection was a spiritual resurrection, i.e. they said in other words that the resurrection was past (p. 158 ἐξαλοῦνται ἐκ τῶν μνημείων οἱ νεκροὶ τουτέστιν ἐκ τῶν σωμάτων τῶν χοϊκῶν ἀναγεννηθέντες πνευματικοὶ οὐ σαρκικοί, and the whole passage).

(8) Though the genealogies referred to by St Paul are not so distinctly traced in the Ophite system, as painted by Hippolytus, as in later Gnostic sects, still there are evidences of these. Compare especially the hymn, which, as Hippolytus says, contains a summary of all their mysteries (p. 174 νόμος ἦν γενικὸς τοῦ παντὸς ὁ πρῶτος νόος· ὁ δὲ δεύτερος ἦν κ.τ.λ.). And other accounts of the Ophites are very full on this characteristic of the sect (cf. Neander *Ch. Hist.* ii. p. 109 Engl. transl. *ed.* Torrey).

There is therefore sufficient correspondence between the two systems to enable us to conclude that the heresy combated by St Paul in the Pastoral Epistles was identical with the heresy of the Ophites, or at least partook largely of an Ophite character.

[1865.]

XII.

ST PAUL'S HISTORY AFTER THE CLOSE OF THE ACTS.

Printed from Lecture-notes.

XII.

ST PAUL'S HISTORY AFTER THE CLOSE OF THE ACTS.

THE conclusion, at which we have arrived in the last section, assumes St Paul's release from his captivity at Rome. We must suppose that he resumed his active missionary labours, and that these were terminated by a second captivity ending in his martyrdom, of which the Second Epistle to Timothy sounds the knell. In the present section it will be my business, *first*, to show that there are sufficient grounds independently for assuming this release, and *secondly*, considering this as established, to sketch out his movements by the help of the record in the Pastoral Epistles.

I. Of this release, with the subsequent events, there is no intimation in the New Testament beyond the notices in the Pastoral Epistles which seem to demand it. In the memoir of St Luke there is not the slightest intimation of the future. The Epistles of the First Roman Captivity hover between hope and fear, between anticipation of release and forebodings of condemnation. They contain nothing which leads directly to the result we are seeking.

One passage indeed has been adduced as conclusive against a subsequent visit of St Paul to Ephesus; and as, by surrendering this visit, we should be surrendering all the advantages gained by the assumption of his release, and should be thrown back upon our difficulties with respect to the Pastoral Epistles, it is important to consider what is the value of this argument. St Paul in his farewell address to the Ephesian Elders on the eve of the First Captivity, says[1], 'And now, behold, I know that ye all, among whom I have gone preaching the kingdom of God, shall see my face no more.' This is supposed to be inconsistent with a later visit to Ephesus, and *pro tanto* with his release from captivity. But in no other province of history would it be allowable to convert a presentiment, however strongly expressed, into a fact; and as this is purely a personal matter, inspiration does not enter into the question. A presumption might indeed have been founded on this expression, if no intimation existed of a release; but the notices in the Pastoral Epistles to the contrary are in themselves more than sufficient to set this presumption aside. Then again, in what infinite difficulties does this supposition involve us! To the Romans he says; 'I will pass by you into Spain[2].' This however, it may be said, was before the conviction (or the revelation) declared to the Ephesian elders had seized him. What are we to say of the expressions scattered through the Epistles of the First Captivity? Why does he waver between hope and fear, if the fatal result was certain? Why does he entreat the prayers of his converts for his release, if he knew that release to be absolutely impossible? Writing to the Philippians he says that he trusts in the Lord, that he himself also will come shortly[3]. Nay, he even affirms positively that he will be released. 'Having this confidence,' he says, 'I know (τοῦτο πεποιθὼς οἶδα) that I shall abide and continue with you all[4].' Why is the οἶδα to be regarded as decisive in the one case, and disregarded in the other? But it may be urged that the supposed revelation did not negative his release *in toto*, that it is limited, that it referred only to his revisiting these Churches of Asia Minor. To this too St Paul's own language furnishes a reply. He bids Philemon 'prepare him a lodging' at Colossæ, he 'trusts that through their prayers he

---

[1] Acts xx. 25 καὶ νῦν ἰδοὺ ἐγὼ οἶδα ὅτι οὐκέτι ὄψεσθε τὸ πρόσωπόν μου ὑμεῖς πάντες.

[2] Rom. xv. 28.

[3] Phil. ii. 24.

[4] Phil. i. 25.

shall be given unto them¹'—language which he could not have
held, if he had had a revelation to the contrary. And if here
again it be urged that he might have gone to Colossæ without
revisiting the neighbouring Church of Ephesus, to this we
should reply, *firstly*, that when the inference from οἶδα is pared
down to these dimensions, we have obtained such a concession
as will explain the notices in the Pastoral Epistles, for, though
a visit to Ephesus is much more probable, a visit to the
neighbourhood would suffice; and *secondly*, that it will be felt
that so limited an inference is meaningless, and of course valueless to those who refuse to allow the release of St Paul.

But though the New Testament, with the single exception
of the Pastoral Epistles, is silent about this release, it is most
satisfactorily established from external tradition.

CLEMENT OF ROME [† c. A.D. 96], a contemporary of the
Apostles, after mentioning several incidents in St Paul's life,
and saying that he had preached in the East and the West,
adds that he was 'a teacher of righteousness unto the whole
world', and, before his decease 'reached the furthest bounds of
the West and bore testimony before the ruling powers' (ἐπὶ τὸ
τέρμα τῆς δύσεως ἐλθὼν καὶ μαρτυρήσας ἐπὶ τῶν ἡγουμένων).
Considering that Clement was writing from Rome, and bearing
in mind the common significance of the expression 'the extreme
West'² at the time, as referring to the Pillars of Hercules³, we

¹ Philemon 22.

² For the expression, referring to
the western extremity of Spain, the
pillars of Hercules, comp. Strabo ii. 1
(p. 67) πέρατα δὲ αὐτῆς (τῆς οἰκουμένης)
τίθησι πρὸς δύσει μὲν τὰς Ἡρακλείους
στήλας, ii. 4 (p. 106) μέχρι τῶν ἄκρων
τῆς Ἰβηρίας ἅπερ δυσμικώτερά ἐστι, iii.
1 (p. 137) τοῦτό (τὸ ἱερὸν ἀκρωτήριον)
ἐστι τὸ δυτικώτατον οὐ τῆς Εὐρώπης μόνον
ἀλλὰ καὶ τῆς οἰκουμένης ἁπάσης σημεῖον·
περατοῦται γὰρ ὑπὸ τῶν δυεῖν ἠπείρων ἡ
οἰκουμένη πρὸς δύσιν, τοῖς τε τῆς Εὐρώπης ἄκροις καὶ τοῖς πρώτοις τῆς Λιβύης,
iii. 5 (p. 169) ἐπειδὴ κατὰ τὸν πορθμὸν
ἐγένοντο τὸν κατὰ τὴν Κάλπην, νομίσαν-

τας τέρμονας εἶναι τῆς οἰκουμένης...τὰ
ἄκρα, *ib.* (p. 170) ζητεῖν ἐπὶ τῶν κυρίως λε-
γομένων στηλῶν τοὺς τῆς οἰκουμένης ὅρους
(these references are corrected from
Credner's *Kanon*, p. 53), and see Strabo's whole account of the western
boundaries of the world and of this
coast of Spain. Similarly Vell. Paterc.
i. 2, 'In ultimo Hispaniae tractu, in
extremo nostri orbis termino.'

³ It is instructive to mention some
interpretations by which the force of
these words has been evaded: (1) 'to
his extreme limit towards the west,
(Baur *Paulus der Apost.* p. 230, Schen-
kel *Studien und Kritiken* p. 71, Otto

can scarcely be wrong in concluding that St Paul was released from captivity and fulfilled his purpose, expressed years before, of visiting Spain[1].

It might be urged indeed that Clement has here the passage in the Epistle to the Romans in his mind, and that he assumes the intention was carried out. But seeing that at least one of the facts mentioned in the context—the Apostle's seven captivities ($\dot{\epsilon}\pi\tau\acute{a}\kappa\iota\varsigma$ $\delta\epsilon\sigma\mu\grave{a}$ $\phi o\rho\acute{\epsilon}\sigma a\varsigma$)—is not recorded in the New Testament, he must be deriving his information from independent sources, as indeed, living at Rome and having perhaps known the Apostle personally, he was very competent to do. And it may be argued further that this fact obliges us to prolong the Apostle's labours beyond the captivity with which the Acts closes.

2. Two generations later (c. A.D. 180), the anonymous writer of the MURATORIAN CANON gives the following account of the Acts of the Apostles. 'Luke comprises in detail in his treatise addressed to the most excellent Theophilus the incidents in the lives of the Apostles of which he was an eye-witness. As he does not mention either the martyrdom of Peter, or the journey of Paul to Spain, it is clear that these took place in his absence[2].'

Pastoralbr.) taking the word subjectively, (2) 'the sunset of his labours' (Reuss *Gesch. des N. T. Schrift.* p. 124) explaining metaphorically, (3) 'to the boundary between the East and West' (Hilgenfeld *Ap. Vät.* p. 109, Schrader *Paulus*), (4) 'to the goal or centre of the west' (Matthies *Pastoralbr.*), (5) 'before ($\dot{v}\pi\grave{o}$ for $\dot{\epsilon}\pi\acute{\iota}$) the supreme power of the west' (Wieseler *Chron. der ap. Zeitalt.* p. 533, followed by Schaff *History of Apost. Ch.* I. p. 400). Such attempts are a strong testimony to the plain inference which follows from the passage simply interpreted. Had the expression been $\dot{\epsilon}\pi\grave{\iota}$ $\tau\grave{a}$ $\tau\acute{\epsilon}\rho\mu a\tau a$ $\tau o\hat{v}$ $\kappa\acute{o}\sigma\mu o\upsilon$, it might be explained (as Meyer proposes) as a rhetorical exag-

geration, but not as it stands. [See the notes on the passage in *Apostolic Fathers*, Pt. I. Vol. II. p. 30 *ed.* 2, from which the above are expanded.]

[1] It has been urged (e.g. by Davidson *Introd.* II. p. 101 *ed.* 1) that Clement cannot have meant this, because in that case Eusebius (*H. E.* iii. 4) would certainly have adduced the passage, which he does not. To this the reply is twofold: (1) that all arguments drawn from the silence of a writer are in the highest degree precarious; and (2) that we are quite as competent to judge what Clement meant, as Eusebius was.

[2] 'Lucas obtime Theofile (*l.* optimo Theophilo) comprindit, quia (*l.*

3. EUSEBIUS speaks of St Paul's release and second visit to Rome, which ended in his martyrdom, as a common report (λόγος ἔχει)[1]. It is true that he goes on to confirm this report by a false interpretation of 2 Tim. iv. 16, explaining the two apologies there mentioned of the Apostle's two captivities; but the worthlessness of his own comment does not affect the value of the tradition on which it is founded, and which must be held quite distinct[2].

4. In his Epistle to Dracontius, ATHANASIUS holds up for imitation the earnestness of the Apostle of the Gentiles, whose zeal prompted him 'to preach as far as Illyricum, and not to hesitate to go even to Rome, nor to take ship for Spain, so that the more he laboured the greater reward he might receive for his labour[3].'

5. CYRIL OF JERUSALEM, in his second catechetical lecture upon the Holy Spirit, adduces as a witness of the power of the Spirit St Paul's conversion, and his missionary labours, which he names in the following significant order, Jerusalem, Illyricum, Rome, Spain[4].

---

quae) sub praesentia eius singula gerebantur sicuti et semote passionem Petri evidenter declarat, sed et profectionem Pauli ab urbe ad Spaniam proficiscentis, *Fragm. Murat.* (pp. 19, 40 *ed.* Tregelles Oxon. 1867; Westcott *Hist. of Canon* pp. 517, 528 *ed.* 4). The drift of the latter part of the sentence seems to have been generally misunderstood. I take 'semote' to be opposed to 'sub praesentia eius,' in the sense 'at a distance,' 'in his absence.' Other solutions, either in the way of interpretation or of correction of the text, may be found in Routh *R. S.* p. 394, Bunsen *Anal. Antenic.* I. p. 125, Westcott p. 528, Credner *Kanon* p. 141 (*ed.* 1860) and Wieseler *Chron.* p. 536.

[1] Eus. *H. E.* ii. 22, τότε μὲν οὖν ἀπολογησάμενον αὖθις ἐπὶ τὴν τοῦ κηρύγματος διακονίαν λόγος ἔχει στείλασθαι τὸν ἀπόστολον, δεύτερον δ᾽ ἐπιβάντα τῇ

αὐτῇ πόλει τῷ κατ᾽ αὐτὸν τελειωθῆναι μαρτυρίῳ.

[2] Meyer's inference (on Romans *Einl.* § 1, p. 15) from Origen's silence that he was ignorant of this release is quite arbitrary. At least it did not strike Eusebius so, who quotes Origen in the following words: Τί δεῖ περὶ Παύλου λέγειν ἀπὸ Ἱερουσαλὴμ μέχρι τοῦ Ἰλλυρικοῦ πεπληρωκότος τὸ εὐαγγέλιον τοῦ Χριστοῦ, καὶ ὕστερον ἐν τῇ Ῥώμῃ ἐπὶ Νέρωνος μεμαρτυρηκότος; (*H. E.* iii. 1).

[3] Athanas. *Ep. ad Dracont.* § 4, I. p. 265 *ed.* Bened. διὰ τοῦτο καὶ σπουδὴ τῶν ἁγίων (l. τῷ ἁγίῳ) μέχρι τοῦ Ἰλλυρικοῦ κηρύττειν καὶ μὴ ὀκνεῖν μηδὲ εἰς τὴν Ῥώμην ἀπελθεῖν, μηδὲ εἰς τὰς Σπανίας ἀναβῆναι, ἵνα ὅσον κοπιᾷ τοσοῦτον καὶ τοῦ κόπου τὸν μισθὸν μείζονα ἀπολάβῃ.

[4] Cyrill. Hier. *Catech.* xvii. pp. 276, 7, ἀπὸ Ἱεροσολύμων μὲν καὶ μέχρι τοῦ Ἰλλυρικοῦ πεπληρωκότα τὸ εὐαγγέλιον·

6. EPIPHANIUS, in the account which he gives of the succession of the episcopate at Rome, explains his theory of the appointment of Linus, Cletus and Clement as bishops in the lifetime of the Apostles Peter and Paul by the frequent journeys which the Apostles had to take from Rome, and the impossibility of leaving the city without a bishop. 'For Paul,' he says, ' even went as far away as Spain, and Peter was frequently superintending Pontus and Bithynia[1].'

7. JEROME appeals to the testimony of older writers in support of his statement of St Paul's release from his first imprisonment, which was arranged in God's providence 'that so he might preach the gospel of Christ in the West also[2].'

8. THEODORE OF MOPSUESTIA speaks in the plainest way of St Paul's two visits to Rome in the reign of Nero. After relating how he was sent as prisoner there on his appeal from Festus, he goes on to say that he was ' set free by the judgment of Nero and ordered to depart in safety. But after stopping two years at Rome, he departed thence and appears to have preached to many the teaching of godliness. However, coming a second time to Rome, while still stopping there, it happened that by the sentence of Nero he was punished with death for his preaching of godliness[3].' The passage is somewhat obscure owing to its survival in the Latin version only.

9. When we come down to the time of PELAGIUS, we find the release from the first imprisonment generally main-

---

κατηχήσοντα δὲ καὶ τὴν βασιλίδα Ῥώμην καὶ μέχρι Σπανίας τὴν προθυμίαν τοῦ κηρύγματος ἐκτείναντα.

[1] Epiphan. *Haer.* XXVII. p. 107 *ed.* Pet. ὁ μὲν γὰρ Παῦλος καὶ ἐπὶ τὴν Σπανίαν ἀφικνεῖται, Πέτρος δὲ πολλάκις Πόντον τε καὶ Βιθυνίαν ἐνεσκέψατο.

[2] Hieron. *de Eccles. Script.* §5, Vol. II. p. 823 *ed.* Vallarsi, 'Sciendum autem in prima satisfactione, necdum Neronis imperio roborato, nec in tanta erumpente scelera, quanta de eo narrant historiae, Paulum a Nerone dimissum, ut evangelium Christi in

occidentis quoque partibus praedicaret'; cf. *Comm. in Amos* v. 8, 9 Vol. VI. p. 291.

[3] Theod. Mops. *Argum. in Eph.* I. p. 116 *ed.* Swete, 'Inde judicio Neronis liberatus, securus abire jussus est. duobus vero annis commoratus Romae, exinde egressus, multis pietatis doctrinam praedicasse visus est. secunda vero vice Romam accedens dum illo adhuc moraretur, contigit ut sententia Neronis ob praedicationem pietatis capite puniretur.'

tained. Commenting on the Apostle's request to Philemon 'to prepare him a lodging,' he says: 'Here it is shown that on the first occasion he was sent away from the city'; though of the journey to Spain he speaks more doubtfully[1].

10. THEODORET, commenting on the Apostle's expression of confidence addressed to his Philippian converts that he would abide and continue with them, remarks: 'and the prediction was fulfilled; for at first he escaped the wrath of Nero.' Then, after quoting the passage in 2 Tim. iv. 16, 17, and appealing to the last verses in the Acts, he continues: 'Thence (i.e. from Rome) he departed to Spain, and carried the divine gospel to the inhabitants of that part also, and so he returned, and was then beheaded[2].' Other references to his release and visit to Spain are given below.

On the statements of Eusebius and later writers however no stress should be laid. Even if it were clear that they relied on some independent testimony, and did not found their belief on deductions—in some cases erroneous deductions—from St Paul's own language, they are too far removed from the time of the events to be of any real value as guides. With Clement and the author of the Muratorian fragment the case is different. The former wrote from Rome, at a place where and at a time when the memory of the Apostle's labours was fresh, and his testimony is explicit, so far as relates to St Paul's preaching in the West. The latter, though living at a later period, is a witness of some importance, for he too was probably a Roman[3], and he distinctly attests the journey to Spain. Indeed, so irre-

---

[1] Pelagius Comm. in Philemon v. 22, 'hic ostenditur quia prima vice sit ex urbe dimissus'; in Rom. xv. 24, 'utrum in Hispania fuerit incertum habetur.'

[2] Theodoret Comm. in Phil. i. 25, Vol. III. p. 451 ed. Schulze, καὶ τέλος ἡ πρόρρησις ἔλαβε· διέφυγε γὰρ τὸ πρῶτον τοῦ Νέρωνος τὸν θυμόν... ἐκεῖθεν δὲ εἰς τὰς Σπανίας ἀπελθών, καὶ τὸ θεῖον κἀκείνοις προσενεγκὼν εὐαγγέλιον ἐπανῆλθε, καὶ τότε τὴν κεφαλὴν ἀπετμήθη:

in Ps. cxvi. Vol. I. p. 1425, ὕστερον μέντοι καὶ τῆς Ἰταλίας ἐπέβη, καὶ εἰς τὰς Σπανίας ἀφίκετο, καὶ ταῖς ἐν τῷ πελάγει διακειμέναις νήσοις τὴν ὠφέλειαν προσήνεγκε: in 2 Tim. iv. 17, ἀπολογισάμενος ὡς ἀθῶος ἀφείθη καὶ τὰς Σπανίας κατέλαβε καὶ εἰς ἕτερα ἔθνη δραμὼν τὴν τῆς διδασκαλίας λαμπάδα προσήνεγκε.

[3] His use of the expression 'ab urbe,' referring to Rome, shows this.

sistible has this evidence appeared to impartial critics, that the release has been accepted as a fact by many writers who cannot be suspected of any bias towards this result—by Hug, for instance, who places the Pastoral Epistles earlier in St Paul's life, and by Ewald, who denies their genuineness entirely.

But it has been urged that, though there is evidence for the journey to Spain after the Apostle's release, there is none for another visit to the East. This is true, if the notices in the Pastorals themselves are not to be put in evidence; but even then, how does the case stand? St Paul, while still a prisoner but anticipating his release, expresses his intention of visiting the Philippians again, and writes to Philemon at Colossæ to prepare him a lodging. He does obtain his release. In the absence of evidence either way, is it not more probable that he did fulfil his intention of visiting Macedonia and Asia than the contrary?

II. Assuming then that St Paul was released from his first captivity at Rome and resumed his missionary labours, we shall have to sketch in the events which took place between this date and his final imprisonment, from the notices in the Pastoral Epistles, aided by such probabilities as circumstances suggest. If an intelligible and reasonable account of St Paul's doings during this interval can thus be given, we shall have found a possible place for the Pastoral Epistles, and shall have furnished an answer to objections raised from the point of view of historical unaccountability; and, in the absence of full and direct information, nothing more than this hypothetical solution can be expected.

Before entering into details, however, we must clear the way by settling two main questions; *first,* what was the probable length of this interval; and, *secondly,* supposing that St Paul visited both East and West, in what order did he make these journeys.

(1) According to the chronology I have adopted[1], St Paul arrived in Rome early in the year 61. The closing verses of

---

[1] See above, pp. 217 sq., 222.

the Acts speak of his remaining there without any change in the circumstances of his captivity for two whole years[1]. This brings us to the beginning of the year 63 at least. Here St Luke's narrative ends abruptly; so that we are without information as to what occurred afterwards, but the natural inference is that at the end of the two years there was a change in the prisoner's condition—a change either for the better or for the worse, but a change of some sort. Perhaps the most probable supposition is that his trial came on then. If so, we may place his release not later than the summer of 63, at all events it must have taken place between that date and the summer of the following year, for the great fire which broke out in July 64 was a signal for a fierce persecution of the Christians in Rome, and a teacher of the hated religion so zealous and so distinguished could not have escaped the general fate, had he still remained a prisoner.

The data for determining the close of the period are still more vague. Ecclesiastical tradition fixes the martyrdom of St Paul in Nero's reign, and this is probable in itself, for, after the tyrant's death, the Romans were too much occupied with their own political troubles to pay any attention to the Christians, even supposing the succeeding emperors were animated by the same bitter spirit. It cannot therefore have been later than June 68, the date of Nero's death. Now, when we examine the Pastoral Epistles with a view to obtaining some result, opposing considerations present themselves. On the one hand, their marked difference in style leads us to prolong the interval between them and the earlier Epistles as far as possible, while on the other hand the mention of Timothy's youth is an ever-increasing difficulty as we postpone the date of the letters addressed to him. On the whole, perhaps, the later consideration must give place to the former. The death of the Apostle will then be placed at the very close of Nero's reign, and the Pastoral Epistles will have been written in the year 67 or 68.

[1] Acts xxviii. 30, 31.

(2) Next, as to the order in which St Paul visited the East and West. On the whole, it is probable that he went eastward immediately after his release. It is true that he had intended, when he first thought of visiting Rome, to proceed thence westward to Spain[1]. But circumstances might have occurred in the intervening period of about five years to alter his purpose and determine him to revisit the troubled Churches of Asia, before he entered on a new mission field in the far West. Such is the impression left by his language to the Philippians and to Philemon[2].

But if it is probable that St Paul was in the East immediately after his release, it is certain that he was there towards the very close of his life. The notices of his transactions in the East scattered through the Pastoral Epistles reach continuously to the time of his second imprisonment at Rome, which ended in his death. If this be so, the visit to Spain and the West must have intervened between two visits to the East. For these incidents there is ample time in the four or five years which elapsed before his martyrdom.

We obtain then

(i) A visit to the East, probably brief, according with his intention expressed to the Philippians and to Philemon.

(ii) The fulfilment of his long-cherished purpose of preaching in Spain and the West.

(iii) A return to the East.

Eastward then the Apostle hastens after his release. First of all perhaps he revisited the Macedonian Churches, fulfilling his promise to the Philippians. We may imagine him next

---

[1] Rom. xv. 24, 28.

[2] Phil. i. 24; Philem. *v.* 22. This conclusion however must not be regarded as absolutely certain. It may be that we should not press the ταχέως of Phil. ii. 24. And the injunction to Philemon to prepare him a lodging may point rather to the certainty than to the nearness of the visit. It is as if the Apostle had said, 'You may certainly expect to see me. I shall myself observe what treatment Onesimus has received from you.' With delicate tact, the Apostle's language, suggested by some slight misgiving, assumes the form of an appeal to Philemon's hospitality and kindly feeling towards himself.

directing his steps towards the Churches of Asia and Phrygia. The unhealthy tone of religious speculation in these districts needed correction. And to Colossæ moreover he was drawn by a personal motive. He was anxious to assure himself that Onesimus was fully restored to his master's favour, and to carry out his undertaking of staying with Philemon. We can scarcely suppose that he left these regions without a brief visit to the Church of Ephesus, which had occupied so much of his time and thoughts; and it is possible that some of the notices in the Pastoral Epistles refer to incidents which occurred on this occasion, though it is on the whole more probable that they took place on a later visit.

We may conjecture also that, before he left the neighbourhood of the Ægæan, he laid the first foundations of a Church in Crete. There was in this island a large Jewish population[1]— a circumstance which would press itself on the Apostle's attention. Possibly also St Paul's anchorage there[2] on his voyage to Rome may have been accompanied by incidents which dwelt on his mind, and stimulated his desire to preach the Gospel in Crete. At all events a few years later we find a Christian Church established here, and, if its foundation is to be attributed to St Paul, no occasion is more probable than this of his first visit to the East after his release.

Having thus taken a rapid review of the Churches of the East, the Apostle hastened to fulfil his long-postponed intention of visiting the hitherto unexplored region of Spain. There was a considerable Jewish population settled in many of the towns on the Spanish coast[3], and the Apostle would make this his starting-point. This course had many advantages in itself, but a deeper principle of obligation commended it to the mind of the Apostle, who seems to have held sacred the maxim, 'To the Jew first, and then to the Gentile.' Whether St Paul

---

[1] Philo. *Leg. ad Caium* ii. p. 587 (ed. Mangey), οὐ μόνον αἱ ἤπειροι μεσταὶ τῶν Ἰουδαϊκῶν ἀποικιῶν εἰσιν ἀλλὰ καὶ νήσων αἱ δοκιμώταται, Εὔβοια, Κύπρος, Κρήτη.

[2] Acts xxvii. 7–12; esp. *v.* 9, ἱκανοῦ δὲ χρόνου διαγενομένου.

[3] See Remond *Ausbreitung des Judenthums* § 31.

extended his labours in the West beyond the limits of Spain must remain a matter of speculation. At the close of his life we find him sending Crescens on a mission to Gaul—for so we may perhaps understand by 'Galatia[1]'—and if this interpretation is correct, it would seem to imply some previous communication with this region. It is highly probable indeed that, either on his way to or from Rome, he should have visited the famous port of Marseilles[2], and having once set foot in Gaul, he would naturally avail himself of the opportunity of furthering his Master's cause. At all events, the Churches of Spain and Gaul were founded at a very early date, so that Irenæus appeals to them[3] along with others, as witnesses of the primitive tradition in matters of doctrine. On the other hand, had he remained long either in Spain or Gaul, we should have expected to find in those parts a more direct tradition of his visit[4].

Moving eastward, perhaps passing through Rome, the Apostle may possibly have visited Dalmatia, for with this region again we find him in communication at the close of his life[5]. If so, he may have continued his journey along the Adriatic coast to Epirus, so that, by wintering at Nicopolis on a subsequent occasion[6], he purposed renewing an intimacy already formed, thus following out his general practice of confirming the Churches of his founding.

We find the Apostle then in the East once more. The slight fragmentary notices in the Pastoral Epistles may be pieced together variously, so that any particular plan of his journey must be more or less arbitrary. The object of framing such a plan is to show that it is possible to give a consistent and intelligible account of his movements, on the supposition of

[1] 2 Tim. iv. 10; see *Galatians* pp. 3, 31. On Crescens see esp. Gerarius *Mogunt. Resp.* p. 225, and on the early Church in Gaul, Neander *Ch. Hist.* i. p. 116 (Eng. transl. by Torrey).

[2] See the interesting speculations of Blunt *The First Three Centuries*, p. 184 sq. (1861).

[3] Iren. *Haer.* i. 10. 2.

[4] The journey to Britain must be abandoned, as highly improbable, though maintained with a patriotic urgency by many able advocates (Stillingfleet, Burgess, etc.); see the references in Soames *Anglo-Saxon Church*, p. 21 sq. (1844).

[5] 2 Tim. iv. 10.

[6] Tit. iii. 12.

his release; and under the circumstances no more than this can reasonably be demanded. The scheme which I shall give differs from those generally adopted in assuming that the winter which he purposed spending in Nicopolis was in fact spent in Rome[1]. We may suppose that his abrupt arrest and imprisonment frustrated his previous plans. In this way the events are gathered within narrower limits of time; and, the Pastoral Epistles being thus brought into closer chronological connexion, the striking coincidences of thought and language between them are the more easily explained. This arrangement of the incidents seems to me slightly more probable than any other, but I lay no stress on it.

Once in the East then, he would naturally revisit the Churches of Phrygia and Asia, which had caused him so much anxiety. There he found that his gloomiest anticipations had been realised. Grievous wolves had indeed entered the fold, as he had predicted years before. His personal influence had gone. 'All in Asia turned away from him[2].' Phygellus and Hermogenes are especially named among these timid or recreant Christians. There was one bright exception however in Onesiphorus, whose attentions—repeated afterwards when the Apostle was a prisoner in Rome—are gratefully recorded[3]. It was probably at Ephesus too and on this occasion that St Paul encountered the opposition of Alexander the coppersmith[4]. And this is perhaps the same Alexander whom, together with Hymenæus, the Apostle 'delivered unto Satan, that they might learn not to blaspheme[5].' If we are right in assigning all these notices to this one occasion, it would seem that the Apostle's residence was more or less prolonged. Altogether the visit was one of bitter trial. It was evident that the clouds were gathering about the Church, and that a period of storm and tempest was imminent.

From Ephesus the Apostle turned northward into Mace-

---

[1] Thus the winter of Titus iii. 12 becomes identical with that of 2 Tim. iv. 21.

[2] 2 Tim. i. 15 sq.

[3] 2 Tim. i. 15–17; cf. iv. 19.

[4] 2 Tim. iv. 14.

[5] 1 Tim. i. 20.

donia. At the same time he left Timothy behind to preside over the Church there in his absence[1]. He would gladly seek consolation after these sad experiences in the affection of that Philippian Church, of which he entertained the most tender remembrance, and which more than once had relieved his wants[2].

What country St Paul visited next, we cannot say; it is not unnatural to suppose that, following his old route, he would turn towards the Churches of Achaia. Somewhere about this time we may perhaps place the writing of the *First Epistle to Timothy*. Its exact time and place cannot be ascertained, but the following data should be observed. (1) It cannot have been written very long after St Paul left Ephesus, as the whole tenour of the Epistle shows. It betrays a nervous anxiety such as might be expected from one who had recently delegated a very arduous task to a young and inexperienced successor. Such advice to have any value must be given at once, and indeed the Apostle's ardent temperament would admit of no delay in a matter so important. (2) It would seem to have been written before the incidents occurred which St Paul relates to Timothy in the Second Epistle[3]. When the letter was written, St Paul hoped to revisit Ephesus soon, but foresaw that he might possibly meet with some delays[4].

About this time he also visited Crete. A hypothetical account of the origin of this Church I have given already[5]. Having been recently founded, its organization was still very imperfect; and, as St Paul himself could not stay to do all that was needful, he left Titus behind him to complete his arrangements there[6].

From Crete we may suppose that he went to Asia Minor, and somewhere about this time he directed a letter of advice and exhortation to Titus. For ascertaining the time of writing of the *Epistle to Titus* we have the following data. (1) As in

[1] 1 Tim. i. 3.
[2] See above, pp. 249, 260.
[3] e.g. iv. 9–13, 20.
[4] 1 Tim. iii. 15.
[5] See above, p. 431.
[6] Tit. i. 5.

the case of the First Epistle to Timothy, it cannot have been written long after St Paul left Crete. (2) Tychicus was still with him when he wrote; and therefore it is before the point of time noted in 2 Tim. iv. 12. (3) He has no forebodings of his coming fate, for he purposes wintering at Nicopolis, not expecting to have his movements constrained[1]. (4) On the supposition that this winter is identical with that mentioned in his Second Epistle, the year cannot have been far advanced now. There is time for him to despatch a messenger to Titus, for Titus to join him (at Corinth or Nicopolis) and to leave him again for Dalmatia, for him to reach Rome himself, for several incidents at Rome, e.g. his trial, etc., for him to despatch a messenger from Rome to Timothy, for Timothy to join him in Rome; all this before the winter.

In this letter he tells Titus that he will send Artemas or Tychicus—perhaps to act as his deputy—and bids him hasten to join him at Nicopolis. He asks him to provide Zenas the lawyer and Apollos with the necessaries for their journey[2].

From this point onwards we can trace the Apostle's course westward with some degree of continuity[3]. We find him at Miletus, where he dropped Trophimus on account of illness[4]. Hence perhaps he despatched Tychicus to Ephesus[5]. Miletus was a convenient point from which to communicate with Ephesus, as he had found it on a former occasion[5], and we may conjecture that, having abandoned his purpose of revisiting Ephesus, he sent Tychicus to Timothy to inform him of this[7]. From Miletus he sails northward to Troas, where he lodges with Carpus[8]. What were the intermediate stages, we do not know, but we next find him at Corinth, where he leaves Erastus behind[9]. He was now on his way to Nicopolis—probably the

[1] Tit. iii. 12.
[2] Tit. iii. 12, 13.
[3] The journey is the reverse of that in Acts xx. 13 sq.
[4] 2 Tim. iv. 20.
[5] 2 Tim. iv. 12. Tychicus and Tro-

phimus were Ἀσιανοί; cf. Acts xx. 4, xxi. 29.
[6] Acts xx. 17.
[7] 1 Tim. iii. 14.
[8] 2 Tim. iv. 13.
[9] 2 Tim. iv. 20.

city of that name in Epirus, where he purposed passing the winter. Whether he reached Nicopolis or not must remain uncertain. A probable, though a conjectural, account seems to me this. While he was at Corinth, his old enemies, the Jews, informed against him, as the leader of the hated sect of malefactors, who had roused the indignation of Rome; and on this information he was seized and imprisoned and ultimately carried to the Metropolis to await his trial[1].

Meanwhile, finding his plan of wintering at Nicopolis frustrated, he despatches his messenger—probably Artemas[2], since he had left Tychicus behind[3]—to Titus in Crete to join him, not in Nicopolis, as he had intended, but either in Corinth or in Rome itself, whither he was soon to be conveyed. At all events Titus did join him at some point in his route[4].

Arrived at Rome, the Apostle found himself almost deserted. Onesiphorus, who lived in Ephesus[5], and whose kind services the Apostle had experienced during his stay there, coming to Rome sought him out and with some difficulty found him[6]. But these friendly offices ceased with the departure of Onesiphorus. Of all his more intimate friends and companions in travel Luke alone remained with him[7]. Titus had gone to Dalmatia, Crescens to Gaul, probably despatched thither by the Apostle on some missionary errand. Demas had forsaken him, and gone to Thessalonica, probably his native place[8]. Certain Christians of Rome, Eubulus, Pudens, Linus and Claudia, join in the salutation, but these must have been comparative strangers[9]. In this forlorn condition he writes his *Second Epistle to Timothy*. He urges Timothy to join him as soon as

---

[1] We know that Nero was in Greece at this time, and that he was still there in August 67, though he was recalled to Rome towards the close of the year by Helius (see Clinton *Fasti Romani* I. p. 50). Perhaps the Emperor himself sent the Apostle to the capital.

[2] Tit. iii. 12.

[3] 2 Tim. iv. 12.

[4] 2 Tim. iv. 10.

[5] 2 Tim. iv. 19.

[6] 2 Tim. i. 17.

[7] 2 Tim. iv. 9 sq.

[8] See above, p. 247.

[9] [On the supposed connexion of Pudens and Claudia with Britain see *Apostolic Fathers* Pt. I. *Clement of Rome* I. p. 76 (1890)].

possible[1], at all events to come before the winter sets in and while the sea is yet navigable[2]. At the same time he charges him to perform a commission at Troas; he had left his cloak with some books and parchments, and he requests Timothy, as he passes, to fetch these[3]. He evidently contemplates that Timothy will follow the coast to Macedonia, and then take the great Egnatian Road from Philippi to Dyrrachium and cross over the straits thence to Italy. It was perhaps already late in the season, and a voyage on the high seas was hazardous. Timothy is to pick up Mark on the way and to bring him with him[4]. Timothy appears to be still at Ephesus, for the Apostle in this letter salutes the household of Onesiphorus, doubtless resident there[5]; he also salutes Aquila and Priscilla[6], and they too seem to have had connexion with Ephesus[7].

The legal proceedings have already commenced when the Apostle writes. He has had his first hearing, and has a respite for a time[8]. But he is full of gloomy forebodings, or rather he foresees but one termination to the trial. And here, with the notes of his dying strain ringing in our ears, we take leave of the Great Apostle.

[1862.]

[1] 2 Tim. iv. 9.
[2] 2 Tim. iv. 21.
[3] 2 Tim. iv. 13.
[4] 2 Tim. iv. 11.
[5] 2 Tim. iv. 19, i. 16. Onesiphorus

himself seems to be absent (i. 17).
[6] 2 Tim. iv. 19.
[7] 1 Cor. xvi. 19.
[8] 2 Tim. iv. 16.

INDICES.

INDEX OF PASSAGES.

INDEX OF SUBJECTS.

Cambridge:

PRINTED BY C. J. CLAY, M.A. AND SONS,
AT THE UNIVERSITY PRESS.